CAMBRIDG

Books of enduring scholarly ~~~~

History

The books reissued in this series include accounts of historical events and movements by eye-witnesses and contemporaries, as well as landmark studies that assembled significant source materials or developed new historiographical methods. The series includes work in social, political and military history on a wide range of periods and regions, giving modern scholars ready access to influential publications of the past.

Lollardy and the Reformation in England

James Gairdner (1828–1912) was one of the foremost authorities of his day on the Tudor period. This magisterial four-volume survey (originally published 1908–1913) argues that the impetus for the English Reformation came from the Lollard movement of the late fourteenth century. A prolific researcher and editor, Gairdner devoted his career to English history, and his study is both meticulous and factually sound. His critics, however, were quick to observe that the Lollard hypothesis was tenuous, and this mature work is most valuable today to those interested in the history of Reformation scholarship. Focusing on the more immediate causes of the Reformation, Volume 2, published in 1908, considers the rise of German Protestantism, the dissolution of the monasteries, the history of the English Bible and the influence of Katherine Parr and the New Learning, concluding with the death of Henry VIII in 1547.

Cambridge University Press has long been a pioneer in the reissuing of out-of-print titles from its own backlist, producing digital reprints of books that are still sought after by scholars and students but could not be reprinted economically using traditional technology. The Cambridge Library Collection extends this activity to a wider range of books which are still of importance to researchers and professionals, either for the source material they contain, or as landmarks in the history of their academic discipline.

Drawing from the world-renowned collections in the Cambridge University Library, and guided by the advice of experts in each subject area, Cambridge University Press is using state-of-the-art scanning machines in its own Printing House to capture the content of each book selected for inclusion. The files are processed to give a consistently clear, crisp image, and the books finished to the high quality standard for which the Press is recognised around the world. The latest print-on-demand technology ensures that the books will remain available indefinitely, and that orders for single or multiple copies can quickly be supplied.

The Cambridge Library Collection will bring back to life books of enduring scholarly value (including out-of-copyright works originally issued by other publishers) across a wide range of disciplines in the humanities and social sciences and in science and technology.

Lollardy
and the Reformation
in England

An Historical Survey

VOLUME 2

JAMES GAIRDNER

CAMBRIDGE
UNIVERSITY PRESS

CAMBRIDGE UNIVERSITY PRESS

Cambridge, New York, Melbourne, Madrid, Cape Town, Singapore,
São Paolo, Delhi, Dubai, Tokyo

Published in the United States of America by Cambridge University Press, New York

www.cambridge.org
Information on this title: www.cambridge.org/9781108017725

This edition first published 1908
This digitally printed version 2010

ISBN 978-1-108-01772-5 Paperback

Lollardy and the Reformation in England

MACMILLAN AND CO., Limited
LONDON · BOMBAY · CALCUTTA
MELBOURNE

THE MACMILLAN COMPANY
NEW YORK · BOSTON · CHICAGO
ATLANTA · SAN FRANCISCO

THE MACMILLAN CO. OF CANADA, Ltd.
TORONTO

Lollardy and the

Reformation in England

An Historical Survey

BY

JAMES GAIRDNER, C.B.

HON. LL.D. EDIN.

VOL. II

MACMILLAN AND CO., LIMITED
ST. MARTIN'S STREET, LONDON
1908

CONTENTS

BOOK III
THE FALL OF THE MONASTERIES

BOOK IV
THE REIGN OF THE ENGLISH BIBLE

CHAPTER II

CHAPTER III

CHAPTER IV

ERRATA

Vol. II

Page 85, line 9, after " Henry VIII." insert a comma.
,, 97-100. Cancel these two leaves.
,, 103, line 8 from bottom, for " was a dandy, and " read " dressed in indecorous fashion ; "
,, 105-6. Cancel this leaf.
,, 119, lines 23, 24, for " their brother canons " read " the canons," and in lines 24, 25 strike out " for they belonged . . . (the Augustinian)," which is wrong.
,, 157, line 8 from bottom, for " Tyburn " read " Tower Hill."
,. 227, line 20, for " began " read " committed to the press."
,, 227, line 21, for " where " read " but."
,, 257-60 to be cancelled.
,, 261, line 2 from bottom, after " end " place a comma, and for " of " read " 1st."
,. 273, lines 29, 30, for " fully . . . that Coverdale " read " gives strength to our surmise that Coverdale went to the Netherlands by the statement that he."
,. 289, line 20, after " For " insert comma.
,, 301, line 5 (first line after quotation), strike out " only."
,, 308. Note correction already made at p. 506 at end of Index.
,, 317. lines 16-19. The sentence " But . . . to comply " is not accurate. It should be :—" But this the Elector would not let him do, and when the news of Anne Boleyn's fate reached Germany, he himself cared less about the disappointment."
,, 317. The footnote 2 should be amplified by adding " Cp. Georg Ellinger's German *Life of Melancthon*, p. 327."
,, 447, line 6, for " But probably the date is fictitious. and " read " The date, perhaps, may be genuine, but."

Index

BOOK III

THE FALL OF THE MONASTERIES

CHAPTER I

MORE'S writings, we may well believe, were not altogether ineffective in the discouragement of heresy, although it was so much encouraged by the Court. It was, no doubt, essential to the King's purpose that the Pope and the clergy should be reviled and their authority impugned as much as possible. But this did not make the divorce of Katharine or the marriage with Anne Boleyn more popular; and the enforcement of the Act of Supremacy, though it made resistance hopeless, did not reconcile Henry's subjects to an unprecedented breach in the unity of Christendom. On the contrary, it aroused a deep sympathy with the patient victims of tyranny, of which the King himself was not by any means unconscious; and the leading note of his whole policy from that time was an effort to convince himself and others that in throwing off his allegiance to Rome he was merely vindicating the independence of his realm, and that he made no breach whatever in the spiritual unity of Christendom. He had his own spiritual advisers in his own kingdom, and whatever was done as regards religion and the faith was done after full consultation with them. Nor did either he or they impugn one vital doctrine.

Resentment of the King's tyranny.

To vindicate this position, while it was necessary, for the sake of his policy, to put to cruel deaths the most saintly men in his kingdom, was of course not

3

an easy matter; and, in fact, the very cause which led him on to his peculiar line of action had become the greatest obstacle to its success. " Thou art the cause of this man's death," he might very well say to Anne Boleyn of Sir Thomas More; only he should have blamed his own infatuated passion rather than the poor weak woman who at first had really withstood its vehemence for a considerable time. But she, or her influence, was undoubtedly the cause of the death, not only of Sir Thomas More, but of Bishop Fisher and Reynolds and the three Carthusian priors. Nor was the legal butchery even yet at an end, though the passion for Anne Boleyn had long been on the wane; for the law, however tyrannical, must be upheld, else respect for him who got it passed would very soon pass away. It was no secret to him, nevertheless, that he had greatly lost the esteem and affection of his subjects; he could not be ignorant of that, when he was ruling by terror and not by love. Yet he could not have imagined—what was unknown till our own day—how privy conspiracy, even among the courtiers whom he least suspected, was endeavouring to procure an invasion of the kingdom.[1]

As a means of establishing better feelings between him and his subjects the sacrifice of Anne Boleyn was sure to take place before many years were over. Her indiscretions and her insolences aggravated the general feeling against her. Even her uncle, Norfolk, spoke of her with utter disgust.[2] She hated the Princess Mary, and even ventured to tell the King he would have to get rid of her one day, as he had got rid of Bishop Fisher. " She will be my death or I hers," she would say; " but I will take care that she shall not laugh at me after I am dead." [3]

This insolence of an upstart for whose sake the old order of Church and State had been completely

Arrogance of Anne Boleyn.

---

[1] See *L. P.*, VIII. Pref., pp. ii. iii.
[2] *L. P.*, VIII. 1.   [3] *L. P.*, IX. 873.

subverted did not make men warm upholders of change in matters of religion. Even before royal supremacy over the Church had been vindicated by such cruel martyrdoms there was deep disaffection everywhere. Lord Hussey and Lord Darcy had been eager to inform the Imperial ambassador in secret that everybody in England would gladly welcome an invasion by the Emperor, even to rescue from danger Queen Katharine and her daughter Mary, and restore them to their proper positions as queen and princess. Indeed, Darcy was confident that he could raise the North against the Lutheran policy that the King seemed bent on pursuing; and if the King of Scots at the same time would invade the northern counties, while the Emperor sent a force to the Thames, it would be so much the better.[1] Other noblemen confirmed the statements of general disaffection; and even the King's Chamberlain, Lord Sandes, pretending sickness as an excuse for retiring from Court, sent a secret message to Chapuys to say that the King had lost the hearts of all his subjects, and that if the Emperor only knew the state of matters in England he would surely not delay to come to the relief of an oppressed nation.[2]

Secret disaffection of noblemen.

Now, if this was the state of matters even before those cruel and savage executions done to vindicate royal supremacy, what was it likely to have been after they had taken place? Men spoke, of course, with bated breath as far as they dared speak of it at all. England was tongue-tied, and we need look for no direct expression of her feelings; but abroad, we know perfectly well what was thought of those brutalities. The news of the execution of Prior Houghton and his companions seemed very outrageous to the papal nuncio in France, who was informed besides that the whole of London was displeased at it.[3] From Venice, too, the English ambassador reported

Public feeling shocked, at home and abroad.

[1] *L. P.*, VII. 1206.   [2] *L. P.*, VIII. 48.   [3] *L. P.*, VIII. 726.

that it was considered extreme cruelty and against all honest laws of God and men. He had never seen Italians so vehement about anything.[1] At Rome, of course, it was most deeply felt of all; and it aroused a feeling not only of indignation against the tyrant, but also of such admiration for his victims that some of the cardinals said that they envied such a death.[2] Such was the feeling for the first martyrs of the new Act, even before the further butcheries of More and Fisher. Yet in England men could say nothing. The King's power was irresistible; and if he insisted on vindicating his ecclesiastical supremacy by such savage methods, what was to be done?

It was a perplexing question. A whole nation could not be expected to imitate the example of Reynolds, and Hale, and the three Carthusian priors, and Bishop Fisher, and Sir Thomas More. How many could calmly face the prospect of strangulation, the ripping knife, the block, to yield their testimony to the belief that there was a law above the laws of Parliament and the will of a despotic king? The great majority could retain that belief, yet give a qualified oath with which the authorities were content. Even More's noble-hearted daughter, Margaret Roper, did that, and would have persuaded her father to do it too. What was compulsory surely could not be wrong, especially with the reservation, "as far as lawful." Even Convocation had made a somewhat similar reservation when it acknowledged the royal supremacy, though the reservation was afterwards treated as nil by Parliament, which cited the acknowledgment without the qualification as a warrant for "the Act of Supreme Head." Churchmen might repent too late the concessions that they had made; but Convocation, under Warham's guidance, had not really sanctioned in full the supremacy which Henry claimed. There was something, no doubt, in the

---

[1] *L. P.*, VIII. 874.   [2] *L. P.*, VIII. 786, 807.

way they recognised it, too much akin to that religion of casuistry by which Henry himself would fain have justified his divorce ; and, indeed, it was the religion of casuistry which now was on its trial. But what else but casuistry was at the bottom of this whole divorce question, which ended in acts of schism? The supreme authority of the Roman pontiff was an authority to determine cases of conscience before an external tribunal. Sweep away the casuistry of the canon law and the Pope's authority was gone. Put down the Pope's authority by the strong hand, and casuistry might still fairly plead that the subjects of a realm could not be condemned for doing the best they could under trying circumstances. Besides, royal authority, as well as papal, had always been regarded as sacred, and it was hard to leave it to the individual to draw the line between them.

So when the King's authority came in conflict with the Pope's, very serious and perplexing questions were raised, even in regard to ethics. Prior Houghton himself sought the best advice, and Father Fewterer, the head and confessor of the great monastery of Sion, was entirely against his yielding to royal supremacy. But when he saw the result of the counsel he had given him, Father Fewterer deeply reproached himself. " I beseech you to forgive me, most gentle brethren," he said, when on his deathbed, to eight of the remaining Charterhouse monks, who, indeed, had been sent to him on purpose that he might cure their obstinacy : " I am guilty of the death of your reverend Father, of which I was the cause ; for I encouraged him in his resolution to die in the cause for which he suffered, and for which you are brought hither. Now, however, I am of another mind, and I perceive that the cause is not one for which we are bound to suffer death." [1]

The Carthusians had remained singularly steadfast

Questions of conscience.

[1] Chauncy's *Historia aliquot Martyrum Anglorum* (ed. Doreau), p. 114.

even after the awful death of their venerated prior.
The daily services continued as of old in that quiet
retreat outside the city and Smithfield. The convent,
indeed, could not think of proceeding to elect a new

Efforts to
bring the
remaining
Charter-
house
monks to
conformity.
prior;[1] for even on the day of Prior Houghton's
martyrdom they were visited by Thomas Bedyll, clerk
of the Council, who brought with him a bundle of books
and "annotations," written against the primacy of "the
Bishop of Rome" and even of St. Peter, showing that
all the Apostles were equal by the law of God. He conversed for an hour and a half with the vicar and procurator of the House (Fathers Humphrey Middlemore and
William Exmew, two of the three who were afterwards tried with Fisher and suffered three days before
him), and he left the books and annotations for the
edification of the convent to bring them to conformity;
but the vicar and procurator sent back the books
next day without any message either by word or
writing. Bedyll was then confined to bed by a fever,
and, sending for the procurator to come and speak to
him, asked whether he and the vicar and others had
examined the books. The procurator said that he
and the vicar and Newdigate (the third of the above-
mentioned trio) " had spent the time upon them until
9 or 10 of the clock at night, and that they saw
nothing in them whereby they were moved to alter
their opinion." Bedyll pointed out the danger of this
opinion, " which was like to be the destruction of
them and their house for ever," but they showed
themselves quite unmoved and ready to meet the
fate that they were soon to undergo. Worse still,
when he asked the procurator whether the rest of
the brethren were of like opinion, he said he was not
sure, but believed that they were all of one mind.
Bedyll then told him he believed they were inspired
by "the spirit which appeared before God and said

---

[1] *L. P.*, VIII. 585 is out of place. It was in 1536 that Father Trafford was
forced upon the convent as prior.

he would be a false spirit in the mouths of the prophets of Achab," and he wrote to Cromwell with remarkable unction :—

Finally, I suppose it to be the will of God that as their religion had a simple beginning, so in this realm it shall have a strange end, procured by themselves and by none others. And albeit they pretend holiness in this behalf, surely the ground of their said opinion is hypocrisy, vainglory, confederacy, obstinacy, to the intent they may be seen to the world, or specially to such as have confidence in them, more faithful and more constant than any other." [1]

These disgraceful words are at least a tribute to the high repute in which the Carthusians were held for constancy to their profession. The King undoubtedly felt that if he could only succeed in getting such men on his side he need hardly fear serious opposition from any other quarter. And a curious report got abroad shortly after this that the King himself had gone in disguise to the Charterhouse to persuade the monks to compliance—a statement which, strange though it be, seems really to be tolerably well authenticated. For not only was it believed by Francis I., who told it as a fact to the papal nuncio at his Court, but the same nuncio read a statement to the like effect in a letter shown him by the Imperial ambassador at the time.[2] It seems also to be corroborated by some later traditions to be mentioned presently, notwithstanding an important discrepancy. For it would appear that there was at least one of those Carthusian monks on whom the King might hope to bring his own personal influence to bear. Sebastian Newdigate had been, in past years, a gentleman of his privy chamber, " and not a little favored by him "—in so much that his sister, Lady Dormer, greatly feared that he would be corrupted by a dissolute Court. But when he himself perceived its moral dangers, to which the

The King said to have visited the Charterhouse himself.

---

[1] Wright's *Suppression of the Monasteries*, pp. 40, 41.
[2] *L. P.*, VIII. 837.

King's determination to seek a divorce fully opened his eyes, he resolved to take refuge in a monastic life under the habit of a Carthusian.[1] Coming to the Charterhouse, therefore, with the memory, doubtless, of pleasant hours of social intercourse in the past, the King seems to have made one effort to rescue at least Newdigate from the awful fate by which he was determined to vindicate his law of supremacy. But not only had the sunshine of royal favour lost its power over Newdigate's mind, but the terrors of Prior Houghton's fate were counterbalanced to him by the prospect of that " crown of life " which faithfulness unto death would secure for him.

The Carthusian Chauncy, who lived through those terrible days and reproached himself afterwards for not having had the courage to be a martyr like some of his brethren, says that three weeks after the slaughter of Prior Houghton and his fellows, some ignoble men got authority from the King's Vicar-General Cromwell still further to afflict the monks, and seized the persons of Middlemore, Exmew, and Newdigate, whom they threw into a prison reeking with filth, where they were bound with iron chains about their necks and legs to posts and pillars.[2] Chauncy's narrative, though written from memory many years after, is for the most part minutely accurate, and bears the test of comparison with contemporary documents to a degree almost beyond expectation. But one little point is here omitted, and its omission really attests his accuracy still further. Three weeks from the date of Prior Houghton's martyrdom bring us to the 25th day of May; and from the indictment of Middlemore, Exmew, and Newdigate it is clear that they were taken from the Charterhouse to Stepney, where Cromwell had a

Seizure of three more Carthusians.

---

[1] See the *Life of Jane Dormer* (edited by J. Stevenson), pp. 19-23.
[2] Chauncy's *Historia aliquot Martyrum Anglorum*, p. 107. The statement is confirmed by a fragment among the collections of Camden and Stow. See *L. P.*, VIII. 895. See also what the Bishop of Faenza says, No. 846.

mansion, on the 25th day of May, and there each of
them, in reply, of course, to a question put to them all,
declared severally, " I cannot, nor will, consent to be
obedient to the King's Highness as a true, lawful, and
obedient subject, to take and repute him to be Supreme
Head in Earth of the Church of England under Christ."
These are the words charged against them when they
were brought to trial on the 11th June;[1] and it
must have been immediately after this repudiation
of royal supremacy that they were thrown into the
Marshalsea prison—for that was their place of confinement.[2]

There, in their horrible dungeon, chained in an
upright position, which allowed no rest for the body,
they spent dismal days and nights for a whole fortnight; and it was there, according to later tradition,
that the King went to visit them in disguise. So it
is stated in the *Life of Jane Dormer*, and also in
the MS. of Father Transam belonging to the English
Carthusians now at Parkminster,[3] both of which,
though written in the middle of the seventeenth
century, appear to be generally trustworthy. It is
not likely, however, that the nuncio in France,
writing at the time, was misinformed about the
place; for though it is probable enough that the news
of an incident which took place after the 25th May
in London would have reached Abbeville, where the
nuncio was with the French Court, before the 6th
June, and that the place might have been misreported,
yet it is much more credible that the King should have
visited the Charterhouse than have entered a noisome
prison to reason with a man who was actually suffering from the horrors of such a constrained position.

After a fortnight of this misery it must have been
a real relief to the three monks to be transferred, as

[1] *L. P.*, VIII. 886.
[2] *Life of Jane Dormer*, p. 27, where, besides the place of confinement being
named, it should be noted that the date is given quite accurately, 25th May.
[3] See Hendriks, pp. 99, 170, 310.

they were apparently, on the 8th June, to the Tower, even though they were to be brought thence three days later in the custody of Sir Edmund Walsingham to their trial at Westminster. That took place on the 11th, and as juries by this time knew that they could only refuse to convict at their own peril, sentence was passed the same day. They were executed at Tyburn with the usual barbarities on the 19th. Bishop Fisher had been condemned just two days before, and was to suffer on the 22nd.

Their martyrdom.

It would have been strange if these severities had produced no effect, especially as there were one or two weak brethren in the community to whom the rigour of the discipline had been almost too great a trial in times less exceptional. Their grievances presently were to find freer utterance. But the spirit of the brotherhood as a whole was singularly maintained. One John Whalley was put for a time in possession of their house, a man not long afterwards made paymaster of the King's works at Dover, and a little later Master of the Mint. A preacher named Rastell had been sent to persuade the monks, but they had laughed at him. Whalley thought he knew better how to convert them. First, he tells Cromwell, get some honest, loyal, and learned men to stay with them ; then get Roland Philips, the famous preacher, vicar of Croydon, Dr. Buckmaster, and others " of the popish sort," to preach to them in open audience against their superstitions, but not to be suffered to speak to any of them alone. After which Archbishop Lee of York, Bishop Gardiner of Winchester, Bishop Tunstall of Durham, and other bishops of similar proclivities, should likewise preach to them. The undoubted attachment of such men to the old order of the Church would add force to their advocacy of royal supremacy, to which they themselves had consented.[1]

[1] Willingly or unwillingly, the whole bench of bishops had taken the oath of supremacy between the 10th February and the 1st June (*L. P.*, VIII. 190,

This advice seems to have been acted on to some extent, but the vicar of Croydon's sermon does not appear to have given complete satisfaction, for it "touched in parable" the King and Cromwell and the Archbishop of Canterbury.[1] But the Archbishop of York (Lee) made himself serviceable otherwise than by preaching to the London brethren (if, indeed, he ever did so). For in July he was in the North and called before him the Prior of Mountgrace, one of the houses of the Order in Yorkshire, whom he found "very conformable," and much comforted to hear that by that time the London Charterhouse and other houses of his religion were "stayed." The Archbishop was also of opinion that Dr. Horde, Prior of Hinton, a man considerably esteemed throughout the Order, who had apparently acknowledged the royal supremacy, should be sent to all the different houses to persuade them. But this advice seems not to have been taken, for Prior Horde had certainly shown "untowardness in certain things," and was not quite the man to do the work.[2]

On the 29th May Whalley had received orders from Cromwell to take from the monks such books as the statutes of Bruno "and such like doctors."[3] They were to be deprived of all means of reference even to the statutes on which their rule was founded. Whalley was assisted in the work by Jasper Filoll, a servant of Cromwell's, who also took up his abode in the house, and continued there after he was gone. In September Filoll reported on the expenses of the establishment. He found that the demands of the lay brethren were more than the revenue of the house could stand. Wheat had risen 4s. 3d. a quarter, and malt 20d. ; and yet

311, 494, 803). The only exceptions were Llandaff (a foreigner), no doubt deprived by this time, like Ghinucci of Worcester and Campeggio of Salisbury, and the newly appointed successors to these two last, Latimer and Shaxton.

[1] *L. P.*, VIII. 600, 602.

[2] *L. P.*, VIII. 1011. Comp. Nos. 402, 778. For particulars about Prior Horde see *The Somerset Carthusians*, by Miss E. M. Thompson.

[3] *L. P.*, VIII. 778.

they expected, he said, to have the same fare as in
times past, with the old bounteous distribution of
bread, ale, and fish to strangers in the buttery, "and
to their servants and vagabonds at the gate." This
was out of the question.[1]

There had been a very rainy summer—a calamity,
as people thought, due to the King's misdeeds—
followed by a very bad harvest, and on the 2nd October
Filoll followed up his suggestions by the following
"instructions," which he forwarded to Cromwell :—

If it be the King's pleasure and yours that this Charterhouse shall stand without a prior as it now doth, it seemeth
then, saving your mastership's correction, to be very necessary
to minish the number of the cloister monks, and also of the
lay brothers, at the least by so many as hath not, ne will not,
confess the King to be their Supreme Head under God here
in earth, and that will not renounce all jurisdiction of the
Bishop of Rome, and of all his laws that be contrary to the
good laws of the realm.

That done, it seemeth to be necessary that they shall sit
daily in their fraytowr, and four of them at a mess of meat,
and that so done that meat that now serveth twelve persons
will serve then twenty persons honestly.

It seemeth also to be convenient that their lay steward,
and other their lay servants and strangers, should eat flesh
in their hall and parlour, contrary to their old ill custom.

Also, if any of the cloister monks list to eat flesh it were
pity to constrain him to eat fish; for such constrained abstin-
ence shall never be meritorious.

It is no great marvel though many of these monks have
heretofore offended God and the King by their foul errors;
for I have found in the prior and proctor's cells, three or four
sundry printed books from beyond the sea, of as foul errors
and heresies as may be; and one or two books be never
printed alone, but hundreds of them. Wherefore, by your
mastership's favor, it seemeth to be much necessary that
their cells be better searched; for I can perceive few of them
but they have great pleasure in reading of such erroneous
doctors, and little or none in reading of the New Testament
or in other good books.

---

[1] *L. P.*, IX. 283.

Also Master Bedyll and Mr. Doctor Crome in this vacation time called Rochester and Fox before them, and gave them marvellous good exhortations by the space of an hour and more, but it prevailed nothing, but they left those two froward monks as erroneous as they found them; wherein was much lack of grace.

Also, William Marshall gave lately to be distributed among all our monks twenty-four English books named *The Defence of Peace.* Many of them received those books and said if their president would command them or license them to read it, then they would so do, or else not. The third day following all they save one sent home their books again to me, saying that their President had commanded them so to do. Yet at more leisure Dampne[1] John Rochester was so fair entreated to read one of them that he took the book and kept it four or five days, and then burned him; which is good matter to lay to them at the time when your pleasure shall be to visit them.

Where in every office of the house there is set one or two lay brothers, it is thought that they be not profitable to the house but much prodigal, every one of them to the other and to their friends elsewhere.

Also the lay servants of that house be but like Abbey men, and will do but as they list; and they be the common messengers for bearing and bringing of letters, tidings, and credence to and fro the convent in the cloister; and every of the said lay servants hath a key to the cloister door, to come and to go, and let in and let out their friends at their pleasure.

One man there hath the convent seal of twenty houses in London, and his writing is much suspicious, for it is razed in twenty words; and the tenths decayeth and he is bound to reparations, and is not able to repair them, for he hath long owed £18 to this house and yet oweth it; and also he hath forfeited £40 to this house for not keeping his covenants.

There be also other tenants, and one of them hath two or three houses without any lease of them, and they maketh their under-tenants at their will, and driveth those tenements to ruin; and they will take no warning to avoid. And some of those tenements will be let with reparations borne by the tenant, and good surety therefor.

Your Mastership's pleasure and commandment known, all these matters may be reformed well enough and in short space.

---

[1] "Dampne" or "Dan," equivalent to the Latin *dominus.*

Memorandum, for Fogwell pound, it is like to be destroyed by the means of an ill tenant that hath no lease therein, for he is a very poor and wilful young man, that doth steal and destroy carps there, to the treble value of his rent; and yet that pound is no part of his covenant, but he hath free entry thereto and shutteth out all other the owners.

Master Maydwell, otherwise called the Scottish Friar, hath at mine instance lain three nights in the Charterhouse to examine certain books which I think to be much erroneous. I beseech your Mastership that I may know your pleasure whether he shall tarry here any longer or nay. The man is very honest, but he hath no money to pay.[1]

This Scottish Friar, Master John Maydwell, had been employed to preach to the brethren, and they were at first content to give him a hearing, but next day sent him word that they would not hear him again as he preached against the worship of images and was a blasphemer of Saints.[2] Presently an "Order for the Charterhouse"[3] was drawn up, putting the house under five or six temporal governors, two or three of whom were to be present at every meal and lodge there at night. They were to call before them all the members and servants of the house, and tell them that the King had pardoned all their heresies and treasons committed before that day, but that they should die without mercy if they offended again. They were to take the keys from the procurator and other officers, and govern the house, receiving all the rents and making all the payments. They were to call the monks individually before them at different times, use all persuasions and offer dispensations to those willing to leave the Order, with stipends for a year or two till they had found livings, and so forth. It seems to have been after this that, as we learn from Chauncy, two seculars appointed by Cromwell to have charge of the place, living very comfortably themselves, reduced the by no means

A new "Order for the Charterhouse."

---

[1] MS. Cott., Cleopatra E iv. ff. 36, 37.
[2] *L. P.*, IX. 283. [3] *L. P.*, IX. 524.

luxurious diet of the monks, leaving them to starve
on slender allowances of cheese or some such food,
and called in bullies who jeered at and buffeted them.[1]
Everything, in short, was done to depress, intimi-
date, and demoralise the community. Dan Thomas
Salter, who had of old been given to complaining of
his brethren,[2] had been imprisoned by Prior Houghton
for some breach of discipline, and was willing enough
to invoke Cromwell's aid for his release.[3] Whalley
recommended Cromwell to set him at liberty,[4] which
no doubt he did; and afterwards he and Dan John
Darley informed Jasper Filoll that they would fain
be out of the cloister with Cromwell's favour. At
the same time Dan Nicholas Rawlyns, with some help
from Archbishop Cranmer, procured from the new
authority a capacity to leave his Order, but had to
borrow secular garments from other priests to go
abroad in the world with.[5] Applying to Cromwell
for this dispensation, he poured forth sentiments
which he durst not utter inside the convent. He
had heard, he wrote, that the King, Lords, and
Commons, who had a conscience and a soul to keep
as well as himself, had enacted that the King should
be Supreme Head of the Church of England, for not
consenting to which their Father Prior and others
had suffered death. But he desired to express his
loyalty, though his brethren who suspected him for
it would wonder at him like a company of crows or
daws at a tame hawk. He complained, moreover,
that, contrary to the statutes, he had not even had a
half-year's probation before entering the Order, and
that his health could not stand the fasting and watching. There were not six monks in the cloister, he
said, but had some infirmity or other.[6]

---

[1] *Hist. aliquot Martyrum*, 109. This could not have been till after the
13th October, at which date they seem to have fared tolerably well. See
L. P., IX. 597.   [2] Chauncy's *Hist.*, pp. 81, 82.
[3] *L. P.*, VII. 246.   [4] *L. P.*, VIII. 601.
[5] *L. P.*, IX. 283, 284.   [6] *L. P.*, IX. 1150.

A curious story is told of Dan John Darley in earlier days, which seems slightly overdrawn. He one day murmured at his scanty fare, especially at the fish diet, declaring that he would rather eat toads. He straightway had an opportunity, not at all to his satisfaction, for his cell was invaded with such a number of toads that they jumped after him whenever he turned in it, leaped upon his plate when he dined, and were his companions in bed. If he threw one into the fire it jumped out unhurt, and when he took one up with the tongs for that purpose it emitted such a smell that he was forced to desist. Even other monks in the cloister smelt that horrid odour; and the toads continued in his garden for the space of three months, as he himself used to relate with great grief of heart.[1]

John Darley's vision.

Dan John Darley, no doubt, had a fevered imagination; but what he imagined during that troubled year, 1535, was a thing that got noised outside the monastery and gave sensible discomfort to Cromwell, who, as the King's minister, did his utmost to prevent the spread of the story. Nevertheless it got abroad, even as far as Rome, that the Charterhouse of London had been the scene of revelations from a deceased person, showing the glorious crown of martyrdom that had been won by the Cardinal of Rochester and the saints who had preceded him.[2] Dan John Darley had, in the spring before Prior Houghton's execution, attended the deathbed of another of the house named Father Raby, and had said to him, "Good Father Raby, if the dead may come to the quick, I beseech you to come to me"; and Raby, just before he died, said "Yea." The rest must be told in the words of Dan John Darley himself:—

"And since that I never did think upon him to St. John's Day, Baptist, last past. Item, the same

<hr>

[1] Chauncy, pp. 83, 84.　　　　[2] *L. P.*, ix. 681.

day at 5 of the clock at afternoon, I being in contemplation in our entry in our cell, suddenly he appeared to me in a monk's habit, and said to me, ' Why do ye not follow our Father?' And I said, ' Wherefore?' He said, ' For he is a martyr in heaven next unto angels.' And I said, ' Where be all our other Fathers which died as well as he?' He answered and said, ' They be well, but not so well as he.' And then I said to him, ' Father, how do ye?' And he answered and said, ' Well enough, but prayer both for you and other doth good.' And so suddenly vanished away.

" Item, upon Saturday next after, at 5 of the clock in the morning, in the same place in our entry, he appeared to me again with a long white beard and a white staff in his hand, lifting it up, whereupon I was afraid ; and then, leaning upon his staff, said to me, ' I am sorry that I lived not to I had been a martyr.' And I said, ' I think ye be as well as ye were a martyr.' And he said, ' Nay ; for my lord of Rochester and our Father was next unto the angels in heaven.' And then I said, ' Father, what else?' And then he answered and said : ' The angels of peace did lament and mourn without measure' ; and so vanished away." [1]

It was not pleasant, certainly, for the King and his chief minister when even a weak brother of the Charterhouse could utter stories like this. But his dream does not seem to have stirred him to emulate the martyrs, and no doubt the attentions he received from Whalley and Filoll increased his desire to be relieved from the obligation of his monastic vows. He was secure, moreover, of filling another post at Salisbury ; [2] and it may be presumed that with Cromwell's good leave he quitted London and went thither.

---

[1] Wright's *Suppression of the Monasteries*, pp. 34, 35.
[2] *L. P.*, IX. 284.

Another weak brother was won over to the King's service in a more effectual fashion; and as he was really a man of great ability I must give some little account of him. In 1534, when the oaths of the Charterhouse monks were taken by Bishop Roland Lee, one of those nineteen brethren who were priests was Andrew Borde. His physical constitution was not such as to endure easily the severities of the Carthusian rule. He wrote himself to the Prior of Hinton, "I am not able to bide the *rugorosytè* of your religion." The close air and confinement especially disagreed with him, and perhaps it was partly for this reason that about the year 1520 he procured from Rome a dispensation to leave the Order, though the reason assigned for it was that he might be made suffragan to the aged Bishop Sherburn of Chichester. This office he never exercised, and he remained a Carthusian, but seems to have had licence to go abroad, and he studied medicine in various schools on the Continent. After his return to England he served for some time as physician in attendance on Sir Robert Drury, when, in 1530—the year in which Wolsey was sent northward to his See of York—the Duke of Norfolk sent to have his advice, it would seem rather urgently, in the absence of Dr. Buttes, the Court physician. Borde, feeling himself "but a young doctor" then, though he could not have been very young in years, undertook the case with some anxiety; but his patient recovered, and Borde was called to the King's presence. It was probably owing to royal intercession that Prior Batmanson then procured for him from the Grande Chartreuse a dispensation from his "religion"; and this, no doubt, enabled him to go a second time beyond sea and visit the most approved universities and schools "to have a true cognition of the practice of physic." He took counsel with the most eminent physicians of the day with the view of writing "a

Andrew Borde.

dietary of health" for the Duke his patron's use. But he was home again, and in his cloister, as we have seen, on the 6th June 1534, when Bishop Roland Lee visited the house in company with Sheriff Kytson, and he took the oath of supremacy along with his fellow monks. He was certainly not one of the most unwilling.

In fact, it is clear that by this time his loyalty to the Order was suspected among the brethren. He was kept in prison strictly and was compelled, as he afterwards explained to Cromwell, to write at their request to Prior Houghton in the Tower; for which he hoped Cromwell would pardon him. "For I could never know nothing of no manner of matter but only by them"—such was his excuse, and he was thus led "stultitiously" to do as many of the others did, knowing "neither the King's noble acts" nor Cromwell's authority as the King's Vicegerent. But Cromwell not only set him free but gave him, as he said, "clearness of conscience," and he fully recognised "the ignorance and blindness" which he had shared with his fellow monks. In short, royal supremacy suited him very well as a means of emancipation from monastic discipline, though he still remained a Carthusian monk with licence to travel abroad. For he presently crossed the sea again; and by June 1535, seven weeks after his prior had suffered at Tyburn, and while Bishop Fisher was in the Tower after sentence awaiting execution on Tower Hill, he wrote from Bordeaux to Cromwell, saying that he had " perlustrated" Normandy, France, Gascony and Bayonne,[1] Castile, Biscay, Spain, and part of Portugal, and had returned through Aragon and Navarre to Bordeaux. And as one result of his travels he was compelled to inform Cromwell that he had heard by "divers credible persons" of all those

[1] "Byon" in MS., which has been misread "Lyon" and given as 'Lyons" in *L. P.*, VIII. 901.

countries, and also of Rome, Italy, and Germany, that
the Pope, the Emperor, and other Christian princes,
all but the French King, were dead set against the
King his master; that fleets and armies were everywhere preparing, and that England had few friends
in those parts of Europe.

From Bordeaux Andrew Borde traversed the south
of France into Dauphiny, where he visited the chief
house of his Order, the Grande Chartreuse, having a
little business to do there both for himself and for
the King of England. The solitude of the great
monastery was no doubt favourable to his designs.
The monks could have known nothing of Henry's
cruelties to their brethren, or of Paul III.'s determination, already formed, to deprive him of his
kingdom if he could but obtain the aid of temporal
princes to carry out the sentence. They had just
elected a new Grand Prior, by name John Gailhard,
whom Andrew approached as an English Carthusian,
declaring that though he had a licence to leave
his house procured for him by Father Batmanson,
his conscience was not satisfied without visiting the
General of the Order, and being assured that he was
fully "dispensed with the religion." He then told
him something about the affairs of the Order in
England, but evidently without saying a word about
the fate of Prior Houghton, which, indeed, it is just
possible that he might not have heard of himself,[1]
indicating that there were disputes between the King

He visits the Grande Chartreuse,

[1] This seems difficult to believe considering the indignation which it
aroused on the Continent, even at Venice, as we have seen above. But
Borde had doubtless left England the year before, and the news might not
have reached the south of France, where perhaps efforts were made to stop
its diffusion. It is curious that writing (no doubt) from the Grande
Chartreuse, on the 2nd August 1535, when there was no prior at the head of
the London Charterhouse, he addresses his letter "to Master Prior and the
Convent of the Charterhouse of London, and to all priors and convents of
the said Order in England." And even after he had reached London, in
August or September, he wrote to Cromwell referring to a licence he had "to
depart from the religion" granted to him by "the Prior of the Charterhouse
of London last being." Did he really mean Houghton, or was he thinking
of his predecessor Batmanson?

and the monks, which a letter from the head of the
Order would tend to pacify. The Grand Prior gave and obtains
him all he wanted, and enabled him to write to his letters
from the
brother Carthusians at home that the Father of the Grand
Head Charterhouse exhorted them "in any wise" to Prior.
obey their King, being sorry to hear that there had
been "wilful and sturdy opinions among them to the
contrary." The Grand Prior was also induced to
make Thomas Cromwell and the Bishop of Coventry
and Lichfield brothers of the religion, apparently on
the supposition that they would be mediators with
the King in behalf of the Order; and a mutilated
letter to the Bishop still exists which he entrusted
to Borde to take home with him. It is dated at the
Chartreuse, 1st August 1535.

Having achieved this grand object Borde lost no
time in coming home, and was with Cromwell at
Bishop's Waltham in September. In the following
spring we find him in Scotland, studying and practising physic "in a little university or study named
Glasgow."[1] But the rest of his career and correspondence do not greatly concern our subject, except
that it is interesting to note that he was unable to
collect debts due to him in London, where they called
him an apostate and a good-for-nothing fellow for
leaving his Order.[2]

How the monks still left in the London Charterhouse were dealt with appears pretty clearly in a
letter addressed to Cromwell by the obsequious Bedyll
written from Otford — no doubt, from Cranmer's
house there—on the 28th August 1535,[3] beginning
as follows :—

As I am greatly bounden to you, so I commend me heartily
to you. I am right sorry to see the foolishness and obstinacy

[1] L. P., x. 605.
[2] L. P., xi. 297, which may possibly be a year or two later than 1536,
where it is placed. The whole of Borde's letters are printed by Dr. Furnivall
in the Early English Text Society's Extra Series, No. 10.
[3] L. P., vii. 1090. See correction of date in viii. 200. The text is
printed in State Papers, i. 422.

of divers religious men, so addict to the Bishop of Rome and his usurped power that they contemn all counsel, and likewise jeopardie their bodies and souls and the suppression of their houses, as careless men and willing to die. If it were not for the opinion which men had, and some yet have, in their apparent holiness, which is and was, for the most part, covert hypocrisy, it made no great matter what became of them, so that their souls were saved. And as for my part, I would that all such obstinate persons of them which be willing to die for the advancement of the Bishop of Rome's authority were dead indeed by God's hand, that no man should run wrongfully into obloquy for their just punishment. For the avoiding whereof, and for the charity that I owe to their bodies and souls, I have taken some pains to reduce them from their errors, and will take more if I be commanded specially, to the intent that my sovereign lord the King's Grace should not be troubled or disquieted with their extreme madness and folly. I mean this by divers of the Charterhouses, and chiefly at London, but also by others, as by divers of the friars at Sion which be minded to offer themselves in sacrifice to the great idol of Rome. And in their so minding they be cursed of God, as all others be which put their trust and confidence in any man concerning everlasting life. And in case they had not such confidence in the Bishop of Rome they would never be so ready to lose their temporal life for him and for his sake, which is the great impostor and deceiver of the world.

Bedyll wishes the steadfast Carthusians were dead.

The writer of these shameful words was not a mere secular tool of the King and Cromwell. He was Archdeacon of Cornwall, advanced, of course, by royal favour, and he had been strenuously doing the King's work as a churchman. He had been getting the clergy to preach the King's title as Supreme Head of the Church, and he had received reports of the partial success with which this new duty had been enforced in the great monastery of Sion to which Dr. Reynolds had belonged. This house was a very special foundation, of the Order of St. Austin as reformed by St. Bridget of Sweden, and the full number of its regular inmates was eighty-five, of whom no less than sixty were nuns living in a separate wing of the building. The whole staff was ordained to consist of thirteen priests (corresponding to the number of the Apostles, including St. Paul) and seventy-two disciples, among whom the males were four deacons and eight lay brethren. Of the thirteen priests one was the Confessor, the head of the whole house, and of the sixty nuns one was Abbess.

Bedyll reports to Cromwell, as follows, what Mr. Mores, surveyor of the lands of Sion, had informed him about the success of the efforts to compel the monks to preach the King's title. The Confessor (Father Fewterer) had done as required and had preached twice since a visit which Bedyll had paid to the place in company with the Bishop of London (Stokesley). Master David Curson had done the same, though he once brought in the words *mea culpa* out of frame— perhaps by inadvertence. On Sunday last, however, one Whitford had preached—one of the most wilful, Bedyll calls him—and said nothing about the King's title. On St. Bartholomew's Day one Ricot complied with the order, but said that he who commanded him so to preach should discharge his conscience— thus laying the responsibility either on the Bishop of London or on the Confessor. But when he began The monks to declare the King's title, nine of the brethren, of Sion will not hear whose names Bedyll gives, immediately left. Bedyll the King's seriously thought that as Cromwell was then at a title declared; distance it would be better to forbid them preaching at all till his return, or else to see that those who did preach did their duty in declaring the King's title, and that others did not go away from the sermon. He suggested also that some of the King's servants thereabouts should be present at their sermons and report them.

I have shown already how Father Fewterer on his deathbed repented of having counselled resistance to the King's supremacy. Here we find him already

but a few
are
brought
to con-
formity.
submissive in August 1535 ; and it is to be noted that
two of the nine rebellious brethren who left the church
during Ricot's sermon were afterwards brought to
conformity by Bishop Stokesley. Their names were
Copynger and Lache. The course of events brought
home to them a lesson which, however they disliked
it at first, seemed to have real arguments in its favour;
and like Father Fewterer himself, they were anxious
to persuade the Carthusians to give up resistance to
the royal will. By that time, probably, the London
Charterhouse had got a new prior, not, certainly, of
its own election. In April 1535 the Royal Commissioners for the valuation of spiritual benefices in
Nottinghamshire sat in the Carthusian priory of
Beauvale, and declared to the monks that the King
was of right Supreme Head of the Church. The prior
was then absent in London ; but William Trafford,
proctor of the house, answered boldly, " I believe
firmly that the Pope of Rome is Supreme Head of the
Church Catholic," and on being asked if he would
stand to his words, he replied, " Even to death." He
wrote down the words himself, and was committed to
the custody of the Sheriff, who was one of the Commissioners.[1] But William Trafford, too, experienced
a change, however it may have come about ; and just

A new
prior is set
over the
brethren.
a twelvemonth later, in April 1536, he was appointed
by Cromwell Prior of the London Charterhouse, on
which he went up to pay his respects to his patron
with a letter of recommendation from Henry Man,
Prior of Sheen, another convert to royal supremacy.[2]

It was about this time, certainly in 1536, that
Copynger and Lache, writing partly in behalf of
Father Fewterer, endeavoured to dissuade the brethren
of the London Charterhouse from continuing their
resistance to royal supremacy. The writers urged
them to believe that their own conformity and that

---

[1] *L. P.*, VIII. 560, 692.
[2] *L. P.*, VIII. 585, which is misplaced in 1535.

of others was conscientious, and not dictated by fear of bodily pain, penury, death, or shame, or worldly loss. They found arguments to absolve all doubts and scruples. If any of the Carthusians would not obey the power [1] that God had set to be obeyed, "his prince, I mean," says the writer, "nor his prelate," if he had learning to defend his position, he could be answered. Obedience was due to a prince or prelate if it was not expressly against the law of God. They had considered the matter much, and given papers containing the result of their labours to the Prior of Sheen. They had found arguments both in the Old and the New Testament in favour of the King's authority, and none whatever for "the Bishop of Rome's." As to the supremacy, if there was any Church in England the King was supreme. St. Paul counselled obedience to the higher power. It was true that the King did in the spiritualty what other princes had not done before ; but this was not against God's law, for it was admitted that the Pope might license a layman to be judge in a spiritual cause, and if so it was lawful for a prince to be judge in spiritual causes, and so forth.[2]

Were such reasonings sound ? To men who upheld that the Pope had a divine authority as head of a universal Church, of course they could never be so. To us it may appear that there was a good deal of truth in them. But it is clear enough that to religious men of that generation—even to the very men who were using these arguments — they would have appeared of little weight but for the formidable coercive power by which royal supremacy was enforced. Yet there was a far greater trial than that

[1] The word in the MS. looks very like "priour," written with a contraction over the p to represent "ri," and it may very well be that the writers were thinking of the new prior Trafford, whom most of the Carthusians would not acknowledge. But if we ignore the ambiguous contraction, the word is simply "pour," *i.e.* power, which harmonises better with the sense.

[2] *L. P.*, VIII. 78, misplaced in 1535. The letter is printed in full, but not very accurately, in Smythe's *Historical Account of Charterhouse*, pp. 64-70.

Conflicts of feeling. of coercion itself—the tears and groans and expostulations of kinsmen and friends urging the most steadfast to abandon the fundamental principles of their Order. The way, indeed, was free for any of them to leave the Order itself. "But, thank God," says Chauncy, "such was their holiness of life, their constancy of mind, their modesty in speech, their cheerfulness of countenance, their alacrity in doing, their moderation in all things, that all who saw them were confounded. Though bereft of an outward prior, and made orphans without a father, yet to each of them his conscience was a prior, inwardly directing and instructing them in all things."[1] Troubled, no doubt, at meeting with such resistance, Mr. Secretary Cromwell was "much busied" about the Charterhouse monks, and it was difficult to "get him in a good mood" for other subjects.[2]

The process by which some monks in different Orders were subdued to the King's will was a gradual one. In December 1535, Copynger and Lache of Sion had not yet been brought into conformity. But hopes were entertained of important conquests, even in the great monastery to which they belonged. Among the monks the King's clerical tools, Richard Layton and Bedyll, even with the aid of Dr. Buttes and Shaxton, the Queen's almoner, were as yet making little progress in persuasion ; but with the nuns things looked somewhat better. Lord Windsor had a sister and some relations among them, whom he was naturally very anxious to win over to compliance. The conversion of the Confessor, of course, was a great assistance. On the 16th the Confessor and Bishop Stokesley came into the women's chapter-house, and both declared to them that upon their consciences and the peril of their souls they considered that the ladies ought to consent to the King's title. This promised to smooth matters, and Layton and Bedyll fancied they saw an easy way to victory. They

[1] *Historia aliquot Martyrum*, pp. 110-11.   [2] *L. P.*, IX. 950.

desired such of the ladies as agreed to acknowledge
the King's title to sit still, and those who refused it to
leave the chapter-house. Not one of the nuns left her
seat. But this did not exactly mean complete agreement; more probably the feeling was that Layton
and Bedyll had no proper authority to address them.
One Agnes Smith was urgent with several of the The nuns
other sisters not to allow their convent seal to be will not
attached to any act of submission; and apparently submit.
she prevailed, for among the numerous monastic
acknowledgments of supremacy in the Record Office
we do not find one of the monastery of Sion, not even
of the nuns.[1]

As to the Carthusians, it was suggested by Bishop
Hilsey, whom the King had appointed as Fisher's
successor in the See of Rochester, that the monks
should be taken to Paul's Cross every week to hear
the sermon there, "that their hearts might be
lightened by knowledge, their bodies escape such
pains as they were worthy to suffer, and their souls
escape the judgment of God for such demerits as their
ignorant hearts had conceived."[2] This highly spiritual
advice seems to have been acted upon, for by
Cromwell's orders one Sunday morning four of the Four Car-
Charterhouse monks were seized during the celebra- thusians
tion of mass, carried out of the convent, and taken mass,
to St. Paul's to hear a bishop preach, who was
probably no other than Hilsey himself. They were
brought to the usual place in custody of the Sheriffs
of London, and after the sermon they were sent
home again. But they were not edified by what
they heard.[3]

It appears, indeed, that one of the four who was
to have been taken to hear the sermon was that day
the celebrant at the mass, and the officers had the
grace to let him go on with the function. They put
another in his place to make up the number. But

[1] *L. P.*, ix. 986.   [2] *L. P.*, ix. 989.   [3] Chauncy, p. 111.

now it was resolved to use stronger measures, and the four whose names had been put down to be taken to Paul's Cross were seized on the 4th May 1536, the
and sent to the North.
anniversary of the prior's martyrdom, and sent to two other monasteries belonging to the Order in the North. "For four entire years," says Chauncy (that is to say, from 1534 to 1537), "we had to endure very special troubles during the months of May and June, though by no means left in peace at other seasons."[1] The four monks who were thus dealt with were, first John Rochester and James Walworth—these two were sent to the Charterhouse of Hull; and next, John Fox and Chauncy himself, who were committed to that of Beauvale in Nottinghamshire. "The King's councillors then thought," says Chauncy, "to lay hands on those who were left, as if they had been without wall, or bars, or doors. And they came with gaping mouth to seize and disperse the flock; but, blessed be God, who did not give them a prey to their teeth, they remained immovable and steady upon a rock." The councillors then sent eight of them to the Bridgettine house of Sion to hear the exhortation of the dying Father Fewterer, of which we have already heard. But though some of them were half persuaded at the moment that he was right, when they got back to their own house they were again firm in resisting the royal counsels. The opposition of the brethren was undoubtedly strengthened by corporate feeling, and the consciousness that weakness in one or two of them would have encouraged the King to put the rest to death.[2]

Archbishop Lee of York, however, had already won over the priors of the Carthusian houses of Hull and Mountgrace. They and other heads of houses had come to him for counsel what to do in times of so great peril, and he had always counselled them to do as he himself had done, and many others "both great

---

[1] Chauncy, p. 112.   [2] *Ibid.*, pp. 113, 114.

learned men and taken for good men." " The priors
of Hull and Mountgrace," he wrote to the King, " were
sore bent rather to die than to yield to this your royal
style, but I have persuaded both to change their
opinions."[1]

Just after this, by the middle of March 1536, the
Act had been passed for the suppression of all the
smaller monasteries with revenues under £200 a
year. With what pressure the servile Parliament
was induced to pass this measure we need not inquire. There was a tradition in a later generation,
that a comprehensive measure on these lines had
been in contemplation some years before, and that
Convocation had been urged to consent under threat
of the King's displeasure, but that Bishop Fisher
had warned them in a fable that the axe which cut
down small trees would in time leave a whole forest
bare.[2] We cannot well feel much certainty of the
truth of this story, but we are in no great danger of
error if we regard the royal visitation of the monasteries set on foot in the autumn of 1535, as having
been designed to smooth the way for a large confiscation of monastic property. Of this I shall speak
more at large in the next chapter. Here suffice it to
say that two principal agents, Dr. Thomas Legh and
Dr. Richard Layton, commissioned by the King's
Vicegerent, Cromwell, traversed the West, South, and
North of England in the course of a few months,
visiting the monasteries, giving injunctions which it
was hard to keep, and which were well calculated to
promote applications to Cromwell for dispensations,
and sending reports of gross scandals and disgusting
impurities which they professed to have discovered in
two-thirds of the houses they visited. That these
reports were ever seen by the persons accused, or
that they were ever submitted to Parliament, as
historians for a long time believed, there is no evidence

*The sup-
pression of
the smaller
monas-
teries.*

[1] *L. P.*, x. 93, 99.   [2] Ortroy, pp. 222-4.

whatever to show; and apart from the questionable characters of the visitors and the extreme rapidity with which they did their work, a good deal can be shown to discredit several of their statements in detail. Reports, moreover, of a totally different character were made not very long afterwards by a number of the local gentry in different counties, acting under a royal commission. But the general effect of the reports of the Visitors was declared by the King himself to the House of Commons, which he seems to have visited on purpose, and the bill for the confiscation of the smaller houses was passed with a preamble declaring (quite against the tenor of the secret reports) that while vice and abominable living abounded in houses where there were fewer than twelve inmates, good discipline prevailed in larger monasteries, to which it would be advisable to transfer the demoralised brethren of those smaller houses.[1]

At the same time there was a judicious provision in the Act, that the King might grant, by patent under the Great Seal, licences to certain of those minor monasteries to continue—a faculty of which he made use in a considerable number of instances, when a sufficient sum of money was offered by those interested. This was frequently done by neighbours, for of course houses whose revenues were so small could not easily afford the sum that was requisite; but the monasteries, on the whole, were popular, and many of them in particular situations discharged specially useful functions, or were endeared by old associations to families of wealth and rank. Hull Charterhouse was one of those for which intercession was made. The townsmen of Hull thought it deserved to stand on account of the virtuous living and hospitality of the monks; and though its revenues were under £200 a year it was spared for a payment

[1] Stat. 27 Hen. VIII. c. 28.

into the Exchequer of £233, 6s. 8d.[1] It would hardly have been so if the prior and his brethren had not been persuaded to accept the royal supremacy ; against which, evidently, Rochester and Walworth stood alone in their protest.

It would seem that John Rochester, after the death of Prior Houghton, must at least have held an informal position among the brethren in London as a monk of special zeal. Early in August, Cranmer as Archbishop had sent for him and Nicholas Rawlins to converse with them and bring them over. With Rawlins he succeeded, but he was obliged to send Rochester back to the Charterhouse unaltered in his devotion to Rome.[2] Later, as we have seen, Bedyll and Crome bestowed long exhortations upon him and Fox to no purpose, and when copies of *The Defence of Peace* were given to the monks, he apparently was the " president " to whom they referred the question whether they should read the book, and at whose command they returned the volumes unread to Filoll. On further exhortation he consented to read over one copy himself, but after keeping it four or five days he burned it.[3] He and Walworth, of whose previous history less is known, remained in the Hull Charterhouse during the great commotions in the North in the winter of 1536-37. With these risings they do not seem in any way to have been mixed up. The risings themselves, indeed, were mainly due to the general dislike of heresy and of the first steps taken in the suppression of the monasteries. But these Carthusian monks, living within their cloisters, were not insurgents and did not favour insurrection. It was the laity who were alarmed at the new tendencies of things, more than any monks or clergy. The legislation of the

The Carthusians.

The Northern Risings.

[1] *L. P.*, x. 980. Comp. Gasquet's *Henry VIII. and the English Monasteries*, ii. 530 (ed. 1888-89).
[2] *L. P.*, VIII. 283.   [3] See above, p. 15.

last Parliament had been revolutionary and destructive of ancient authority ; and the insurgents, perfectly loyal to the King, wished the removal and punishment of wicked councillors like Cromwell and Riche, and of heretical bishops like Cranmer and Latimer. They wanted a free Parliament to revise the recent revolutionary legislation, and to relieve them of the fear of new inordinate confiscations. And so formidable was the revolt that Norfolk, sent to quell it, was obliged to temporise. He quieted the people by a promise, which he was understood to have given by authority, that there should be a free Parliament in the North of England for the consideration and redress of grievances.

But there soon appeared reasons for doubting the good faith of the Government, and there was serious danger of a new commotion in the North, of which Hallom's attempt to get possession of Hull was one of the first indications. Indeed, new commotions did occur, even after the failure of this and of Bigod's rebellion in Yorkshire, in the region farther west, south of Carlisle. The Duke of Norfolk came down again into the North, not, as had been expected, to complete the pacification of which he had given hopes, but to administer severe punishment to all new offenders. He was called to Carlisle by the disturbances in the West, and after doing " dreadful execution " there, returned to Newcastle and so into Yorkshire, where he visited Hull in the middle of March and was at York a little later. At Hull he seems to have called Rochester, and probably Walworth also, before him, when Rochester said he was ready to prove that the King had been deluded by false counsel to assume the title of Supreme Head. This he told the Duke he had already declared to Bedyll and others in London, and he even sent a letter to Norfolk [1] after the Duke had left Hull, asking

[1] *L. P.*, xii. i. 778.

that he might have an opportunity to put the matter
before the King himself. He trusted that Norfolk's
influence might be of use in this, as it had already
been on a very important point not long before. For
it was through Norfolk that the King had "staid
Purgatory"—a point which deserves a word or two
of retrospective notice.

In June 1534, when the encouragement of heretical
preachers was important to support the Anne Boleyn
marriage against the Pope, Archbishop Cranmer issued
an order to the clergy of his Province, inhibiting all
persons from preaching either for or against Purgatory
and some other disputed doctrines for one year.[1]
Like order, of course, was taken for the province of
York, where Archbishop Lee mentions that the year
was to expire at Whitsunday 1535.[2] A definite
decision was expected to be promulgated by that
time as to the sort of doctrine that was to be sanctioned by royal authority. But the time was allowed
to lapse, and Archbishop Lee received instructions in
January 1536 still to avoid contrariety in preaching
against novel opinions, but to repress the temerity of
adherents of "the Bishop of Rome."[3] When Parliament met next month the members were abundantly
supplied with a number of new printed books designed
to provoke legislation against images, adoration of
Saints, and the doctrine of Purgatory.[4] In the spring
the bishops held conferences on the subject with
Cranmer at Lambeth ; but before the end of April the
King came to a determination about it, and preachers
were ordered to avoid new opinions and return to the
old fashion of preaching.[5] That this decision was due
largely to the influence of Norfolk, Father Rochester's
letter shows, and it is what we might otherwise pretty

[1] *L. P.*, VII. 464, 871. From the date of Chapuys's letter (871) it is clear
this order was given some time after the inhibition, No. 463, which was in
Easter week.
[2] *L. P.*, IX. 704.
[3] *L. P.*, X. 172.
[4] *L. P.*, X. 282. Comp. 528, 619.
[5] *L. P.*, X. 601, 752, 831.

well expect. Norfolk was always in favour of old orthodoxy, as far as he might be allowed to support it.

But to be asked to send to the King an obstinate Carthusian, who, when refreshed with proper diet— for it seems that he was much debilitated at the very time he wrote—hoped to maintain in the face of royalty that the title of Supreme Head was unlawful, was altogether out of the question. In writing to Cromwell, Norfolk wondered how the man was ever sent into those parts at all, when he had shown his opinion to Mr. Bedyll and others in London. Why was he not put to execution there?[1] His letter, of course, which the Duke forwarded to Cromwell, showed him in the opinion of the Council to be a rank traitor, and the Duke was instructed, if he persisted in his opinions, to deal with him as such. A month later the Duke, who had been at Sheriff-hutton, returned for a day to York and had before him Rochester and Walworth, indicted for denial of the King's supremacy.[2] They were hanged in chains at York on the 11th May.[3]

Two more Carthusian martyrs.

Just one week later came a great crisis in the London Charterhouse. Under a new prior, placed over them by Cromwell to bring about compliance with the King's will, persuasions, of course, were not wanting, and Archdeacon Bedyll, backed up by Richard Gwent, the Archdeacon of London, pressed them harder than before, and succeeded in bringing about a division in the community. Nineteen of the monks were won over, and unwillingly joined the prior in taking the oath of supremacy. They took it, as Chauncy plainly says, against their consciences, with qualifications which they were allowed to make, and hoping that their compliance would avert the complete destruction of their house. But ten others

In London some submit, some die in prison.

---

[1] *L. P.*, XII. i. 777.   [2] *L. P.*, XII. i. 846, 1156, 1172.
[3] Chauncy, p. 118.

remained refractory. Two documents were drawn up by a notary of the submission on the 18th May 1537.[1]

The ten who remained faithful to their principles were allowed but eleven days' rest. On the 29th May they were committed to the filthy prison of Newgate, where with stench and squalor they all of them but one gradually succumbed to fate. The single survivor three years later, on the 4th November 1540, was brought out to suffer a martyrdom like that of his prior—the brutal punishment awarded to high treason.[2]

The conformity of the majority did not save the house from ultimate extinction. On the 10th June it was surrendered by Prior Trafford in the name of the convent, with a formal confession that the majority had provoked the King by their offences, and deserved the severest death as well as the confiscation of the property of their priory, and that they thought it best to throw themselves upon the King's mercy.[3] Four days later Archdeacon Bedyll informed Cromwell, in the following cold-blooded letter, of the process which was gradually going on in Newgate :—

My very good Lord, after my most hearty commendations, it shall please your Lordship to understand that the monks of the Charterhouse here at London, which were committed to Newgate for their traitorous behaviour longtime continued against the King's Grace, be almost despatched by the hand of God, as it may appear to you by this bill enclosed; whereof, considering their behaviour and the whole matter, I am not sorry, but would that all such as love not the King's Highness and his worldly honor were in like case. My Lords, as ye may, I desire you in the way of charity, and none otherwise, to be good lord to the prior of the said Charterhouse, which is as honest a man as ever was in that habit (or else I am much deceived), and is one which never

---

[1] *L. P.*, XII. i. 1232, 1233 ; Chauncy, p. 115.
[2] Chauncy, pp. 116, 117. See correction of date in *Annotations*, p. 145.
[3] *L. P.*, XII. ii. 64.

offended the King's Grace by disobedience of his laws, but
hath labored very sore continually for the reformation of
his brethren, and now at the last, at mine exhortation and
instigation, constantly moved and finally persuaded his
brethren to surrender their house, lands, and goods into the
King's hands and to trust only to his mercy and grace. I
beseech you, my Lord, that the said Prior may be so entreated
by your help that he be not sorry and repent that he hath
feared and followed your sore words and my gentle exhortation made unto him to surrender his said house, and think
that he might have kept the same if your Lordship and I had
not led him to the said surrender. But surely I believe that
I know the man so well that how so ever he be order[ed] he
will be contented without grudge; he is a man of such charity
as I have not seen the like.

As touching the house of the Charterhouse, I pray God,
if it shall please the King to alter it, that it may be turned
into a better use, seeing it is in the face of our world, and
much communication will run thereof throughout this realm ;
for London is the common country of all England, from
which is derived to all parts of this realm all good and ill
occurrent here.

From London the 14th day of June.

By your Lordship's at commandment,

THOMAS BEDYLL.

The enclosure is as follows :—

There be departed :—Brother William Greenewode, Dan
John Davye, Brother Robert Salt, Brother Walter Peereson,
Dan Thomas Greene.

There be even at the point of death :—Brother Thomas
Scryven, Brother Thomas Reedyng.

There be sick :—Dan Thomas Johnson, Brother William
Horn.

One is whole :—Dan Bere.[1]

So it appears that it was only by " sore words " on
the part of Cromwell, as well as " gentle exhortation "
on that of Bedyll, that Prior Trafford, who a year
before he was made head of the house had expressed

---

[1] MS. Cott., Cleop. E iv. 217. Printed in Ellis' *Letters* (1 S. ii. 76) and
Wright's *Suppression of the Monasteries*, p. 162. But Wright omits the
enclosure, and Ellis misreads two names in the list.

himself as ready to die for the Pope's supremacy, was induced both to make the surrender and get his brethren's consent almost to the very thing that they had taken an unwilling oath in order to avoid. It was important that he should be rewarded for his submissiveness in such a way that he should not repent it. In his behalf, at least, Bedyll could write " in the way of charity."

Did Prior Trafford not repent it? We have no record of his feelings.[1] The one thing which is beyond all question is that the surrender was forced. The King had set his mind on the complete suppression of the Charterhouse, had got Prior Trafford's aid to win over as many of the brethren as possible to consent to the act, and was determined to get rid of the rest by a process of slow murder in Newgate. It appears that an old MS., preserved long ago among the English Carthusian exiles, gave an obituary of those poor sufferers, showing the date on which each of them departed to God ; and the record is in complete conformity with the above list. William Greenwood died on the 6th June, John Davy on the 8th, Robert Salt on the 9th, Walter Pierson and Thomas Green on the 10th, Thomas Scriven on the 15th, and Thomas Reding on the 16th ; while Richard Beer—the only one above described as " whole " on the 14th June—did not die till the 9th August; and Thomas Johnson, though sick on the 14th June, held out till the 20th September.[2] That some of them lived so long after a time excited the King's astonishment, who suspecting, what was indeed the case, that private sympathy had come to the aid of the afflicted, caused a stricter watch to be kept over them. For in truth a kind-hearted young woman named Margaret Clement, whose mother had been

Forced surrender of the house.

[1] He got only a pension of £20 a year for his pains. Dugdale's *Monasticon*, vi. 10.
[2] Hendriks, 228.

brought up in Sir Thomas More's household, had bribed the jailor to get access to them, and, disguising herself as a milkmaid, came to them "with a great pail upon her head full of meat, wherewith she fed that blessed company, putting meat into their mouths, they being tied and not able to stir, nor to help themselves; which having done, she afterwards took from them their natural filth." But when the stricter watch was instituted the jailor durst not allow her the same free access as before. Nevertheless, by importunity and by the force of bribes, she prevailed with him for a time to let her go up upon the roof, just above their cells, and, removing some of the tiles, she was able to let down by a string some meat in a basket and approach it to their mouths as they stood chained against the posts. It was a troublesome operation, and the poor prisoners after all could not feed themselves very effectually. The danger of discovery, moreover, was such that the jailor at length refused to let her come any longer.[1]

There were still two monks of the London house, John Fox and Maurice Chauncy, who, having been removed, as we have seen, to the priory of Beauvale in Nottinghamshire, had not even yet acknowledged the supremacy. In August 1537 that priory was visited by Henry Man, prior of Sheen, a Carthusian whom the King, having won him over to his supremacy, had appointed visitor of his own Order, along with John Mitchel, prior of Witham. They found Fox and Chauncy "very scrupulous in the matter concerning the Bishop of Rome," though they were not obstinate and willingly agreed to confer upon the subject with Copinger, who, since Father Fewterer's death, had been appointed, of course by royal authority, Confessor of Sion in his room. They were

---

[1] Morris's *Troubles of our Catholic Forefathers* (1 Ser.), i. 27, 28. This kind-hearted lady died at an advanced age at Louvain, where she had been for more than fifty years Superior of the convent of St. Ursula.

accordingly sent up to Sion, where they appear to have had lengthened discussions with the new Confessor; to whom also William Broke and Bartholomew Burgoyn, two of those monks still in the London Charterhouse who had once been sent to Sion to hear Father Fewterer's dying exhortations, wrote to thank him for the great pains he took with them, hoping that he would succeed in their conversion. "We have not forgotten," they said, "the pains and patience and longanimity that ye had with us when we were with you, and how hard it was, and in a manner impossible, to us to follow your counsel. But in process of time we did follow your counsel, thanks be to Jesu. This we write, for we suppose it to be thus with our brethren; and if it be thus, we instantly desire you to continue your good patience to them. . . . Glad would we be to hear that they would surrender their wits and consciences to you, that they might come home, and as bright lanterns show the light of religious conversation amongst us, as they can right well, to God be glory." [1]

The reader can judge from words like these what lengthened arguments it required to overcome conscientious scruples and subvert an ancient order. But we cannot blink the fact that the ancient order was in the end effectually subverted, and even conscience cannot bind a man to a dead master or a woman to a dead husband. The moral influence and political power of Rome were tottering to their fall. The moral influence might in part revive, and did so; but the political power was going, if not actually gone. In this very year, 1537, Cardinal Pole had been sent by the Pope as Legate to go to the Low Countries and watch matters in England, where rebellion had broken out in opposition to the King's revolutionary measures. A papal legate had hitherto been honoured in all countries as the ambassador of

Cardinal Pole's abortive mission.

[1] Hendriks, pp. 232-6.

the most sacred Power on earth. But such was Henry's extraordinary influence over secular princes that neither Francis I. nor Mary of Hungary, the Regent of the Netherlands, durst give a public reception to one whom the King of England denounced as a traitor to himself, and whose delivery to him as such he had the audacity to demand. Neither Francis nor Mary of Hungary desired to offend the Pope; but to offend Henry VIII. would have been more dangerous still, and they begged Pole's indulgence for not receiving him. Pole accordingly, after making a public entry into Paris in the French king's absence, went on to Cambray, and from thence, after waiting some time, was escorted hastily to the security of Liège without having accomplished anything.

The King of England was thus an absolute sovereign in his own realm. There was no power on earth to control him within or without the kingdom; and it is no wonder that the scrupulous Fox and Chauncy at length yielded to Copinger's arguments and took the oath of supremacy—a weakness with which Chauncy ever afterwards reproached himself as a grievous sin. They were partly reconciled to it, as their brethren had been, by the belief that their submission on this point would preserve the monastery from being utterly suppressed. In so thinking they were deceived. The work begun in 1536 under the Act of Parliament for suppressing the smaller monasteries was continued two years later by other processes, till in the year 1540 not a single monastery was left in England. On the 15th November 1538, within a year after Fox and Chauncy had taken the oath and been restored to their old priory, the monks were turned out of the house and pensioned.[1] Their old home of piety was turned into a brothel and a place of wrestling matches; the church was made a repository

End of the
London
Charter-
house.

[1] Chauncy's original date of 1539 is corrected by his last editor, Doreau. See Pref. p. xxi.

for the King's tents, and the altars were profaned as gaming tables. At last, six years after the expulsion of the monks, the place was at least purified, the buildings being given to a courtier, Sir Edward North, who turned them into a private residence, converting the church into a dining-room and pulling down all the cloister.[1]

[1] Chauncy, pp. 119, 120.

CHAPTER II

VISITATION AND SUPPRESSION OF MONASTERIES

Magnitude of the change caused by the overthrow of papal authority.

THE overthrow of papal authority in England, which was the great achievement of Henry's reign, has brought about such enormous results, not merely in this, but, since then, in every country in Europe, that we can hardly realise what a stupendous task he undertook, and with what difficulty he carried it through. Royal supremacy over the Church within any realm, whether recognised by that name or not, is really a universal principle now. The sovereign authority is supreme over all persons and over all causes, whether ecclesiastical or civil. A jurisdiction termed ecclesiastical may still remain, but it is not the ecclesiastical jurisdiction of the Middle Ages, when bishops had their own courts and cited heretics before them *virtute officii*, without interference from any other power. As Selden put the matter in his *Table Talk*, "There is no such thing as spiritual jurisdiction—all is civil; the Church's is the same with the Lord Mayor's." The same, he meant, as to the supreme determining power, though there might be a distinction in the tribunal according to the nature of the cause. But as to all jurisdiction being civil, it is scarcely so in one sense ; for civil authority could not stand alone without a religious sanction.

'We are well satisfied, indeed, that there are no Church tribunals now independent of the State ; but we hardly realise that a result which we consider so

wholesome was due in the first instance to unex-
ampled tyranny and oppression. Nor was it the
work of a mere commonplace tyrant; for no such
character would have found the existing system any
very great impediment to his lust, his selfishness, or
his caprice. Henry was at once a casuistical and a
self-willed tyrant, professedly observant of law, but
determined to carry his point at any cost. He had
with great difficulty forced Convocation to acknowledge his supremacy, and they had only done so with
a qualification which they considered essential. He
got Parliament to ratify it without the qualification. He procured the most merciless enactments
against any who should deny it; yet even Parliament, like Convocation, would not do what was
required without putting in a qualification of its own.
The parliamentary qualification in the statute was
designed to protect those who did not deny the
supremacy "maliciously." But the lawyers treated
the word as superfluous, just as Parliament had
ignored the qualification inserted by Convocation.
And so the heads of martyrs fell on the block, or
their bodies were suspended on the gibbet. And all
this was done, in the first place, to justify the King's
marriage with Anne Boleyn, and, after Anne Boleyn's
fall, to justify the King's own enactments.

Yet even with all this the result was but imper-   Difficulty
fectly achieved. We have followed the process so far   with which
to the extinction of one religious house—the house   achieved.
which undoubtedly offered most resistance to the
royal claims. But the monasteries, without outspoken opposition, were a far greater obstacle than the
bishops and Convocations. In the Convocations the
Church of each province seemed to have but one
neck, as Caligula wished the Roman people had, and
the bishops were helpless after their Convocations had
yielded. All of them, except the Spaniard who was
Bishop of Llandaff, took the oath of supremacy within

the space of little more than three months. But the
monasteries still remained—scores of houses often in
a single county, besides those which clustered about
the suburbs of great towns, and the friaries within
the precincts of such towns. Of the friars, indeed,
one Order had already been suppressed, namely, the
more strict Order of Franciscans, who were called
Observants. Bound to the rule of St. Francis in all
its rigour, unable to possess property, and incapable
of being seduced by the ordinary allurements which
wealth and power can place in the way of other men,
the Observants were popular mainly on account of
their known fearlessness and independence. But it
was just these qualities which made them specially
objectionable to the King. On Easter Sunday, 1532,
the year before he married Anne Boleyn, Friar Peto,
preaching before him at Greenwich, warned him
against sycophants who, like the lying prophets of
Ahab, encouraged him in evil counsels, and also
against the danger he incurred of excommunication
if he put away his true wife, Katharine. The King
vainly remonstrated with him at a private interview,
and no less vainly endeavoured, in Peto's absence
next Sunday, to correct the impression made, by
getting a chaplain of his own to preach a contrary
doctrine in the same place. The royal chaplain was
answered by another of the friars, the Warden of the
Greenwich brethren, who, for his boldness, was told
by a nobleman that he deserved to be put in a sack
and thrown into the Thames. "Make these threats
to courtiers," replied the Warden ; "the way lieth as
open to heaven by water as by land." [1]

If the King were to have his way, such a dangerous
Order, it was clear, must be suppressed. One of the
earliest measures taken two years later for enforcing

[1] The accounts of this episode, given by Sanders, and before him by
Harpsfield (*Pretended Divorce*, pp. 202-205), are quite in accordance with the
strictly contemporary and independent reports of the Imperial and Venetian
ambassadors (*L. P.*, v. 941 ; *Venetian Calendar*, iv. No. 760).

the royal supremacy, as may be seen in a State paper of the period, had special reference to the control of the friars and the regulation of preaching. The following is the abstract of this document given in the Calendar of State Papers :—

All the Friars of every monastery in England must be assembled in their chapter house and examined separately concerning their faith and obedience to Henry VIII., and bound by an oath of allegiance to him, Queen Anne, and her present and future issue. They must be bound by oath to preach and persuade the people of the above at every opportunity. They must acknowledge the King as Supreme Head of the Church, as Convocation and Parliament have decreed. They must confess that the Bishop of Rome has no more authority than other bishops. They shall not call the Bishop of Rome Pope, either privately or publicly, or pray for him as such. They shall not presume to wrest the Scriptures, but preach the words and deeds of Christ sincerely and simply, according to the meaning of Holy Scriptures and Catholic doctors. The sermons of each preacher must be carefully examined, and burned if not Catholic, orthodox, and worthy of a Christian preacher.

Preachers must be warned to commend to God and the prayers of the people, first the King as Head of the Church of England, then Queen Anne with her child, and lastly the Archbishop of Canterbury, with the other Orders of the Clergy. Each house must be obliged to show their gold, silver, and other moveable goods, and deliver an inventory of them. Each house must take an oath, under their convent seal, to observe the above orders.[1]

To confess the King to be Supreme Head of the Church of England was a thing that friars of any Order had never done yet ; but means were taken to compel them. The King, wielding powers which had hitherto belonged to the Pope, first appointed the Prior of the Austin Friars in London (Dr. George Browne) as Provincial of the whole Order of Friars Hermits in England, and Dr. John Hilsey as Provincial of the whole Order of the Dominicans, or

How the friars were brought under control.

[1] *L. P.*, VI. 590, from MS. Cott., Cleopatra E iv. 11.

Friars Preachers ; then gave these two jointly a commission to visit the houses of all Orders of friars whatever—not only their own two Orders, but the Franciscans, Carmelites, and Crossed Friars—to inquire into their lives and morals and fealty to the King, and to lay down injunctions for their future conduct, calling in the secular arm, if necessary, to enforce obedience.[1] Of course Browne and Hilsey were men well suited to serve the King's purpose, or they would not have been selected; and each of them had his reward in a bishopric not very long after. The lessons of compliance which it was their function to teach were, moreover, strongly recommended to attention by the fact that two Observant Friars, Rich and Risby, Wardens of the houses at Richmond and Canterbury respectively, had been hanged at Tyburn in April as abettors of the Nun of Kent. Yet the efforts of Browne and Hilsey were but subsidiary to those of other agents by whom it was hoped to bring the friars, especially the Observants, into complete subjection.

Those worthy associates, Bishop Roland Lee and Thomas Bedyll, little more than a fortnight after the execution of the Nun's adherents, had got the prior, convent, and novices of Sheen to take the oath required by the statute, and had done their best to persuade the Observants of Richmond to do the like. With these they confessed that after repeated conferences they had been unsuccessful, and had despaired of influencing them till the 7th May, when they passed on to Sion. It was just three weeks and a day before their visit to the London Charterhouse, and their success in swearing the whole inmates of one Carthusian house at Sheen encouraged them to look for further conquests. They began to think that the Observants of Richmond would be

[1] *L. P.*, vi. 530, 587 (18).

more pliable, and meanwhile they would see what they could do with the brethren and sisters of Sion before they went on to London. They were not successful, and, as we have seen already, their first visit to the London Charterhouse on the 29th May had to be supplemented by a second visit from Bishop Lee in company with Sheriff Kitson on the 6th June, in order to produce a very marked effect. When by these means the qualified oath had been procured from the London Carthusians, Bishop Lee and Bedyll were directed once more to turn their attention to the Observants; but, as the following letter shows, their zeal met with very little success.

BISHOP LEE AND BEDYLL TO CROMWELL

Please it you to understand that on Saturday last, about 6 of the clock, we received your letters by the Provincial of the Augustine Friars,[1] according to the which letters we took our journey forthwith towards Richmond, and came thither betwixt 10 and 11 at night. And in the morning following we had first communication with the warden and one of the seniors named Sebastian, and after with the whole convent, and moved them by all the means and policies that we could devise to consent to the articles delivered unto us by the said Provincial, and required the confirmation of them by their convent seal. Which warden and convent showed themselves very untoward in that behalf; and thereupon we were forced to move the convent to put the matter wholly in the arbitrament of their seniors, otherwise named discreets, which were but four in number, and that they four having full authority to consent or dissent for them all and in the name of them all, should meet us at Greenwich this day in the morning and bring their convent seal with them; and so they did. And when we came to Greenwich we exhorted the convent likewise to put the whole matter in the hands of their seniors or discreets, to the intent to avoid superfluous words and idle reasoning, and specially to the intent that if the discreets should refuse to consent, it were better, after our minds, to strain a few than a multitude.

---

[1] Dr. George Browne.

But at Greenwich we could in no wise obtain to have the matter put in the discreets' hands and arbitrament, but the convent stiffly affirmed that where the matter concerned particularly every one of their souls, they would answer particularly every man for himself. And when, after much reasoning and debating, we required to have their final and determinate answer, which we demanded of every one of them particularly, we found them in one mind of contradiction and dissent from the said articles, but specially against this article, *Quod episcopus Romanus nihilo majoris neque auctoritatis aut jurisdictionis habendus sit quam cæteri quivis episcopi in Anglia vel alibi gentium in sua quisque diocesi.*

And the cause of their dissent, as they said, was by reason that that article was clearly against their profession and the rules of St. Francis, in which rules it is thus written, as they showed unto us: *Ad hæc per obedientiam injungo ministris ut petant a domino Papa unum de Sanctæ Romanæ Ecclesiæ cardinalibus, qui sit gubernator, protector, et corrector istius fraternitatis, ut semper subditi et subjecti pedibus Sanctæ Ecclesiæ ejusdem stabiles in fide Catholica paupertatem et humilitatem, et secundum Evangelium Domini nostri Jesu Christi, quod firmiter promisimus observemus.* Whereunto three answers: First, that St. Francis and his brethren at the beginning were dwelling in Italy under the obedience of the Bishop of Rome, as all monks not exempt be under the obedience of the Bishop of Canterbury, and therefore it were no marvel that St. Francis would his brethren to be obedient to the Bishop of Rome, being their prelate; at which time of St. Francis, and long after, there were none of his Order in England, and therefore these words were not meant by friars of England. The second answer that we made was this, that the chapter of St. Francis' rule which they allege maketh mention of ministers, and that they should desire of the Pope to have one of the cardinals which should be governor, protector, and corrector of their brotherhood; and we showed them that in our opinion that chapter [was] no part of St. Francis' rule, but was forged sithence and planted into the same by some ambitious friar of that Order, for, as we supposed, the name of ministers was not found out or spoken of when their rule was confirmed; and it is [not?] to be thought that St. Francis, being a holy man, was desirous to have a cardinal to govern and correct his brethren. Thirdly, we affirmed unto them that they were the King's subjects and that by the law of God they owed him their entire obedience; and that the Pope and St. Francis and they themselves, with their vows, oaths, and professions, could take away not one jot of the obedience which they owe to the King by God's law. And we showed them that none of the King's subjects could submit himself or bear obedience to any other prince or prelate, without the King's consent. And if he did he did the King's Grace great injury and offended God, breaking his laws commanding obedience towards princes. And in this behalf we showed that the King, being a Christian prince, was a spiritual man, and that obedience which they owed to the King by God's law was a spiritual obedience and in spiritual causes; for they would be obedient but only in temporal causes. But all this reason could not sink into their obstinate heads and worn in custom of obedience of the Pope,—albeit we further declared unto them that both Archbishops of this realm, the Bishops of London, Winchester, Durham, Bath, and all other prelates and heads, and all the famous clerks of this realm, have subscribed to this conclusion *Quod Romanus pontifex non habet majorem jurisdictionem ex sacris literis in hoc regno Angliæ quam quivis alius externus episcopus.'* All this notwithstanding, their conclusion was, they had professed St. Francis' religion, and in the observance thereof they would live and die. Sorry we be we cannot bring them to no better frame and order in this behalf, as our faithful minds was to do, for the accomplishment of the King's pleasure. From the Mile's end, the 15th day of June.

By yours assuredly, Roland Co. et Lich.

Your own, Thomas Bedyll.

Addressed : To Master Secretary.[1]

Since reasoning like the above was of so little avail, a new process was applied, and, two days later, two carts full of friars passed through the city on their way to the Tower.[2] In August matters were carried a step or two further. "Of seven houses of Observants," writes Chapuys on the 11th, "five have been already emptied of friars because they have refused to swear to the statutes made against the Pope. Those in the two others expect also to be expelled."[3]

Suppression of the Observants.

---

[1] MS. Cott., Cleopatra E iv. 40.   Printed by Wright, *Suppression of the Monasteries*, pp. 41-44.
[2] *L. P.*, VII. 856.   [3] *L. P.*, VII. 1057.

The persecuted brethren found means to send a memorial to the King;[1] but of course it was altogether useless. In a very short time the two remaining houses were cleared, and their inmates distributed in other Franciscan monasteries of the Conventual, or less strict Order, where they were kept locked in chains and worse treated than they would have been in ordinary prisons.[2] Thus the whole Order of the Observants in England was suppressed.

All this, be it observed, was before the tyrannical view of Supremacy had even been endorsed by Parliament; for the session in which the Act of Supreme Head was passed only began in November following, and, as we have seen, Parliament showed itself anxious to protect those who did not offend "maliciously." But together with this came Acts of Attainder against More and Fisher for refusing the oath to the succession (which they did only on account of its preamble), and the severe Act of treasons already mentioned, enacted to prevent speaking against the marriage with Anne Boleyn. It was in the following year, 1535, that all this fearful legislation began to bear fruit, and the world was horror-struck at the executions of England's best and noblest sons. But after More's head had fallen on Tower Hill in July legal butcheries ceased for a while. The government even of the Church in England was now a despotism against which it was hopeless to contend; and the foundations had to be laid for a new order of things without much risk of interference from abroad.

It was in truth a new order of things even from the passing of that Act of Supremacy; for never had such pretensions been advanced before by any English sovereign, or in any English sovereign's name. But the development of that new order was

---

[1] *L. P.*, VII. 1063.
[2] *L. P.*, VII. 1095. Cp. Wriothesley's *Chronicle*, i. 25.

not a matter that could be left to time and circumstance. The beginning of the year 1535 had seen Cromwell appointed Vicegerent of the King in spiritual matters, to carry out a policy within the Church as well as within the State, of which he seems himself to have been the great deviser. Bent merely on satisfying a despotic master with a view to his own advancement in wealth and power, he never allowed considerations of humanity or justice to stand for a moment in his way. In January he received a commission for a general visitation of churches, monasteries, and clergy throughout the kingdom; but nothing was done in the matter during the first half of the year while those awful executions were going on. In July, however, while he was with the King in the West of England, the two monastic Visitors whom he had appointed, Dr. Legh and Dr. Layton, started on their work. They had both, as Layton confessed, been preferred to the King's service by Cromwell and looked upon him as their only patron; and in the North Country they had both of them "familiar acquaintance," within ten or twelve miles of every monastery, by whom they could find out every scandal, "so that no knavery could be hid from them."[1]

Cromwell appoints Visitors for the monasteries.

They had both, moreover, shown their fitness for the work required by taking part in the examinations of More and Fisher in the Tower; and so had John Ap Rice, a notary, who was set to accompany Dr. Legh upon his travels. The three worthies did not agree very well together at first. Dr. Legh visited over again the monastery of Bruton which had already been visited by Layton, and complained that Layton had not been strict enough elsewhere, in restraining the heads and brethren from leaving the precincts. Complaints on the other hand reached Cromwell of Legh's ostentatious insolence, which he blamed Ap

[1] *L. P.*, VIII. 822.

Rice for not reporting. Ap Rice agreed that Legh was too insolent and pompous, but he thought Cromwell had seen evidence of the fact himself in London. "Wherever he comes," wrote Ap Rice, "he handles the fathers very roughly, many times for small causes, as for not meeting him at the door, where they had warning of his coming." He was young and intolerably conceited, and, moreover, took exorbitant fees of the houses he visited; while at every election he demanded the altogether unheard-of sum of £20. He made all the monks afraid of him; and he departed in some matters from the instructions given him in his dealings with them. Still it would not do for Cromwell to punish him and so discredit the wisdom of his own appointment; it would be better, Ap Rice thought, first to admonish him gently.[1]

Ap Rice, indeed, as he confessed, had some personal reasons of his own for this suggestion. Legh had acquaintance with so many rufflers and serving-men that he could make him very uncomfortable if he suspected that he was giving information against him. But as to the taking of fees, Legh, no doubt, had learned much of the arts used by Cromwell himself when he suppressed the small monasteries for Wolsey's colleges. Moreover, if his strictness was complained of, Legh had a good deal to say for himself. Ap Rice, it seems, thought it was excessive that not even the heads of monastic houses were allowed to go out of doors. Many of those houses, he remarked, were supported by husbandry, and would be quite unable to live if their heads were never to leave their precincts. The head of a house was chosen expressly for his ability in business matters, and was to do duty in providing for all the rest that they might be released from secular cares and devote their attention the more freely to their religious

[1] *L. P.*, IX. 138, 139, 167, 621, 622, 630.

duties. Even the monks of the Charterhouse required to have a proctor, and their prior had to go abroad on the business of the house.[1] But Legh considered that he was not bound to take such matters into consideration. He merely followed his instructions, treating heads and members alike, which would have a most beneficial effect in making them feel the King's ecclesiastical power, and apply either to the King himself or to Cromwell for relief. Even when his instructions were modified by Cromwell, who wrote to allow him at discretion to let the heads go abroad quietly on the business of their houses, he declined to relax his orders till he had spoken with Cromwell himself, thinking not only that it might give occasion to the juniors to complain of unequal treatment, but that it would be for Cromwell's own advantage to compel the seniors thus to seek his favour and the King's.[2]

By and by Legh and Ap Rice ventured to submit their joint counsel to Cromwell on a higher subject. The visitation of monasteries was but one department of the Vicegerent's functions, and it could not be effectually carried on without encroachment on the regular functions of the bishops. On the 18th September royal letters were despatched to the two archbishops to inhibit their suffragans from visiting their dioceses, as the King intended a general visitation of the whole kingdom. Even Cranmer did not at once act upon this mandate. Probably he made some remonstrances, the bishops themselves very naturally being much disturbed at the idea that their functions were to be suspended; and it was only on the 2nd October that he sent the required inhibition to the Bishop of London.[3] It was Legh and Ap Rice who had drawn up the inhibitions, and, anticipating the remonstrances of the bishops, they wrote to Cromwell on the 24th September giving six

Episcopal visitations inhibited.

---

[1] *L. P.*, IX. 139.   [2] *L. P.*, IX. 265.   [3] *L. P.*, IX. 517.

reasons in justification of the step. 1st, As the King was now acknowledged as Supreme Head of the Church of England (though he had always been so), the only way to give effect to his title was by taking all jurisdiction into his own hands for a season. 2nd, If this were not done the bishops would imagine they had not received their jurisdiction from the King. 3rd, They must either have it by the law of God, or from "the Bishop of Rome," or from the King. If the first, let them show it by Scripture, which they would hardly be so unwise as to attempt. If the second, let them exercise it still if they thought meet. If the third, why object to its resumption by the King? 4th, They might say they had "prescribed against the King"—that is to say, they might urge the plea of prescription; which, no doubt, they would, though the law was against them, and for that very reason it was well to interrupt their visitation. 5th, If they exercised their jurisdiction, it would undoubtedly be according to the canon law, which was now abrogated in England; so Lee and Ap Rice considered that the jurisdiction should be given them from the King with the laws for executing it. 6th, When they challenged jurisdiction as theirs by right, it was clear that they would refer it to some one else than the King if they only dared.[1]

The very tenor of these arguments shows the greatness of the revolution which two upstarts—mere creatures of Cromwell—had taken upon them to urge on a not unwilling master. Not a vestige of authority was to be left to the bishops which was not avowedly derived from the King as the only source. The whole form of ecclesiastical jurisdiction was to be changed, and the bishops must submit to an innovation which sensibly lowered their dignity and repute among the people. Suggestions were made about the same time by other councillors for bringing ecclesiastical

[1] *L. P.*, IX. 424.

causes under the cognisance of temporal judges.[1] The way, at all events, was clear for Legh, Ap Rice, and Layton to visit the monasteries at their pleasure.

Their commission, at first, does not seem to have extended to the Universities of Oxford and Cambridge, though the colleges might have been considered in that day somewhat in the light of monastic bodies. Legh wrote to Cromwell from Wilton on the 3rd September urging him to consider well whom he sent to those universities, " where either would be found all virtue and goodness or else the fountain of all vice and mischief."[2] The person Cromwell actually sent to visit Oxford, however, was Layton, who must *Layton and Legh visit the Universities also.* have arrived there about a week after Legh wrote this letter from Wilton ; and Legh himself writes from Cambridge on the 21st October.[3] So the two universities were successively subjected to the discipline of the two chief monastic Visitors ; and in this new field, as in the former, Layton was at work before his colleague, armed with full authority to bring about a new state of things.   In this business, indeed, he seems to have had colleagues, though we do not know their names, for in the report of their joint doings to Cromwell he uses continually the plural pronoun " we."   But we can hardly doubt that he himself was the chief moving spirit, and his account of what was done is lively reading.   In Magdalen College where they found one lecture of divinity, two of philosophy (moral and natural), and one of Latin, they added a lecture in Greek.   In New College they established one Greek and one Latin lecture, and the like at All Souls, but they found Corpus Christi was so provided already.   They established a Latin lecture at Merton and another at Queen's.   The revenues of the other Colleges were insufficient to support such lectures, and

[1] *L. P.*, IX. 119.   [2] Wright's *Suppression*, p. 66.
[3] *L. P.*, IX. 350, 651.

their students were enjoined under a penalty to resort daily to the lectures thus established.

So far the Visitors had provided for the future study of Latin and Greek, and of moral and natural philosophy. But the real revolution was in the abolition of the study of the canon law and scholastic theology. "We have set Duns in Bocardo," Layton continues, "and have utterly banished him Oxford forever with all his blind glosses," adding that he was now nailed up upon posts for public use "in all common houses of easement." "And the second time we came to New College, after we had declared your injunctions, we found all the great quadrant court full of the leaves of Duns, the wind blowing them into every corner. And there we found one Mr. Greenfield, a gentleman of Buckinghamshire, gathering up part of the said book leaves, as he said, therewith to make him sewelles or 'blawnsherres'[1] to keep the deer within the wood, thereby to have the 'better cry with his hounds.'" In place of a canon law lecture the Visitors instituted one on civil law to be read in every college, hall, and inn. To complete their great reform they imposed new regulations on students sent up from the monasteries, prohibiting their resort to taverns or alehouses, and laundresses from visiting their chambers — to the great distress, as Layton understood, "of all the double honest women of the town."[2]

Legh's injunctions for Cambridge[3] are less interesting than Layton's account of his own at Oxford. The University, he himself said, approved them highly "except three or four Pharisaical Pharisees."[4] The injunctions were in Cromwell's name, who had just

---

[1] The meaning of these terms is pretty well conveyed by the words which follow. A "sewell" was a figure with papers fluttering in the wind like a scarecrow to frighten deer. A "blancher" was either a man or any inanimate device to serve the same purpose.
[2] Wright's *Suppression of the Monasteries*, pp. 70-72.
[3] *L. P.*, IX. 664.　　　　　　　　[4] *L. P.*, IX. 694.

been made Chancellor of the University in place of
the martyred Fisher, and we may place what value
we please on Legh's assurance in writing to him :
" They say you have done more for the advancement
of learning than ever Chancellor did." [1]
    As to the general character of the monastic visita-
tion, it is scarcely necessary to say much ; for though
the amount of monastic impurity may be a subject of
debate, it is now generally agreed that it was not an
honest investigation.   But a few specific illustrations
may not be out of place.   The nature of the commis-   Instruc-
sion given to the Visitors is briefly described by Abbot   tions given
Gasquet as follows :—   monastic
visitation.

    They were furnished with a set of eighty-six articles of
inquiry and with twenty-five injunctions, to which they had
power to add much at their discretion.   The articles of inquiry
were searching, the injunctions minute and exacting.   Framed
in the spirit of three centuries earlier, unworkable in practice,
and enforced by such agents, it is easy to understand, even
were there no written evidence of the fact, that they were
galling and unbearable to the helpless inmates of the
monasteries.   We may give a passing notice to one or two of
these regulations, as they show the spirit which actuated
those who framed them.   All religious under twenty-four
years of age, or who had been professed under twenty, were
to be dismissed from the religious life.   Those who were left
became practically prisoners in their monasteries.   No one
was allowed to leave the precincts (which even in the larger
monasteries were very confined as to limit) or to visit there.
In many instances porters, who were in reality gaolers, were
appointed to see that this impossible regulation was kept.
What was simply destructive of all discipline and order in
the monasteries was an injunction that every religious who
wished to complain of anything done by his superior or any
of his brethren was to have a right at any time to appeal to
Cromwell.   To facilitate this the superior was ordered to find
any subject the money and means for prosecuting such an
appeal in person, if he so desired.[2]

---

[1] L. P., IX. 708.
[2] Gasquet's Henry VIII. and the English Monasteries, i. 255-6.

The results of all this interference appear naturally in Cromwell's correspondence, and, considering how completely that correspondence seems to have been preserved, we are almost surprised that the evidences of demoralisation procured were not greater. Many, doubtless, were the houses in which the monks were still loyal to their superiors, and good discipline was still kept up in spite of the insidious efforts of Cromwell and the Visitors to destroy it. But as to the demoralisation we must not leave the reader to general inferences without positive examples.

At Worcester, William Fordham had occupied seven years before the office of cellarer to the Cathedral Priory. He incurred debts in the name of the monastery to the extent of £280, and borrowed money, likewise in the name of the monastery, which he converted to his own use, while the prior, attending the Convocation in London, was arrested for payment of his bills. He also incurred a disease which speaks ill for the kind of life he led, and the house was charged with payments for his cure. Under these circumstances it is not wonderful that he was removed from his post and a new cellarer appointed. But the priory was visited by Legh and Ap Rice in the end of July, and on the 1st August Fordham wrote to Cromwell commending the pains taken by his Visitors, trusting that they would report that he had lived religiously, and declaring that "the saddest men" of the monastery wished him restored to his office. In his time, he said, no lawsuits had gone against the house, but during the seven years since his removal they had lost £200. His final plea to Cromwell, however, was undoubtedly the most effective. "If your Lordship will restore me" (Cromwell, however, was not a lord at that time) "I will give you 100 marks." Four weeks later he was given to understand that Cromwell had "spoken good words of him," and that his suit was successful. He accordingly writes to Cromwell to express his thanks, and as he hears that "some of the brethren" were applying to men of honour to speak for them, he himself will rely entirely upon Cromwell, whose administration, he says, was so much to the comfort of the King, the Queen, and all their subjects. In this reign, he ventured to say, no man had suffered but he had confessed himself he had deserved to suffer, and many who had suffered might have lived if they would under such a benignant King. "His most merciful pardon was ready; it was but their own folly. All this realm may it well know."[1]

The reader will hardly require any criterion besides his own words by which to judge the sycophant. He was answered by a letter from the convent to Cromwell, signed by the sub-prior (the prior, William More, had got into trouble, as we shall see) and six-and-twenty of the monks, giving the reasons why he was dismissed from the cellarership, which, one would think, were sufficiently weighty. But it is true, as Fordham himself wrote, that he had supporters within the monastery, whether "the saddest men" of the community may perhaps be open to question. Legh in his visitation of course had his ears open to complaints, and ordered the prior, with three of his brethren, to appear before Cromwell in the beginning of August. Cromwell was at that time in the West Country, with the King, and even when he got home in October the prior remained in custody at Gloucester.[2]

It would seem that in spring the prior had imprisoned a refractory monk named John Musard for appealing to Cranmer's visitation. Musard could not have been detained very long; for in July, when the King was at Gloucester, and his Vicegerent, Cromwell, at Winchcombe, he took the opportunity of visiting them both and reporting the treasonable

---

[1] *L. P.*, IX. 6, 204, 653.   [2] *L. P.*, IX. 656.

conversation of some of the monks who had railed at the King and Queen Anne and upheld the authority of the Pope. For this, however, he complains that his "unkind master," and some of the brethren, "conspired against him," and made such a report of him to Cromwell that he was again imprisoned at Worcester, this time by Cromwell's orders. Even Legh and Ap Rice joined in accusing him; and as, apparently, Cromwell had acted on their information, he wrote to Cromwell himself for a further hearing. He wrote also to the King, showing that his father and brothers had devoted themselves to the service of Henry VII., who made two of them Yeomen of the Crown, and one had been slain at the siege of Boulogne; and he further intimated that sixteen of his near relations were ready any day to set upon four-and-twenty of his Grace's evil willers.[1] At the election of Latimer as bishop he could take no part, having been expelled by the Chancellor as an excommunicate, and he wrote to Cromwell that another of the monks deserved such treatment better, —Thomas Blockley, who stole out of his cell a letter conveying an accusation of treason. Dr. Legh, he said, had stated openly that Blockley was "comperted" by many of the convent for incontinency and as a sower of discord among them, yet nothing had been laid to his charge, and it was suspected that he had bribed Dr. Legh and Master Ap Rice.[2] Such was the imputation he did not scruple to make against Cromwell's Visitors, and it certainly was not inconceivable.

With all this he was unable to win favour, and remained still in prison in January following, writing new representations to Cromwell of the maladministration of the monastery under the prior and his last predecessor.[3] But he had succeeded in getting his

[1] L. P., IX. 51, 52, 108.   [2] L. P., IX. 497.
[3] L. P., X. 216.

prior into trouble for treason, and the Lord Chancellor sent down a Commission of *oyer and terminer* to investigate the case.[1]   The prior remained for some time in custody.[2]   The King himself, however, manifested some disposition to restore him to his office, and on this subject Cromwell asked the opinion of Latimer as his bishop, who, however, gave it as his opinion that if "that great crime" was proved against him, it was a pity even to spare his life.[3] Nothing, apparently, could atone in Latimer's eyes for the fact of a man having countenanced the Pope's authority against the King's.   The King himself, however, was more merciful in this case than Latimer, and was content to accept the man's resignation, and to give him a pension, and, it would seem, a comfortable living besides.[4]

The prior's chief accuser was Dr. Roger Neckham, whom he had deposed from the office of sub-prior.[5] In pleading to Cromwell that the prior's case might be carefully examined, Lady Margery Sandys declared that he was a true monk to God and the King, and also that his accuser, Neckham, was sufficiently well known.[6]   The prior had been elected by the unanimous vote of the convent, and had received his appointment from Fox, Bishop of Winchester, without giving a penny for his promotion.   Nevertheless he knew well enough the altered ways of the world, and, as Lady Margery wrote, was prepared to give Cromwell in ready money as much as any other man. It would have been useless interceding for him without such an intimation.   Of course Musard and Neckham were strong supporters of the dismissed cellarer Fordham.

Now let us look at the effects of the visitation on another large West Country monastery.   At Winch- at Winchcombe;

---

[1] *L. P.*, IX. 90 (p. 26), 151, 165.   [2] *L. P.*, IX. 304.
[3] *L. P.*, X. 56.   [4] *L. P.*, X. 311, 597 (8), 1272 ; XVII. 14.
[5] *L. P.*, IX. 52 (2).   [6] *L. P.*, IX. 656.

combe was a monk named John Horwood, who generally used the signature of " Placet," or " Placidus." On the 20th August he begins a correspondence with Cromwell by informing him that the monastery had lately been visited by the King's Commissioners, to whom he felt bound in conscience to report some things,—especially about a certain book which he was ready to send to Cromwell, and which one Master Cannonis, dwelling near Salisbury, had borrowed of him long ago. But he also desired counsel what to do about certain ceremonies for exalting " the Bishop of Rome." Encouraged by the Visitors, he asked Cromwell for orders to bring in books touching " the Bishop of Rome's " authority, St. Patrick's Purgatory, miracles, and so forth, by which simple souls were confounded.[1] In another letter he asks for authority to seize any books about Purgatory, and mentions particularly one, " freshly limned and fair written," of which the matter is but " dry dreams "; also a book of Alverius, in which the power of the Pope is so magnified that he was made equal to the Holy Trinity. He advises that his brother, Overbury, should be commanded to preach the Royal Supremacy every Sunday before the convent, and have his chamber, books, and fire; and that he himself should have authority to compel every monk to preach it and to teach it to others.[2] This was pretty well for a subordinate. One asks in amazement, if his request was granted, what amount of authority was left to his abbot. Clearly, none at all.

No wonder that in his next letter, dated 9th September, he declares that his proceedings are disliked by the convent. He was counted a wretch, he said, because he had made a little treatise against the usurped power of " the Bishop of Rome." His brethren, it seems, attached far too great importance

[1] *L. P.*, ix. 134.   [2] *L. P.*, ix. 135.

to their three vows, " the efficacy " of which Cromwell had " discreetly declared " to them when he was with them.[1]   But, however unpopular they made him in the convent, his efforts to please Cromwell had gained some personal comforts for himself, for Cromwell had ordered that he should be excused from rising at midnight.   This had created all the more grudge against him ; yet his much-enduring abbot, who was obliged to tell him so, was, he said, very good to him.   The abbot knew very well that he could not endure the rigour of the religion, the fasts, the " frayter," and other observances.   He begs Cromwell, therefore, to get him a capacity to take a benefice without changing his habit.   Bishop Roland Lee could have got him one at one time, but he trusted to the favour of Cromwell and his abbot, who had already allowed him the cure of a little village of forty souls, though not worth quite £4 a year.   " Such a thing," he wrote, " were most quiet for me, which I may serve and keep my bed and board, and go to my book in the monastery." [2]

He got leave to visit Cromwell in September when he was in attendance on the King at Waltham, and apparently obtained a commission about books such as he desired, or nearly so.   He was evidently greatly indebted in these matters to Dr. Layton.   " You cannot love your servant Dr. Layton too well," he writes to Cromwell, and he goes on to tell how he was proceeding with his commission.   " I have sought many old books and ragged pamphlets *de Purgatorio, pro et contra.*"   He had also found a letter to Pope John against pride and covetousness.   He had scribbled in haste a small quire against prayers for the dead, and some other points.   He had got hold of a book of Alverius, *de Planctu Ecclesiæ,* " which some thought smelt of the Popish pannier," and so forth.[3]

---

[1] *L. P.*, IX. 321.   [2] *L. P.*, IX. 322.   [3] *L. P.*, IX. 723.

There are also two letters to Cromwell from his "brother Overbury," above mentioned, for whom he desired powers to assist him in forcing the Royal Supremacy upon the convent. These are written in a hand so exactly like his own that it is really very difficult to distinguish between them.[1] It may be desirable to give the text of these letters in full :—

WILLIAM OVERBURY TO CROMWELL—I
Jesus Christus.

Honorable Master Secretary, I meekly commend me unto your goodness, as the true subject ought to the power which is ordained of Almighty God. For to you is given ministration of God next under the King's Highness; to the which power of ministration every Christian man in this realm of England ought truly without any feigning meekly to obey, and not for fear but for safeguard of conscience. And for my poor part, because I would knowledge myself in heart, word and deed to be a true obediencer and faithful subject to this high power which is given to the King's Grace immediately next to God, as excelling and forepassing all other, and to you as the faithful minister under him : Wherefore by God's own words you and all such true ministers that truly doen minister under this power (which was not given by any man's trade or invention, but only by God) be called well-doers. There is no power but only of God, who ever preserve you. Scribbled in great haste, the 16th day of September.

By your obiencer,

WILLIAM OVERBURY.

Addressed :—" To the very honorable Master Secretary unto the King's Highness, with reverence this be delivered."[2]

---

[1] Perhaps he really wrote with his own hand in Overbury's name, although both signed the Supremacy, or appear to have done so. He was certainly obliging enough to write a letter to Cromwell in the name of one John Persons, who appears to have been a servant or dependant on the abbey, complaining of the abbot for not allowing him to be in the town of Winchcombe to work for his living. The only cause of complaint the abbot had against him, Persons writes—that is to say, Placidus writes for him—was that he waited on one of the monks (of course Placidus himself) to London, when he was commanded by Cromwell to bring up certain books to him (*L. P.*, IX. 1137). The handwriting of this letter is undoubtedly that of Placidus himself. [2] *L. P.*, IX. 381.

This letter is written in a beautiful regular hand, which is quite exceptional in its neatness, and no one certainly would believe that it was " scribbled in great haste."

WILLIAM OVERBURY TO CROMWELL—II

Emanuel.

Faithful, trusty and dearly beloved minister unto the high power of Almighty God, of that which you have ministration under our Sovereign Lord the King, here in earth, the only high and supreme Head of this His Church of England, grace, peace and mercy be evermore with you. Laud and thanks be to God the Father Almighty for the true and unfeigned faith that you have in our sweet Saviour Jesu. Paul, the true preacher of Christ, saith *Fundamentum aliud nemo potest ponere præter id quod positum est, quod est Jesus Christus.* Whosoever believeth Jesus Christ to be only Saviour of the whole world, pacifier of God's wrath, mediator between God and man, the bearer of sins and the true Lamb of God, that taketh away the sins of the world, hath now set this foundation. Therefore it is to be trusted upon that where Christ is the foundation, there must needs follow the edifying and building of good works as testimony of the true foundation. Also Christ saith *Ego sum ostium.* He entereth in by this door, the which feeleth the truth and, preaching the same to others, followeth and keepeth it himself. Paul 9 Corin.[1]:—*Væ enim mihi est si non evangelizavero. Necessitas enim mihi incumbit. Si enim volens hoc ago, mercedem habeo. Si autem invitus, dispensatio mihi credita est. Quæ est ergo merces mea?* etc. This doth some take upon them, diligently executing the office of the ministration of the word of God, plainly, sincerely, following the gracious will and mind of our gracious Sovereign Lord the King, being only high and Supreme Head of this Church of England, to whose high power, given unto him from God above, it pertaineth by the ordinance of Almighty God, to send workmen into the harvest or vineyard of this His Church, of the which his Grace is the only high Head and governor next God. *Quomodo audient sine prædicante? Quomodo vero prædicabunt, nisi mittantur? Sed non omnes obediunt Evangelio.* For there be many perverse men which do dilaniate the flock of Christ—yea, and of them which

[1] The passage is in 1 Cor. ix. 16-18.

seem to men to be the pillars or bearers up of the Church, which doth rather diminish the faith than anything augment it.

I have many things which I would fain declare to your goodness; but I consider your great and manifold cure and business, and mine own impediments by the custom and trades of men ordained that let me, not only this time in this my rude scribbling to you, but also almost at all times, from both study and exercise of the Holy Gospel, the true faith and doctrine of the which I pray God augment to His honor; who ever preserve and keep you. Amen.

Your obediencer,

WILLIAM OVERBERY.[1]

The address of this letter, which was doubtless on a fly-leaf, has not been preserved, but there is no question whatever that it was addressed to Cromwell as the King's Vicegerent in spiritual things. It is not exactly pleasant to dwell on an exhibition of arrant hypocrisy; but that some few monks, finding that, willingly or not, they and their brethren had to live under a new allegiance, were only too ready to give that new allegiance a religious sanction is no more than the necessities of the case would naturally lead us to expect. Yet historic, if not religious, sympathy must deplore the sad ruin of monasticism—a system whose great aim was to remove men from worldly and demoralising influences—when we see it in its last days helpless before tyranny, obliged even to harbour within the cloister some traitors who made a religion of worldliness and subservience to earthly power.[2]

[1] The original of this letter is in MS. Cott., Cleop. E vi. 261. It is printed by Strype in *Ecclesiastical Memorials*, I. i. 316.

[2] As for John Placidus, I presume that he got his benefice; for though he signed with his brother monks the acknowledgment of the King's supremacy in August 1534 (*L. P.*, VII. 1211 (42)), his name does not appear in the pension list of the monastery in December 1539 (*L. P.* XIV. ii. 728). Or rather, he is one of seven monks who signed the supremacy in 1534, and who were not pensioned at the dissolution; for it is curious that every monk of this monastery was pensioned under a different surname from that which he used in his

Yet one more documentary illustration may be permitted, to show how the new state of matters affected abbots, who, having hitherto had undisturbed control of their houses, could even have called in the aid of the civil power at any time to prevent the escape of disaffected brethren seeking to run away. Now it was a different story when a monk desiring to lodge a complaint against his superior had facilities given him by the authorities to go up to London. It is thus the Abbot of Brewerne in Oxfordshire writes to Cromwell : [1]—

The Abbot of Brewerne to Cromwell

Right worshipful and my very singular good master, I have me heartily commended unto your good mastership, most instantly desiring you of your help and counsel, which I shall deserve by God's grace. So it is, as I am informed, that I was indicted three times at Oxford the 6th day of this present April. First was for a riot, the second of ravine (?), the third of murder. I know no cause why they should so do, I take God to record. As for the riot, they lay it unto me because I perceived by one that told me privily Easter day at afternoon that one of my monks, which is now in London, he intended that night of Easter day at midnight to take his journey, as I heard, towards London, and I sent one of my servants to my friend Master Whyteney, which dwelleth within two miles of me, desiring him to send two or three servants of his with my servant, to watch till after midnight for the same monk a quarter of a mile fro the Abbey ; and so he came about midnight with a horse which one of the sheriff's servants lent him to take his journey upon ; which servant was commanded by his master to wait on me because I have but few servants and am amongst them every day in jeopardy of my life. But that servant of the sheriff's hath done there much hurt in giving my monks

(marginal note:) at Brewerne Abbey.

---

signature. One or two of the seven may have died in the meanwhile, but I suspect that Placidus got the benefice he so much wanted ; for there were only two Johns who received pensions, the prior and the sub-prior, and he can hardly be identified with either of them.

[1] This letter has unhappily been omitted by oversight in the *Letters and Papers*. It is in MS. Cott., Cleop. E iv. 100.

evil counsel, and of a very likelihood by his master's setting on. So that night my servant with Master Whyteney's servants took the monk and carried him to Master Whyteney's unto they knew my pleasure; and for so taking of my monk (as I perceive) they have indicted me of a riot. And so the Monday in the morning my convent had knowledge that their messenger was so taken, they raised a great many of lewd fellows abroad in the country, which came to my abbey and threatened to pluck me out of my house unless I would fet the monk again. And so they kept me in to my chamber all day till even song time, and I dare in no wise come out. So the said Master Whytteney had knowledge how I was dealt withal; he being of the fee of the house, as injoined in patent with his father-in-law, Master Robert Wye, as stewards of our courts, he could do no less but come to me with his servants, intending hurt to no man. So, soon after his coming, which was about three of the clock, many of his neighbours, which heard that he had gone to Brewern, came after him; and after that came the sheriff, whom I had sent for in the morning, and he was greatly discontented because Master Whyteney was there; and for that cause they have indicted the said Mr. Whytteney and all that came with him for a unlawful assembly. Therefore, in the honour of God, be good unto me and to my friends, for the sheriff is heavy master to me and to as many as taketh part with me. For such as came to pluck me out by the head, as they said they would, were nothing spoke to; but such as would have holp me if need had required, were indicted; and the sheriff, as I heard, gave evidence himself and panelled a quest for the same at his pleasure; whereby I think he did wrong. Therefore, for the love of God, be good unto me in this my heinous business, and I shall deserve your pains with my heart and prayer, as knoweth Almighty God my whole mind, who ever preserve you. Fro Brewern, the 9th day of April.

All yours unfeigned,

THE POOR ABBOT OF BREWERN.

If monks ought to have been protected by their rule and the respect in which it had always been held from the evil influences of a secular tyranny, even more so should nuns have been; but it is only too evident that they were not. Nuns under twenty-five years of age were turned out of their convents, and one of the commissaries sent on this business (no doubt Dr. Legh) addressed the ladies in an immodest way. They rebuked his insolence, and said he was violating their apostolic privileges; but he replied that he himself had more power from the King than the whole Apostolic See. The nuns, having no other appeal, made their remonstrance to Cromwell; but he in reply said these things were but a prologue of that which was to come.[1]

So the occurrence was reported at the time by Chapuys in England to Dr. Ortiz, the Imperial agent at Rome; and Sanders, who though then only eight years old, was much better informed and more accurate about many things when he wrote than past historians have believed, says distinctly that Legh, as a means of discharging the duties imposed upon him, solicited the nuns to breach of chastity, and that he spoke of nothing more readily than of sexual impurity; for the visitation was appointed expressly for the purpose that the King might catch at every pretext for overthrowing the monasteries.[2]   The tradition of this abominable procedure, as is shown even by the Protestant historian Fuller, was kept alive for some generations by the just indignation of Roman Catholics; and Fuller himself reports as a fact circumstantially warranted by the tradition of papists, the story of one of those base attempts in a nunnery some miles from Cambridge.   It is, moreover, quite evident that Fuller himself, with every desire to discredit the story, was far from being convinced that it was altogether untrue.   If false, indeed, the tradition must have been very elaborately supported by further falsehood; for it is stated that one of the agents afterwards confessed to Sir William Stanley, who served in the Low Countries in the time of Queen Elizabeth, "that nothing in all his life lay

Dr. Legh's conduct towards nuns.

---

[1] *L. P.*, IX. 873.
[2] *Historia Schismatis Anglicani*, p. 105 (ed. Cologne, 1628).

more heavy on his conscience than this false accusation of those innocents."[1]

It was on the 4th June 1535 that Dr. Richard Layton, Clerk of the Council, wrote to Cromwell desiring a commission for himself and Dr. Thomas Legh to visit the North of England as Cromwell's commissaries in the general visitation which was then resolved upon. As many were likely to apply for such offices, he assured Cromwell he would find no more trusty agents anywhere. Cromwell, he said, required instruments such as would be to him another self, and as they both owed their preferment in the King's service to him, he might be perfectly sure of their "true hearts and minds." There was not a monastery or cell in the North "but either Dr. Legh or I," he wrote, "have familiar acquaintance within ten or twelve miles of it, so that no knavery can be hid from us in that country." They would also find friends and kinsfolk ready to assist them "if any stubborn or sturdy carle might perchance be found rebellious." Layton, moreover, had drawn up articles of inquiry for such a visitation twelve months before, which would serve to detect all abuses hitherto cloaked and coloured by so-called reformers; for each particular religious rule had "by friendship found crafty means to be their own visitors," who intended no real reform, "but only to keep secret all matters of mischief," and who hastened the ruin of the monasteries by selling their jewels and plate at half their value for ready money. Such was the purport of his letter.[2]

Again he wrote to him that the diocese of York had not been visited since Wolsey's time, and within

---

[1] Fuller's *Church History* (ed. 1845), iii. 385. Compare what is said before in pp. 382-4. The nunnery may have been Chatteris. Fuller says "within twelve miles of Cambridge," but miles as commonly computed were generally much longer than our statute miles. The penitent Visitor was, no doubt, Ap Rice.

[2] Wright's *Supp. of the Monasteries*, pp. 156, 157.

the province there were many things that required
reformation, especially among the exempt monasteries.
Archbishop Lee forbore to do anything, awaiting the
King's visitation; but if Layton were sent thither,
with Blitheman as registrar, he could finish the whole
province by Michaelmas, while Dr. Legh could finish
by the same time the counties of Huntingdon and
Lincolnshire and the diocese of Chester—that is to
say, of Coventry and Lichfield.   The matter was
urgent, for if Cromwell deferred the visitation till he
had leisure, it was to be feared that day would never
come, and if he waited till Lammas, when the Archbishop of Canterbury had finished his visitation, the
year would be far spent.   The Archbishop and his
officers would be very glad if Cromwell did not visit
at all.   But there was no better way of beating the
King's authority as Supreme Head into the heads of
that rude northern people, who were more superstitious than virtuous.   Towards the end of this
second letter he writes that Cromwell will never know
what he can do till he tries him.[1]

The desired commission was given to Legh and
Layton, and even something more.   It would have
been a pity, no doubt, to confine the functions of such
useful tools to a visitation of the North of England,
when they had to pass through the South, or at least
the Midlands, in order to get there.   So they were
to take the South of England first, each going by a Circuits
different route and collecting what information he of the Monastic
could get that would be serviceable for the King's Visitors.
purpose.   Leaving the Court in Gloucestershire,
Layton visited, among other places, Bath and Bristol
before he came to Oxford and revolutionised the
university studies in the manner we have seen.   He
then visited in Surrey and Sussex, and was at Sion
monastery in December, where he got one Bishop to
preach and declare the King's title, though he pro-

[1] *L. P.*, VIII. 955.

fessed to have discovered many gross scandals against
him the day before, and he intended to make further
inquiry about intercourse between the monks and
the nuns.[1]   Meanwhile his colleague Legh, after
passing through Wiltshire and Hampshire, visited
Reading, Chertsey, and Merton Abbeys, came to
London at Michaelmas, and went on through Cambridgeshire and Bury St. Edmunds to report on the
houses on his way into Norfolk and Suffolk.   Very
foul reports were transmitted to Cromwell by both
Visitors of the state of many of the monasteries ; but
it is noticeable among other evidences tending to
discredit these statements that whereas Dr. Legh,
when he visited Chertsey, found a considerable
number of the monks guilty of the grossest possible
impurity, Bishop Gardiner and Treasurer Fitzwilliam
had not long before visited the abbey by the King's
orders and found nothing wrong.[2]   That Bishop
Gardiner was at all anxious to overlook immorality
within his own diocese there is certainly no reason to
believe.

From the Eastern Counties Dr. Legh turned
towards the Midlands and met his colleague Layton,
by appointment, at Lichfield about Christmas.   From
that time the two journeyed in company, and were at
York together on the 11th January 1536.   They had
each done a very considerable amount of travelling,
to say nothing more, between August and the New
Year.   At York, on the 11th, they were with the
Archbishop, whom they enjoined to preach the
King's prerogative and to get other capable men to
do the same ; also to bring up to Cromwell " his
first, second, and third foundations whereupon he
enjoyeth his office and prerogative power, with the
grants, privileges and concessions given to him, and
to his See appertaining."   Dr. Legh had no doubt

*Their
injunctions
to the
Arch-
bishop of
York.*

---

[1] *L. P.*, IX. (see index).   Wright's *Supp.*, pp. 47, 48.
[2] *L. P.*, IX. 472.

that when Cromwell read them he would find many things worthy of reformation ; and, moreover, that if the King and Cromwell would take like order with other bishops it would greatly " edify " those under their government in Christ and his teaching, and enlighten many poor, blind, ignorant persons.   It would, moreover, tend to the preservation of their loyalty to the King and his successors—of course meaning his issue by Anne Boleyn, about whose succession there might well have been misgivings.[1]

It was Dr. Layton, however, who appears to have handled Archbishop Lee most rigorously, examining him closely about his communications with the General Confessor of Sion ; and the Archbishop wrote a letter to Cromwell the same day in his own exculpation.[2]   Layton seems now to have been in his element.   He had discovered worse abominations in the religious houses of Yorkshire, even than in the South ; and he fully expected, as he wrote, when he began that day with the great Abbey of St. Mary's at York, " to find much evil disposition both in the abbot and the convent."[3]

The two Visitors next wrote a joint letter from Richmond on the 20th, showing that they had deposed the Abbot of Fountains for notorious profligacy, theft, perjury, and squandering the goods of his house.   They warned Cromwell, however, that if the Earl of Cumberland knew that the monastery was vacant, he would urge the claims of the cellarer to be made abbot ; but they considered him unfit, for reasons which Layton knew Cromwell would agree with when he had an opportunity of explaining them.   In fact there was not a monk resident in the house fit for the place, in their opinion, and they recommended to Cromwell one Marmaduke, then resident on a prebend at Ripon,

They depose the Abbot of Fountains, and recommend for his successor one who will pay well for the place.

---

[1] Wright's *Supp.*, pp. 95, 96.   [2] *L. P.*, X. 93.
[3] Wright's *Supp.*, p. 97.

" the wisest monk within England of that coat and well learned, 20 years officer and ruler of all that house, a wealthy fellow which will give you 600 marks to make him abbot there, and pay you immediately after the election without delay or respite." Perhaps we may surmise from these words the nature of the cellarer's disqualification, which the Visitors would not commit to paper. There is a sentence further on in the letter which is not a little significant : "And we suppose that many other of the best abbots mo, after they have communed with your mastership and us will come to like preferment."[1] We can imagine pretty well what was the most important element in such conversation.

Before the end of January the two Visitors had entered the Bishopric of Durham, where the gentle Bishop Tunstall received them with peculiar honour, and on their departure sent a large company of his servants to escort them from Auckland half way to Durham Abbey. Legh felt particularly pleased. "Both we and our company," he wrote, "had large rewards, thus setting an example to the people, and especially to the abbots, of their duty towards their prince, and how they ought to accept him as their Supreme Head." Since the King had conquered him in argument on this subject five years before, Tunstall had not only become submissive to royal supremacy himself but a strenuous supporter of the doctrine. He had been preaching it in various parts of his diocese, with the result that no part of the realm was in better order in that respect, and Legh strongly recommended that the King or Cromwell should urge him to write a book upon the subject, so many learned men would be guided by his opinion. This advice was backed up by Layton, who was quite astonished at the Bishop's learning and power of argument in discussing the question. He had

Their conversation with Bishop Tunstall.

[1] Wright, 100-102.

imagined he himself knew all that could be said about it; " but when I heard his learning," he wrote, " and how deeply he had searched into this usurped power, I thought myself the veriest fool in England." [1]

On the 3rd February they were at Whitby, where they expected to get the abbot to resign; but he declined to do so, and they left a set of the usual injunctions, so hard to keep that the abbot wrote to Cromwell for their relaxation. By one of them he was bound to provide horse and money for any of his brethren who wished to go to Cromwell to complain that the injunctions were violated. He really thought a monk desiring to complain might first show his complaint to himself before four or six of his seniors. [2]

The Abbot of Whitby.

The whole visitation seems to have been completed in February. The report of the Visitors was drawn up opportunely for the last session of Henry VIII.'s "Long Parliament," which began on the 4th of that month, and continued its sittings till Good Friday, the 14th April, when it was dissolved. [3] By the middle of March the Act had been passed for the dissolution of all monasteries under £200 a year in value. [4] In the preamble of this statute [5] it was strangely declared that vice was daily practised in small monasteries of monks, canons, and nuns, where the number of the religious persons was under twelve; that all the visitations for the last two hundred years had failed to correct the evil, and that the only cure was to suppress such houses and transfer the inmates to larger and better regulated monasteries, where they might be compelled to live religiously. These statements, it was said, were vouched for by the " compertes " of the recent visitation, as well as " by sundry credible informations "—

[1] _L. P._, x. 182, 183.   [2] _L. P._, x. 238, 239.
[3] _L. P._, x. 669.   [4] _L. P._, x. 494.
              [5] Stat. 27 Hen. VIII. c. 28.

The Act of Suppression of the smaller monasteries professedly founded on the reports of the Visitors.

a beautifully vague expression to justify an act of plunder. But there is no clear evidence that these " compertes," or findings, of the recent visitation were submitted to Parliament. They seem rather to have been private and confidential communications transmitted to Cromwell, accusing a large number of monks and nuns in different monasteries (who were never heard in their own defence) of very gross impurities. A *Compendium compertorum* for the province of York and the diocese of Coventry and Lichfield still remains, drawn up in the hand of Ap Rice, the registrar who accompanied Dr. Legh.[1] There also exist two similar documents in the same hand relating to the monasteries in Norwich diocese. Neither of these papers bears out the statement that the smaller monasteries were more disorderly than the large; but if the reports were at all trustworthy, many of the large houses as well as of the small were dens of infamous vice.

The reports, however, will hardly command much credit from the student of contemporary State papers. That abuses may have existed in some monasteries, and that impurities from laxity of rule may not have been effectually dealt with, are facts that we might presume as probable from the infirmity of human nature; but before we can believe that the abominations were anything like so gross as were reported, we ought to have better evidence of the honesty and truthfulness of the Visitors than appears, even in the light of their own reports. Some of those filthy revelations, indeed, are of a nature that could only have been known, if true, through the confessional, and that any of the monks or nuns chose Legh or Layton for a confessor is past belief. But to estimate the value of the inquiry, even in a general way, we should require to know the processes used, and of these the evidence is very unsatisfactory. That the visitation

[1] *L. P.*, x. 364.

was deeply resented by most of the houses there is very little doubt. Legh and Ap Rice themselves confessed that the greatest houses were "so confederate by reason of their heads being mere Pharisees" that they could get no "compertes." If that were the temper of many of the monasteries, what sort of attitude would they or others have maintained when questioned by Visitors for whom they had no respect? Ap Rice considered the Abbey of Bury St. Edmunds to be confederate and determined to confess nothing.[1] So also Dr. Layton found the Abbey of Leicester. The abbot there, he said, was an honest man, but his canons most obstinate and factious. He proposes, therefore, to call some of them before him, object to them unnatural crimes, and on their denial, descend gradually to less heinous offences.[2] If this was the process used in other cases, what likelihood is there that a true result was elicited? The worst was surmised at the beginning; each monk was supposed to be guilty before he was found innocent, and how far his indignant disclaimers were regarded we do not know. Very likely many remained silent before a judge whom they did not acknowledge, and silence may have been taken as tantamount to a confession of guilt. It is to be presumed, moreover, that in their rapid survey of the houses—far too hurried to have been anything like a judicial inquiry—the Visitors occasionally accepted mere gossip and scandal as if they had been well-ascertained facts.

There may have been cases, indeed, where the monasteries had sufficient reason to dread inquiry. The nunnery of Crabhouse in Norfolk, anticipating the coming of the Visitors, sold its lands and goods, and the inmates prepared to desert the house and go away before the visitation.[3] The Visitors found that the prioress and three nuns had children;[4] which may

[1] Wright, p. 85.   [2] Ibid., p. 93.
[3] L. P., IX. 808.   [4] L. P., X. 364 (p. 144).

have been the case, though the testimony is suspicious. This nunnery was at Wiggenhall on the Ouse, some miles above Lynn, in a marshy country, perhaps not sufficiently looked after. We know, in fact, that there had been scandals there in times past, and now there may have been new ones.[1] But the possibility that in the whole of England there may have been a few ill-regulated monastic houses with unchaste inmates is no argument against the character of the monasteries as a whole.

The labours of the Visitors, however, had supplied the King with all the information he required— possibly even more than he expected—in order to make up a case to go before Parliament. And how Use made he used their report we know almost in detail. For of the the presumption is a very strong one that the follow- Visitors' report. ing extract from a contemporary letter refers to the introduction of the measure for the suppression of the smaller monasteries :—

> On Saturday in the Ember week [2] the King's Grace came in among the burgesses of the Parliament, and delivered them a bill, and bade them look upon it and weigh it in conscience; for he would not, he said, have them pass on it nor on any other thing because his Grace giveth in the bill, but they to see if it be for a common weal to his subjects and have an eye thitherward. And on Wednesday next he will be there again to hear their minds.[3]

There is a fine Tudor irony in the proceeding. The House of Commons had been jealous of its privi- leges even in Wolsey's time, and hesitated at first, it is said, to admit the Cardinal, at least with his whole

---

[1] At an episcopal visitation of this house in 1514 two of the nuns reported that Dame Agnes Smyth had children in the priory, and she herself confessed that one Simon Prentes got her with child. At the next visitation, six years later, the report was, "Omnia bene juxta facultates."—Jessopp's *Norwich Visitations* (Camden Soc.), pp. 108-110, 168.

[2] The letter is dated 13th March and refers to Ember week in Lent, in which the Saturday would be the 11th March. The writer is one Thomas Dorset.

[3] Wright's *Suppression*, pp. 38, 39.

train, when he brought a message from the King.[1] But the privileges, as understood in that age, were saved, alike when Wolsey entered the House and now when the King himself did. Neither Wolsey nor the King himself remained to hear a debate ; each simply left a message. But the message in this case required an answer by the following Wednesday. They were to use a perfectly independent judgment, but on Wednesday following the King would come again to know what conclusion they had arrived at. A House composed, as we have seen, completely of dependents of the Court, knew perfectly well what that meant.

It had already been rumoured, as early as the 3rd March, that a measure was in contemplation for the suppression of abbeys and priories under 300 marks (that is, £200) a year in value, or having fewer inmates than twelve.[2] But the bill, though thus clearly foreshadowed, both in its effect and in its preamble, had evidently not yet been introduced; and it is not unlikely that its introduction was delayed ten days on account of the very unpopularity of the proposal. On the 18th March, Chapuys writes to the Emperor that it had passed the legislature.[3] The Act was one of various schemes talked about for augmenting the revenues of the Crown; along with which the King was also considering how to employ robust mendicants in public works, such as the making of Dover harbour [4]—a work of high import-

Act for the suppression of the smaller monasteries.

[1] Roper's *More*, pp. 20, 21 (ed. 1817).   [2] *L. P.*, x. 406.
[3] *L. P.*, x. 494 (p. 200). It may be noted that the Wednesday on which the King promised to pay a second visit to the House of Commons would be the 15th March. We unfortunately have not the Journals of the House of Lords for this year, which would have shown the day when the bill came up from the Commons and the day it was passed.
[4] Compare with last reference the passage immediately following the extract already made from Thomas Dorset's letter in Wright, p. 39 : "There shall be a provision made for poor people. The gaols shall be rid, the faulty shall die, and the other shall be acquit by proclamation or by jury and shall be set at liberty and pay no fees ; and sturdy beggars and such prisoners as cannot be set a-work shall be set a-work at the King's charge, some at Dover and some at the place where the water hath broken in on the land, and other mo places. Then if they fall to idleness, the idlers shall be had before a justice of the peace," etc.

ance, of course, for the defence of the kingdom in case an invasion were attempted to give effect to a papal interdict. What was thought of these other measures does not much concern us; but as to the suppression of the smaller monasteries the tradition remained to the days of Sir Henry Spelman, a hundred years later, that even this subservient Parliament only agreed to it under the gravest possible menaces.[1]

On the other hand, we have the contemporary evidence of Latimer, not unfrequently referred to as evidence of the gross demoralisation of the monasteries, that "when their enormities were first read in the Parliament house, they were so great and abominable that there was nothing but 'Down with them'!" To weigh this testimony truly, however, we must consider the time at which it was uttered and the general drift of the argument the speaker was employing. It is contained in the second sermon preached by Latimer before King Edward VI. One great object of the preacher was to maintain the fulness of the royal authority, even though the King was under age—to answer those who, because Edward was but a child, said, "Tush, this gear will not tarry; it is but my lord Protector's and my lord of Canterbury's doing." He accordingly descants on the high duties of a king, and, among other things, on the importance of encouraging sound scriptural preaching, even by promoting learned laymen to the work while negligent bishops and clergy should be displaced. "But I fear one thing," he says; "and it is, lest for a safety of a little money, you will put in chantry

What Latimer said about it.

---

[1] "It is true that Parliament did give them to him, but so unwillingly (as I have heard) that when the bill had stuck long in the Lower House and could get no passage, he commanded the Commons to attend him in the forenoon in his gallery, where he let them wait till late in the afternoon, and then, coming out of his chamber, walking a turn or two amongst them, first on the one side and then on the other, at last, 'I hear,' saith he, 'that my bill will not pass, but I will have it pass, or I will have some of your heads,' and without other rhetoric or persuasion returned to his chamber. Enough was said, the bill passed, and all was given him as he desired."—Spelman's *History of Sacrilege*, ed. 1853, p. 206.

priests to save their pensions." Chantries had by
this time been put down and their priests pensioned
off; but the pensions were discontinued when benefices
of equal value were provided for them. And though
Latimer did not object to this in the case of chantry
priests who could preach, he did not like it as a mere
piece of economy. "I will tell you," he continues,
"Christ bought souls with his blood, and will ye sell
them for gold or silver? I would not that ye should
do with chantry priests as ye did with the abbots
when abbeys were put down. For when their enormities were first read in the Parliament house, they
were so great and abominable that there was nothing
but 'Down with them!' But within a while after,
the same abbots were made bishops, as there be some
of them yet alive, to save and redeem their pensions.
O Lord! think ye that God is a fool and seeth it
not? And if He see it, will He not punish it?"[1]

It is doing no more than justice to Latimer's
zeal for righteousness to quote this passage at
length; for he distinctly points to a shameful blot
on past administration. And therein let us follow
him, seeing that he helps us so greatly to weigh the
specious pretence of morality used as a justification
for the suppression of the smaller monasteries.
"Their enormities," forsooth, "were read in Parliament," and were "so abominable that there was
nothing but 'Down with them'!" Whether this was
a general cry that rose spontaneously from the whole
House of Commons we are not concerned to inquire.
Latimer seems to have accepted the official theory,
and been willing to believe without question a great
deal of the vile scandals that it was alleged had come
to light. But the thing at which he was indignant, as
an honest man might well be, was that the very
abbots who were accused of keeping disorderly houses
and perhaps indulging in gross sins themselves, were

[1] Latimer's *Sermons* (Parker Soc.), p. 123. Cp. pp. 117-22.

promoted to bishoprics in order to save their pensions. If the accusations against them were true, surely they did not deserve pensions at all, much less bishoprics.

How much people in general believed of what the Visitors professed to have discovered matters little to our purpose. There are always many whose ears are open to scandal, and whose judgment is not much exercised in sifting the true from the false. And that vague scandals were often repeated about monastic life in general there is very little doubt. But a point which deserves some consideration is, How much was there to go upon in the way of tangible evidence, either substantial or misleading? In the What was said about it in Queen Elizabeth's days. reign of Elizabeth it was plausibly asserted that the Visitors had returned " a book called the Black Book, expressing of every such house the vile lives and abominable facts, in murders of their brethren, in sodomies, in whoredoms, in destroying of children, in forging of deeds and other infinite horrors of life, in so much as, dividing of all the religious persons in England into three parts, two of these parts at the least were sodomites; and this appeared in writing with the names of the parties and their facts. This was showed in Parliament, and the villanies made known and abhorred." [1]

" What became of this Black Book?" various writers have asked. We have a " book," or what would have been called a book in the sixteenth century —indeed, three " books," the largest of which extends to thirty-three pages—containing the record of what the Visitors professed to have discovered in the province of York and the two dioceses of Coventry and Lichfield and of Norwich. Of this *Compendium Compertorum* I have already spoken, and I have no doubt whatever that this was " the Black Book" the Elizabethan writer had in view; but, foul as it is, with a most unspeakable foulness, even this docu-

[1] Wright's *Suppression*, 114.

ment does not by any means justify the numbers
stated to have been tainted with gross impurity. It,
moreover, says nothing about murders of the brethren,
destroying of children, or forging of deeds. In fact,
it is pretty evident that these further accusations
were the growth of time and of old nourished prejudices
after the monks had passed away. If they had no
opportunity of vindicating themselves, even in the
days of Henry VIII. by being brought face to face
with their accusers, they were still more defence-
less after they were dead, in an age prejudiced
against monasticism. And if the scandals reported
in that age so greatly exceeded what was written in
the *Comperta* themselves, we must beware of accepting without criticism even what seems to rest on
contemporary authority.

That the *Comperta* themselves were shown in
Parliament is not a necessary inference from Latimer's
words above quoted ; for what was read in Parliament
may not have been the original records. An official
statement ostensibly founded on them would have
answered all the purpose, and how far it went beyond
generalities we cannot tell. Still, it is possible enough
that the *Compendium* itself may have been produced
in Parliament and extracts from it read. We have,
however, another official statement proceeding from
the King himself, which seems to go a good way
beyond what we find in the *Compendium* ; for if we   What the
are to believe the King's own express statement,   King him-
confessions of abominable vice were signed by the   self said.
monks with their own hands.

To estimate this evidence, however, we must note
the circumstances under which it was given. Little
more than half a year after the passing of the Act
a formidable rebellion broke out in Lincolnshire,
in which the insurgents complained chiefly of the
character of the King's ministers and of the suppression of the monasteries. They sent up messengers to

the King with a list of their grievances, and received forthwith a lengthy reply carefully composed by the King himself, in a tone so extraordinary that only a considerable extract can do it justice. The following is the text of the passages which specially relate to these subjects :—

First, we begin and make answer to the fourth and sixth articles, because upon them dependeth much of the rest. Concerning choosing of Counsellors, I never have read, heard or known that princes' counsellors and prelates should be appointed by rude and ignorant common people, nor that they were persons meet nor of ability to discern and choose meet and sufficient counsellors for a prince. How presumptuous then are ye, the rude commons of one shire, and that one of the most brute and beastly of the whole realm, and of the least experience, to find fault with your Prince for the electing of his counsellors and prelates, and to take upon you, contrary to God's law and man's law, to rule your prince, whom ye are bound by all laws to obey and serve with both your lives, lands and goods, and for no worldly cause to withstand! The contrary whereof you, like traitors and rebels, have attempted, and not like true subjects as ye name yourselves.

As to the suppression of religious houses and monasteries, we woll that ye and all our subjects should well know that this is granted us by all the nobles, spiritual and temporal, of this our realm, and by all the Commons in the same by Act of Parliament, and not set forth by any counsellor or counsellors upon their mere will and fantasy, as ye full falsely would persuade our realm to believe. And where ye allege that the service of God is much diminished, the truth thereof is contrary, *for there be no houses suppressed where God was well served, but where most vice, mischief, and abomination of living was used ; and that doth well appear by their own confessions subscribed with their own hands in the time of their visitations.* And yet we suffered a great many of them (more than we needed by the Act) to stand ; wherein, if they amend not their living, we fear we have more to answer for than for the suppression of all the rest. And as for the hospitality for the relief of the poor, we wonder ye be not ashamed to affirm that they have been a relief of poor people, when a great many, or the most part, hath not past four or five religious persons in them, and divers but one, and which spent the substance of the goods of their houses in nourishing of vice and abominable living. Now what unkindness and unnaturality may we impute to you and all our subjects that be of that mind, that had liever such an unthrifty sort of vicious persons should enjoy such possessions, profits and emoluments as grow of the said houses, to the maintenance of their unthrifty life, than we, your natural prince, sovereign lord and King, which doth and hath spent more in your defences of our own than six times they be worth?

The truthfulness of all this seems to be on a par with its urbanity. Not a single house suppressed where abominable vice was not practised! Even supposing that, against all reasonable probability, vice reigned universally in houses which did not possess £200 a year of revenue, the King's Visitors had not, with all their diligence, traversed more than the half of England, and that half very hastily; so there was no means of judging the characters of half the houses suppressed. In fact, the total number of houses actually visited was not nearly one-third of all the monasteries of England; so there could have been no report at all against two-thirds of the houses suppressed. Yet the King boldly alleges that not a single house was suppressed which was not vicious, and declares that their suppression weighs less on his mind than the fact that he had spared a few in hope of their amendment; which he did, indeed, for pecuniary considerations, though he did not say so, neighbours offering occasionally considerable sums that useful monasteries might stand. And what a fine touch in the end about the King having spent of his own money more than six times the value of those smaller monasteries in defence of the realm, when he had laid on oppressive taxes, followed by a forced loan of which he got Parliament to relieve him from repayment! The truth is that there never was a time in his whole reign when Henry was in more serious danger from rebellion, and he was not at all scrupulous about the means he used to tide over a temporary difficulty.

Defama-
tion gave
a pretext
for sup-
pression.

The defaming of the monasteries was simply a step towards their suppression and the confiscation of their endowments; and apart from the gratification of avarice, their suppression was a necessary step in the policy which the King and Cromwell had been carefully engineering. Popular prejudice served them well in some things, but popular prejudice against the monasteries was by no means vehement. So far as it touched the religious Orders at all, it went against the wealthy heads of houses, as against wealthy lords in general. And the King was not slow to avail himself of such prejudices when they could find a respectable mouthpiece. Such a mouthpiece he found at this time in Latimer, who had been made Bishop of Worcester in the preceding autumn. It may almost seem to us that Latimer, rising by Court favour at the beginning of his career, was a different man from Latimer denouncing peculation and immoral government under King Edward VI. But in truth, though the two sides of his character have different aspects, there is no moral incoherence in his career. He was a man who had his weaknesses and his prejudices, but in the main was entirely honest. We must look at him, however, now on his weak side, rather too much elated by Court favour. The contemporary letter from which an extract was given touching the King's introduction of the bill for the suppression, was written by a London clergyman named Thomas Dorset to the Mayor of Plymouth and three of his fellow townsmen. It is a rather lengthy news-letter, almost entirely about Church matters, and at the beginning relates to the examination of some clergymen at Lambeth "before the three bishops of Canterbury, Worcester, and Salisbury" (Cranmer, Latimer, and Shaxton), showing how at this time the power of examining for heresy was given over to the newly promoted dignitaries who upheld royal supremacy. And how bold these men of the new school had now become in speaking against the old, whether clergy or laity, appears well by the paragraph immediately preceding that which we have already extracted :—

On Sunday last the Bishop of Worcester preached at Paul's Cross, and he said that bishops, abbots, priors, parsons, canons resident, priests and all were strong thieves—yea, dukes, lords and all. The King, quod he, made a marvellous good Act of Parliament that certain men should sow every of them two acres of hemp; but it were all too little, were it so much more, to hang the thieves that be in England. Bishops, Abbots, with such other, should not have so many servants, nor so many dishes, but to go to their first foundation, and keep hospitality to feed the needy people,—not jolly fellows with golden chains and velvet gowns, ne let them not once come into the houses of religion for repast. Let them call, Knave Bishop, Knave Abbot, Knave Prior, yet feed none of them all, nor their horses, nor their dogs. . . . The Bishop of Canterbury saith that the King's Grace is at a full point for friars and chauntry priests, that they shall away all that, saving those that can preach. Then one said to the Bishop that they had good trust that they should serve forth their life times, and he said they should serve it out at a cart then, for any other service they should have by that.

Latimer's abuse of the bishops and clergy.

That a revolution was to be made in religious matters by strong coercion was perfectly evident; and this process naturally had the approval of Cranmer, Latimer, and Shaxton, who had all three been made bishops for the express purpose of supporting the new style of spiritual government. Of the three, it would seem that Latimer devoted his energies to it with the least misgivings. Honest as he undoubtedly was throughout his career, he cannot be classed among those clear-sighted and incorruptible heroes who discern sources of mischief before they come to maturity, and set themselves to oppose moral and social danger before it becomes widespread. A man of old-fashioned ideas generally, a popular preacher who set forth morality with merry stories, no one would ever have thought of calling him a great divine, and the last thing he was likely to do was to take a leading part in a religious revolution. Nor, in truth, did he take the lead; he simply followed a course marked out for him. He believed in the ability and clear-sightedness of the King and Cromwell; his devotion to his sovereign saw no clear line of limitation; and he was rather intoxicated to find important functions given him, to which he could hardly have aspired when he was first presented to the benefice of West Kington in Wiltshire "by the King at the suit of Cromwell and Dr. Buttes" more than four years before he was made a bishop. Invited to preach before the King and in London about that time, he was delated for heresy and protected by courtiers; yet he was obliged, in spite of favour, to make his submission to Convocation. Now, however, he had his revenge, and was more free with his tongue.

In June a new Parliament met, and Convocation, as usual, met at the same time. The last Convocation had experienced cruelty and suffering enough at the King's hands. It had been forced to make an enormous contribution, which was accepted only as a fine to expiate the grievous sin of the clergy in acknowledging Wolsey's legateship, and it had been driven to that qualified acknowledgment of the King's supremacy, which, as has been sufficiently shown, was interpreted by Parliament as unqualified, and enforced by a cruel statute, followed by merciless and unjust executions. Now the subjection of the clergy was to be further exemplified. Cromwell presided in Convocation as the King's Vicegerent—nay, even Cromwell's deputy in his absence,—and Cranmer appointed Latimer to preach before the assembled divines, giving him thereby an opportunity to pay off old scores against them. In the two Latin

He preaches before Convocation.

sermons which he then delivered he certainly did not spare them. Without calling them to their faces "strong thieves," as he had done at Paul's Cross, he asked what one good thing they had done for seven years past. They had burned a dead man and tried to burn a living one. They had been compelled against their will to allow the circulation of good books. It was the King who had done some good by admonishing them to preach oftener; and it was time now to reform spiritual abuses, for the number of holy days was excessive, and images, pilgrimages, and relics served but to encourage superstition. He also glanced at Purgatory as a fiery furnace that burned away people's pence. Thus the lines of a new Church policy were indicated. But Convocation, however ineffective its voice might now be, endeavoured to take a way of its own, and still showed considerable independence of spirit in denouncing what it considered popular errors and heretical outcries, some of which Latimer's sermon distinctly favoured.

To return, however, to the subject of the monasteries. On the 24th April, more than a month after the passing of the Act for the suppression of the smaller houses, commissions were sent out to a number of gentlemen in each of the counties to take certain preliminary steps towards putting it in force. Certain special officers, viz. an auditor, a particular receiver, a clerk of the register of the late visitation, and three other discreet persons to be named by the King in every county, were to visit the different houses, show their commission, and declare to the governors the statute of dissolution. They were then to swear the governors and officers of each house to make declaration,—first, of the Order to which the house belonged, and whether it was a cell (for cells of great monasteries were to be spared), and, if so, they were to deliver a privy seal to the

92 LOLLARDY AND THE REFORMATION BK. III

governor to appear before the Chancellor and Council
of the newly constituted Court of the Augmentations ;
secondly, what number of religious were in it, " and
the conversation of their lives," how many were
priests, and how many were willing to go to other
houses, or take capacities, and also how many servants or other dependents belonged to the house ;
thirdly, they were to value the lead and the bells ;
fourthly, to call for the convent seal and muniments,
make an inventory by indenture with the governor
of all the ornaments, plate, jewels, household stuff,
farm stock, and so forth, with the debts owing by
and to them.   Then, after some necessary injunctions, they were to survey the demesnes, and certify
the clear yearly value, and what woods, parks, forests,
and commons belonged to each house.[1]

The "new
survey" of
the monas-
teries.   The returns made of this " new survey," as it was
called, for several counties are extant ; and it is not
a little singular that the characters given of the
monks by these royal commissioners are almost
uniformly good.   Occasionally, the inmates of some
of the most defamed monasteries in Legh and
Layton's *Comperta*—as in the cases of the monks of
Garadon and the nuns of Gracedieu in Leicestershire,
were reported to be all of good conversation.   In
neither of these two houses, moreover, was there a
monk or nun who desired to leave—a fact which
enhances the credit of the later report.   At Coxford,
in Norfolk, where, according to the Visitors, one
William Nevell confessed impurity, the commissioners found that there were only three monks, all
priests of good name, who, however, desired dispensations to leave.   At Bromholm, where the Visitors
had found the prior and three monks (who, in fact,
were all the house) impure, the commissioners found
them all " of very good name and fame."   Moreover,
at the nunnery of Crabhouse above mentioned, which

---

[1] *L. P.*, x. 721.

had only four inmates, all of whom, according to the Visitors, had had children, the report of the commissioners was of all four, that "their name is good, as is commonly reported." On this, however, it must be remarked that another hand has written at the top, "Their name is not good."[1] In this particular case, apparently, the first report of the commissioners was made without sufficient inquiry.

But, on the whole, it will surely be admitted that no reliance whatever is to be placed on the foul reports of the Visitors, which were clearly intended for no other purpose than to afford a pretext for the parliamentary suppression of the smaller monasteries. It is further evident that that measure was exceedingly unpopular and one of the main causes of the two, or rather three, successive rebellions which broke out in Lincolnshire, Yorkshire, and the North of England between the beginning of October 1536 and the middle of February following. For more than four months there were intermittent outbreaks, at times quieted by false assurances, soon after perfidiously violated,—outbreaks punished with a brutal, unsparing severity which left very little heart in the people for renewed disturbances. So the monastic system in England was broken down and the unpopular legislation was carried into effect. The pretence that no further suppression was contemplated than that of the smaller monasteries did not endure two years. Strong intercession, indeed, was made for many of the smaller monasteries, and, as I have already said, considerable sums were paid to the Exchequer that they might be spared, for there was a special provision in the Act allowing the King to spare those he thought fit. But after a brief respite there began a process of surrenders, even of the larger monasteries, which one by one fell into the King's hands also, till finally the abbots of

Destruction of the monastic system.

[1] Gasquet's *Overlooked Testimonies.* See *Dublin Review*, April 1894.

three great houses who were not inclined to follow
suit, were accused of treason, as a few other abbots
had already been before them, with the result, which,
as contemporary memoranda show, was fully determined on before their trial, that they were found
guilty and hanged. The houses themselves, in all
such cases, were, by an arbitrary stretch of the law,
confiscated on account of the attainder of their
heads,—just as part of the property of the See of
York had been confiscated on the fall of Wolsey.

Note.—That the tradition recorded by Sir Henry Spelman
of the King's arbitrary conduct towards Parliament is by no
means improbable we may judge, not only by the fact that
the parliamentary suppression was one great cause of the
Northern rebellions, but also by the unpopularity of the far
less extensive suppression of small monasteries effected by
Wolsey, notwithstanding that he did it at great personal
cost to himself under the authority of papal bulls and royal
licences, and the object was to apply the revenues to the
foundation of two colleges for the education of youth, the
one at Oxford and the other at his native town of Ipswich.
In Roy's bitter satire against Wolsey, " Rede me and be not
wrothe," we meet with the following passage :—

> I am sure thou has hearde spoken
> What monasteries he hath broken
>   With out their fownders consentis.
> He subverteth churches and chappells,
> Takynge a waye bokis and bells
>   With chalesces and vestmentis.
> He plucketh downe the costly leades
> That it maye rayne on saynctis heades,
>   Not sparynge God nor oure Ladye.
> Where as they red servyce divyne
> There is grountynge of pigges and swyne,
>   With lowynge of oxen and kye.
> The aultres of their celebracions
> Are made pearches for henns and capons,
>   De foylynge them with their durt.
> And though it be never so prophane,
> He is counted a good christiane,
>   No man doynge hym eny hurtt.[1]

---

[1] See Arber's reprint of the ballad, p. 113.

The whole number of monasteries suppressed by Wolsey was twenty-nine. Those suppressed by Parliament, even deducting those which had special licences to continue, were two hundred and fifty-eight.

APPENDIX TO CHAPTER II

The real condition of the monasteries as regards purity has of late become a question of much discussion; but exact evidence is clearly impossible to attain, and the accuracy of any general estimate will always no doubt be impugned, more or less from *a priori* impressions.   Scandalmongers were far more outspoken in those days than they would have been if controlled by a law of libel, and the social life of England as a whole was probably no better than that of other countries.   Domestic feeling was killed by feudalism. The ties of marriage were little regarded in high life; the middle classes were corrupted by their superiors, and many of the secular clergy, bound to celibacy, formed uncanonical unions with women, or even lived in sinful relations with married women deserted by their husbands.   That vice should be so prevalent in the world, and not find its way into the monasteries—harbours of refuge though these might be considered—was hardly to be expected; and we know that it was by no means completely excluded.   But a more sober estimate of the degree to which it actually prevailed there may be found by comparing, where it is possible to do so, the *comperta* of the Royal Visitors of 1536 with the results of episcopal visitations not many years before.

This is possible, at least, in some houses in the diocese of Norwich, and we have already made the comparison in the case of Crabhouse in Wiggenhall.   But before proceeding to a more extended comparison, it should be observed that the object of these episcopal visitations was not, generally speaking, merely to correct immorality.   It was to correct anything whatever that was wrong—whether chanting in the choir was too quick or the tiling of an outhouse was in decay; to hear complaints, even against heads of monasteries, whether an abbot or prior was too severe, or whether a lazy monk shammed illness and lay too long abed in the morning; for good monks got up in the night to go to lauds.   Quarrels, of course, come out in evidence occasionally, and as to more

Results of the Royal Visitation in Norwich diocese compared with episcopal visitations before it,—

serious things they could not well be kept out of sight. Consequently they do appear sometimes, but certainly nothing like so frequently as they do in the reports of the King's Visitors.

at Hick- For example, those Visitors at Hickling found six monks
ling, unchaste, and three of them with women. We have the records of four episcopal visitations from 1492 to 1532, and various complaints are made at three of them, as, that servants are ill paid, lights not kept up, and that there is no schoolmaster; but not a word about unchastity. In 1520 nothing is reported amiss at all. In 1532 the chief thing to be looked to in that lonely country seems to be danger from ill neighbours, and the bishop orders clubs to be provided

Thetford, for the defence of the priory! At Thetford (a place of old renown, once the East Anglian bishop's see) there was a priory and a nunnery also, both in great decay and very poor. But out of four visitations the only hint of unchastity is in 1514, when the prior is suspected with the wife of Stephen Horham. In the others there were either no complaints or very trivial. In 1536, however, the King's Visitors not only found that one canon confessed theft and one impurity, but among the nuns they alleged that one had confessed incontinence. They suspected, however, that the canons were confederated as there were seventeen of them! But this statement, even as to the number, seems not a little doubtful; for the priory, which was found to be in decay in 1514 and 1520, consisted in 1532 only of the prior and three canons with three novices. And even in 1534 when the brethren acknowledged the King's supremacy they numbered only seven, including the prior.[1] The report of the Visitors, however, was written only for the King's information.

Wymond- At Wymondham, indeed, we find a house which seems to
ham. have been always more or less unruly. In 1492 it was found, among other things, that divine offices were celebrated *morose*—in a grumbling sort of a way; that monks bought and sold like merchants; that they did not study, but hunted with hounds and hawks, and left the cloister without the abbot's leave for their own amusement. The rules of the Benedictine Order were not kept, and the walls of the monastic enclosure were not in good repair. The abbot, John Kyrtelyng (an old man, doubtless, for he had been abbot

---

[1] Rymer, xiv. 514-15.

one-and-twenty years),[1] was compelled to hand over the administration to William Batell, with whom he made an agreement for a pension, a mansion-house to live in, and various allowances from the monastery, which certainly ought to have made him very comfortable. In 1514 the abbot's name was Thomas Chamberlen. He complained that some of the monks broke the locks of the cloister—he could not tell who the offenders were ; that William Bury the prior, with some of the other monks, broke up a chest and carried off evidences of the house without his leave ; that the same prior plucked a dish from a servant and disposed of it *ad libitum*. Prior Bury, however, had his own complaint against the abbot, who kept the offices of cellarer and sacrist in his hands, giving the poor monks not enough to eat and drink; that the abbot did not pay the "Juste money"; and that a number of other things were unsatisfactory. One monk on the Eve of St. John Baptist had declared that a man would not rise with body and soul on the Day of Judgment. Others wore shirts and long hose. One Hengham was suspected with Agnes Hoberd. The daughters of a certain widow came suspiciously to the chamberlain's room. The precentor took away books to the injury of St. Mary's mass, etc. But Dan John Harleston gives a very unfavourable character of Prior Bury and says he is a malicious man. He drew a sword last Lent on Dan Richard Cambridge and would have killed him if Harleston had not stopped him. He maliciously broke the clarichord of Dan John Hengham, and would have hit him with a stone in the abbot's presence ; and so on. The depositions testify general disorder ; and Prior Bury, when Dan Richard Cambridge threatened to report him to the bishop, not only for the attempt against himself with the sword but for other irregularities, answered contemptuously, "Tell my lord and my lady both, for I care not." This seems to suggest that the bishop himself had a " lady," which, indeed, I cannot quite disprove. The notice of Bishop Nix in Godwin's *Bishops* is not favourable to his character, but on what evidences it was based is not clear. At this time, however, Bishop Nix must have been nearer seventy than sixty years old, and if he required a " lady," it was probably as a nurse rather than in any other capacity. In 1520 matters at Wymondham were not very much better, and Dan Richard Cambridge was

---

[1] Dugdale, iii. 327.

reported as given to drink. But some improvement had begun, the abbot being John Holt, titular Bishop of Lydda, a learned man and friend of Sir Thomas More. And in 1526 this improvement seems to have been maintained. Prior Bury, indeed, still remained, and, curiously, no one complained of him this time; but the abbot, William Castilten, seems to have been a capable man, and four of his monks report that he corrects everything and all is well. He and the cellarer, Thomas Thaxsted, however, say that Thomas Osmund is a getter-up of quarrels between him and the brethren. In 1536 the Royal Visitors here found four cases of impurity among the professed. There were eleven monks including the abbot in 1534.[1]

Previous history of Wymondham.

The previous history of this abbey, we may observe, was a little peculiar. Till the year 1448 it had been a cell of the great abbey of St. Albans, the abbot of which, by name John Stoke, caused one of his monks, Stephen London, with whom he had personal disagreements, to be made prior there. But this Stephen became so popular both with his brethren and with Sir Andrew Ogard, "his founder," that Abbot Stoke's jealousy was roused and he endeavoured to remove him. The prior and Sir Andrew, however, successfully petitioned the King for leave to obtain a bull from the Pope to erect Wymondham into an abbey; which was done, and Stephen London became the first abbot.[2] He certainly was one who could speak his mind very decidedly, as a letter of his to Abbot Stoke bears witness; and I suspect Abbot Stoke deserved every word of the strong rebuke he gave him. Stephen London was evidently a good and capable ruler; but the same could not be said of his successors a little later. Things do not seem to have been improving, even inside monasteries, in the latter half of the fifteenth century.

At St. Albans itself in the end they became far worse. John Stoke had succeeded a really great abbot, Whethamstede, who resigned after twenty years' rule, overburdened with anxieties. After Stoke's death Whethamstede was elected again, and he at once instituted a register of things done in the abbey, and thereby became an historian of the civil war, of which St. Albans itself witnessed the first conflict. After Whethamstede's day there was a sad moral decline, and

---

[1] *L. P.*, vii. 1121 (61); x. 364.
[2] Dugdale, iii. 326; Amundesham, ii. 366 (Rolls Series).

under Abbot Wallingford, though he set up a printing press in the Abbey and presented it with a fine altar-screen and other costly gifts, occurred those fearful scandals which called for the interference of Archbishop Morton at the beginning of Henry VII.'s reign, when this, the oldest of Benedictine abbeys in England, infected two neighbouring nunneries with its own impurities.[1]

Now let us look at a nunnery. At Blackborough the Royal Visitors in 1536 found the prioress and two others "suspected" of incontinence. What was the previous record of this house? In 1514 the prioress, whose name is not given, said she had nothing to report. Dame Margaret Gigges said all things were well, both as to services and repairs, though it was true the prioress did not render any accounts, to save the expense of an auditor, but only (as another sister observes) reported verbally the state of the house to the sisters. Others agreed generally that things were well; but Margaret Hollins, who was president and sacrist, considered that the buildings of the church and cloister required repair; while Agnes Grey said that they did not keep up the number of sisters required by their founder; they were in debt, and had not had a sub-prioress for four years. In 1520 all was reported well and an inventory exhibited. In 1532 Elizabeth Dawny, the prioress (the same whom the Royal Visitors "suspected" of incontinence four years later), said all was going on as well as the resources of the house permitted; but Margaret Gigges, who by this time had been made sub-prioress, said the church was ruinous with age and they could not afford workmen to rebuild it. No unfavourable criticisms were elicited from any one of the eleven sisters examined; but one replied in answer to a question that a Black Friar of Lynn came to confess them. Such is the substance of three visitations of a house that was clearly decaying as regards the means of keeping it up. But do these reports convey any idea that it was governed by an immoral prioress or that it was at all likely to harbour immorality?

Again, let us take another kind of community, consisting neither of monks nor nuns, but of canons. At Coxford Priory the Royal Visitors in 1536 found that one canon, William Nevell, confessed impurities. Here, perhaps, we may suspect that the confession was genuine; but it is worth while looking at the previous history of the house. There

(margin: Blackborough.)

(margin: Coxford.)

----

[1] See Vol. I. pp. 269 *sq.*

seems to have been a struggle to keep it up. In 1492 there were a prior and seven canons, and the visitor, Archdeacon Goldwell, commissary of the Bishop of Norwich, found first that the infirmary was not open for the use of the sick, and the refectory was too cold for the canons to dine in comfort; that it would be advisable to have a teacher of grammar for the juniors; and that the brethren had not fitting recreations. That was all. In 1514 things were certainly going wrong. John Mathew, the prior, said the morning mass was not celebrated; the brethren were disobedient, quarrelsome, and incorrigible; Dan John Berdon had three or four times taken flight and was now incarcerated. Dan John Nightingale, the sub-prior, said that silence was not observed, that the prior did not render accounts yearly, that the refectory was in decay, and they had no infirmary—complaints repeated by another canon. Dan John Froste, however, said all was well, and so said Thomas Birde and three others; while Richard Andrew stated that the prior did not rise in the night-time except at the four principal feasts. The Bishop on this gave injunctions with a view to better management. In 1520 there was a marked improvement. The establishment seems to have consisted at that date of the prior, John Mathew, the sub-prior, John Nightingale, five canons, and three *professi* not even in minor orders. The prior complained about an annuity given by the house to one Nicholas Hare, who did not discharge the office for which it was given. The sub-prior said that a yearly account of the state of the house was not rendered, but all else was well; and each of the canons, examined separately, agreed that all duties were done truly, both in temporal and in spiritual things, and that the prior was very attentive to the weal of the house. In 1526 John Mathew is still prior, and admits that an account is not rendered yearly of the state of the house; his sub-prior, Nightingale, adds that to his knowledge it has not been usual to do so for forty years. Two priests and one deacon, who seem to be all the remaining canons, say that all things are going on well. But in 1532 a scandal is for the first time revealed. Prior Mathew and another prior, Mr. Rawlens, have passed away, and now the prior is Henry Salter, who has not been a year in office, but promises to render an account by the end of the year. He says, however, that Dan Robert Porter had a child with which the house is burdened, and that he was corrected for this by

Prior Rawlens—statements which are confirmed by Dan John Graye. The sub-prior, however, Dan William Nevell, simply says that all things are done well *juxta facultates,* with which John Graye agrees also, and the guilty Robert Porter and two novices say the same.

That is the last episcopal visitation, and it is remarkable that the Royal Visitors four years later are silent about Robert Porter's misconduct, but find that William Nevell has confessed unchastity; which may, no doubt, be true, or it may be (just as likely) that the Royal Visitors in their hasty visitation, confused the names of Nevell and Porter—accuser and accused.

Again, let us look at the story of Buckenham Priory, where in 1492 were a prior and seven canons. By the visitation of that date it appears, first, that the prior did not show a yearly account as he ought to do (this, it will be observed, was a very common neglect, condoned in many houses by the brethren); then, that there was not perfect charity among the brethren, that they had not a good supply of fish on fast days, and that the prior was not impartial. In serious matters he did not take counsel but did everything after his own mind. He had pawned a gilt cup worth eight marks. If a brother was sick he got no one to tend him in the infirmary. He had leased the dairy to the detriment of the house. The brethren did not keep the refectory except in Lent and Advent. The victuals in the kitchen were not good. The house and walls of the priory were decayed. Finally, one Isabella Warner came suspiciously often to the priory, and something was suspected between her and the sub-prior, Thomas Beverley. The bishop "continued"—that is to say adjourned—this visitation, first till the following Wednesday (it was in October), and then till the 9th July next after, which would be the following year; but whether he gave any injunctions even then does not appear. In 1514 the prior, John Milgate, and the sub-prior, Thomas Beverley, complain of certain disobedient canons, and others report slight irregularities, while three say that all is well. In 1520, except that one canon did not appear and was pronounced contumacious, all seems to have been going on well. By the bishop's leave the neighbouring parish churches of St. Benet, Old Buckenham, and St. Andrew were served by the brethren. In 1526 Milgate is still prior, as, indeed, he was to the last, and all is reported well by everybody, except some misconduct on the part of a servant, and a complaint

Bucken-ham.

by the novices of the smallness of their stipends. In 1532 all is found well except that some of the young canons leave the cloister after complines. Some wear shoes "with horns," and a canon who serves the cure of Stamford is declared by one of the brethren to be unfit. The bishop's injunctions are that the canons shall retire to the dormitory at once after complines, and not leave it without licence. The south doors are to be shut. No canon is to wear "lascivious" shoes, and none is to serve a secular cure without the bishop's licence. Not one of the last three episcopal visitations shows anything worse than this little dangerous tendency of canons to imitate the fashions of the day with "lascivious" shoes. But four years later the Royal Visitors find Prior Milgate himself incontinent with a single woman and two of the canons unchaste in another way. If these accusations were just, it seems a little strange that Prior Milgate's frailty was never discovered in any of the previous two-and-twenty years.

It is true, the monasteries we have been considering were chiefly in country districts—even Wymondham could hardly have had much of a town about it. But Norwich was a kind of metropolis of the Eastern Counties, a busy populous city, the attractions and excitements of which had un-

Norwich Cathedral priory.

doubtedly their influence upon the inmates of the Cathedral priory; and it is certainly of some interest to know how far the report of the Royal Visitors here is likely to have been justified. Now it may be supposed that a cathedral priory, being so closely connected with a bishop's see, was under more complete episcopal control than an ordinary monastery. But in truth the very reverse was the case; for the prior was the real acting head, who was commonly very jealous of the bishop's interference, and many are the cases in monastic history of vehement disputes between a bishop and the prior of his cathedral convent. Such a prior, indeed, required to be a man of special sagacity and moderation, not only to keep his subordinates in order but to maintain his own firmly, and at the same time respectfully, against his diocesan if necessary. But a prior would sometimes exalt his own authority too much, without improving the discipline. The story of Norwich priory from the year 1492 is certainly not that of a well-ordered community. In Bishop Goldwell's visitation in that year it was found, among other things, that women spent the night within the precincts of the monastery; that the sub-sacrist went out at night and sat too long with a tailor and his wife, spending money profusely; that the sacrist sold the jewels of the monastery; that laymen sat at the common table with the brethren, and that the monks walked about in church talking with women of bad fame. The bishop's injunctions, intended to meet these abuses, began by requiring due respect for his own authority, annulling the ordinances of a previous prior, and forbidding such reverence as was due to a bishop to be paid to a prior or any other. They then enjoined the masters of the novices to desist from some new style of teaching that they had introduced, and return to the old accustomed fashion. The modern statutes were to be erased from the books, and viands good and sufficient in quantity were to be served to the canons. For the worst scandals, touching the admission of women within the monastery, he only warned the brethren that the statutes of his predecessor, Bishop Bateman (about a century and a half old), were still binding and must be observed.

When Bishop Nix visited the priory in 1514 matters were certainly worse. Among the *comperta* it is stated that the brethren are not studious after they are promoted to the priesthood; that their friends visit them in their chambers and not in the parlour; that suspected women come to the monastery; that the sub-prior sets a bad example as regards religion and chastity; that a certain monk had got an unmarried woman with child, and that the priors of the dependent cells were in many ways remiss. One of these last the bishop ordered to be dismissed, and after some other injunctions he "continued" the visitation until the following Lent. Six years later, in 1520, there seems to have been a decided improvement. Prior Robert Catton showed his account, which proved that the monastery was out of debt; there were no scandals, and the bishop's injunctions were only framed to correct minor irregularities. But in 1526 things had got worse again; the sub-prior was too easy in relaxing penances, the precentor was neglecting his duties. One monk was a dandy, and another played cards and dice when penance was enjoined to him. Dr. Reppis or Repps (who was soon afterwards made Abbot of St. Benet's Hulme, and, later, Bishop of Norwich) is accused of having embraced the wardrober's wife, even in the presence of others. There is a great tangle of complaints, but we do not know what they all came to; for the bishop "continued" his visitation from June to August, and there is no record of final proceedings. In 1532 we hear of various irregularities but nothing of unchastity.

After these varying reports that of the Royal Visitors in 1536 does not seem so incredible. Only one monk was found to have had intercourse with a woman, though four others were found to be impure.

St. Benet's Hulme.

A change from the populous city of Norwich to the lonely swamps, amid which then rose the great Abbey of St. Benet's Hulme, is really as great a change as the county of Norfolk could show. It is not wonderful that in such a country the prior in 1532 says he was allowed to wear shoes and hose (*calcei et caligæ*) instead of boots (*ocreæ*) by the abbot's leave, on account of an ailment in his legs. The situation was, in truth, most uninviting, and the monks were not as numerous as those of the Cathedral; just twenty-four, including the abbot and prior, signed the Supremacy in 1534. Yet the abbot was one of the mitred abbots who sat in Parliament, and probably the very fact that he was often called away from the monastery had an injurious effect upon its administration. Scandals and irregularities certainly appear in all but one of the four episcopal visitations. But in 1520, under the effective discipline of Abbot John Salcot, otherwise named Capon (who unfortunately earned promotion afterwards to two successive bishoprics by doing the King's dirty work), everything was reported well, except by one brother who made a slight complaint against the prior. Neither is there anything much amiss in 1526, except that one brother is presented for laziness in lying abed and evading matins on pretence of illness. The bishop proposed to send him to his own prison at Norwich; but Abbot Salcot intercedes for him that he may have another trial. At the last episcopal visitation, in 1532, Salcot having been promoted to the Abbacy of Hyde near Winchester, Dr. Repps was abbot in his place, and there is certainly an appearance of order having been let down somewhat. Prior Scottowe, whose tender legs required indulgence, did not rise to matins. His negligence, however, is complained of; for owing to it the juniors did not keep silence or observe ceremonies, but strolled outside the monastery. The third prior, Thomas Stonham, hunted in the morning after matins, going out at three or four o'clock; and there were far too many dogs, who ate up what should have been given to the poor. The sacrist was accused of defaming his brethren at meal times. These are the principal complaints.

But we hear nothing about unchastity, of which the Royal Visitors four years later declared four of the monks to be guilty.

The two worst monasteries in the diocese, according to the report of the Royal Visitors, must have been the priories of Pentney and Westacre. These two houses were about equal in size, each consisting in 1534, when the Supremacy was signed, of a prior and sixteen canons. Now, in all the episcopal visitations Pentney bears an absolutely spotless Pentney. character. Generally the canons are agreed that there is nothing whatever to report; but complaints crop up once of the want of a schoolmaster, and another time of an inefficient tutor. "Of Pentney," says Dr. Jessopp, "during the five centuries that it lasted, we hear nothing but good reports, and the canons of that house kept up their character to the end." Yet the Royal Visitors did not scruple to report that the prior, Robert Codde, and five of the canons were unchaste; and in the case of the prior they said they knew, from the confession of the Abbess of Marham, that she had a child by him. This looks bad; but if the Abbess of Marham had so misconducted herself, it may well be that she told a lie in accusing the Prior of Pentney as her seducer. Marham seems to have had a bad name. Not only are the Royal Visitors very specific about the failings of these nuns, of whom four besides the abbess, by their account, had borne children, but even the Commissioners of what was called "the new survey," who report so much more favourably of the monasteries generally, describe this house as "of slanderous report."[1] The fact was probably due to its being exempt from episcopal visitation as a Cistercian nunnery. As regards the accused Prior of Pentney, however, we have not only the favourable report of those Commissioners in his case, but a special intercession that was made for him to Cromwell: "We beseech your favour," wrote Richard Southwell and Robert Hogen, "for the Prior of Pentney, assuring you that he relieves those quarters wondrously where he dwells, and it would be a pity not to spare a house that feeds so many indigent poor, which is in a good state, maintains good service, and does so many charitable deeds."[2] The house itself consisted of nine priests, who were, by the report of the Commissioners, "of very honest fame and good religious persons who do

---

[1] See Gasquet in the *Dublin Review* for April 1894.
[2] *L. P.*, x. 563 ; also xi. 518.

desire the King's licence to continue and remain in religion."[1]

Westacre. At Westacre there were certainly complaints of irregularities of various kinds in five different visitations; in three of which are charges of impurity. In 1514 improper intercourse is hinted at between the prior and the wife of John Smyth. In 1526 one monk is accused of unnatural crimes; and in 1532 the butler is reported as having illegitimate issue supported by the priory. These scandals undoubtedly make more plausible for this house the double report made by the Royal Visitors in 1536, the first statement aspersing nine canons with impurity, one of them with various women; the second statement accusing Prior Wingfield and another canon of what could only have been learned, if true, from their own confessions, and imputing to another canon adultery with a married woman, and to another connection with two women and unnatural crime besides.

There are a few other monasteries besides in the diocese of Norwich, in which the results of episcopal and royal visitations may be compared. But perhaps the above examples may suffice. Whoever would pursue the subject further will find the episcopal visitations printed by Dr. Jessopp in one of the Camden Society's publications.[2] From the reports as a whole we can certainly see that monasteries differed greatly in character, and we can understand what the inmates themselves regarded in each case as the things most requiring amendment. It is impossible to rise from the perusal without a feeling that vice, sometimes even gross vice, did make its way at times into these retreats for piety; but that many of them were deeply tainted, or were allowed long to continue so, does not seem to me a justifiable inference from these very frank revelations.

---

[1] Gasquet, *u. s.*
[2] *Visitations of the Diocese of Norwich, A.D. 1492-1532.* Edited by the Rev. A. Jessopp, D.D., 1888.

CHAPTER III

WITHOUT entering into many details of the suppression
of the larger monasteries, which, as already mentioned,
was mainly effected by individual surrenders, a few
examples of what was going on, and of the methods
practised, may be desirable. But in the first instance
it is as well to take note of the chronology of the Chronology
other important events that were taking place. of events.
Katharine of Aragon had died on the 7th January
1536, to the great satisfaction of her inhuman husband,
who was relieved of any fear that the Emperor would
make war on England to secure justice to his aunt.
Her rival, Anne Boleyn, was beheaded on the 19th
May following, and the King married his third wife,
Jane Seymour, on the 30th of the same month. In
the summer the work of suppressing the smaller
monasteries began; and in October broke out the
Lincolnshire insurrection, succeeded by one in Yorkshire, which was quieted by false assurances. These
very serious outbreaks were largely due to the measures
taken against the monasteries, and they might have
had a very different result if Reginald Pole, now at
Rome, whom the Pope had created a cardinal, and
designed to send as legate into England, or as near it
as possible, had been able to start sooner on his
mission. Rebellion in the North, however, had already
been subdued or disarmed before he left Rome, and

when he afterwards passed through France, and then through Flanders, where he was obliged to turn to Liège for an asylum, neither Francis I. nor Mary of Hungary dared to receive him as legate, for fear of incurring the enmity of Henry, who denounced him as a traitor to himself, and even demanded his extradition.

Thus in 1537 England was still cut off from Rome, and the hope which had begun to be entertained at Anne Boleyn's fall of bringing Henry and his kingdom back to the unity of Christendom was altogether frustrated. The bishops and leading divines of England held a Council, in which they drew up a manual of religious teaching called *The Institution of a Christian Man*, published with the King's sanction, though not by his express authority as Head of the Church, for he professed that he had found no time to examine it carefully. It was clearly a tentative effort towards a system of religious instruction which ignored the Pope's authority, but nevertheless could not be impugned as heretical. In October of the same year Queen Jane Seymour gave birth to a son, the future Edward VI., and died a few days after.

As yet, since the suppression of the smaller monasteries, none of the greater had surrendered except Chertsey, which consented to be extinguished with a view to a larger monastic foundation. But just at this time it would appear that Cromwell and the Duke of Norfolk had arranged together to obtain Dissolution of Lewes Priory. from the King a grant of the possessions of the Priory of Lewes, which they found means to get the prior to give up into the King's hands. How the prior was reconciled to this is not difficult to conjecture. In his visitation in 1535 Layton professed to have found great immorality at Farleigh in Wiltshire, a cell of Lewes, and to have gathered matter sufficient to bring the Prior of Lewes into great danger if the testimony against him was true.[1] Later on he visited

[1] *L. P.*, IX. 42.

Lewes itself, where he made the sub-prior confess treason in his preaching, and then denounced the prior as a perjured traitor; the prior all the while kneeling and imploring him not to report his conduct to Cromwell. Layton, nevertheless, summoned him to appear before Cromwell on All Hallows Day, wherever he and the King might happen to be at that date, bringing the sub-prior along with him.[1] The only result, however, appears to have been that the prior was very sufficiently tamed. He remained in possession of his house for two years longer, receiving letters from Cromwell from time to time to give up this or that farm belonging to the priory to some nominee of the King or his Vicegerent.[2] Occasionally, indeed, the orders were contradictory in favour of different applicants, owing to the multitude of suitors and the confusion of public business; but the poor prior did his best to give satisfaction, till now it was proposed to make him give up the priory and all its possessions to the King.

The first steps taken towards the extinction of this monastery will be seen by the following letter, which has an interest of its own besides :—

THE DUKE OF NORFOLK TO CROMWELL

My very good Lord, with most hearty thanks for your venison. These shall be to advertise you that where I perceive by your letter ye would know how I sped with the King's Highness yesterday;—first, at my coming to his Majesty I used myself, though, peradventure, not wisely, yet after mine accustomed manner, plainly, exhorting his Highness to take in good part the pleasure of Almighty God in taking out of this transitory life the Queen our late mistress, and to recomfort himself with the high treasure sent to him and his realm, that is to say, the Prince, with many other persuasions to advise him to tract no longer time than force should drive him unto to provide for a new wife, by whom, of likelihood,

---

[1] *L. P.*, IX. 632.   [2] *L. P.*, XI. 214, 373, 448, 583.

more children might be brought forth to our most rejoice and consolation. After that I most humbly thanked his Majesty for that I perceived by your good Lordship he was content to give unto us Lewes if we might bring the bargain to pass, saying and rehearsing further, concerning your service done to him, no less than I said to you in your garden. And further, that I should be fully contented with that ye should have two parts and I the third; whereunto his answer was, as ye showed unto me he said to you, that he thought the same well bestowed upon us. Surely I found his Highness not only better Lord to us both than for my part I have or can deserve, but also desirous, as I might by his words and gesture perceive, that we might compass this matter to our contentations. Many other communications was between us, too long to molest you withal; and therefore [I] shall forbear writing thereof unto our next meeting. And as concerning order to be taken for our business here, Mr. Comptroller [1] can declare the same unto you, being present at that matter only. And as for the third part, I will remain in the determination I told you of. And thus most heartily fare you well. From Hampton Court, the 4th of November.—Yours assuredly, T. NORFOLK.

Addressed: To my very good Lord, my Lord Privy Seal.[2]

The matter having been thus arranged, the Prior of Lewes came up to London, and on the 12th November at the Rolls " acknowledged a fine " (that is to say, made a conveyance) both of Lewes priory and of its cell, Castleacre, " though it is thought," writes Cromwell's servant Polsted, " that the latter does not pass by the fine." There were legal scruples in the matter, it seems, whether there were moral ones or not. " It is now fully resolved," Polsted adds, " that there shall be no such preamble to the deed." We shall see what this means by and by. The prior, it is further stated, affirmed that the Duke of Norfolk had promised him all the goods and one-half the debts due to the monastery.[3] A formal surrender was required besides the fine, and it was duly

---

[1] Sir William Paulet, Controller of the Household.
[2] *L. P.*, XII. ii. 1030. [3] *L. P.*, XII. ii. 1062.

executed by the prior and convent on the 16th, and acknowledged the same day before one of the clerks of Chancery. The like surrender was made and acknowledged by the prior and convent of Castleacre on the 22nd, and both convents executed further deeds of conveyance to the Crown, each on the day of surrender. Then, the whole property being thus in the King's hands, a grant was made to the Duke on the 22nd December of Castleacre and its possessions in fee simple. The parent house of Lewes with its possessions was granted to Cromwell in like manner on the 16th February following.[1]

Thus fell the most ancient monastery of the Cluniac Order in England, a house founded by William, Earl Warrenne, within twelve years of the Norman Conquest, and possessing a clear yearly revenue, as certified at the great valuation three years before the suppression, of over £920.[2] Cromwell had the larger share of the plunder, and knew well what he meant to do with it. Early in March, Lord Lisle's correspondent Husee writes to inform his master that Mr. Polsted was going into Sussex to "dissolve" my lord's house of Lewes, and was expected to be away for a fortnight.[3] Polsted probably took with him an Italian engineer named Giovanni Portinari, with seventeen workmen, who had instructions to pull down the priory church—this was the way it was to be "dissolved." On his arrival, the Italian found the church larger than he had been given to expect. It was 420 feet in length, 69½ feet in breadth from the entrance to the middle, and 150 feet in the middle portion; the height was 63 feet. The circumference within was given as 1558½ feet; outside, 1512 feet.[4] The wall in front was 10 feet thick, and at the sides 5 feet. The wall of the

Description of the building.

---

[1] *L. P.*, XII. ii. 1101, 1311 (30); XIII. i. 384 (74).
[2] See Dugdale's *Monasticon*, v. 1.
[3] *L. P.*, XIII. i. 421.
[4] Strange that the inside circumference should have measured more than the outside! But such was Portinari's report.

steeple, which was on one side of the front, was 10 feet thick. There were thirty-two pillars, eight of them very large, of which four supported a lofty roof after the fashion of a belfry, the other four a still higher one, where five bells were hung. Each of these eight pillars was 14 feet thick, 45 in circumference; the other twenty-four were 10 feet thick, 25 [1] in circumference. The height of the roof in front of the great altar was 93 feet, and of that in the middle of the church where the five bells were hung 105 feet.[2]

Such a fine massive building surely deserved to be spared; but the Italian, when he had taken the measure of the work, assured his employer that all should be pulled down. They began on Friday the 15th, cutting the wall behind the high altar, where there were five chapels and four pillars supporting a vault over the altar. Their plan was to cut down under the foundations and put in props, which afterwards it was proposed to burn or to blast with powder as might seem most advisable. The business might take eight or ten days at the longest, but the whole fabric would by that time be demolished. As a matter of fact it took them just a week before they pulled down the four pillars and the five chapels behind the altar, and on the 24th there was still a very high vault with four great pillars to throw down. But no doubt it would soon be done, and on Tuesday (the 26th) they would begin melting the lead.[3]

All was to be demolished; but there must have

---

[1] So in Portinari's letter; but perhaps 35 was meant, as pillars 10 feet thick must have been over 30 feet in circumference.

[2] *L. P.*, XIII. i. 554, 590. Morison's translation of this letter is careless. The passage, "I told your Lordship of a vaute *on the ryghte syde* of the hygh altare," should be "*behind* the high altar"; *drieto* is the word. But the worst inaccuracies are in the measurements given at the end, some of which are omitted altogether, while the length of the church is made only 150 feet ("cl. fote"), when it is expressly given in the original as 140 yards, or 420 feet. Wright's editing also is inaccurate here and there, and in one passage where the paper is decayed he has completed a word erroneously. The reading must have been, to correspond with the original, "A Tuesday they *begin* (not *began*) to cast the ledde."

[3] *L. P.*, XIII. i. 554, 590.

been on the property some pleasant residence, which
Cromwell desired for his son Gregory ; who, in point
of fact, writes to him from Lewes on the 11th of
next month to tell him how he and his wife are
pleased alike with the house and the situation. A
little later they had to remove for a time in consequence of an epidemic of plague, but they soon
returned.[1]

Thus was one great monastery absorbed by private
greed. Somewhat different was the case of Bisham
or Bustlesham, of which the King had got William
Barlow made prior in the spring of 1535.[2] In January
1536 Barlow, retaining this priory, was made Bishop of
St. Asaph's, and translated to St. David's in April
following. In July of the same year he granted his
monastery of Bisham to the King by charter under
the convent seal. But a year later, in July 1537, the
abbot and convent of Chertsey were induced to
surrender their monastery to the King with a view to
the re-erection of Bisham and its more munificent
re-endowment as a mitred abbey.[3] Chertsey had been
visited in September 1535 by Dr. Legh, who transmitted to Cromwell a special *compendium compertorum* for that particular monastery much of the
same character as the reports on other places, though
Gardiner, Bishop of Winchester, in whose diocese it
lay, along with Mr. Treasurer Fitzwilliam, had made
a special visit to it not long before by the King's
command, and had reported that all was well there.[4]
The Visitors, however, found no other fault with the
abbot himself, John Cordrey, except that he had
alienated some of the property ; and as to the foul
charges which they made against thirteen of the
monks (nearly the whole convent), nobody seems to
have believed them. At all events, the surrender
was signed by the abbot and fifteen monks on the

Change
made at
Bisham.

---

[1] *L. P.*, XIII. i. 734, 1059, 1281. [2] *L. P.*, VIII. 553, 596.
[3] *L. P.*, XII. ii. 220, 1311 (22). [4] *L. P.*, IX. 472.

6th July 1537, with a view, as above shown, to the re-endowment of Bisham.

The new foundation, as set forth in the charter which was granted on the 18th December following, was to be called "King Henry the Eighth's new monastery of Holy Trinity of Bustelesham." But its career was a very short one; for on the 19th June 1538 Abbot Cordrey surrendered it to the Crown, just as he had surrendered Chertsey. So that it existed exactly six months, and then was extinguished for ever.

It may have been one object with the King in a design so soon laid aside to show more fully his competence to exercise papal functions in England by giving the new abbot the right to wear a mitre. But in 1538 he was beginning to force monasteries in general to surrender. At first, indeed, he would fain have prevented the least suspicion being entertained that any such general dissolution was intended. The monastic Visitors might again be stirring; but their movements need not be so interpreted. Valuable results might still be obtained from a line of action that they had already begun. For Legh and Layton in their late visitation had reported not only on the vices which they alleged were practised in the monasteries, but also on their superstitions. What discoveries, in this matter, had they not made—discoveries, it is true, of things very well known and laughed at by superior intelligence. How many fragments of the Holy Cross, how many phials of the Blessed Virgin's milk! How many places were noted for pilgrimages: the shrine of St. Chad at Lichfield, that of St. Ethelburg at Thurgarton, that of St. William at York, not to speak of others. And with or apart from pilgrimages, how much quackery! Men went to Repton in Derbyshire to visit St. Guthlac and his bell, which they put on people's heads to alleviate headache. Very likely, the journey thither had that effect and the bell did no particular harm. The nuns of Gracedieu had the girdle and part of the tunic of St. Francis, which were supposed to help lying-in women. Other localities, too, possessed relics with the like property, as Meaux in Yorkshire, which had the girdle of St. Bernard, and Newburgh, which had the girdle of St. Saviour; while Holm Cultram in Cumberland had at least a necklace called an *Agnus Dei* with the like beneficial virtue.[1] Surely it was important to purify religion from superstition, especially when the King's revenues might be augmented by so doing!

In 1538 both Legh and Layton were started on their old work again, visiting monasteries, but privately charged to take surrenders of them also, when convenient. In the very beginning of January, Dr. Legh took the surrender of Muchelney Abbey in Somerset. A month later he was at Chester, where he got the old and infirm Abbot of St. Werburgh's to resign on his coming. In another month, after visiting some houses in Yorkshire, he had reached the borders of Scotland and taken the surrender of Holm Cultram; from which he proceeded afterwards through the Midlands. We need not follow his whole progress in detail.[2] Meanwhile his fellow, Layton, had likewise resumed his functions, accompanied this time by Robert Southwell, Attorney of the Court of Augmentations. To proceed on a circuit with such a colleague was rather calculated to raise disquieting suspicions; and when they reached Barnwell Priory in Cambridgeshire, it was hinted that they were going to suppress that priory on their way into Norfolk, and all other monasteries wherever they came. It was of great importance to stop such rumours as this, or the monks would find various devices to prevent the property getting into the King's clutches. So Layton boldly denounced the

The Visitors again on circuit:

deny that they are going to suppress Barnwell, or monasteries generally.

[1] *L. P.,* x. 364.   [2] See *L. P.,* XIII., references in index.

report as a slander against the King, and charged the abbots that they should not, for any such vain babbling, sell, waste, or alienate any of their property.[1]

In point of fact, the Priory of Barnwell was spared for ten months longer, and Layton and Southwell seem to have taken no surrenders till they came to Westacre in Norfolk, which they two and Sir Thomas L'Estrange had a special commission to take into the King's hand. For this, it would seem, there were plausible pretexts. Westacre was rather a small house, having only eight canons besides the prior, and the property was much encumbered. The prior and canons, indeed, were somehow got to confess in a formal document signed by them, and with the convent seal attached, that they had forfeited all right to the monastery and its possessions by the way they had administered their property. "Stirred by grief of conscience to great contrition for their manifold negligences, enormities, and abuses of long time practised by them and their predecessors under the pretence and shadow of perfect religion"—such are the words, briefly condensed, of the exordium— they admit that their course of life has been "to the grievous displeasure of Almighty God and the crafty deception and subtle seduction of good Christian people, not only in omitting the execution of observances that they were bound by their vows to their founders, the King's progenitors, to maintain, but also in letting their property be dilapidated. Prostrate at the King's feet, to prevent his Highness being any more abused with such feigned devotion, and considering their imminent peril of damnation if they persist, they beg him to accept, of their free gift unprompted, all the possessions and rights they have in their monastery as rightfully belonging to himself by reason of their offences and his Grace's laws; and, without other compulsion than that of their own

They take the surrender of Westacre,

---

[1] *L. P.*, XIII. i. 102.

conscieces, they have declared this before Richard
Layton, LL.D., Archdeacon of Buckingham, Robert
Southwell, Attorney of the Augmentations, and Sir
Thomas Le Straunge, the Commissioners."[1]
The above is the very language of the original
document slightly abridged ; and it seems extraordinary that—though this monastery, very likely,
was not untainted in morals[2]—a prior and eight canons
could have been induced to sign a confession so humiliating, and, we may add, so untrue. For, of course, no
one will readily believe that the document was, as it
professes to be, unprompted ; and if a doubt could exist
about the matter, we shall see presently very distinct
evidence that the abject submission was drawn up by
the Royal Commissioners, and that the canons were
only required to put their signatures to it. The date
was the 14th January in the twenty-ninth year of
Henry VIII. (1538). A surrender was taken on the
following day of all the possessions of the house,
specifying the names of the several manors ; and
the Commissioners reported to Cromwell what they
had done. The monastery, unfortunately, was so
encumbered that they found, with all their legal
astuteness, that it would require some leisure to
" revoke or reduce," for the King's benefit, the " blind
bargains " made, as they said, by the folly of the
governors. It is clear, however, that even property
so encumbered as that of many of the monasteries
was could be relieved of many burdens by the dex-
terity of the Crown lawyers, while of course it was
freed from all the old charges of keeping up hospitality
for wayfarers.[3]
The policy of denying rumours that a general

[1] This document, which is dated 14th Jan. 29 Hen. VIII., has, unfortunately, not been noticed in L. P., though a notice of it will be found
in the list of Acknowledgments of Royal Supremacy in the Record Office
(with which it had been improperly placed) in the Seventh Report of the
Dep. Keeper of the Public Records, App. ii. p. 304. It is numbered 117†.
[2] See p. 106.   [3] L. P., XIII. i. 85, 86, 101

suppression was intended had been impressed upon Layton before he set out on his journey by the wary and unscrupulous Cromwell; but it was only in passing through Cambridgeshire that he was made to feel its vital importance. He not only charged the abbots and priors of the district not to alienate their property from any such idle apprehensions, but commanded them, if knaves would so report, to put them in the stocks; if gentlemen did so, to certify Cromwell and the Council about it. Thus it was made dangerous to suggest what nevertheless was virtually true. "This digression," he wrote to Cromwell, "has hindered us from Westacre; but, if I had not sped it before the dissolution of the same, the abbots and priors would have made foul shifts before we could have finished at Westacre. Your command to me in your gallery in that behalf was more weighty than I then judged. As for Westacre, what falsehood in the prior and convent, what bribery, spoil and ruin contrived by the inhabitants, it were long to write; but their wrenches, wiles and guiles, shall nothing them prevail." It would seem that it was only the terror of what might be in store for them under the unknown complexities of a system of law which was sure to be strained in its interpretation, that induced the prior and convent to put their hands to the humiliating submission.

After the surrender of Westacre, it was a month and a half before Layton and his colleague took any similar step. People, of course, might have formed their own opinions, and rumours might have grown in spite of official denials and threats. Perhaps they were maturing a new policy, or taking counsel how to make their position stronger in their further proceedings. Again they obtained a special commission for themselves and a local gentleman, and on the 1st March they were at Northampton, along with Sir William Parr, uncle of the lady who afterwards

and, some time later, of St. Andrew's, Northampton.

became Henry VIII.'s last queen. The monastery of St. Andrew's, Northampton, was one of those that Layton had already visited little more than two years before, when he reported that though its revenue was £400 a year it was very much in debt, that the lands were sold or mortgaged, and that the rents of the farms were received beforehand under bonds for the payment of various chantries. But the prior, he said, was a Bachelor of Divinity, " a great husband," and a good clerk, and if he were promoted " to a better thing " the King might take the monastery into his hands and recover all the lands again. He added that if the King agreed, he would suggest the matter to the prior on his own return from the North.[1] This was in December 1535. Now on the 2nd March 1538 the surrender was actually made by the prior and canons ; and the manner in which it was taken was precisely the same as in the case of Westacre. That is to say, it was preceded by a similar humiliating avowal of infidelity to their trust, dereliction of duty, and fear of damnation by professedly conscience-stricken canons. Only, in this case the confession was far more lengthy and more abject. Like their brother canons of Westacre—for they belonged to the same Order (the Augustinian)—they professed to be moved with great contrition for the enormities and abuses of which they and their predecessors had been guilty " under the pretence and shadow of perfect religion." The exordium, in fact, was the same, word for word, showing clearly that it was not drawn up in the cloister either of Westacre or of Northampton. But the depth of abasement, long drawn out, which was put into the mouths of the Northampton canons can only be gauged by a comparatively minute extract or two. Here are the exact words in one passage :—

[1] Wright's *Suppression*, 92, 93.

But as well we as others our predecessors called religious persons within your said monastery, taking on us the habit or outward vesture of the said rule, only to the intent to lead our lives in an idle quietness and not in virtuous exercise, in a stately estimation, and not in obedient humility, have, under the shadow or colour of the said rule and habit, vainly, detestably, and also ungodly, employed, yea rather devoured, the yearly revenues issuing and coming of the said possessions, in continual ingurgitations and farcings of our carayne [*sic*] bodies, and of others, the supporters of our voluptuous and carnal appetite, with other vain and ungodly expenses, to the manifest subversion of devotion and cleanness of living. . . . Which our most horrible abominations and execrable persuasions of your Grace's people to detestable errors, and our long covered hypocrisy cloaked with feigned sanctity, we revolving daily and continually pondering in our sorrowful hearts, and thereby perceiving the bottomless gulf of everlasting fire ready to devour us if, persisting in this state of living, we should depart from this uncertain and transitory life ; constrained by the intolerable anguish of our conscience,[1] etc.

What are we to think of so much abasement and so much confession of hypocrisy and sin where Layton himself had found no great enormities two years before, although he was then on the lookout for them wherever he went ? We might readily suspect the genuineness of the document, as the original is not known now to exist, and we have only two manuscript copies of a later age, besides the text printed early in the seventeenth century. But the fact that some such document was obtained from the convent is clear from the words of the Royal Commissioners themselves, who also show distinctly how falsely it pretends to be the spontaneous act of the prior and canons, when they write to Cromwell : " We have taken a release and a deed of feoffment of the monastery of St. Andrew's in Northampton to the King's use, and an humble submission of the prior and convent, *as we*

---

[1] See the full text in Weever's *Funeral Monuments*, pp. 106-110.

suppose, to the King's honor and contentation, referring our diligence and doings therein to your judgment." [1]

A letter written the same day by Southwell, apart from his fellow-commissioners, to Cromwell, lets us a little further behind the scenes. It is quite clear that the policy at first laid down for Layton and Southwell was to procure successively from individual monasteries acknowledgments that they had not fulfilled the purposes for which they were founded, and that consequently their houses and endowments might lawfully be resumed by the King. Something of the kind had evidently been intended even at Lewes, but afterwards was not thought advisable, and the " preamble to the deed," as we have seen, was omitted. Now, however, the plan was put in force, and it was evidently thought that the same form, or nearly the same, would suit the purpose in each individual case, the documents being so worded as to show that there was no enforced suppression, and that each was merely an individual case. Experience, however, showed that some variation was necessary ; and thus it is that Southwell writes :—

The policy pursued.

" Although, my very good Lord," he begins, " that there wanted here some part of the occasions comprehended in the submission of the late monastery of Westacre, as concerning the clear alienation of the possessions belonging to the same, with such like, yet found we here of other (that I suppose been in the more part of the residue that at this day stonden) sufficient enough for the fulfilling of *the submission that now we send your Lordship in the place of the other that wanted*, so as by the variety of occasions this book in the more part or all is altered from the other in matter, as by the perusing thereof your Lordship shall well perceive, which I humbly beseech

[1] Wright's *Suppression*, p. 168.

you that it may like you to do. And though it shall
seem tedious, or the over-reading unworthy, yet shall
I eftsoons humbly beseech you to accept it in good
part, and for a perfect demonstration of *my good will
to have made the better*, in case my knowledge had
extended thereto."[1]

And a little further on he adds :

" Sir, these poor men have not spared to confess
the truth, as ye shall well perceive, whereby in my
poor mind they deserve the more favor, and I daresay
in their hearts [they] think themselves rather to have
merited pardon by their ignorance than praise or laud
for their form of living."

We seem to get a little nearer the truth in that
last sentence than the abject petition brings us.
The monks clearly thought that in the new order of
things the best they could do was to submit and
make terms for their pensions (which Southwell
further tells us that he had arranged with them
" as easily to the King's charge,"[2] as he could
manage), and they accordingly confessed as much
as was required of them, humiliating as the confession was. Still, it is a mystery why Layton
and Southwell alone were instructed to proceed in
this wise, for the King had other agents doing
kindred work elsewhere, and already, on the 29th
Surrender January, the well-known abbey of Boxley in Kent
of Boxley surrendered.[3] It does not appear by whom the
Abbey. surrender was taken, but on Thursday, the last day
of the month, Walter Henley, who had just been
made solicitor of the Augmentations on the promotion of Robert Southwell to be attorney of that
court,[4] arrived there to survey the lands and goods
of the monastery by order of Mr. Chancellor Riche,
and handed over the property to the keeping of
one Ralph Fane, a servant of Cromwell.[5] In

---

[1] Wright's *Suppression*, pp. 171-2.   [2] *Ib.*, p. 173.
[3] *L. P.*, XIII. i. 173.   [4] *L. P.*, XIII. i. p. 582.   [5] *L. P.*, XIII. i. 195, 229.

making his survey Henley was assisted by John Ashton, auditor of the same court, and Geoffrey Chamber, receiver-general, so that we may presume nothing escaped examination which made for the King's purpose. There was an obvious intention to destroy the credit of a place to which pilgrimages had been made. The monastery was defaced and the images pulled down. Particular attention was naturally paid to the famous "Rood of Grace"—a crucifix in which the eyes and nether lip had been made to move by machinery. That there was any real deception about it is by no means evident, even from the account of Geoffrey Chamber himself; but when the image was loosened from the wall, and the engines and old wire and "old rotten sticks" in the back by which the movements were effected, were brought to light, an excellent subject was obtained for the denunciation of monkish abuses. Geoffrey Chamber, indeed, says even at the time that the discovery was "not a little strange" to him and others present; but we can hardly suppose that he, at least, met with anything very unexpected. He tells us something still more strange when he goes on to say that the abbot and some old monks whom he examined declared that they knew nothing of it.[1] They must certainly have known of the performances the figure had been made in past times to go through, even if, as has been suggested, it was an old-fashioned automaton long disused,—a theory with which the "old wire" and "old rotten sticks" seem to agree. Perhaps what the abbot and the old monks meant was, that the apparatus was now so antiquated that they really did not know how it had been worked.

Geoffrey Chamber knew well how to use the discovery. Considering, as he says, the devotion paid to the image by the people of Kent in times past, he took it with him to Maidstone on Thursday the

The Rood of Grace.

---

[1] *L. P.,* XIII. i. 231.

7th February, which was a market-day, and showed it to the people, who, by his account, had the matter in wondrous detestation and hatred, so that (he would venture to say)[1] if the monastery had to be defaced again they would pluck it down or burn it.[2]   He then brought the thing up with him to London, where it was to do some further duty.   "The Rood of Grace," writes John Husee on the 23rd to his master Lord Lisle, the Deputy of Calais, "shall stand to-morrow at Paul's Cross during the sermon time, and there the abusion shall be divulged." The "abusion," of course, was pretty well known to all intelligent people, even before it was "divulged," and Lord Lisle at Calais understood perfectly well what was meant.   What ideas the ignorant vulgar may have entertained about it may, perhaps, be a question ; but the veriest numskull could hardly have taken a puppet for anything but a puppet, or supposed that its motions were controlled by anything but mechanism. Those, however, who hated monasticism, or loved to expose ecclesiastical abuses, were delighted at seeing the work done for them by authority of the King himself.   How the promised exposure was actually made we learn from a letter written by John Hoker of Maidstone to the Reformer Bullinger of Zurich, of which the following is a translation :—

Dagon of Ashdod is everywhere falling.   That Bel of Babylon is now broken to pieces.   There was found of late

---

[1] It is perhaps desirable to quote the very words of the letter :—" Who, I dare say, that if the said late monastery were to be defaced again (the King's Grace not offended) they would either pluck it down to the ground or else burn it ; for they have, the said matter in wondrous detestation and hatred, as at my repair unto your good lordship and bringing the said image with me,—whereupon I do somewhat tarry, and for the further defacing of the said late monastery,—I shall declare unto you " (Ellis's *Original Letters*, Third Series, iii. 169).   Printed also by Bridgett, in *Blunders and Forgeries*, pp. 171-2.   When an official of Henry VIII. says " I dare say " in a matter like this, we must not take it for granted that he is stating an undoubted matter of fact, though of course there were many people among the mob that would readily have given effect to his words.

[2] *L. P.*, XIII. i. 231.

a wooden god of the Kentish men, a hanging Christ who might have vied with Proteus himself. For he knew well how to nod with his head, wink with his eyes, wag his beard, bend his body to reject and to receive the prayers of those who came to him : This, while the monks were falling on his account, was found in their temple, surrounded with a multitude of offerings, and enriched by gifts of linen, wax candles, &c. A sagacious man, brother of our Nicholas Partridge, smelt the deceit, and, fixed as it was against the wall, he loosened the image from its place. The arts, the impostures came to light, and the wonderful juggler is caught. There were hidden pipes everywhere in a body full of holes, and a wire was drawn through the chinks by the operator, the whole being skilfully concealed by thin plates. Thus he had made a great profit by deluding the people of Kent, indeed of all England, for ages past. Being laid open, he first offered a spectacle to my people of Maidstone, exhibiting himself from an elevated place to a dense crowd of people, some laughing heartily, some almost as mad as Ajax. The stroller was brought hence to London. He visits the Court and the King himself—a novel guest; no man, indeed, salutes him. Lords, dukes, marquises, earls, collect about him with the laughter of the Court. They come from a distance, stand round about him, stare and look him through and through. He acts, he scowls with his eyes, he turns away his face, he distends his nostrils, he sets back his head, he bends his back, he assents and denies. They see, they laugh, they wonder, the theatre resounds with voices, the cry rises to heaven. It is hard to say whether the King himself was more pleased that the imposture was exposed, or grieved at heart that the poor people had been deluded for so many years. What need of many words ? The matter was referred to the Councillors, and some days later at London, the Bishop of Rochester [1] preached a sermon. The Kentish Bel, set upon a high pulpit, stands opposite Daniel. He again opens himself ; he again acts his part skilfully in public. They wonder, they are enraged, they are stupefied, ashamed to have been so basely deceived by an idol. And when the preacher grew warm and the Word of God secretly worked in the hearts of the audience, they hurled the wooden trunk head foremost into the thickest of the crowd. And now were heard manifold cries of various persons ; it is seized, torn, rent in pieces, cut

---

[1] Hilsey.

up into atoms and fragments; at last it is thrown in the fire. And so he made his end.[1]

This is certainly a very artistic presentation of the matter, and we must remember that it was meant for use abroad. The reader, for one thing, may attach what value he pleases to the statement that the King hardly knew whether more to rejoice at the exposure or to grieve at the long deception. That was a piece of information which would go down well at Zurich whither it was addressed. The following further statements contained in another letter to Bullinger were, of course, intended for the same market. The writer, then living at Frankfort, was no other than that Nicholas Partridge, whose brother was so active in the business of detaching the image from the wall. So we might presume that his information came direct from an agent who was anxious to justify his conduct. Yet he himself is silent about his brother, and gives no other authority for his statements than that of an anonymous German :—

A certain German, who belongs to one of the merchant companies residing in London, has told us marvellous stories respecting some saints, who formerly had fixed and immoveable abodes at a distance from London; namely, that they have now ridden to London and performed most astonishing things in a numerous assembly. Concerning the bearded crucifix of Kent, called in our language "the Rood of Grace" near Maidstone, he told us that while the Bishop of Rochester was preaching at Paul's Cross to a most crowded congregation of nobility and others, in the presence, too, of many other famous saints of wood and stone, it turned its head about, rolled its eyes, foamed at the mouth and poured forth tears down its cheeks (!). The bishop had before thundered forth against these images; those satellite saints of the Kentish image acted in pretty much the same way. It is expected that the Virgin of Walsingham and St. Thomas of Canterbury, and likewise some other images, will soon perform their miracles in the same place, which, of what

---

[1] Burnet's *History of the Reformation* (Pocock's ed.), vi. 194-5.

character they are, you may, I think, judge for yourself. For the trickery of the wicked knaves was so publicly exposed in the image of that crucifix, that every one was indignant against the monks and impostors of that kind, and execrated both the idols and those who worshipped them.[1]

The story here has evidently grown in volume; Growth of for if the King's own agents at Paul's Cross managed the legend. to work such miracles with the "idol" as to make it shed tears and foam at the mouth, they did more than the monks themselves are recorded ever to have done. It is interesting, however, to know from this letter of an Englishman abroad, written on the 12th April, that it was even then expected that Our Lady of Walsingham and St. Thomas of Canterbury would likewise be brought to London to give account of themselves. They were not, in fact, sent up till some months later, but the crusade against superstition was even now actively going on. On the 21st March, John Husee in London writes to Lord Lisle that "pilgrimage saints goeth down apace," among others Our Lady of Southwick, the Blood of Hailes, and St. Saviour's, Bermondsey; and on the next day, writing to Lady Lisle, he tells her that most of the Saints to whom pilgrimages and offerings were wont to be made were already taken away. "I doubt," he adds, "the resurrection will after."[2]

It is to be regretted that the story of the final exhibition of the Rood of Boxley at St. Paul's has not been recorded by any eye-witness, and our earliest information on the subject is derived entirely from letters written by Englishmen abroad, or prepared by them for a foreign market. But there are two other such letters that refer to it, neither of them dated either as to time or place, but both of

---

[1] *Original Letters* (Parker Soc.), pp. 609, 610. The original Latin text is given in a separate volume (*Epistolæ Tigurinæ*, pp. 395-6), and I have ventured to correct a word or two in the translation to make it more literal.

[2] *L. P.*, XIII. i. 564, 580. Cp. also 514; and Wriothesley's *Chronicle*, i. 77.

them written, no doubt, about the same time as Partridge's letter and not improbably from the very same place, that is, Frankfort. One of the writers, John Finch, refers, like Partridge, to a German merchant as his authority, and though he gives the story more fully, it looks rather as if it came from the very same informant. The other writer, William Peterson, treats the matter much more briefly; but a certain characteristic touch makes us suspect here too a common source of information. For the words of this second writer are as follows :—

As to the news which you desire of me, I have not any, except that the images which formerly used to work miracles in England, are now, as I hear, broken in pieces, and the imposture of the priests is made known to every one. And to mention to you one idol and imposture in particular, you must know that there was in England an image, which at certain times used to move its mouth and eyes, *to weep* and to nod in sign of dissent or assent before the bystanders. These things were managed by the ingenuity of the priests standing out of sight; but the imposture is now notorious to every person in England.[1]

Surely it must have been the German merchant that first credited the image with shedding tears. Perhaps John Finch, whom I now proceed to quote, though he took in a great deal of the merchant's story, had some discreet misgivings about this part, for he does not mention it :—

A certain German merchant here, who is well acquainted with the English language, told me as a certain fact that all the images which used to work miracles by the artifices of the Devil and his angels, that is to say, the monks, friars, fisheaters, and others of that stamp, were conveyed on horseback to London at the command of the Bishops; that a public sermon was preached from the pulpit of St. Paul's to the congregation assembled in Christ; after which a certain image brought away from Kent, and called in English "the

---

[1] *Original Letters* (Parker Soc.), p. 604.

Rood of Grace in Kent," was first exhibited. The preacher, the Bishop of Rochester, explained all the trickery and imposture in the presence of the people. By means of some person pulling a cord, most artfully contrived and ingeniously inserted at the back, the image rolled about its eyes, just like a living creature; and on the pulling of other cords it gave a nod of assent or dissent according to the occasion. It never restored health to any sick person, notwithstanding great numbers afflicted with divers diseases were carried to it and laid prostrate before it, unless some one disguised himself of set purpose and pretended to be sick; in which case it would give a nod, as though promising the restoration of health, that it might by this means confirm its imposture. Then again, by some other contrivance unknown to me it opened and shut its mouth; and, to make an end of my story at once, after all its tricks had been exposed to the people it was broken into small pieces, and it was a great delight to any one who could obtain a single fragment, either, as I suppose, to put in the fire in their own houses, or else to keep by them by way of reproof to such kind of impostors. After this Bishop Latimer, in the West country,[1]

---

[1] On reference to the original in the *Epistolæ Tigurinæ* I have altered the translation of this passage, as I think Dr. Hastings Robinson, who edited these Zurich letters in English, was mistaken in supposing that the writer was still describing what was done at St. Paul's, and that the words *in Occidentali parte* referred to the west part of the church. Bishop Latimer's diocese was in the west part of the country. And I am rather inclined to suspect that the writer of the letter himself made a mistake, attributing to Latimer what was more probably the work of his brother bishop, Shaxton of Salisbury, also a western diocese. For the same superstition, with the number of oxen doubled (which is a trifle), is related of the Rood of Ramsbury which was in Shaxton's diocese, as we read in a contemporary ballad :—

> " The swete Rode of Rambisbery
> Twenty myle from Maumbysbery
>   Was oftimes put in feare ;
> And nowe, at the laste,
> He hath a brydling caste,
>   And is become I wote not wheare.
>
> Yet hath it been saide
> His virtue so wayde
>   That XVI oxen and mo
> Were not able to cary
> This Rode from Rambisbery
>   Though he toke seven horses also.
>
> Whiche is a great lye,
> For, the truth to trye,
>   His virtue is not worth a beane ;

carried in his hand a small image and threw it out of the church, though the inhabitants of that country constantly affirmed that eight oxen would be unable to remove it from its place. There were, after this, exhibited many other tricks of the same kind, by which the simple were imposed upon by the priests; so that the ignorant people now call them mere conjurors, and despise their contrivances, objecting the deceits they practised against them as long as the tower of Babel was safe, which being now undermined, is daily threatening an overthrow.[1]

Silence of some contemporary chroniclers. It is singular that no notice is taken of the Rood of Boxley either in the contemporary *Chronicle* of Hall or by the continuator of Fabyan, nor yet in the *Greyfriars Chronicle*. We might suppose reasons for its omission in the last; but Hall and Grafton were just the sort of chroniclers to whom the story of such an exposure would, one would have supposed, have been particularly agreeable. The only strictly contemporary chronicler who notices it seems to be Wriothesley, who, however, supplies us with what we may presume to have been the official view, though written, no doubt, long after the event. His account is in these words :—

This year in February there was an image of the crucifix of Christ, which had been used of long continuance for a great pilgrimage at the Abbey of Boxley by Maidstone in Kent, called the Rood of Grace, taken from thence and brought to the King at Westminster, for certain idolatry and craft that had been perceived in the said Rood; for it was made to move the eyes and lips by strings of hair, when they would show a miracle, and never perceived till now. The Archbishop of Canterbury had searched the said image in his visitation, and so, at the King's commandment, [it] was taken thence, that the people might leave their idolatry that had been there used. Also the said rood was set in the

---

For one man toke him downe,—
From his churche and towne
Thre men conveyed him cleane."

This ballad is entitled "The Fantassie of Idolatrie," and I shall speak of it a little further on.

[1] *Original Letters* (Parker Soc.), pp. 606, 607.

market place, first at Maidstone, and there showed openly to the people the craft of moving the eyes and lips, that all the people there might see the illusion that had been used in the said image by the monks of the said place of many years time out of mind, whereby they had gotten great riches in deceiving the people, thinking that the said image had so moved by the power of God, which now plainly appeared to the contrary.

The writer, who was in the service of Lord Chancellor Audeley, undoubtedly intended to justify what was done by authority and to cultivate popular prejudice ; but though the statement of the case is not in all respects accurate—as, for instance, in what is said of the archbishop's visitation—the details given of the " idolatry and craft " are really of a very modest kind, and would suggest no very elaborate artifices were it not for the words, " when they would show a miracle," and " never perceived till now." Nor can we attach much value to suggestions of this kind, considering the quarter from which they come.

The simplest statement of what was done at the final exhibition of the image is that of honest John Stow the chronicler, who was always careful to collect intelligence, and never wrote for effect. We might, indeed, almost reckon him among contemporaries ; for he was thirteen years old at the time and, being a regular Londoner, very likely witnessed the scene. But he betrays no excitement about it ; and his sober record of what took place seems to contain all that is really essential. It is as follows :—

The 24 of February, being Sunday, the Rood of Boxley in Kent, called the Rood of Grace, made with divers vices to move the eyes and lips, was showed at Paul's Cross by the preacher, which was the Bishop of Rochester, and there it was broken up and plucked in pieces.[1]

There is, however, one point more to be considered in a passage actually written at the very time con-

[1] Stow's *Annals*, p. 575.

cerning this celebrated image. When Northampton Priory was surrendered a month later in the manner we have seen, Southwell wrote to Cromwell as follows :—

> Whether there was cause why that Boxley should re-cognise as much or more it may please you to judge, whom it also pleased to show me the idol that stood there, in mine opinion a very monstrous sight.[1]

If the monks of Boxley had been for ages prac-tising a very gross deception upon the people, there surely would have been cause why they should have made some such contrite submission as the Priory of St. Andrew, Northampton ; nor would it have been wonderful if they had really recognised " as much or more." But no such submission seems to have been required of them ; and with all the alleged indigna-tion elicited by the exposure of their jugglery, it is remarkable that not one of them was punished for it. On the contrary, the abbot and his monks were all liberally pensioned[2] — a fact which pretty clearly shows that they made no opposition to the dissolu-tion of the abbey. Opposition, clearly, would have been futile, and they thought it well to make the best terms they could for themselves. They disclaimed all responsibility for the automaton and, apparently, their claim was admitted. It was not a manufac-ture of recent date, and, after all, we may be pretty sure, it was a very harmless piece of mechanism. Although a different account of its origin was pub-lished, it may not unlikely have been fashioned in old days by some monk with a mechanical turn ; for in-genious pieces of mechanism were sometimes made in monasteries. And it would seem that there were both in monasteries and cathedrals other images not altogether dissimilar in character. As, for example,

"The Rood" a harmless piece of mechan-ism.

---

[1] Wright's *Supp.* p. 172.
[2] See Bridgett's tract, *The Rood of Boxley*, p. 44, giving the amounts of the pensions.

there was at that very time in St. Paul's, though not brought up for judgment till after Edward VI.'s accession, " a picture (*i.e.* an image) of the Resurrection of our Lord, made with vices, which put out his legs of sepulchre and blessed with his hand, and turned his head." This with some other images was broken to pieces on Advent Sunday 1547, after a sermon by Bishop Barlow on " the great abomination of idolatry in images."[1]

After the surrender of St. Andrew's monastery at Northampton the plan of procuring a forced confession of delinquencies at the different monasteries appears to have been abandoned. Most houses, no doubt, yielded easily enough without it. Indeed, Butley in Suffolk surrendered to Dr. Petre on the very same day (1st March)[2] that Northampton made its humiliating submission to Dr. Layton ; and besides these agents, who travelled up and down the country with remarkable alacrity, there were several others engaged in the work during the whole of that year and the next. Surrenders of monasteries, destruction of images, and exposure of superstitions were the main doings of the year 1538 especially. It is not my purpose to follow the acts in detail. But there is one notable monastery the circumstances of whose fall revealed touching stories of what had passed during the last few years within its walls ; and from these we may well infer the similar painful struggles that took place in many other houses.

The Abbey of Woburn surrendered on the 8th May to Dr. Legh and to Mr. Williams, Master of the King's Jewels. Williams, it may be mentioned, had already been at Bury St. Edmunds and elsewhere, plundering shrines for the benefit of the King's treasury.[3] Before taking their surrender the two Commissioners informed the abbot and monks that they were accused of

Surrender of Woburn: accusations against the abbot and monks.

---

[1] Wriothesley's *Chronicle*, ii. 1.   [2] *L. P.*, XIII. i. 393.
[3] *L. P.*, XIII. i. 192, 484.

various crimes, amounting, indeed, to high treason; on which they appear to have felt that there was nothing for it but to address a very humble submission to the King, expressing their great grief that any such things should be said of them, and placing themselves, their house, and goods, at the King's mercy.[1] The charges were investigated at the monastery, four days later, by Legh and Williams and Dr. Petre, and the depositions taken are extant.[2]

From these it is sufficiently evident that there were traitors among the monks—not traitors against the King, but against the abbot to whom they owed obedience. The poor old abbot—Robert Hobbes was his name—had been suffering from a painful disease just before Easter, and had wished that God would take him out of the world, and that he had died with the good men who had suffered heretofore, meaning Bishop Fisher, More, and their fellow-martyrs. On Passion Sunday he exhorted some of the brethren to charity, and he besought them never to consent to give up the monastery or to change their habits. The question of Royal or Papal Supremacy was a sore one. He had said to the curate of the Lady Chapel at Woburn: " Sir William, I hear say ye be a great railer. I marvel that ye rail so. I pray you, teach my cure the scripture of God, and that may be to their edification. I pray you leave such railing. Ye call the Pope a bear and a bawson.[3] Either he is a good man or an ill. *Domino suo stat aut cadit.* The office of a bishop is honorable. What edifying is this to rail?"

To revile the Pope, however, even within the walls of a monastery, was now considered the part of a loyal subject; to call him Pope was not permissible. Monks, like other people, must learn to call him " Bishop of Rome," and the name of " Pope " was to

---

[1] *L. P.*, XIII. i. 955, 956.   [2] *L. P.*, XIII. i. 981.
[3] A " bawson " meant a badger (animal) or an insolent person.

be erased in all service books. In this duty Sir William, the parish priest of Woburn Chapel, was a little too zealous for his abbot, who rebuked him for using a knife to rase the Pope's name out of the canon, telling him to do it simply with a pen, for "it will come again one day," he said. Sir William answered that in that case they could put it in again, but he trusted never to see that day. Such language pained the abbot extremely. He said that if Sir William railed so much against the Pope he was no meet chaplain for him. "It is a perilous world," said the abbot; "St. Bernard calleth the See of Rome *pastor pastorum*, but now it is of another trade."

Towards the close of the year 1537 a false report of the King's death had got abroad and was general over the South of England and some part of the Midlands. Dan John Croxton, otherwise called West, deposed to the way it was received within the abbey. He had been in the shaving house, he said, during the Christmas holidays with Dan Robert Woburn and others, when Dan Laurence Bloneham reported that the King was dead. Croxton answered at once that the King was well, and advised Bloneham "to leave his babbling." Bloneham replied, "Croxton, it maketh no matter what thou sayest, for thou art one of the new world." Croxton retorted, "Thy babbling tongue will turn us all to displeasure at length." Bloneham then said, "Neither thou nor yet any of us shall do well as long as we forsake our head of the Church, the Pope." "By the mass," replied Croxton, "I would thy Pope Roger were in thy belly or thou in his, for thou art a false perjured knave to thy Prince." Bloneham indignantly rejoined, "By the mass, thou liest. I was never sworn to forsake the Pope to be our head, and never will be." "Then," said the other, "thou shalt be sworn in spite of thine own heart one day, or I will know why nay."

Sir William Sherbourne—that was the name of the

priest of the Lady Chapel above referred to—gave
evidence himself before the Commissioners. He had
only possessed that benefice since midsummer of the
previous year (1537), at which time he had a discussion with the abbot about the refusal of the Germans
to attend the Council summoned to Mantua. The
abbot gave him a copy of the excuse offered by the
Germans to take to Sir John Mylward of Toddington [1]
to examine and report upon. Mylward read it over,
and two days later came and said that the Germans
were heretics. How could they be so, asked Sherbourne, seeing that they owed no obedience to the
Bishop of Rome, but only to the Emperor, who was
Supreme Head of the Church of Rome ? The Emperor
had not, indeed, so proclaimed himself as their own
King had done in England, but he was so, and he did
not disapprove of the Germans taking him for their
Supreme Head. Sherbourne also reported how his
abbot had reproved him for speaking against the
Pope's authority, and how he had said that the
Carthusians and More and Fisher had been taken
away in order that naughty heretics might have their
swing.

Sir John Mylward's opinion on Church matters,
it thus appears, was highly esteemed by the abbot.
Mylward, as the abbot himself confessed, had once
lent him a treatise of his own making, containing the
statements of various weighty authorities *de Potestate
Petri*, which the abbot got copied before returning.
It was sad for Abbot Hobbes when these things came
to light, and he tried hard to show that his meaning
was inoffensive. He was accused, moreover, of
neglecting, when he preached, to declare the King's
title as Supreme Head of the Church, and he could
only say that his omission was not due to malice but
only " for a scrupulous conscience that he then had,

[1] He was master of a hospital at Toddington. See *Valor Ecclesiasticus*,
iv. 211.

considering the long continuance of the Bishop of Rome in that trade being, and the sudden mutation thereof." He was very sorry if he had offended. Evidently he was not a man of the same clearness of head or firmness as Bishop Fisher or Sir Thomas More ; but he felt with some diffidence what they felt strongly. He had, indeed, bent to the prevailing tyranny, and not only acknowledged the King's supremacy but compelled his sub-prior, Dan Ralph Woburn, to do the same under threat of sending him up to the Council if he refused.[1] Such was the statement of the sub-prior himself, who professed to have come afterwards to a better state of mind by reading such books as Tyndale's *Obedience of a Christian Man* and *The Glass of Truth.*[2] Still, the abbot could not quite believe that royal supremacy would last. He had only bent in weakness to a power which he could not resist at the time, but which he believed would pass away. But when the news came of the deaths of the Carthusians and their fellow-martyrs the terror inspired by their fate moved him to acts of no ordinary solemnity. Assembling the monks in the chapter house, he commanded them to repeat the psalm *Deus, venerunt gentes* (Ps. lxxix), and said, "Brethren, this is a parlous time. Such a scourge was never heard sith Christ's Passion." He added that it was certainly for their offences, and that if they repented God would take vengeance on their enemies the heretics. The psalm was said every Friday, with the versicle *Exsurgat Deus*, after the Litany, the monks prostrate all the while before the altar. *A scene within the abbey.*

The poor abbot could hardly realise that even in these sad orders and acts of government he was making the situation more difficult for himself.

---

[1] *L. P.*, x. 1239. This document seems to be misplaced in 1536. It must surely be of June 1538—just a little later than the other depositions.

[2] A pamphlet published by the King in 1531 in defence of his pleas that marriage with a brother's wife was unlawful and that he ought not to be cited to Rome.

Monks were too well aware of the state of the world
outside their walls, and that a new era had begun in
which abbots were of small account. What wonder,
then, that some of them murmured at this new discipline of humiliation? Disaffection of monks towards
their abbot was not half so serious a thing as disaffection towards the King, and expressions of sympathy
with the recent martyrs were in themselves most
dangerous unless a whole convent were firmly united
not to betray each other. Such was certainly not the
state of matters at Woburn. And yet in another
year it seemed as if the storm had blown over. The
abbot had even friends at Court, or one friend, at
least, who, dissolute enough in life, and related to
the haughty Anne Boleyn for whose sake the world
had been thus turned upside down, did not in his heart
at all admire the revolution. This was her cousin, Sir
Francis Brian. On Anne's fall, he had been sent for
by Cromwell in great haste " upon his allegiance ";
but if there was any momentary doubt that he might
be involved in the fate of his kinswoman, it was soon
dispelled. For Brian remained in high credit, and
when the Court afterwards repaired to Ampthill
(apparently in September 1536 [1]) he not only invited
the Abbot of Woburn to come and visit him there,
but on his arrival greeted him, in the presence of
Lord Grey of Wilton and others, with the words :
" Now, welcome home, and never so welcome ! " The
abbot, greatly astonished, asked why, and he said he
would explain at leisure. Brian then told him how
he had cleared himself, and how friendly he found
Cromwell to both of them. " You are much bound,"
he told the abbot, " to pray for his lordship." " Why
so ? " again the abbot asked, and Brian assured him
that Cromwell had spoken in his favour to the King.

[1] The Court was at Ampthill at least from the 19th to the 28th September.
See *L. P.*, XI. 469, 519 (19, 20, 22), 943 (4, 22). Even in August Sir Francis
had negotiated with the abbot for Cromwell in some matters. *L. P.*, XI. 326.

So now, it would almost seem, the clouds had altogether dispersed, and Brian congratulated the abbot as a friend.

But if the abbot's heart was somewhat lightened, as no doubt it must have been for a time, it was by the delusion which so many shared that the King, having got rid of Anne Boleyn, would now return to the communion of Rome and the spiritual unity of Christendom. Even when the Act for the dissolution of the smaller monasteries began to be put in execution, he was hopeful of better times. He enjoined his monks to sing daily after lauds *Salvator Mundi, salva nos omnes,* and to use certain other versicles and collects at every mass, assuring them that if they did so with good and pure devotion, God would so handle the matter that it should be to the comfort of all England. "And surely, brethren," he added, "there will come once a good man that will re-edify these monasteries again that be now suppressed, *quia potens est Deus de lapidibus istis suscitare filios Abraæ.*" The progress of events, unfortunately, did nothing to encourage such beliefs. But even when required to deliver up his bulls to Dr. Petre (for no documents emanating from Rome were to be allowed to remain) he had them all copied first, in order that if by the mediation of princes the King should hereafter be reconciled to the Pope, they might again be ratified.

What was his dismay in the beginning of 1538 when he found that new suppressions of monasteries were taking place! "Mercy, God! it is a wonderful thing," he said, "that the King's Grace cannot be content with that his Parliament have given him, but ever more and more plucketh down the holy monasteries which his predecessors and other noble founders have ordained to the honor of God for their souls' healths, and endowed with possessions to the intent that religious persons should pray for them and maintain alms and hospitality for poor men. And his Grace as yet hath built no house of prayer, not so much as one chantry for himself, that I know." Yet this, the abbot said, could not come of himself, for a better prince to the Church and Commons of his realm never was; and though the Lord Privy Seal (Cromwell) seemed to be the maintainer of these wretched heretical books that he set forth *cum privilegio regali*, neither the King nor he knew the pestilent heresies contained in them. Thus did Abbot Hobbes speak his mind while trying not to offend. As to the suppressions themselves he also said, " It is an unmerciful thing thus to put down the houses of God and expulse the inhabitants from their living, yea and many one from their life too." [1]

Need it be said what became of the abbot? He was tried, apparently at Lincoln, along with Laurence Bloneham, or Peck, and the sub-prior, Ralph Woburn, or Barnes, and all three received the usual sentence for high treason.[2] The abbot was hanged, tradition says, on an oak-tree in front of his own abbey,[3] and probably the others along with him, as was also a Bedfordshire parson—no very near neighbour of theirs —John Henmersh, vicar of Puddington.[4]

The abbot hanged, and others also.

We may now leave the reader to picture for himself what was taking place within the walls of many other monasteries during the few last years of their existence. We have, indeed, no other such touching records, and the reason probably is that there were really but few of those houses in which insubordination, notwithstanding all the encouragement it received, was really very prevalent. For abbots and priors to yield up their houses was comparatively a small matter.

[1] All the above information, except where otherwise noted, is from *L. P.*, XIII. i. 981. The latter part has been compared with the MS.

[2] The entry of their attainder is on the Controlment Roll, 30 Hen. VIII. m. 16 *d.*, with three notes in the margin of " Tᵃ et Sˢ " (*trahatur et suspendatur*).

[3] Dodd's *Woburn*, p. 38.

[4] Gasquet's *Henry VIII. and the English Monasteries*, ii. 202.

To yield quietly when resistance can do no good is the part of common sense, and stern duty itself can have little to say against it. Monasteries, even when fully tolerated, were often heavily burdened with debt ; and when hemmed in with new restrictions by a power which could not be withstood, it is no wonder that the abbots and priors consented, without more ado, simply to give up their trusts. The work was going on rapidly now in this year, 1538, and continued to go on steadily during the next year as well, till the three great abbots who would not surrender, having each gone through the form of a trial, though his execution was determined beforehand, were hanged, each apparently close to his own monastery, as a quiet warning of what was to be expected by any others who should dare to oppose the King's will. In the course of little more than two years every one of the larger monasteries was suppressed.

Progress of the suppression.

No less successful was the King's crusade against superstition, so triumphantly begun by the exposure and destruction of the curious toy of Boxley. When Bishop Hilsey preached on that occasion at Paul's Cross he was careful to show in his sermon "how other images in the Church used for great pilgrimages hath caused great idolatry to be used in this realm, and showed how he thinketh that the idolatry will never be left till the said images be taken away and that the boxes that they have to gather the devotions of the people were taken away first, so that they should have nothing used to put the charity of the people in ; but if there were any persons that would offer to such images, that the said offering might be given incontinent to poor people, and that the people should be showed how they should offer no more to the said images. He doubted not but then in short time they would grant that the said images might be taken away. Also he said how he confessed a woman twenty years ago in Oxford, which woman was the miller's wife by the Abbey of Hailes, in Gloucestershire, and how she showed him how the abbot of the same place had given her many jewels that had been offered there at the Holy Blood "—a precious phial containing, as was supposed, the blood of Christ— " and how he would have given her one jewel which she knew very well hanged about the said Holy Blood, and said to the abbot that she would not have that because she was afraid, because it hanged by the Holy Blood. And the abbot said, ' Tush, thou art a fool, it is but a duck's blood.' And this the said bishop showed that it was true, as he besought God he might be damned if it were not so as he said ; and also how he had showed the King and the Council of the same, and that it should be known more openly afterward." [1]

The "Blood" of Hailes.

Whatever opinion we may be inclined to form of the veracity of Bishop Hilsey in reporting this disgraceful anecdote to the multitude, there can be no doubt at all as to the object with which it was done. Hilsey was already, and had long been, fully committed to the King's service, not as a mere loyal subject, but as one of the two Royal Visitors of the Orders of Friars—that is to say, he filled a post which could only be filled by a zealous supporter of royal supremacy and opponent of papal authority. His object was to promote the King's Church policy in this war against superstitious relics ; and if the disclosure—nay, the open publication of an alleged confession made to him as priest—could be of any use in this way, he was not the man to stick at a trifle from considerations of mere delicacy. The woman, indeed, and the wicked abbot himself, may both have been dead, and the disclosure not altogether illicit by the rules of the confessional, supposing that the story itself was true ; but it could hardly be considered edifying or beneficial to public morality.

[1] Wriothesley's *Chronicle*, i. 75, 76.

On the other hand, if the tale was a fiction—which, in spite of the bishop's strong asseveration to the contrary, may appear not incredible,—it was assuredly well devised for depreciating the relic as much as possible, and even more than was altogether right. For, as will be seen hereafter, the liquid inside the phial certainly was not a duck's blood, whatever it was; and though an immoral abbot may possibly have cared little about its real character, we can hardly imagine even such a one giving away with a light heart an object so highly esteemed, with an excuse which none but a ribald scoffer would have dared to utter.

The existing Abbot of Hailes, Stephen Sagar, was not a man to countenance superstition. About this time he came up to London, first, as he told Cromwell in writing, personally to thank him for persistent acts of kindness, one of which seems to have been recommending him to the King as a royal chaplain;[1] secondly, to express his satisfaction that he lived in a time of enlightenment when the King had done so much to promote the true honour of God; and thirdly, most of all, out of perplexity what to do about this celebrated relic. He durst not put it away of his own authority, and he was afraid lest he should be suspected of having at times changed the liquid in the phial, renewing it with drake's blood. Whether he wrote this before or after Bishop Hilsey's sermon does not appear; but the double suggestion by abbot and by bishop, of the blood of a duck or drake, shows sufficiently the kind of suspicion that might easily be imputed, and which, in fact, was very often expressed by the irreverent. The abbot protested that the liquid had never been renewed to his knowledge, and that it had been kept for nearly forty years by a monk who was almost eighty, and who would make the same answer.[2] Nor is there any reason to doubt

---

[1] *L. P.*, XII. i. 1323.　　　　[2] *L. P.*, XIII. i. 347.

the statement, for it was, in truth, a relic some centuries old, and not unlikely to have come from the Holy Land, as one of its greatest revilers said it had done.[1]

The abbot's journey to London, however, was not a little due to another cause which he omitted to mention in his letter to Cromwell. His bishop had evidently spoken to him on the subject of the relic, and his bishop was Latimer. Some time after his return home Latimer wrote of him to Cromwell by the ugly designation of "the Bloody Abbot," insinuating that he had an eye to the precious things in his abbey, a good portion of which he seems to have pawned to pay the expenses of his journey. Latimer accordingly warned Cromwell to see to it lest all the jewels of the house should be thus "surveyed" away without his knowledge.[2] Cromwell, however, required little warning in matters of this kind. The abbot had already given a private undertaking to surrender his monastery when required, and before his return from London Dr. Layton had compelled him to give a bond of £500 that he would alienate no movables, and make no grant under the convent seal from the date of this "privy surrender."[3] After he had returned to Hailes he wrote to Cromwell to thank

[1] William Thomas, who was clerk of the Council under Edward VI., and was beheaded under Mary for an attempt against the Queen's life, writes thus in his book called *The Pilgrim*, edited by Froude in 1861 : "In a certain monastery called Hailes there was a great offering to the Blood of Christ, brought thither many years agone out of the Holy Land" (p. 38). This, perhaps, may have been true as to the origin of the relic ; for it was procured in Germany in 1267 by Edmund, Earl of Cornwall, who brought it to England with a written account of it drawn up by Pope Urban IV. See Dugdale's *Monasticon*, v. 686. Whether the monks were guilty of the trick, imputed to them on p. 39, of turning the glass to show a thick side or a thin, as they proposed to work on the superstitious fears of a beholder, I do not undertake to say. But the utter dishonesty of the following passage deserves to be noted : "And what blood, trow you, was this ? These monks (for there were two especially and secretly appointed to this office) every Saturday killed a duck and revived therewith this consecrated blood, *as they themselves confessed, not only in secret, but also openly, and before an approved audience.*" How untrue this was we shall see presently. But this story Thomas expressly says that he propagated in Italy.
[2] *L. P.*, XIII. ii. 186. [3] *L. P.*, XIII. ii. 481.

him for his " inestimable goodness," and to urge again his perplexity about the relic. The case which contained " the Blood" still stood where it did in the fashion of a shrine, and he feared it might cause abuse to weak consciences. He begged, therefore, that he might be allowed to put it down " every stick and stone," so as to leave no remembrance of " that forged relic" as long as the King was pleased that the house should stand. The silver and the gold in it, he said, were not worth £40, scarcely £30.[1]

The answer to this was a commission issued by the King on the 4th October to Bishop Latimer, Prior Holbeche of Worcester, the abbot himself, and Richard Tracy, to examine and report upon the relic. They accordingly held an investigation on the 28th October, in the presence, as they wrote, of a great multitude of people. The Blood, by their report, " was enclosed within a round beryl, garnished and bound on every side with silver." Latimer himself wrote that it was "wondrously closely, and craftily enclosed and stopped up." They had it opened before the people, and taken out of the beryl, when it was found, on close examina- *Its nature* tion, to be " an unctuous gum coloured." In the *examined.* glass it had certainly looked red and somewhat like blood, but taken out of the glass it was yellow like amber. So it was clearly not duck's blood, nor any blood at all. It stuck like gum or bird-lime. The Commissioners enclosed it in red wax, sealed with their seals, and locked it in a coffer, leaving it in the abbot's custody under indenture, and giving the key to Richard Tracy till the King's pleasure was known what to do further. In due course they were instructed to send it up to London, which Latimer accordingly did, but what became of it there we are not informed.[2] Presumably it was simply thrown away.

Relics and images had been coming up to London

[1] *L. P.*, XIII. ii. 409. [2] *L. P.*, XIII. ii. 709, 710, 856.

that year in considerable profusion. Soon after the destruction of the Rood of Grace and the removal of various other images of "pilgrimage saints," it was expected that images, even of Our Lady of Walsingham and St. Thomas of Canterbury, would likewise be sent up to perform miracles before a London audience,[1] and in the course of a few months they were certainly sent up at least. Nor was the spring well over before a very notable example had been made of a great image from North Wales which in that country had attracted superstitious reverence. Hundreds of pilgrims had come in a single day to make offerings to Darvelgadarn, of kine, oxen, horses, or money. It was said that he was powerful even to fetch damned souls out of hell; and Mr. Elis Price, whom Cromwell had appointed Commissary-General for the diocese of St. Asaph, felt that he could not but consult his lordship how to correct such a gross abuse. In three weeks he received an answer, and in spite of the remonstrances of the parson and parishioners, who offered him £40 to let the image remain, he took it down and had it forwarded to London.[2] Here it had a very special part to play, not merely as an example of superstition, but as the means used of punishing in one case disloyalty to the King's religion. To explain the matter, however, we must part company with Darvelgadarn for a moment.

The image Darvelgadarn.

In years past John Forest, one of the Franciscan friars of Greenwich, had been Queen Katharine's confessor, and of course was entirely opposed both to the King's divorce and to the Royal Supremacy. But early in 1533, when Anne Boleyn's star was in the ascendant, Richard Lyst, a false brother in the convent, seeking Court favour, reported to Cromwell his "unkindness and duplicity" towards the King. Cromwell then called Forest before him, but did not succeed

Story of Friar Forest

---

[1] *L. P.*, XIII. i. 754.   [2] *L. P.*, XIII. i. 694, 863, 864.

in making him tractable. A Frenchman newly elected provincial of the Grey Friars was spoken to, and Friar Forest was removed to a distant house of the same Order.[1] In 1534 he was probably in the Tower with Abell, Queen Katharine's chaplain, when they wrote to each other letters of encouragement and religious consolation.[2] He wrote also from his prison to Queen Katharine, expressing his determination to die for his religion, which he expected soon to do. And Katharine wrote to him in the like spirit, deeply regretting to lose her beloved spiritual father, whom she would rather precede than follow in his martyrdom. He was not, however, destined immediately to meet his fate ; and when the Observants were suppressed in the autumn of 1534, he seems to have been treated like the rest of that Order who opposed the King—handed over to the custody of that other branch of the Franciscans called the Conventuals, who were less rigid in adhering to the original rule of St. Francis. In the houses of these Conventuals the Observants were kept in irons, suffering torments at the hands of brethren, worse, as it was reported, than those of ordinary prisons.[3]

Forest was placed in the London house of Conventuals. There his constancy for a time gave way. He disowned the authority of the Pope, and was placed at ease. He resumed his old functions and heard confessions. But new difficulties arose when he had to give spiritual advice to others. Was Royal Supremacy right in spiritual things ? Had More and Fisher and the Carthusians deserved their fate as traitors, or earned an undying crown as martyrs ?

[1] *L. P.*, VI. 116, 168, 309, 334, 512.
[2] *L. P.*, VII. 129-34. Abell's letter, No. 133, must have been written, apparently, not at the end of January, as suggested by the reference in the footnote, but later. He was, indeed, committed to custody at Bugden on the 19th December 1533, but he was not lodged in the Tower till the 24th February 1534 (*L. P.*, VIII. 1001), and if he had been there thirty-seven days he must have been writing on the 1st April.
[3] *L. P.*, VII. 1095 (p. 425).

Forced thus to consider the question anew, he felt no doubt about the answer. Those men had died for the cause of the Church like St. Thomas of Canterbury, and he had no doubt their souls were in heaven. How, then, could he excuse himself, or explain himself even, to his own penitents, who knew that he had renounced the Pope's authority? He himself was driven to confess to them, and told one of them, who revealed the fact on examination, " that he had denied the Bishop of Rome by an oath given by his outward man, but not in the inward man." He acknowledged a double obedience, to the King by the law of God, and to the Pope by his rule; but he urged men in confession to remain steadfast to the old faith; and when there was a talk of friars being compelled by the King to change their habits, he had expressed his opinion that he might not lawfully do so at the King's commandment, but only at the Pope's. When he said that he believed in the Catholic Church, he understood that Church to be the Church of Rome.[1]

These things came out upon inquiry, and he was proceeded against for what was now accounted heresy. Declaring that he would abide by the judgment of the Church, he submitted to various examinations, and abjured before Cranmer at Lambeth on the 8th May. He was then ordered to do public penance at Paul's Cross on the following Sunday, the 12th, when Bishop Latimer was to preach the sermon. But meanwhile he intimated that he would not undergo the penances, and when the day arrived no persuasions could induce him to do so. He was then committed to Newgate till the 22nd, when he was brought to Smithfield with the alternative either to abjure or to be burned. Latimer again was there to preach before him; but after the sermon he declared

---

[1] *L. P.*, XIII. i. 880, 1043 ; Hall's *Chronicle*, p. 825 ; Wriothesley's *Chronicle*, i. 78, 79.

that an angel from heaven could not persuade him now to believe otherwise than he had believed all his life. He even told Bishop Latimer to his face, and with undoubted truth, that seven years before that time he would never have dared to preach in the way he had just done.[1]

He was not tied to a stake, as was usual with heretics. He was suspended by iron chains from a pair of gallows, and beneath him was placed the great wooden image, Darvelgadarn, an effigy of a man-at-arms with a little spear in his hand and a casket of iron hanging from his neck by a riband. The image was then set on fire, and Forest was burned in the same flame. The place of the execution had been carefully railed round to bar out the vast crowd which came to witness the spectacle, and the Lords of the Council, and the Mayor and Aldermen of London, with other gentlemen, beheld it from a long scaffold erected near St. Bartholomew's Hospital Gate.[2] *He is burnt along with Darvelgadarn.*

The war against images, it seems, was taken up by the mob, and that same night after midnight, "the Rood at St. Margaret Pattens by Tower Street, was broken all in pieces, with the house he stood in, by certain lewd persons, Flemings and Englishmen, and some persons of the said parish."[3]

What wonder if "lewd persons" went beyond what was strictly legal or expressly authorised? In June, Latimer wrote to Cromwell about the image of the Virgin in his Cathedral: "I trust your Lordship will bestow our great Sibyl to some good purpose, *ut pereat memoria cum sonitu*. She hath been the Devil's instrument to bring many, I fear, to eternal fire. Now she herself, with her old sister of Walsingham, her young sister of Ipswich, with their other two sisters of Doncaster and Penrice,[4] would make a *The image of the Virgin at Worcester.*

---

[1] *L. P.*, I. 687, 897 ; Wriothesley's *Chronicle*, i. 78-80.
[2] Wriothesley's *Chronicle*, i. 80, 81 ; Hall, p. 826.
[3] Wriothesley, i. 81.
[4] In Glamorganshire, another image to which pilgrimages were made.

jolly muster in Smithfield; they would not be all day in burning."[1]   That the worship of images which had so long prevailed was sinful, as being nothing less than the idolatry forbidden in the Decalogue, had always been the teaching of the Lollards, and Lollardy was coming into favour now, though it was no longer called by that name.   As a mere school of thought it was tolerated under the name of "the New Learning"; and it was sufficiently popular to give the King some support in measures for the robbery of shrines, the destruction of images, and the putting down of pilgrimages.   Not that there was any idea at this time of a general destruction of images; but where they had been decked with costly jewels and become the objects of pilgrimage, the King's treasury was manifestly capable of being enriched by their removal.

In July came the time that Latimer had been looking forward to, when Our Lady of Walsingham and Our Lady of Ipswich were both sent up to London;[2] and next month Cromwell sent down orders into Wales for the removal of the image of Penrice "as secretly as might be."[3]   It was not expedient, evidently, to do such things openly.   This image, too, was sent up to London, and about the same time those of St. Anne of Buxton, in Derbyshire, and St. Modwen of Burton-on-Trent.   One

Other images sent up to London.

[1] Latimer's *Remains*, p. 395 (Parker Society).   A year before, Latimer, as bishop, had caused the image to be stripped of its jewels and ornaments.   On which one Thomas Emans addressed it, "Lady, art thou stripped now? I have seen the day that as clean men hath been stripped at a pair of gallows as were they that stripped thee."   He then entered the chapel, said his prayers, and told the people, "Ye that be disposed to offer, the figure is no worse than it was before, and the lucre and profit of this town is decayed through this" (*L. P.*, xii. ii. 587).   The story, which the editor of Latimer's *Remains* cites from Herbert's *Henry VIII.*, that Our Lady of Worcester, when stripped, turned out to be the statue of some bishop, does not well agree with this.   It was certainly a mere piece of scandal, the source of which may be traced to a very dishonest document described in *L. P.*, xiv. i. 402 (p. 155) as an "Official Account of the Reformation."   This document will be found in Collier's *Church History* (Records, No. xlvii.), the passage in question being printed at p. 170 in vol. ix. (ed. 1841).

[2] *L. P.*, xiii. i. 1376, 1501.   [3] *L. P.*, xiii. ii. 345.

Sir William Basset, a local gentleman, spoken of as a servant of Cranmer's, had been very active in those parts, and, on receipt of instructions from Cromwell, had not only taken charge of those two images and sent them up, but had " defaced the tabernacles where they stood," taken away the " crutches, shirts, and sheets with wax offered," charging the keepers to allow no more offerings to be made, and, as a final measure, had locked up and sealed the baths and wells of Buxton that none might bathe there till he had word of Cromwell's pleasure. All to put an end to the " fond trust " people had in those images! Rheumatic patients were to be debarred the use of those beneficial waters, because there was superstition mixed up with it.[1]

In the beginning of September a far more notable act was done, alike to enrich the King's treasury and to outrage the most cherished sentiments connected with objects of this kind. Of all pilgrimages in England, of all pilgrimages, it might be said, in the whole world, what one was more celebrated than that which formed the subject of Chaucer's *Canterbury Tales*? Of all shrines in Christendom what one was more astonishingly rich and beautiful than that of St. Thomas of Canterbury? It was the marvel of all Europe, enriched with costly gifts of English gentlemen and foreign princes. At the very end of August it had been visited and wondered at by Madame de Montreuil, a lady who had gone to Scotland with James V. in the suite of his first Queen, Madeleine, and was then returning to France. Great attentions were paid her by official persons, and she was shown both the shrine and the head of the Saint himself.[2] A week later the work of pillaging and destruction had begun. According to Sanders, the gold, silver, and precious stones from the shrine filled six-and-twenty large ox-wagons, as the King's receiver had acknow-

Spoliation of Becket's shrine.

[1] *L. P.*, XIII. ii. 244, 256.   [2] *L. P.*, XIII. ii. 257.

ledged, and it was certainly reported at the time
that at least twenty cart-loads were carried from
Canterbury to London. But apparently all this could
not have been from the shrine alone, which contained
no silver at all, gold being the least valuable material
in it. Stow says that the spoils of the shrine filled
two great chests, so heavy that it was all six or
seven strong men could do to convey one of them
out of the church at a time. The value of the whole
booty is faintly suggested by a payment at this
time, duly entered in a book of royal expenses, of
£23 : 16s., partly for rewards to monks and officers
of the Cathedral, partly to servants and labourers
" travailing about the disgarnishing of a shrine "
there.[1]

The spoliation of such a famous shrine must
certainly have appeared to Englishmen, as it did to
foreigners, a peculiar scandal. But if we are to
believe a story reported on high authority abroad,
Henry had taken a very extraordinary step to justify
the outrage. He had called the dead Saint before
some tribunal, and had him pronounced contumacious
for non-appearance and condemned as a traitor!
If anything like this took place, of course it was a
piece of solemn mockery; nor is there any authentic
record of the process. There has, indeed, been published the text of such a citation and of such a judgment; but the documents bear distinct evidences of
fabrication. Still, the story must not be too lightly
dismissed; for, strange as the process may seem,
something of the sort might really have seemed
requisite as a preliminary to the spoliation. If the
King was now the supreme spiritual authority in his
kingdom, it was for him to judge whether Becket
was really a Saint or not. No one, indeed, called his
saintship in question but the King himself and his
courtiers; but the authority that moved the doubt

[1] *L. P.* XIII. ii. 1280, f. 34 b ; XIV. i. 1073.

must judge the doubt, and the result was a foregone conclusion. The way to ascertain whether he was a true Saint or not was to cite him before the King's tribunal, and if he neither appeared—as, of course, he could not—nor anybody else in his behalf—which was almost as unlikely—the Saint would be pronounced contumacious, and on inquiry into his acts it would be found that he was no Saint at all, but a traitor to his King, Henry II. It was therefore, presumably, in accordance with the judgment of some strangely constituted Court, that the bones of the Saint, when his shrine was despoiled, were taken out and burned.[1]

St. Thomas being thus unsainted, his hospital in London called the House of St. Thomas of Acres "was suppressed, and the master and brethren put out, and all the goods taken to the King's treasury" on the 21st October, the day that was wont to be hallowed for the dedication of that church.[2]

On the 16th November a lengthy proclamation[3] was put forth by the King, one part of which was devoted to Becket, to the effect which we have just mentioned. Becket must not be any longer con- *Becket is* sidered a Saint, "as he was really a rebel who fled to *unsainted* France and to the Bishop of Rome to procure the *and his* abrogation of wholesome laws, and was slain upon a *images* rescue made with resistance to those who counselled *pulled* him to leave his stubbornness." This was the way *down.* loyal subjects were henceforth to read one of the most significant events in mediæval history; and popular feeling in later ages has scarcely been more sympathetic. Becket's "pictures," that is to say images, throughout the realm were to be pulled down

---

[1] Wriothesley's *Chronicle*, i. 86. Cp. *L. P.*, XIII. ii. Pref. p. xvi. Some doubts have been raised of late years as to the actual burning of the bones; but the testimony seems to be quite decisive. See Morris on "the Relics of St. Thomas of Canterbury." As to the process, it may be remarked that most of the letters of Chapuys at this particular period seem to have been lost; else we might have had some notice of the fact written at the time in England.

[2] Wriothesley's *Chronicle*, i. 88.   [3] *L. P.*, XIII. ii. 848.

everywhere, his festival no longer kept, and the services in his name were to be razed out of all service books. This, however, was only the final section of a proclamation the main character of which was conservative; for, however revolutionary the King's own proceedings were, it was most important to the vindication both of his old and of his new authority that he should discourage anything like revolutionary proceedings on the part of others. The general contents of the proclamation were as follows :—

(1) To prohibit the import, sale, or publication of English books without special licence, or the printing of such books with annotations or prologues unless they were first examined by the Privy Council or by some authorised person. And even licensed books must not bear the words *cum privilegio regali* without the addition *ad imprimendum solum*.

(2) No one was to print or sell any "books of Scripture" without the supervision either of the King or Council, or of a bishop. Sacramentaries, Anabaptists, or others who should sell books of false doctrine were to be reported.

(3) No one was to reason or dispute about the sacrament of the altar except those learned in divinity. The use of holy bread, holy water, kneeling and creeping to the cross on Good Friday and Easter Day, setting up of lights before Corpus Christi, bearing of candles on Candlemas Day, purification of women, offering of chrisoms and other such things, were to be observed till the King chose to change them.

(4) Priests who were known to have wives or to intend marriage were to be deprived, and those marrying henceforth were to be imprisoned during the King's pleasure.

(5) Archbishops, bishops, and even deacons, were to preach the word of God, showing the difference

between things commanded by Him and the ceremonies used in the Church.

(6) The article about Becket.

It will be seen how completely the King asserted
for himself in this proclamation a supreme spiritual
as well as a supreme temporal sovereignty. All the
authority which had been hitherto derived from the
Pope was henceforth to be derived from him. The
control of religious literature, judgment of heretical
proceedings, the prohibition of discussion on high
subjects, the permission of pious ceremonies of
various kinds till the King thought fit to change
them, the distinction—to be carefully pointed out—
between the commands of God and Church ceremonies
that the King might alter, and finally the judgment
on Becket that he was no Saint—which implied the
King's fitness to decide that question, — all these
things, however different in tendency, were full of
the one great doctrine of the King's spiritual
supremacy. And that was the great point now at
issue, as no man saw more clearly than Henry himself. For as to his subjects, if he allowed old usages,
they did not look upon the sanction as coming from
himself; and what he might do as regards the suppression of monasteries and other unpopular acts—
well, he must be himself answerable for them before
another Tribunal. It was not for subjects to judge
him even in these things.

The only question was whether there was a
tribunal on earth that could bring Henry to
account. He had been excommunicated already, in
1535 ; and no man, surely, could have deserved excommunication better than the perpetrator of those
horrid butcheries of men who upheld his marriage
with Katharine and the sanctity of the Pope's authority ! But what good had been done by his excommunication ? He had never relented in the least ; he
had made the rival princes on the Continent afraid

to receive a papal legate whom he disliked; and now
he had consummated his iniquities by insolently
burning the bones of St. Thomas of Canterbury, the
great defender of the rights of Holy Church against
another tyrant! Rome was filled with horror. But
how to vindicate the Pope's spiritual jurisdiction from
this further outrage more effectually than by the bull

Re-issue,
with an
addition,
of the bull
of excom-
munication
against
Henry.

of 1535 was not apparent. So that bull was only
re-issued with an addition declaring that its execution
had been hitherto suspended from a hope that was
held out that the King might be got to amend; but
now that he had proceeded to those further outrages
(and here the story of the saint's citation and trial
were brought in, with some additional villanies, such
as the plunder of St. Augustine's monastery, from
which he turned out the monks and put in deer in
their places), there was nothing to be done but to
cut off a rotten member from the body of Christ.
So publication of the bull was now decreed, which
might be made, as thought advisable—since it could
not be done in England—at Dieppe or Boulogne in
France, at St. Andrews or Coldstream in Scotland,
or at Tuam or Ardfert in Ireland.[1] To give further
effect to it Pole was again to be despatched to the
Emperor, and a messenger was sent into Scotland
with a cardinal's hat for David Beton, lately made
Bishop of Mirepoix in France. If only the Scots,
the French, and all other Christian nations would
agree to prohibit all commerce with England, the
unhappy country might still be recovered for the
faith.[2]

But all depended upon foreign aid; and what
came of this second mission of Cardinal Pole we shall
see hereafter. Henry meanwhile was very well aware
that Pole was a danger in his path; and not only

---

[1] The bull, which is dated "xvj. kal. Jan." (Dec. 17) 1538, is printed in
Burnet's *Reformation* (Pocock's ed.), iv. 318, and in Wilkins, iii. 840.

[2] *L. P.*, XIII. ii. 1108-1110, 1136.

Pole himself as the Pope's representative, but his whole family as prominent members of the House of York who stood not far off from the succession. There was, in fact, but one family nearer, that of the Marquis of Exeter, a grandson of Edward IV., who had an only son, a lad of twelve years old. On all these the King was keeping watch, knowing well that schemes might be entertained to dethrone him and put one of them in his place. Suddenly, in the end of August, Cardinal Pole's brother Sir Geoffrey was arrested, and, after being kept some time in the Tower, was very closely questioned as to what correspondence he had kept up with his brother the Cardinal, and what conversation he had had with others in England who had expressed a desire for some change in the state of affairs. Pressed by such interrogatories, under fear of torture he was obliged to let out matters which touched his eldest brother Lord Montague, and also the Marquis of Exeter and others. The two noblemen were on this thrown into the Tower, and were presently tried and condemned for high treason, while Sir Geoffrey Pole, having served the King's purpose in this matter, received a royal pardon. He had certainly not informed willingly against his family, and what he had shown ought never to have been accounted guilt; but he knew too well what use might be made of forced confessions, and not long after his arrest he had attempted suicide—no doubt to avoid the misery of betraying those whom he loved. Exeter and Lord Montague were beheaded at Tyburn on the 9th December, while a number of minor persons were hanged the same day as their accomplices.

Executions of the Marquis of Exeter, Lord Montague, and others.

What was their offence? Simply that in private conversation they had expressed dislike of the King's proceedings and hoped to see a change; that they thought Cardinal Pole was right in what he was doing; that they considered that knaves ruled about the King, and feared that they could only be displaced by civil war; and that the Marquis of Exeter, alluding to those knaves, had once said, with clenched fist, " I trust to give them a buffet one day." How much was muttered to the same effect in many other households it did not suit the King's purpose to inquire. Lord Montague, however, wished rather to be out of the way, and had said in confidence to his brother Geoffrey, " I like well the doings of my brother the Cardinal, and I would we were both over the sea, for this world will one day come to stripes. It must needs come to pass one day; and I fear we shall lack nothing so much as honest men." Another thing that he had said in the security of private conversation is well worth the attention of any one who wishes to understand the times: " Cardinal Wolsey had been an honest man if he had had an honest master." [1]

That was the real state of matters. There was no independence anywhere. The nobility had been cowed ever since the execution of Buckingham; the Commons were as yet no power in the State, though the King could use them and even advance their pretensions to suit his own purposes. There was just one other quarter from which freedom and independence might be looked for, and had been looked for in past times not in vain. That was the Church; but even the Church in England was now controlled as it never had been before. Men could only look abroad for help. It was not his own family merely, we may be sure, that " liked well the doings " of Cardinal Pole; at least, it certainly would not have been, if others had known as much about them. While in England bishops and clergy were sworn to the supremacy, and monasteries were dissolved and saints unsainted by a new authority in such matters,

---

[1] *L. P.*, XIII. ii. 979, and the volume (or "part") generally for the story of the arrests, trials, and executions.

and bulls from Rome forbidden, and any acknowledgment of the old spiritual jurisdiction declared treason, the hearts of men, and especially of good men, longed for nothing so much as a reassertion of that spiritual jurisdiction which was acknowledged by all neighbouring countries, and which alone could emancipate them from a demoralising and insufferable thraldom. If England had been so emancipated with foreign aid, even at the cost of civil war, she would, it may be safely said, have been far more grateful for foreign interference than she was even when the father of her present tyrant with French assistance put down Richard III. Indeed, there are not wanting evidences that even a Scottish invasion in behalf of the faith would have been far from inacceptable; and the publication of the papal bull against Henry at St. Andrews or at Coldstream might have been the signal for a movement of far greater moment than anything that had been done in England for a hundred years. Only it would have been tantamount to an act of war.

This chapter has been devoted entirely to the doings of a single year, from the end of 1537 to the end of 1538; and yet the story of that year is incomplete. All that has been related—the beginning made in the suppression of the larger monasteries, the exposure of old abuses, the crusade against idolatry and superstition, the spoliation of shrines and the unsainting of Becket—were but successive steps in putting into practice that royal supremacy which had previously been vindicated in theory by relentless executions. So great a revolution—which few could have believed at first would either have lasted long or been carried so far—took some time to get into working order, and these were parts of the process. But another step taken this year has not yet been mentioned—the unfrocking of the friars. It has been shown how, in 1534, all the different

Orders of friars were subjected to two Royal Visitors, George Browne, Prior of the Augustinian Hermits of London, and John Hilsey of the Black Friars. Both these worthies had by this time been promoted to bishoprics, Browne being now Archbishop of Dublin and Hilsey Bishop of Rochester. Cromwell, however, as the King's Vicegerent in spiritual matters, had obtained for Richard Ingworth, suffragan Bishop of Dover, a commission to visit all the houses, not only of his own Order, the Friars Preachers (or Black Friars), but also those of the Minorites (Grey), the Carmelites (White), the Augustinians, and the Crutched Friars, with power to examine and correct abuses.[1] This was issued on the 6th February 1538; but nothing is heard of Ingworth's proceedings till the 7th April, when he took an inventory of the goods of the Grey Friars of Ipswich, a house which had already been virtually extinguished by the action of its hereditary founder, Lord Wentworth, who, as he wrote to Cromwell on the 1st, had purchased it for himself and his heirs, seeing that the friars had been compelled for very poverty to sell their plate and jewels, as the people would no longer give alms to "such an idle nest of droans."[2]

It seems that the heads of other houses of friars, anticipating that they would share the fate of the monasteries, had been alienating or, in some cases, consuming too freely the property that belonged to them, and the Bishop of Dover received a new commission on the 5th May, with express powers to put the goods of the houses he visited into safe custody and to take inventories of them.[3] With these powers he had visited some of the principal towns of the Midlands, and had reached Gloucester by the 23rd. He had found everywhere poverty, "and much shift made with such as they had before, as jewels selling

---

[1] *L. P.*, XIII. i. 225.   [2] *L. P.*, XIII. i. 651, 699.
[3] *L. P.*, XIII. i. 926.

and other shift by leases." But he had stopped those practices by making indentures and sequestering their common seals; so that now, before the year was out, the communities would almost all be driven to give up their houses for want of means to live. The two friars' houses where he was at Gloucester, were ready to surrender for that reason at once. One of those which he had visited (Atherstone, an Augustinian house) was too poor to pay the costs of their Visitor—a serious matter for the Bishop of Dover! Another Augustinian house, Droitwich, was not able to maintain more than one friar, as everything had been sold. The prior had felled and sold timber, and also sold a gilt chalice of 70 ounces' weight, a censer of 36 ounces, 2 great brass pots (each able, it was said, to seethe an ox whole), with spits, pans, and so forth. Not a bed, nor sheet, nor platter, nor dish was left in the house, and the prior could not furnish a true account of what he had done with everything. But in his coffer the Bishop found eleven papal bulls and above a hundred "letters of pardons," while in all the choir-books the Pope's name still remained unerased. Such a prior, of course, was handed over to custody, and three neighbouring gentlemen were each anxious to get a grant of the house.[1]

(marginal note: Surrenders of their houses taken.)

After this beginning, the Bishop went on to visit in the west and south of England, and in Wales, after which he continued his work in the eastern and in the home counties. As so many friars were going to be turned adrift he desired Cromwell, as the King's Vicar-General, to send down dispensations to allow them to put off their habits. He considered that in this way he was doing them good, as they were quite unable to live. Yet many of them were loth to forsake their houses, especially the Grey Friars. He had more trouble with them, he said, than with any of the

---

[1] Wright's *Suppression of the Monasteries*, pp. 193-5.

others.[1] Meanwhile, Dr. London, Warden of New
College, had received a commission, along with the
Mayor of Oxford and two others, to "look upon"
the friars in that town, and the sphere of Dr.
London's labours was by and by extended to other
places to do similar work.[2] His method was a trifle
more summary than that which the Bishop at first
employed; for he speedily caused all the four Orders
of Friars to change their coats.[3] The change by and
by was made compulsory everywhere, even where it
was not favoured by the heads of particular houses,
as it was by the Warden of the Grey Friars of
London.[4] Of the way in which the order was enforced an interesting example is preserved for us
in the pages of Foxe, who relates it with great
admiration as follows :—

They are compelled to change their coats.

> Hereunto also pertaineth the example of Friar Bartley,
> who wearing still his friar's cowl after the suppression of
> religious houses, Cromwell, coming through St. Paul's Church-
> yard and espying him in Rheines's shop, "Yea," said he,
> "will not that cowl of yours be left off yet? And if I hear,
> by one o'clock, that this apparel be not changed, thou shalt
> be hanged immediately, for example to all others." And so,
> putting his cowl away, he durst never wear it after.

This story is told after some other anecdotes about
Cromwell, the last of which relates how in a no less
summary way he stopped a man in the street and
committed him to prison for a "strange newfangle-
ness" in going "with his hair hanging about his
ears down unto his shoulders," for which, on being
questioned, he pleaded the excuse that he had made
a vow. And after relating these anecdotes Foxe
goes on to lament that magistrates, in the days in
which he wrote, did not put down the "monstrous
ruffs," the "prodigious hose," and the "prodigal, or
rather hyperbolical, barbarous breeches" then preva-

[1] *L. P.*, XIII. ii. 49.
[2] *L. P.*, XIII. i. 1335.
[3] *L. P.*, XIII. ii. 235.
[4] *L. P.*, XIII. ii. 251-2.

lent—the last-named garment seeming "rather like barrels than breeches." "But," he concludes, "here we may well see, and truly this may say, that England once had a Cromwell."

We may say now that England more than once had a Cromwell whose ways were rather drastic. But we are only concerned here with the first, and with his eulogist. If these little anecdotes had been written by an avowed enemy of Thomas Cromwell we might reasonably have suspected that the tyrannical and overbearing character of this upstart minister of Henry VIII. had been a little exaggerated. But as the mode of action he reports seems to Foxe worthy of all commendation, we know what to think both of him and of Cromwell. And now, who was this "Friar Bartley" who came in for such rough treatment? He was a man of some celebrity, better known as Alexander Barclay, for surnames were *Friar* liable to considerable variation in the sixteenth *Barclay.* century. Alexander Barclay,[1] the poet, translator of Sebastian Brandt's *Ship of Fools*, was believed by some, even of his contemporaries, to be a Scotsman, though the fact was uncertain. He was, however, connected with Devonshire, and composed his poetical version of the work just named "in the College of St. Mary Ottery in 1508." By the year 1520 he had become a monk, for he was employed in that year "to devise histoires and convenient raisons to florisshe the buildings and banquet house" at the Field of the Cloth of Gold, and is called, in a letter of the time, "Maistre Barkleye, the Blacke Monke and poete."[2] We know, in fact, that he was a Benedictine at Ely; but not many years afterwards he must have changed his Order and become a Franciscan friar. Later, however, in

---

[1] Dr. Barkley he is called by Wriothesley (i. 82), who, though he does not relate the same anecdote, mentions him particularly as one "which was very loth to leave his hypocrite's coat."

[2] *L. P.*, III. 737.

1528, having apparently caught a little of the contagion of Lutheranism, he escaped abroad and took refuge in Germany, like Roye and Tyndale.[1] Apparently he soon returned and made his peace with the Church.

Barclay was an Observant Franciscan, and when the Observants were suppressed in 1534 he must have been handed over, like Forest, to a house of the Conventual Franciscans. Like Forest, too, he must have obtained a relaxation of treatment by compliance with the Supremacy; but he evidently adhered to his rule as far as might be permitted. He was suffered to go about, and did so still in his friar's weeds, even after they were prohibited, till he met with Cromwell as above, probably in August or September of this year 1538. In October he was in the West Country again—" a frere in somewhat honester weed," as he is described by a country gentleman writing to Cromwell, but creating a good deal of disturbance by his preaching, which did not at all harmonise with what was now expected by the authorities. What was the immediate result of his doing so we know not; but apparently he was obliged to take the world as he found it, and years afterwards he obtained a living in Essex.[2]

We will now leave the story of the friars, and to complete the domestic record of religion in 1538, let us see how Henry VIII. in November exercised his functions of supreme judge in matters of theology. A priest named John Nicholson, who, having been already in trouble for heresy in past years, had

[1] *L. P.*, IV. 4810. The words of the original letter are quoted in Demaus's *Tyndale*, p. 162, as follows : " Edmund de la Pole, who called himself Duke of Suffolk, was demanded of King Philip [of Castile] to be brought into England ; and William Roye, William Tyndale, Jerome Barlow, Alexander Barclay and their adherents, formerly Franciscans of the Observant Order, now Apostates, and also George Constans [Constantine], and many others. who rail against your Grace [Wolsey] ought to be apprehended," etc.

[2] The information contained in Jamieson's biography of Barclay, prefixed to Paterson's edition of *The Ship of Fools* (1874), was amplified in part by me in the Preface to *L. P.*, XIII. ii. (pp. 8-9), and is here further corrected.

adopted the name of Lambert to escape the attentions of the bishops, was indiscreet enough, after a sermon of Dr. John Taylor, a favourer of the New Learning, to seek conference with him on no less weighty a subject than the Sacrament of the Altar. Taylor, unfortunately, referred him to Dr. Barnes, who, though also of the New School, was an adherent of Luther and held very high doctrine on that subject; and Barnes persuaded Taylor to lay the matter before Archbishop Cranmer. The archbishop called Nicholson to his defence, and after a disputation Nicholson appealed to the King. At least this was the history of the case so far as Foxe could ascertain it, for he speaks with a little ambiguity about the last part.[1]

The King agreed to hear him in person. The 16th November was appointed as the day; and the hearing took place in the hall of Wolsey's old palace at Whitehall, still often called York Place.[2] The King took his seat upon a throne with a great assembly of peers and judges on his left, while on the right sat the bishops, "and behind them the most famous lawyers, clothed all in purple, according to the manner." The King himself was clothed all in white, and surveyed the prisoner, who was brought in by a guard of armed men, with a look of great severity. He called upon Dr. Day to declare the causes of the assembly, and Day pronounced an oration, the drift of which was that no man was to imagine that the King, having abolished the jurisdiction of the Bishop of Rome, was going to extinguish religion or give liberty to heretics to trouble the Church with impunity; and that they were not assembled to dispute upon a heretical doctrine but to denounce and condemn it openly. The King then rose to his feet and, leaning on a cushion of white cloth of tissue,

Trial of John Nicholson, or Lambert.

---

[1] Foxe, v. 226-8.   [2] *L. P.*, XIII. ii. 851.

said to Lambert, "Ho! good fellow, what is thy name?"

The poor man, kneeling, said, "My name is John Nicholson, although of many I be called Lambert."

"What," said the King, "have you two names? I would not trust you, having two names, although you were my brother."

"O most noble prince," replied Lambert, "your bishops forced me of necessity to change my name."

Then, being told to proceed to the matter, he began with thanking God who had inclined the heart of the King to hear religious causes himself, as bishops were often guilty of great cruelty and privy murder without the King's knowledge, and he trusted that God, who had abundantly endowed a prince with so great gifts, would bring about some great thing through him. But here the King interrupted him, saying, in Latin, "I came not hither to hear mine own praises. . . . Answer as touching the Sacrament of the Altar, whether dost thou say that it is the body of Christ, or wilt deny it?" And with that the King raised his cap.

"I answer," said Lambert, "with St. Augustine, that it is the body of Christ after a certain manner."

Again the King said in Latin: "Answer me neither out of St. Augustine, nor by the authority of any other, but tell me plainly whether thou sayest it is the body of Christ or no."

"Then I deny it to be the body of Christ," said Lambert.

The King said he would then be condemned by Christ's own words. Then Cranmer was called on to refute ten arguments that he had handed in to Dr. Taylor. While he was discussing the matter, however, Bishop Gardiner, who had been appointed the sixth place in the disputation, joined in, adducing texts which Cranmer had neglected to cite; and after him Tunstall, Bishop of Durham, followed on the same side. Next came Stokesley, Bishop of London, who, if Foxe may be trusted, rejoiced when on the point of death that he had in his time burned fifty heretics. Ten bishops in all had been appointed to dispute the question. The brief winter daylight was gone and torches lighted before the discussion ended, and Lambert was reduced to silence, or saw no good in answering. The King then said to him, "Art thou not yet satisfied? Wilt thou live or die?"

Lambert said that he committed himself wholly to the King's will.

"Commit thyself unto the hands of God," said the King, "not unto mine." He added that he would be no patron of heretics, and bade Cromwell read the sentence.[1]

The hearing lasted altogether from noon to five o'clock. Loyal subjects were powerfully impressed by the scene and the way the King had deigned to discuss matters with a troublesome heretic. "The King's Majesty," wrote Husee to Lord Lisle, "reasoned with him in person, sundry times confounding him, so that he alone would have been sufficient to confute a thousand such. It was not a little rejoicing unto all his commons and to all others that saw and heard how his Grace handled the matter; for it shall be a precedent while the world stands; and no one will be so bold hereafter to attempt the like cause."[2] No less laudation of the King came from Sir Thomas Elyot, in the dedication of his *Dictionary* to Henry VIII., in which he speaks with admiration of "a divine influence or spark of divinity which late appeared to all them that beheld your Grace sitting in the throne of your royal estate as Supreme Head of the Church of England next under Christ, about the decision and condemnation of the pernicious errors of the most

The King as an ecclesiastical judge.

---

[1] Foxe, v. 230-34; Hall, p. 827; Wriothesley, i. 88-89.
[2] *L. P.*, XIII. ii. 851.

detestable heretic, John Nicolson, called also Lambert"; when all men admired "the fulmination of the most vehement arguments" by the King in confutation of his heresies, and also his "wonderful patience in the long sustaining of the foolish and tedious objections of the said Lambert, as also your most Christian charity in moving and exhorting so stubborn a heretic, with the most gentle and persuasible language, to recant." The people, he adds, wept for joy at seeing it.[1] Lambert was burned in Smithfield on the 22nd, six days after his sentence.[2]

There is but one thing more to note in the religious history of England in this year 1538, and it does not concern the religious history of the people. But we may tell it here in the words of the chronicler :—

A German embassy to England. "This year in June came over into England to the King's Grace certain persons out of Germany to entreat of certain Acts concerning the true setting forth of God's Word and the good order of the spiritualty; of whom the head person was a temporal man, well learned, being Vice - Chancellor to the Duke of Saxony with others,—the King admitting Dr. Barnes to be of their party, and for the King's Grace's party the Archbishop of Canterbury, the Bishop of Chichester (Sampson), Dr. Wilson, and three other doctors, which sat every week two or three times concerning the said causes of long continuance."[3]

This reception of a German Protestant mission in England, which had come for the purpose of arranging some common basis in religion, is undoubtedly a matter of great historical interest. It was a failure, indeed, as regards its express object, and produced not the smallest immediate effect on the religion of England. From another point of view,

---

[1] *L. P.*, XIII. ii. 852.   [2] *L. P.*, XIII. ii. 899 ; Wriothesley, i. 89.
[3] Wriothesley, i. 81, 82.

however, it was an event of first-rate importance. For the invitation given to the Germans, and the hopes held out to them of a cordial understanding —hopes that were not completely blighted when the ambassadors returned to their country after a few months' uncomfortable stay in England,—formed another bulwark against the power of Rome, and against any attempt to depose an excommunicated king. Nor were the theological results of the conference by any means forgotten when, in a later period, the Church of England had to formulate her doctrinal position as a Church independent of the Papacy. The story of the mission, however, must be left for another chapter.

CHAPTER IV

GERMAN PROTESTANTISM AND THE ACT OF THE SIX ARTICLES

IT was my aim in the last chapter to give, not exhaustively but by particular examples, as complete an account as might be of all the main facts that affected religion in England in the one year 1538. But to estimate all the agencies at work, we ought to take into account the ballad literature of the period, and more especially of that very year; for though it will scarcely command admiration either as to style, taste, or judgment, it was nevertheless a factor in doing the King's work that should not be overlooked. How much ribaldry might have been expected to spring up spontaneously when once it was known that jests at sacred things were not looked at with disfavour, is not a question of much practical consequence. But the fact is that from the time the King set himself against the Pope there was a special market for such things. In 1533, when Francis I. was endeavouring, as Henry's political friend, to persuade the Pope to delay the sentence of excommunication, the Pope was compelled to pass it the sooner by news that in England his authority had been treated with the grossest disrespect. The King, in spite of a promise given to Francis to take no further steps pending the result of his mediation, had caused scandalous farces to be played in London, in which men in masks went through the streets, arrayed as cardinals, with the most shameless characters, male and female, seated behind them on horseback.[1] It was a part of the royal policy to use such methods of bringing the old ecclesiastical authority into contempt, and in this he received ample aid from his all-powerful minister, Cromwell.

That "valiant soldier and captain of Christ," as Foxe describes him,

as he was most studious of himself in a flagrant zeal to set forward the truth of the gospel, seeking all means and ways to beat down false religion, and to advance the true, so he always retained unto him and had about him such as could be found helpers and furtherers of the same; in the number of whom were sundry and divers fresh and quick wits, pertaining to his family; by whose industry and ingenious labors, divers excellent both ballads and books were contrived and set abroad, concerning the suppression of the Pope and all popish idolatry.[2]

This passage, which was suppressed by Foxe after his first edition, was followed and illustrated by the quotation at full length of one particular sample of these "excellent ballads," entitled "The Fantassie of Idolatrie," the martyrologist passing by "a great sort" of the like matter, which he says he might have brought in as well. This ballad was the work of one William Gray, a servant of Cromwell,[3] and its character deserves consideration. It consists of fifty stanzas, beginning :— *The old religion attacked in ballads.*

> All christen people
> Beyng under the steple
>   Of Jesu Christes faith,
> Marke and drawe nere
> And ye shall here
>   What the holy Scripture sayth.

Then after referring to the Decalogue and other passages in reproof of idolatry, the writer goes on :—

[1] Hamy's *Entrevue de François I. avec Henry VIII.* (Documents, p. ccclxxviii.)

[2] Foxe, v. 403 (from 1st edition).

[3] Cp. footnote at end of the ballad in Foxe, v. 409, with *L. P.*, xvi. 423, p. 213 note.

This should suffise
All those that be wyse ;
    But we, of a stoubourne mynde,
Be so harde harted,
Will not be converted,
    But rather styll be blynde ;

Ronnyng hyther and thyther,
We cannot tell whither
    In offryng candels and pence
To stones and stockes,
And to olde rotten blockes,
    That came we know not from whense ;

To Walsyngham a gaddyng,
To Cantorbury a maddyng,
    As men distraught of mynde ;
With fewe clothes on our backes,
But an image of waxe
    For the lame and for the blynde ;

To Hampton, to Ipswyche,
To Harforth, to Shordyche,
    With many mo places of pryce,
As to our Lady of Worcester,
And the swete Rode of Chester,
    With the blessed Lady of Penryce ;

To Leymster, to Kyngstone,
To Yorke, to Donyngton,
    To Redyng, to the chyld of grace ;
To Wynsore, to Waltam,
To Ely, to Caultam,
    Bare foted and bare legged apace ;

To Saynt Earth a right,
Where, in the dark nyght,
    Many a juglyng cast hath be done,
To Saynt Angers rotten bones,
That ran away for the nones,
    To the crosse that groweth at Chaldon ;

To the good Holy Ghoste,
That paynted poste,
    Abydyng at Basyng stoke ;
Whiche doth as muche good
As a god made of wood,
    And, yet, he beareth a great stroke ;

To the Holy Bloud of Hayles,
With your fyngers and nayles
   All that ye may stretche and wynne;
Yet it woulde not be seen
Except you were thryven,
   And clene from all deadly synne.

There were we flocked,
Lowted and mocked;
   For nowe it is knowen to be
But the blood of a ducke,
That long did sucke
   The thrifte from every degre;

To Pomfret, to Wyldon,
To Saynt Anne of Bucston
   To Saynt Mighels Mount also;
But, to reken all,
My wyttes be too small
   For, God knoweth, there be many mo.

The catalogue does not end here, as we might expect from the last words; but there are some indecencies which we must pass over—indeed, further on they are atrocious. The following additional allusions, however, will interest the reader of the last chapter :—

For the Rode of Grace
Hath lost his place,
   And is rubbed on the gall;
For false devotion
Hath lost his promotion,
   And is broken in peces small.

He was made to jogle,
His eyes would gogle,
   He wold bend his browes and frowne;
With his head he would nod
Like a proper young god
   His chaftes [1] wold go up and downe.

   .   .   .   .   .   .

---

[1] Jaws.

> Also Delver Gathaerne
> As (saieth the Welcheman)
>   Brought outlawes out of hell,
> Is come with spere and shelde
> In harneys to burne in Smythfielde;
>   For in Wales he may not dwell.
>
> Then Forest the fryer,
> That obstinate lyer
>   That wyllingly is dead,
> In his contumacy
> The gospell dyd deny,
>   And the Kyng to be Supreme Head.[1]

Towards the close, as we might expect, there is a little hit at Becket's shrine :—

> Besydes these stockes and stones,
> Have we not had, of late, traytors bones,
>   Thus their trompery to maintain?
> Whiche is a token, verely,
> They go about most earnestly
>   To bryng in superstition again.[2]

Sad doggrel as these verses are, they bring to view many things that time has buried in oblivion, or tradition faintly remembers; and the fact that the writer does not spare superstition is all the more helpful. What a number of pilgrimages to places, the very names of which are not always known to us now! Curious traditions also about saints occur in passages not quoted. Application to St. Syth for a lost purse, to St. Loye to save a horse, to St. Apollinaris " for my teeth " (the saint, it seems, could cure toothache), for the ague to Master John Shorne, who conjured the Devil into a boot, and so forth. At the same time we note the writer's spirit where he seeks to palm upon us the fable of the duck's blood at Hayles as a fact recently ascertained, when it was

[1] The last two stanzas are quoted by Hall in his *Chronicle* (p. 826) with, perhaps, slightly better readings.
[2] Foxe, v. 404-409.

indeed positively disproved. We must be quite prepared, in such matters, for official mendacity.

We now take leave of the domestic records of 1538 to pursue a subject barely touched upon at the conclusion of the last chapter.

Henry had for years been watching the German Lutherans, and sometimes corresponding with them, feeling, even before his actual breach with the Pope, that they might one day be useful to him if the Emperor turned against him, either on his aunt's account or to vindicate the authority of the Holy See. He had evidently watched with peculiar interest the results of the Diet of Augsburg in 1530, and their opposition to the election of Ferdinand as King of the Romans in 1531. They had written to him, indeed, almost immediately after the latter event a letter in reply to which he commended their zeal for the reformation of the Church, but discreetly warned them against restless men too eager to promote a change.[1] In 1533, however, after the death of John the Constant, Duke of Saxony, he offered to place a resident ambassador with his son John Frederic, an honour which the latter wisely declined in order not to offend the Emperor.[2] Then in 1534 he sent a special mission to some of the princes to encourage them to a league against the Pope.[3] Early in 1535 he sent over to Wittenberg Dr. Robert Barnes, who arrived there in March, as Melancthon's letters show,[4] with the view of getting opinions which might be used in favour of his marriage with Anne Boleyn. In this aim Barnes, though popular with the Lutherans, certainly did not succeed, and he soon returned.

But in the autumn of the same year the King sent over a more important embassy. Being then in full expectation of a bull of excommunication from Rome, he sought to neutralise its effects by sending Edward

Henry VIII. and the German Lutherans.

---

[1] *L. P.*, v. App. 7.
[2] *L. P.*, vi. 1079.
[3] *L. P.*, vii. 21.
[4] *L. P.*, viii. 375, 384.

Foxe, whom he had just made Bishop of Hereford, with Dr. Barnes and Dr. Nicholas Heath, to John Frederic, Duke of Saxony, and the Landgrave of Hesse, with a view to a common understanding in matters of religion, which should give them and him mutual support alike against the Pope and against the Emperor. Of some results of this embassy I shall speak more fully hereafter. Here I only sketch the diplomacy. An agreement was soon come to with the princes on one point—that no General Council should be recognised by either party without the consent of both. But the King declined to commit himself and his realm to the principles of the Augsburg Confession until some representative theologians were sent by the Germans to England to confer upon the subject with his own. On the other hand, the Lutheran divines could not be won over to pronounce marriage with a deceased brother's wife, though a wrong thing in itself, to be invalid after it was done; and it may be that their refusal to concede this had something to do with Anne Boleyn's fall.[1]

But, as Bishop Gardiner clearly pointed out when his advice was asked upon the subject, it would have been highly injudicious and against the principles on which the King himself was proceeding in England if he had made a league with princes who were subjects of the Emperor in any such fashion. The King himself was an Emperor in his own country and Head of the Church of England, and the Emperor ought to occupy the like position in his dominions. How could they then make any agreement with Henry without their Head's consent?[2] The King undoubtedly saw the force of these considerations, and, indeed, was guided by them; for it may be safely said that the suggestion of a union with the German Protestants on matters of faith was

---

[1] *L. P.*, IX. 1013-18, 1030; x. 63, 108, 118, 265, 266, 289, 290, 305, 379, 447, 448, 457, 584, 770-71. [2] *L. P.*, x. 256.

intended for nothing but a lure from the first. "My King does not care about religion," said Henry's own zealous advocate, Dr. Barnes, to Luther once [1]— a singularly frank admission from an envoy sent to solicit Lutheran aid for his master. And we need not be surprised that Henry let the Lutherans alone whenever he thought he could do without them. In 1537, however, he published a pamphlet which was most popular in Germany, holding up to contempt the Pope's efforts to procure a General Council. Nothing could have been more agreeable to the German Pro-testant mind, for the Pope had actually issued letters for a Council to meet at Mantua in the May of that year, and had left Rome in April in order to open it, when he was compelled to put it off by the Duke of Mantua's protest that he would require an armed force to protect the city and payment for its support.[2] The German Protestants, meanwhile, had protested most strongly that though they had always desired a free Christian Council, such a place as Mantua could not be trusted, and that the Pope, who had pronounced judgment on them already, had no authority in himself to call a General Council.[3] The King of England's pamphlet accordingly was quite to their mind. It was im-mediately reprinted at Wittenberg, and at least three German translations of it were published in 1537 and 1538, one of them in two editions issued severally at Augsburg and at Strasburg.[4] John Frederic of Saxony and Philip Landgrave of Hesse both wrote to express to him their satisfaction that it agreed so well with the answer they themselves had given to the nuncio and the Imperial ambassador at their Diet at Schmalkalden. In doing so they also took occa-sion to apologise for their own remissness (at which they heard Henry was somewhat dissatisfied) in not having reported this answer to him earlier; and they

The King's pamphlet against the Council summoned to Mantua.

---

[1] *L. P.*, XVI. 106.
[2] *L. P.*, XIII. i. 432, 887, 989.
[3] *L. P.*, XIII. i. 564.
[4] *L. P.*, XII. i. 1310.

assured him that they and their allies in religion were fully alive to his efforts, set forth by that great embassy of learned men two years before, to restore the true worship of God and get rid of the impiety and tyranny of the Bishop of Rome.[1]

It may be doubted, perhaps, whether they were really very grateful for that great embassy, which remained much longer in Germany in the spring of 1536 than there seemed any necessity for, and no doubt put the princes to some cost in entertaining it.[2] But Henry was astute enough to despatch, early in 1538, to their Diet at Brunswick, an agent of his own named Christopher Mont,[3] himself a German, to encourage them to send an embassy to England to take joint measures against the proposed Council and for the establishment of sound religion.[4] An embassy the princes themselves had talked of sending; but there were difficulties in the way—amongst others, that Christian III., the new King of Denmark, not acknowledged as such by the Emperor, nor even by Henry (who had been treating with the city of Lubeck in a way by no means favourable to him), had joined their Gospel league and abolished papal jurisdiction in his kingdoms. The Diet, however, agreed to send two of their divines to England, and ultimately added a third. Mont in vain asked that

German divines sent to England;

Melancthon should be among them; but the three sent were Francis Burchart (Vice-Chancellor of the Duke of Saxony), Dr. George Boyneburg, and Frederic Myconius. They arrived in London on the last day of May.[5]

They were detained in England somewhat longer than they found pleasant. During June and July they had conferences with Henry's divines, and a

---

[1] *L. P.*, XII. i. 1088-89. [2] *L. P.*, x. 584, 677.
[3] His Latin surname seems to have been Montaborinus, or sometimes Montanus, generally abbreviated into Mont.
[4] *L. P.*, XIII. i. 352-3, 367, 648-50, 815.
[5] *L. P.*, XIII. i. 648-50, 815, 985, 1102, 1266.

number of theological papers remain among our archives, which were partly, it would seem, produced by them and partly by the English.[1] On the 5th August they wrote to the King that they felt it necessary to return to Germany, and though they had not arrived at an agreement with regard to some abuses in the Church, which they felt ought to be rooted out, they had made good progress and must content themselves with putting the matter before the King, who would doubtless have it fully discussed by his own divines. The points which they still regarded as heads of papal idolatry were the prohibition of communion in both kinds, the use of private masses, and the enforced celibacy of the clergy.[2] On these subjects the bishops had left it to the King himself to reply, knowing that he intended to do so, as they were afraid to write contrary to the King's mind ; while on other matters, such as matrimony, orders, confirmation, and extreme unction, on which they felt sure that the Germans would not agree with them, except perhaps on the one head of matrimony, they desired Cranmer to draw up a treatise. Henry answered the German envoys, declaring his own view in opposition to theirs on what they considered to be the three great abuses ; but he promised to take further counsel, and hoped to see them again before they left.[3]

The poor Germans, though well entertained in public, were disgracefully ill lodged, rats running about their chambers ; and one of them, Myconius, fell seriously ill in September. But it was only on the 1st October that the King gave them a letter to take to John Frederic of Saxony, praising their erudition and Christian piety, and expressing a hope of good results from what had already been agreed to. He still hoped that Melancthon and other learned men and dismissed with pleasant words.

---

[1] *L. P.*, XIII. i. 1306-1308 ; ii. 166. Also X. 585.
[2] *L. P.*, XIII. ii. 37, 38.   [3] *L. P.*, XIII. ii. 126, 164-65.

would be sent to conclude the matter.[1] Melancthon himself wrote to the King in March and April following, but said nothing about coming to England. He only expressed his satisfaction at Burchart's report of the conferences there, and hoped that they would lead up to a general consent in doctrine among those churches which disowned the tyranny of Rome. Burchart had been loud in the King's praises, and Melancthon, warmly commending his zeal for the Christian religion, trusted earnestly that, as Henry had already begun to put down some superstitions, he would be led to correct such abuses as still remained.[2]

At the same time he naturally expressed himself with a good deal more freedom in a private letter to Cranmer. Why should England retain the impious laws of Rome after getting rid of their author? Why, especially, should the marriage of priests still be prohibited? Why should rites which were manifestly opposed to Scripture be enjoined, and old customs about differences of foods, creeping to the cross, and the like, be vindicated by new sophistries and mystic significations such as Bishops Stokesley and Gardiner loved to produce? Let there be no more follies maintained which tended to nourish superstition.[3]

But Melancthon and his friends were altogether mistaken if they expected Henry to move in this direction. He intended still to make use of them, but quite in a different way. That Burchart went back to his country captivated by the King's affability we can very well believe, for there was a special reason why he should have been so. When he was in England Cromwell had ventured, as if totally unauthorised—a sort of fiction well understood in diplomacy—to suggest to him a marriage between the King's daughter Mary—" the Lady Mary," as she was called at Court, since she was no longer recognised

---

[1] *L. P.*, XIII. ii. 298, 497.   [2] *L. P.*, XIV. i. 613, 666.
[3] *L. P.*, XIV. i. 631.

as Princess—and the young Duke of Cleves.[1] John, Duke of Cleves, and his son William each bore the title of duke, even when the father was still alive; and young William had prospects before him that Henry was not slow to appreciate.   Nevertheless the suggestion of this marriage—a dazzling enough match for a young German prince, even though the King insisted on regarding his daughter as illegitimate— was apparently only intended to raise expectations, and to pave the way for something more momentous. But of this more shall be said by and by.

Henry had at this time real need of friends upon the Continent; for his constant policy, ever since defying the Pope, to strengthen the enmity between Francis I. and the Emperor for his own security, had fairly broken down for the time.   The Pope's efforts to bring the two princes to an agreement had been successful.   A ten years' truce had been negotiated between them at Nice in June 1538, and a subsequent interview at Aigues Mortes confirmed the good impression that old enmities were now laid aside.   The Pope was thus encouraged to despatch Cardinal Pole on a second mission to the Emperor and Francis I. with a view to action against England, either to dethrone King Henry or to bring him once more into submission to the Church.

To make peace with the Church, after all he had done, would have been a serious humiliation to the King; but the situation was alarming.   For he knew that he was thoroughly disliked, both by Francis and the Emperor, besides having undoubtedly lost the hearts of his own subjects generally.   So, if Francis and the Emperor could act cordially together now, this second mission of Pole was pretty sure of success. Of all Englishmen, Pole had best reason to resent Henry's tyranny; for the news of his brother Lord Montague's execution had reached Rome just before

[1] *L. P.*, XIII. i. 1198; XIV. i. 103 (1, 2).

he started, and even his mother had been rudely questioned and placed in confinement, though not as yet committed to the Tower. Yet, bitterly as he felt the wrongs done to his family, it was with no thought of avenging private injuries that he set out from Róme immediately after Christmas 1538, travelling in disguise with few attendants to avoid assassins, whose services, it had not been obscurely hinted, the King of England was quite ready to employ against him. After a long and painful winter journey he reached the Emperor's Court at Toledo in the middle of February 1539, and there was no fear this time that he should be refused access because England chose to regard him as a traitor.

His extradition, indeed, was demanded by the English ambassador, Sir Thomas Wyatt; but the Emperor returned a flat refusal, declaring that even if he had been a traitor to himself, he could not but give audience to one coming as legate from the Holy Father at Rome. Pole, indeed, might well have expected, even on his own account, not only protection but a kindly welcome; for it was but nine months since the Emperor at Villafranca had expressly sought his acquaintance to thank him for the way he had maintained the cause of his aunt, Katharine of Aragon. But kindly feelings now gave place to diplomatic considerations; and though the Emperor treated him with the respect due to a legate, he did not greatly warm to the proposal of taking action against Henry, even by way of forbidding commercial intercourse with England. He required first to be assured that Francis would co-operate with him in such a policy; and Francis, as it soon appeared, required first to be assured that the Emperor would do so with him. For Pole, having withdrawn from Toledo, sent his friend Abbot Parpaglia to the King of France to learn if his coming on such a mission would be acceptable; and Francis, though very polite, con-

fessed that it would be undesirable. Thus the second which is also un-successful.
mission of Pole turned out as unfruitful as the first.

Charles V. knew too well the difficulties of his own
position to be willing to act alone against England, even
in the way of cutting off commercial intercourse, unless
sufficiently assured that he should not act alone. The
Turk outside the Empire, and the Protestant princes
within, always gave him a good deal of trouble, and
of late he was full of further anxieties on the side of
Cleves. Charles, Duke of Gueldres, who had been a
constant source of irritation to the House of Bur-
gundy and to the Empire, died in June 1538, and,
as he had no heirs, his Duchy, by an agreement made
with the Estates, fell to William, the young Duke of
Cleves. The young Duke accepted it, and prepared
to make good his possession against the Emperor,
who claimed it by another title. The elder Duke of
Cleves then died in February 1539, and the Duchy
of Gueldres was in the fair way of being united
with its three neighbours on the Rhine, the Duchies The Emperor's difficulties.
of Cleves, Juliers, and Berg, under one lord. This in
itself was serious enough ; but it was all the more so
as the young Duke's eldest sister, Sibylla, was married
to John Frederic, Duke of Saxony, and though the
young Duke of Cleves himself had not as yet thrown
in his lot with the Protestants, there was little doubt
that he could get important aid from them in a
struggle with the Emperor. The Protestants, moreover, as we have seen, were in league with Christian
III. of Denmark, whom the Emperor regarded as a
usurper, for he had succeeded his father, Frederic I.,
in derogation of the rights of Christian II., the
Emperor's brother-in-law, long ago deposed by the
Estates of Denmark for tyranny, but still alive and
maintained by Charles as the true and rightful king.

So here was an array of dukes and princes whose
countries included the whole course of the Lower
Rhine from the Zuyder Zee to Cologne, and from thence

stretched across Northern Germany to the confines of
Brandenburg, likely to be aided in a revolt, religious
or political, against the Emperor by the actual ruler
of Denmark.   They hardly required sympathy from
England to make themselves dangerous ; but the King
of England required sympathy to ward off dangers to
himself. And it was rather a mistake on Henry's part,
as it was his aim to encourage the Protestant princes
against the Emperor, that at first he, like Charles V.
himself, had declined to recognise the title of the new
King of Denmark, but had played a game of intrigue
in the north of Europe which turned out unsuccessful,
and which it is unnecessary to speak of here.   He
did his best, however, at this time to make amends
for his mistake to Christian III., for the success of
Pole's second legatine mission would have left him
without a friend upon the Continent.   And in very

Henry VIII. desperate.

truth, in the beginning of 1539, he seemed like a
desperate man.   The French ambassador, Castillon,
who was anxious to be recalled, seemed almost afraid
of personal violence at his hands, even though Henry's
own ambassador in France might serve as hostage for
him, for he wrote that he was the most dangerous and
cruel man in the world, and seemed to be in such a
fury that he had neither reason nor understanding left.[1]

It was in this desperate condition that he sent
Mont over once more to see what the German
Lutherans were about, and to ascertain how the two
Dukes of Cleves (for the father was then still alive)
stood affected towards the " Bishop of Rome "; also,
whether, if they were still " of the old popish
fashion," there was any chance of getting them to
change their opinions.   And it was at this time that
Cromwell, of course in concert with the King, gave
Mont his own private instructions suggesting the
match of the young Duke of Cleves with " the Lady
Mary." [2]   Not a word, as yet, had been breathed

[1] *L. P.*, XIV. i. 144 (p. 53).   [2] *L. P.*, XIV. i. 103 (1, 2).

about another and a still more important match; but
Mont also received instructions from Cromwell to An alliance
inquire diligently touching the beauty and other with Cleves suggested.
qualities of the elder of the two daughters of the
old Duke, and if he found that she was a person who
could be "likened unto his Majesty," he might tell
Burchart that Cromwell, for the sake of the alliance
with Germany, would be glad to persuade the King,
not only to marry the young Duke of Cleves to the
Lady Mary, but to marry his elder sister himself.
The King, indeed, had been angling for a wife elsewhere, merely to get one sure friend upon the
Continent. At one and the same time he had been
seeking the hand of the Emperor's niece, Christina,
Duchess of Milan, and that of Mary of Guise, or
any of her sisters that might be found convenient, in
France. But as no favourable answer had come from
Flanders or from France to any of these alternative
wooings, Cromwell believed the King was perfectly
free for a match with Anne of Cleves. Mont, however, was not to speak as if asking her in marriage,
but rather to instigate the Germans to make the
offer, and, if they thought well of it, to suggest the
expediency of sending her portrait to England.

It was in January 1539 that Mont was despatched
to Germany with these instructions. In the middle
of February he and a colleague named Thomas Paynell wrote to Cromwell that they had not been able
as yet to obtain any answer to the principal points of
their charge, except that the Duke of Saxony was
very well pleased with the proposed "affinities," and
would do his best to bring them to effect. Cromwell
replied to their letters on the 10th March, when he
had a piece of important news to communicate,
affecting the common interests of the King and
the German Protestants. The news, in fact, must
have been received in England by the 5th, on
which day Dr. Barnes was despatched with a very

special message to Christian III., the city of Wismar, and John Frederic of Saxony.[1] He was charged to tell them, as Mont and Paynell also were to tell those to whom they were sent, that when Wyatt in Spain demanded of the Emperor that Cardinal Pole, as an English rebel, should be refused entry into his dominions, the Emperor not only said that he could not refuse audience to one thus sent from the Holy Father, even if he were "his own traitor," but, when Wyatt pressed him with the treaties, replied indignantly that he was quite as free to give audience to an English rebel as Henry was to receive emissaries from the Duke of Saxony and the Landgrave, who were the Emperor's rebels, being his vassals, and enemies at the same time to "the Catholic Church of Christendom." Moreover, he knew that Henry had received "letters and orators from the Duke of Holtz" (that is, Christian III.), "usurpator of the kingdom of Denmark, by whose means his brother-in-law, King Christian, is kept tyrannically in prison."[2]

Nothing could have served better than this to make amends for past coolness on Henry's part in not at once recognising the title of Christian III. He had, indeed, done his best to atone for his error a year before; but now he had an opportunity of pointing out that they were both united in a common cause against the Emperor, because he was a danger to them both, and that it would be desirable to form a league against the Papists "for the preservation of the Christian religion." Christian responded in a like spirit, and hoped nothing would deter Henry from maintaining the true Church of God against the false Church of the Bishop of Rome.[3] So the King had secured one valuable friend at least on the Continent.

Henry wins over Christian III. of Denmark.

He also sent two skilful diplomatists, Sir Edward

---

[1] *L. P.*, XIV. i. 441-3.   [2] *L. P.*, XIV. i. 490 (p. 192), 955.
[3] *L. P.*, XIV. i. 956.

Carne and Dr. Nicholas Wotton, with a gentleman of his Privy Chamber, to the young Duke of Cleves (whose father was now dead) to say that he perceived the ill-will entertained towards him and the Evangelic princes by the Emperor at the Pope's instigation, and saw that he meant to use force to deprive him of the Duchy of Gueldres. They were to advise the Duke carefully to consider matters, and to assure him that the King was willing, for old friendship's sake, to make a league with him, offering him a suitable lady in marriage; or perhaps, if the King himself were free from any engagement in that matter, and if a lady suitable for him were found in the Duke's dominions, Henry might be led into considering an overture from him conveyed through ambassadors, with a portrait of the lady. If the Duke seemed well inclined, they might ask for a sight of his elder sister, and assure him that if he could offer reasonable conditions, and Henry was pleased with her, the King would be " glad to honor his house and family with matrimony with her," and make her a liberal dower. Moreover, if a reasonable reciprocity could be established, the King would not hesitate to make a defensive and offensive league with him. But meanwhile, as there were ugly, though not very probable, reports in Flanders of an invasion of England, which the Emperor might undertake at the instigation of " the Bishop of Rome," the King, though reasonably well provided against any sudden attack, would be grateful if the Duke could spare him 100 expert gunners to be kept for a time at the King's cost.[1]

In such wise was the foundation laid for the match with Anne of Cleves. Matrimonial projects and requests for artillerymen went together, for they had a common object; and the King was seeking both guns and gunners in Saxony at the

The match with Anne of Cleves.

[1] *L. P.*, XIV. i. 489.

same time.[1] Theology, moreover, played its part to
the same end,—a subject on which Henry VIII. grew
warm when he perceived that his German friends
were a little slow in responding to his weighty proposals. He employed Cromwell's pen once more in
writing to Mont and Paynell to stir up the Elector of
Saxony and the Landgrave. "For the point concerning the confederation," he wrote, "ye shall
declare unto them that the King's Highness, being
a prince that favoreth the preferment of the Word of
God above all other things in the world, perceiving
sundry practices to be devised and prepensed against
all princes that favored the Gospel, thinking indeed
that like as they have been the first that have in
those parts earnestly sticked unto it, and whom first
of all the cruelty of the enemies of the same would
invade and assay, afore any other, to oppress, sent
you thither to know their minds and intentions
whether they will stick to the same, as his Majesty
doubteth not they will do indeed." It was all out
of the King's ardent desire for their benefit. "For,
thanked be our Lord," the letter goes on, "ye may
affirm unto them, his Majesty feeleth his forces and
strength to be such that in so just a quarrel as the
maintenance of the Word of God is, his Grace trusteth
Christ himself will be so good a protector and shield
to him that he doubteth not but to defend his own,"
etc. We need quote no more of the lengthened-out
hypocrisy, which was all intended to persuade the
Germans that they were more concerned than the
King to enter into a league with him, though the
cause was a common one, as the Pope and his adherents
were most anxious for Henry's overthrow, fearing
that his example might lead other princes to abolish
papal authority in their realms.[2]

[1] L. P., XIV. i. 490 (p. 193).
[2] L. P., XIV. i. 580. For the full text, see Merriman's *Life and Letters of Thomas Cromwell*, ii. 202-206.

No cheering message, however, had yet arrived either from the German princes or from Denmark, when Mary of Hungary, Regent of the Netherlands, intimated to the English ambassadors there that the Emperor had desired her to send for Chapuys, his ambassador in England, who would be best able to advise him on the subject of their negotiations. Three English ambassadors had been at the Brussels Court all through the winter, pressing for the marriage with the Duchess of Milan and other means of strengthening the old alliance between England and the House of Austria. They had wasted a great deal of time, and the Regent Mary and her diplomatic councillors had done the same with them, both sides keeping up an appearance of friendly communication, out of which some substantial result was not altogether hopeless, though unofficial signs were numerous in Flanders that the King and people of England were regarded as heretics, and that it was expected both the Emperor and Francis I. would shortly issue proclamations against commercial intercourse with them.[1] Trade, indeed, had already suffered from an Imperial order published at Antwerp and elsewhere in those parts that no ships should leave the coasts till Easter without the Queen Regent's special licence;[2] and this, though a general order, told most heavily against the English. At such a moment the recall of the Imperial ambassador in England seemed ominous, though it was not accompanied with any intimation of a rupture; and still more unpleasant was the fact that almost at the same time the French ambassador, Castillon, had likewise received his recall—very much to his own satisfaction.[3] It looked almost like an arrangement between France and the Emperor for a simultaneous cessation of diplomatic relations with England.

England fears isolation.

[1] *L. P.*, XIV. i. 337, 418, 433.   [2] *L. P.*, XIV. i. 287.
[3] *L. P.*, XIV. i. 227.

The English ambassadors in Flanders were alarmed lest they should be made prisoners when there was no one in England to represent the Emperor. Henry and Cromwell were still more alarmed lest war should be declared against them, while they had as yet no assurance of support either from Denmark, Cleves, or the Lutherans. They could not forbid the return of either the French or the Imperial ambassador; they could only make remonstrances to each against France and against the Empire being left without a representative in England. And to Castillon, the French ambassador, before his departure, Cromwell, as an act of politic courtesy, thought it advisable to show his armoury, "which he seemed to esteem much," assuring him that there were more than twenty private armouries as well or better furnished within the Kingdom, belonging to lords and gentlemen who would be found ready to do the King service on any emergency. Castillon, as Cromwell wrote to the King, "wondered and said that he thought your Grace the prince best furnished thereof in Christendom"; but what further comments he made in his own mind Cromwell, of course, had no means of ascertaining.[1]

After a brief period of intense anxiety, the English ambassadors obtained leave to return from Flanders just when Chapuys reached Calais, where Majoris, Dean of Cambray, had already arrived on his way to England as Chapuys's successor. But there was an end of the long hypocrisy about forming a closer alliance, and Chapuys, while at Antwerp, put a stop to the secret exportation of arms and gunpowder to England, which had been going on for some time unchecked.[2] Active measures were taken for the defence of the Kingdom, which was believed to be in imminent danger of an invasion. Musters were taken everywhere, mariners were impressed, the coasts were forti-

Alarm of invasion.

---

[1] Merriman, ii. 177.   [2] *L. P.*, xiv. i. 535, 677, 741, 768.

fied, and beacons laid ready to be fired, though orders were given out to beware of false alarms, which would be very mischievous by the effect they would create abroad. Serious misgivings also prevailed for some days as to a great fleet about to sail from Holland. But the fleet proved to be friendly, and presently the King's anxieties were still more relieved by a further incident which he had hardly expected.[1]

Castillon had promised that another French ambassador would come in his place, but no one attached great value to a diplomatic promise. At the end of March, however, a new French ambassador, Marillac, actually did arrive in London, and his first interview with the King, which apparently was on the 31st, completely dispelled the fear of anything like an invasion. The King even ventured to ask if Francis had made any special declaration touching a match that he had suggested through Castillon with a view to an alliance against the Emperor. Marillac confessed that he had not, but said that Francis thanked him for his honourable offer. This answer Francis warmly approved, and urged Marillac to keep the King in good humour, merely telling him, if the subject were again raised, that while Francis was very grateful for his offer, he did not see how to accept it in the existing state of his relations with the Emperor. By the time Marillac had been a month in England a complete change had taken place. The Court, he said, seemed to wear a new aspect, and everybody to be quite delighted.[2]

So Marillac wrote on the 1st May. The King was now perfectly at ease, and had given him a two hours' interview, in which he showed that his satisfaction was further due to a belief that the Emperor would have enough on his hands that year in endeavouring to compose disputes in Germany. For,

A new French ambassador dispels fears.

---

[1] *L. P.*, XIV. i. 398, 400, 529, 540, 564, 573, 615, 652, 655, 682, 691.
[2] *L. P.*, XIV. i. 669, 804, 907-908.

A new
embassy
from the
Lutherans.
in fact, a new German mission had arrived in London a few days [1] before Marillac wrote, Burchart being again at the head of it, and having for his colleague Ludwig von Baumbach, a councillor of the Landgrave. The results, indeed, this time, were by no means satisfactory to the envoys themselves; but the news that they brought, and even the fact of their having come, gave the King perfect assurance that he had nothing now to fear from the Emperor. Henry accordingly received them kindly, and did his best in conversation to nourish their distrust of the Emperor, so that they were induced to believe, at first, that their mission was to be crowned with success. But both the King and Cromwell were slow in coming to business; they were very much occupied with the opening of Parliament, which began on the 28th April. And it by and by became manifest that the business of that Parliament was quite incompatible with the business which these Germans came to promote. For if Henry ever had a thought of even amusing them this time, as before, with the hope of a religious agreement, the news of what was done at the Diet at Frankfort must have completely changed his intention. That Diet had assembled in February, having been indicted by the Emperor, who, with a view to secure peace in Germany, had sent thither as his plenipotentiary, Vesalius, titular Archbishop of Lund in Scania, an old councillor of his brother-in-law, Christian II., the deposed King of Denmark. An agreement was not easily come to—both Catholics and Protestants were suspicious; and the Archbishop had 150,000 ducats sent him by the Emperor to keep an armed force ready at Augsburg in case it

A religious
truce in
Germany;
should be needed. But at last, on the 19th April, a truce was agreed upon for fifteen months, with a

[1] Only two days before, as Marillac thought, but in reality eight days before; for they certainly arrived on Wednesday, 23rd April (*L. P.*, XIV. i. 844, 879). See Seckendorff, iii. 225; and their own account in Merriman, i. 272.

view to a conference for a religious settlement; one
condition of the arrangement being that meanwhile
neither party should receive a new confederate into
its league.[1]

This provision was clearly intended to exclude
England. But even without it the pacification
itself would have made the Germans unserviceable
for Henry's purpose; and when he knew that it had
actually taken place, he made them feel that he considered further negotiation useless. In vain they
begged for a good sum of money to counteract papal
practices and tyranny. The King pointed out that
there was no appearance of reciprocity, and the
ambassadors saw that they must return empty-
handed. Indeed, the case was a good deal worse
than mere failure. For, while they still prolonged
their stay, the discussion on the Six Articles came
on in Parliament, and when the great questions of
the Sacrament and the marriage of priests were under
consideration, they felt that they could not but entreat His Majesty to have regard only to the truth in
such matters. This at once involved them in a
warm debate with the King himself on the subject
of clerical matrimony; and finding at last that their
continued presence in England was useless, they took
leave and departed on the last day of May.[2]

For Henry's policy now was altogether different *which*
from what it had been. Secure of the friendship of *changes the King's*
France, he knew well enough that the Emperor could *policy in*
not afford to quarrel with him, especially if given *England.*
some plausible excuse for not leading that crusade
against him which the Pope desired. The faith itself,
the Emperor might now say, was in no danger under
Henry's rule; the King and the Kingdom, although
they rejected papal authority, were still perfectly

---

[1] Sleidan, Book xii.; Seckendorff, iii. 200-204; *L. P.*, xiv. i. 550, 767, 768, 786.
[2] *L. P.*, xiv. i. 1091-92; Merriman, i. 274-7.

orthodox. And it was not far from the truth; for England was by no means in the same state as Germany. Lutheran views were not in favour among the English people, and, severe as the Act of the Six Articles was, it was by no means unpopular at its enactment. "The people," wrote Marillac, "show great joy at the King's declaration touching the Sacrament, being much more inclined to the old religion than to the new opinions, which are maintained only by some bishops who are little content at the refusal of their request to marry, in order afterwards to convert the property of the Church into patrimony and succession."

It is true, indeed, that the Act was one of singular severity; but severity commended itself to public feeling, which found it difficult, if not impossible, to disconnect heresy from irreverence, and both the one and the other had of late years been far too prominent. That this was to be remedied now was the general belief, even before the first steps had been taken. "This Parliament," wrote John Husee from London to Lord Lisle, "there shall be a thorough unity and uniformity established for the reformation of the Church of this realm." [1] Quite a different "reformation of the Church" from that to which the Germans were looking! But it was, in its origin, a lay movement, not a clerical one. On the 5th, after a speech from the Lord Chancellor, declaring that the King desired above all things the extirpation of diversities of opinion in religion, the Lords appointed a committee consisting of Cromwell as the King's vicegerent, the two archbishops, and six bishops, to take the matter in hand. [2] But, as the bishops appointed were half of the new school and half of the old—for, ever since the establishment of Royal Supremacy, the persons appointed to bishoprics had been all of "the New Learning,"—there was no appearance that they would ever come to agreement. Seeing this, on the 16th the Duke of Norfolk proposed to the Lords Six Articles for their consideration, and suggested that when they had fully discussed them they should pass a penal act to enforce them.[1] Thus the theology of the Church became a matter for the whole House, and not for the bishops alone to consider; and it very soon appeared that, with the exception of the newly made bishops, the whole House intended to stand upon the ancient ways. With these exalted divines, however, the controversy was acute. "There is great hold among the bishops," wrote Husee on the 21st, "for the establishment of the blessed Sacrament of the Altar. The Lords have sitten daily in Council upon the same, and the King's Highness hath been with them sundry times in person." The King's appearance in the House naturally had important results, and some unknown lord writes as follows :— *The Six Articles in Parliament.*

> And also news here. I assure you, never prince showed himself so wise a man, so well learned and so Catholic as the King hath done in this Parliament. With my pen I cannot express his marvellous goodness; which is come to such effect that we shall have an Act of Parliament so spiritual that I think none shall dare say, in the blessed Sacrament of the Altar doth remain either bread or wine after the consecration; nor that a priest may have a wife; nor that it is necessary to receive our Maker *sub utrâque specie*; nor that private masses should not be used as they have been; nor that it is not necessary to have auricular confession. And, notwithstanding my lord of Canterbury, my lord of Ely, my lord of Salisbury, my lords of Worcester, Rochester and St. David's defended the contrary long time, yet finally his Highness confounded them all with God's learning. York, Durham, Winchester, London, Chichester, Norwich, and Carlisle have shown themselves honest and well learned men. We of the temporalty have been all of one opinion, and my lord Chancellor and my lord Privy Seal as good as we can devise. My lord of Canterbury and all these bishops

---

[1] Lord's *Journals*, i. 109.

have given their opinion and came in to us, save Salisbury, who yet continueth a lewd fool. Finally, all England have cause to thank God, and most heartily to rejoice of the King's most godly proceedings.[1]

This account of the matter is noteworthy, for, whatever we think of the writer's style and sentiments, we may take it as more accurate with regard to positive facts than some narratives of later date, which have been too generally accepted. It was natural, of course, to endeavour to make a hero of Cranmer, whose admiring secretary and biographer, Morice, mixing up the story of his conduct in this Parliament with his conduct a little later, has led Foxe and subsequent historians to regard the Archbishop as the one persistent opponent of the Act, "standing, as it were, post alone against the whole parliament, disputing and replying three days together against the said Articles."[2] Cranmer, un-

---

[1] Burnet, vi. 233.

[2] *Acts and Monuments*, viii. 23. Compare Nichols's *Narratives of the Reformation*, p. 248, as to this expression "post alone." In another part of his work (*Acts and Monuments*, v. 264-5) Foxe says that "every man seeing the King's mind so fully addicted, upon politic respects, to have these articles pass forward, few or none in all that parliament would appear, who either could perceive what was to be defended or durst defend what they understood to be true, save only Cranmer, Archbishop of Canterbury, who then, being married (as is supposed), like a constant patron of God's cause, took upon him the earnest defence of the truth oppressed in the parliament; three days together disputing against those six wicked articles; bringing forth such allegations and authorities as might easily have helped the cause, *nisi pars major vicisset, ut sæpe solet, meliorem*; who in the said disputation behaved himself with such humble modesty, and with such obedience in words towards his prince, protesting the cause not to be his but the cause of Almighty God, that neither his enterprise was misliked of the King; and again, his reasons and allegations were so strong that they could not well be refuted. Wherefore the King (who ever bare special favor unto him), well liking his zealous defence, only willed him to depart out of the parliament house into the Council Chamber for a time (for safeguard of his conscience), till the Act should pass and be granted; which he, notwithstanding, refused to do." It is added, that after the Parliament was ended, the King sent Cromwell and the Dukes of Norfolk and Suffolk to dine with the Archbishop at Lambeth to assure him that the King highly appreciated his conduct in that Parliament as that of a wise and learned man, and to beg him not to be discouraged by what had passed in opposition to his arguments.

There is no doubt that the King "bare special favor" to Cranmer, and did not mind the opposition of one who, whatever he said, took care to be so "obedient to his prince."

doubtedly, as a married prelate, had very strong personal reasons for opposing the Act as far as he possibly could. Yet it is evident that he was only one of six bishops who opposed it, and that he, like most of the others, at length gave in to the general opinion, Bishop Shaxton of Salisbury being the most obstinate in his resistance after the others had yielded. Cranmer saw that he must bend to the times. It was not unknown that he had a wife or mistress, in whatever light men might regard her, and his case, unhappily, was not singular in this respect (for it was well enough known, and had been for generations past, that many of the clergy, even prominent men like Wolsey, had female companions by whom they also had children), except that he would fain have called her his wife had he been allowed to do so openly. But this was a laymen's Act of Parliament, and laymen did not mind laying heavy burdens on the clergy, especially when they were justified by the canon law.

The effect of the Act was precisely what the anonymous lord wrote. The preamble declares that *Effect of the statute.* the articles had been submitted to the clergy, and that the King had vouchsafed to come in person into the Parliament, and had " declared many things of high learning and great knowledge touching the said articles "; and that after long debate it was finally determined (1) that the natural body and blood of Christ were in the Sacrament under the forms of bread and wine, and that after consecration no substance of bread and wine remained ; (2) that communion in both kinds was unnecessary ; (3) that priests could not marry by the law of God ; (4) that vows of chastity or widowhood ought to be kept ; (5) that private masses ought to be continued ; and (6) that auricular confession was expedient and ought to be retained. Any persons maintaining opinions against the first article were to be deemed heretics and suffer death by burning without any abjuration, benefit of clergy or sanctuary, with confiscation of all their lands and property. As to the other five articles, any one maintaining opinions against them was to be adjudged a felon and suffer death as such; the same penalty being incurred by any man or woman who, having vowed chastity or widowhood after the 12th July, should actually marry or contract matrimony. All past marriages of such persons, moreover, were declared void; and priests keeping women with whom they had contracted matrimony were declared felons.[1] Here, of course, was the extreme danger of the Act for men like Cranmer, and it is not to be wondered at that he was driven to an artifice such as no priest had ever been compelled to resort to in past times.[2] A proclamation even more rigorous than the Act was issued at the close of the session. Any churchman found to be on too intimate terms with a married woman was to be punished with death; and one so offending with an unmarried woman was for the first offence to lose his goods, both temporal and spiritual; for the second, to forfeit his life.[3]

The extreme severity of the Act was naturally

---

[1] Stat. 31 Hen. VIII. c. 14.

[2] The story of Archbishop Cranmer carrying about in a chest the wife whom he durst not show openly, was supposed at one time to rest only on the authority of Sanders, who was regarded as a malicious libeller. But other much questioned statements of Sanders have lately been proved to rest on conclusive evidence; and this anecdote is vouched for by the earlier testimony of Harpsfield (*Pretended Divorce*, p. 275), derived from a gentleman who was present when the chest had to be conveyed out of danger from a fire at the Archiepiscopal palace at Canterbury (an occurrence which took place in 1543). Parsons also mentions (*Three Conversions*, ii. 371) as a thing testified by Cranmer's son's widow, then alive, that on one occasion when, going to Canterbury, he carried his wife in the chest down the river, the shipmen, who were told to take great care of it as containing my Lord's treasure, after landing it at Gravesend, set it up endlong in the Archbishop's chamber with the head downwards, so that the woman was compelled to cry out for fear of having her neck broken. See footnotes in Lewis' translation of Sander's *Anglican Schism*, p. 181.

[3] *L. P.*, XIV. i. 1207. There was a clause in the Act about priests' concubines in addition to the clauses above mentioned; but the proclamation was still more severe.

resented deeply by all those who sympathised with Lollardy or the New Learning. The name Lollardy, indeed, was by this time almost disused and the expression " the New Learning " had generally taken its place, as putting a better face on the same kind of heresy ; for the New Learning had already received much underhand encouragement from the King in order to checkmate the influence of the clergy, and its votaries were naturally disappointed at an Act being passed so directly against the sort of teaching which they had been zealously promoting. The Act and its operation are accordingly thus described in the work called Hall's *Chronicle* :—

This Act established chiefly six articles ; whereof among the common people it was called the Act of Six Articles, and of some it was named the Whip with six strings, and of some other, and that of the most part, it was named the Bloody Statute; for of truth it so in short time after scourged a great number in the city of London, where the first quest for the inquiry of the offenders of the said Statute sat at a church called Becket's house, now named the Mercers' chapel, that the said quest, being of purpose selected and picked out among all the rest of the inhabitants of the said city, that none thereof might be admitted which either had read any part of the Holy Scripture in English, or in any wise favored such as either had read it or loved the preachers of it: insomuch as this quest was so zealous and fervent in the execution of this Statute, that they among themselves thought it not only sufficient to inquire of the offenders of the said Statute, but also by their fine wits and willing minds, they invented to inquire of certain branches of the same Statute, as they termed it, which was, not only to inquire who spake against masses, but who they were that seldom came unto them ; and also not only who denied the Sacrament to be Christ's very natural body, but also who held not up their hands at sacring time and knocked not on their breasts. And they not only inquired who offended in the Six Articles but also who came seldom to the church, who took no holy bread nor holy water, who read the bible in the church, or in communication contemned priests or images in the churches etc., with a great number of

Account of it in Hall's *Chronicle*.

such branches. This appointed quest so sped themselves with the Six Articles and their own branches that in fourteen days' space there was not a preacher nor other person in the city of name, which had spoken against the supremacy of the Bishop of Rome but he was wrapped in the Six Articles; insomuch as they indicted and presented of suspicion to the number of five hundred persons and above. So that, if the King's Majesty had not granted his pardon, for that by the good Lord Awdeley, Lord Chancellor, his Grace was truly informed that they were indicted of malice, a great many of them which already was in prison had been shortly after scourged in Smithfield with fiery faggots that would have made the best blood in their bodies to have sprung. But most graciously at that time his Grace remitted all; although in the time that these Six Articles endured, which was eight years and more, they brought many an honest and simple person to their deaths; for such was the rigour of that law that if two witnesses, false or true, had accused any and avouched that they had spoken against the Sacrament, there was then no way but death; for it booted not to confess that his faith was contrary, or that he said not as the accusers reported. For they would believe the witnesses; yea, and sometimes, certain of the clergy, when they had no witnesses, would procure some, or else they were slandered.[1]

This is a long extract, but the passage is extremely important, first, because it is the source, not only of much valuable information, but also of a large amount of popular misapprehension concerning the operation of this celebrated Act—misapprehension which has coloured the accounts of Church historians to the present day, notwithstanding what was done long ago by Dr. Maitland, the learned Lambeth librarian, to put the matter in a true light. One thing, however, is evident at the outset. We have here the testimony of a well-informed writer, who writes in perfect security when the days of persecution are over, more than eight years after the passing of the statute, in a spirit of fiery indignation which leads him into long and involved sentences and occasion-

[1] Hall's *Chronicle*, p. 828.

ACT OF THE SIX ARTICLES

ally gets the better of his grammar, whatever may
have been the case with his love of truth. Moreover, without going further than the extract, there
is a strong appearance of bias, especially in the
last words, which seek to fasten upon the clergy,
with the feeble saving clause, "or else they were
slandered," a charge of procuring false witnesses by
subornation of perjury. And there is further an
insinuation that not only was the law itself severe,
but the tribunals which administered it were unjust,
accepting false testimony in the face of honest contradiction, while the first quest strained the law
far beyond its legitimate requirements, and indicted
almost everybody who had been so loyal to the King
as to speak bravely against the authority of "the
Bishop of Rome."

It is right to say that Edward Hall could hardly
have been the author of this passage, for he died in
1547, and it was not till Christmas Eve in that year
that the Act of the Six Articles was repealed.[1] So
that it would seem the statement that the Act
endured "eight years and more" must have been
supplied by the editor, Richard Grafton, when he
printed the work from Hall's MS. in 1548. Indeed,
Grafton himself says, in his preliminary advertise-
ment "To the Reader," that Hall only completed his
work as far as the twenty-fourth year of Henry
VIII., i.e. 1532-1533, leaving after that date a
number of separate papers, which Grafton did his best
to unite and put in order. He adds, however, that
he did this without making any addition of his own
to what Hall wrote—a statement which, evidently,
we must not take too literally, when we find a clause
that must have been written after the author's death.
That clause, at least, if nothing more, must have been
an insertion. But I am afraid Grafton's statement
that he added nothing to what the author had written

Not really Hall's own account.

[1] See Lord's *Journals.*

cannot even generally be relied on. For Hall, however bigoted against the clergy, could hardly have been in his day a reviler of the Six Articles, seeing that he was one of the citizens of London named in 1541 in the commission to carry out the Act, and further that he was one of the witnesses to the confession of Anne Askew, which she made before Bishop Bonner in March 1545.[1] Hall, indeed, however willing to depreciate Church authority at any time, was never the man to depreciate the authority of the law ; and from anything we know of Grafton we may very well suspect that his statement is only an illustration of what Sir Thomas More tells us, that he never found heretics scrupulous about speaking the truth. Grafton, moreover, was the King's printer when the book was issued in the days of Protector Somerset; and, of course, he printed nothing but what was agreeable to the existing Government. Now, under Protector Somerset, there was a very great change in Church policy, and everything that was prohibited and made penal by the Six Articles was expressly sanctioned by Convocation and Parliament ; so that it was just the time to denounce, in the strongest terms, a measure which it would have been dangerous to speak ill of a year before its repeal. Such denunciations, in fact, were positively required, and no doubt were made, on behalf of the Government, to justify what to many minds constituted a serious breach of ancient order. Still, of course, if the Act had all along been felt to be oppressive, the sense of relief at the end of eight years must have been intense, and even a few exaggerations of its past severity might not have been at all unnatural.

Here, however, to go no further than the above extract, we find that the first effects of the Act were little more than a scare. A quest sat at the Mercers' Chapel, the inquisitors being selected from those who

---

[1] See Foxe, v. 440, 543. App. ix.

were not guilty of reading the Bible in English, or
favouring those who did read it ; and the gentlemen
of this quest were so zealous that they went beyond
the statute itself, and inquired into what they called
its " branches." The inquiry, it should be observed,
was entrusted by the Act to commissioners to be
named by the Crown, in every county, who should sit
four times a year. They presented not only those
who spoke against masses but those who seldom came
to them ; not only those who denied Transubstantiation, but those who did not hold up their hands at
sacring time or knock upon their breasts. Nay, they
not only inquired who offended in the Six Articles,
but who came seldom to church, who avoided taking
holy bread and holy water, who read the Bible in
church (some, we know well, read it noisily and
created a disturbance), or in their conversation with
others spoke contemptuously of priests and images.
These subjects the gentlemen of the quest, it seems,
considered " branches " of the Act ; they were anxious,
in fact, that there should be no evasion of the law,
and they possibly went beyond the letter or scope
of the law in their presentments. Still, if they did,
it was at the worst an error of judgment. They
were not judges, but only acted the part of a grand
jury to draw up indictments. And if in a single
fortnight they presented no less than five hundred
citizens of London, we can only conclude that sayings and practices which were still considered
grossly irreverent, had of late years become so
exceedingly common that very numerous prosecutions seemed necessary. But, of course, it was
another thing to carry them out when the evil
had gone so far, and the " good " Lord Chancellor
Audeley (whose character does not stand high in
other things) procured from the King a general
pardon.

So this " Bloody Statute," which, after all, was

not of clerical but of lay manufacture,[1] produced at the first nothing whatever but a scare, and some brief imprisonments. We have already seen from the unbiassed testimony of Marillac, the French ambassador, that the Act was really popular. People did not love the unrestrained licence and offensive bigotry of the men of the New Learning, and were glad to impose some check upon them. From Marillac, too, as a very competent observer, we may learn the real object of the Act, which he explains in a letter to the Constable Montmorency, at the French Court, written on the 13th July. By that time it would seem there was so much change in the international situation, that instead of misgivings being entertained in England as to the attitude of Francis and the Emperor, there were now some misgivings entertained by the Government in France, as to whether England was not thinking of employing the levies so recently raised in her own defence, in an invasion of their country. These rumours, which only arose out of old national prejudice among the ignorant and ill-informed, Marillac was most anxious to assure the Constable were baseless ; and thus he writes :—

The Act really popular.

As to the talk which you have been told this King has set forth in his Parliament of making war on France on pretext of the pension which has not been paid him, be assured, Monseigneur, that this article was never proposed in such terms, as on my honor and life I can affirm, unless it was in secret in the Privy Council of this King ; and it is not likely that such a thing should have been resolved and concluded without some indication being had of it, as there has been of all that has been concluded. And, certainly, Monseigneur, the principal matter put forward by this King was to complain of the Pope, who endeavoured to recall his friends the Emperor and the King (Francis) from alliance with him

---

[1] An anonymous remonstrance against the proposed legislation, which is preserved in the Cottonian MSS. (Cleop. E v. 50 ; see *L. P.*, XIV. i. 971), appears to have originated in Convocation, not in Parliament.

and get them to make war upon him on the pretext that they were all heretics and infidels here ; to show the contrary of which he desired that the opinions which one ought to hold in religion should be determined, in order that every one should know what to hold by, and that Christian princes might perceive that what the Holy Father put forth against him was untrue.[1]

This contemporary diplomatist understood thoroughly the real aim of the Act.   Henry was not really half so much bent on putting down heretical opinions as the title of the Act would suggest ; but sacramental heresies he had always opposed, and at this time he was very much concerned to make it appear to all the world that he was dead against them.   He must have been perfectly aware, however, of the fact referred to in the above passage in Hall's *Chronicle*, that his most outspoken champions among the clergy against papal authority were the men most liable to indictment ; and he had no more notion now than ever of allowing papal authority again.   On the 20th June, Marillac writes to the Constable :— *The King as much against the Pope as ever.*

"The day before yesterday there was acted here upon the river in their King's presence a game of poor grace and much less invention, of two galleys, one of which bore the arms of this King, the other those of the Pope with several Cardinals' hats, as I am told, for I should have considered it against my duty to be there as a spectator.   They made the galleys fight together for a long time, and in the end those of this King were victorious, and the Pope and Cardinals, with their arms, were all thrown in the water, to show by this spectacle to the people that the forces of this King are destined entirely to confound and abolish the power and name of the Holy Father and his adherents." [2] *A poor farce.*

A courtier's account of the same performance is given in Wriothesley's *Chronicle* as follows :—

[1] Kaulek, pp. 114, 115.   [2] Kaulek, p. 105.

"This year the 17th day of June was a triumph on the Thames before the King's palace at Westminster, where were two barges prepared with ordnance of war, as guns and darts of reed, one for the Bishop of Rome and his Cardinals, and the other for the King's Grace, and so rowed up and down the Thames from Westminster Bridge to the King's Bridge;[1] and the Pope [and his Cardinals] made their defiance against England and shot their ordnance one at another, and so had three courses up and down the water. And at the fourth course they joined together and fought sore; but at last the Pope and his Cardinals were overcome and all his men cast over the board into the Thames. Howbeit, there was none drowned, for they were persons chosen who could swim, and the King's barge lay by hovering to take them up as they were cast over the board. Which was a goodly pastime, the King's Grace with his lords and certain ladies standing on the leads over his privy stairs, which was covered with canvas and set with green boughs and roses properly made, so that rose water sprinkled down from them into the Thames upon ladies and gentlewomen which were in barges and boats under to see the pastime. And also two other barges rowed up and down with banners and pennons of the arms of England and St. George, wherein were the sackbuts and waits, which played on the water. And so finished."[2]

This was just after the bill of the Six Articles had passed the House of Lords, and had been sent down to the Commons. When it became law two bishops resigned their sees, Latimer of Worcester and Shaxton of Salisbury. The latter, as we have seen, was

---

[1] The King's Bridge was situated at the eastern end of the new Palace of Westminster, on the river bank, some short distance from Old Palace Stairs, and was so called in contradistinction to the Queen's Bridge or Stairs, situated at the western end of the Palace of Whitehall. Westminster Bridge, mentioned in our text, was another of these river stages, of which there were several on the northern bank of the Thames.—*Editorial Note in Wriothesley.*

[2] Wriothesley's *Chronicle*, i. 99, 100.

the most persistent opponent of the passing of the
bill, even Latimer's opposition, probably, being not
so marked, as the anonymous lord speaks of all the
others having given in except Salisbury. And
Shaxton, most likely, had a personal reason for his
opposition which Latimer had not; for, unless he
married at a later date, he had a wife or mistress
at this time, but Latimer had kept his vow of
chastity. All bishops, however, would be called
on to administer the Act after it became law;
and both Latimer and Shaxton preferred to give
up their bishoprics. They were now in some danger,
and Latimer made his escape to Gravesend, but was
arrested, either there or at Rochester, and brought
back.[1] They were, however, pensioned,[2] and remained
for some years in obscurity, at first in the custody of
two other bishops.

When the news reached Germany of the passing
of the Act, it filled the Reformers there with dismay. Dismay
Melancthon wrote a long and earnest expostulation of the
to Henry,[3] attributing the enactment to the procure- Protestants
ment of the bishops, and grieving to think that the at the Act.
King had been abused by their sophistries, just as
Darius had been induced by his satraps to cast
Daniel to the lions. Of course the remonstrance
had little or no effect; but it was not unheeded, for
Grafton afterwards got into trouble for printing it.[4]

How entirely mistaken Melancthon's idea was
that the bishops were the originators of the Act
we have seen already. It was rather passed by the
laity to correct disorders arising from the fact that
episcopal authority had for some years been paralysed
by Royal Supremacy. Until the bishops' hands were
tied no such Act would have been necessary. Till
then, cases of heresy, sacramental or other, were dealt

---

[1] *L. P.*, XIV. i. 1217, 1219, 1227-28.
[2] *L. P.*, XIV. ii. 236, p. 73.
[3] *L. P.*, XIV. ii. 444. The full text, translated into English, will be found
in Foxe, v. 350.   [4] *L. P.*, XVI. 422, 424.

with simply as they arose, without any general sessions to present offenders, and the prosecutions were comparatively few. Now the numbers presented were simply unmanageable if there had been any design to prosecute in every case. But how

Small effect produced by it.

little the Act was in some cases effectual, even as a scare, we learn from the curious instance of John Harridaunce, the inspired bricklayer of Whitechapel, who, within a week or two after it passed, preached out of his window to an audience collected in the street to hear him between nine and twelve o'clock at night. He also at times preached at the back of his garden, and said in reference to the two bishops who had resigned : " No marvel if the world doth persecute holy men and setters forth of light : for Christ said ' They shall come after Me, which shall persecute the tellers of truth.' " This was pretty bold ; but when a neighbour, a baker apparently, once warned him that he was breaking the commandments of the Council, he answered, " It is as fit for me to be burnt as for thee to bake a loaf." Altogether, Harridaunce confessed, on examination, that he had preached about twenty times in this way, between midsummer and the 13th August.[1]

John Harri- daunce.

This John Harridaunce, whose surname was sometimes ignorantly split in two, and who was called Harry Daunce or Henry Daunce, even by friends who knew him, had been imprisoned two years before for the very same offence. He disturbed the neighbourhood by his preaching, and had done so all the more to spite his parson, who, he said, denounced him as a heretic from the pulpit. When examined on that occasion by the Lord Mayor as to how he had learned to preach, he said that for thirty years he had been seeking to learn Scripture, but could not read or write ; nevertheless, he kept a New Testament always about him. He would begin his sermon, it appears,

[1] *L. P.*, xiv. ii. 42 (1, 2).

"In nomine Patris et *Filius* et Spiritus *Sanctus.* Amen."[1] His imprisonment in 1537 had not in the least deterred him from repeating his performances in 1539. And though a fanatical and illiterate bricklayer might seem hardly worthy of the historian's notice, even when the history of religion is his subject, it would really be a mistake to pass him by as altogether insignificant. For the business of a bricklayer, illiterate though he might be, lent itself readily to the aid of men of the New Learning, in a way that might not at once occur to us. When heretics held secret meetings to read dangerous books at midnight, they would naturally take care to have made "a very secret place to keep them safe in."[2] And this was precisely the service that a sympathetic bricklayer could do them.

Thus in Queen Mary's time, Edward Underhill, "the hot gospeller," tells us what he did when the persecution began :—

Wherefore I got old Henry Daunce, the bricklayer of Whitechapel, who used to preach the gospel in his garden every holyday, where I have seen a thousand people, he did enclose my books in a brick wall by the chimney's side in my chamber, where they were preserved from moulding or mice until the first year of our most gracious Queen Elizabeth, etc., notwithstanding that I removed from thence and went unto Coventry.[3]

Harridaunce, therefore, escaped serious molestation notwithstanding his notoriety and the crowds he sometimes collected, not only during the whole period when the Act of the Six Articles was the law of the land, but even in the trying time of Queen Mary, at least till the persecution began, of which he does not seem to have been a victim. In 1539 the parson

---

[1] *L. P.*, x. 594, 624.
[2] See Dalaber's account of Garret's escape in Foxe, v. 422. Many books were found at that time hid under the earth. *L. P.*, iv. 4004.
[3] Nichols's *Narratives of the Reformation*, p. 171.

of Whitechapel would have taken counsel about him with Bishop Stokesley, but the bishop was on his deathbed.[1] He was, nevertheless, compelled to abjure heresy, no doubt by Bishop Bonner, even in Henry VIII.'s day ;[2] and, like a great many others, did his best for the cause of heresy, even after abjuration.

The Act of the Six Articles, while it was law, was undoubtedly pressed in one or two instances with extreme severity. But it may be said with tolerable confidence that, even in the year when it was enacted, there was not half so much persecution of new religion as there was of old. There was, indeed, a brief pause, just about the time that the Act was passed, in the process of taking forced surrenders of monasteries, which had been going on for more than a year. Only two surrenders seem to have been taken in April, and none at all in May or June. This may have been due to the acute fear of invasion which afterwards passed away. But in July the work began again, a leading agent now being Dr. London, warden of New College, Oxford, whose main qualification for the business seems to have been complete subservience to authority. He had been an eager heresy hunter in 1528 when Garret escaped from Oxford (an incident well known to readers of Foxe), and, as we shall see, he was an eager heresy hunter at a later date. But at present his business was to suppress monasteries, and he had begun in 1538—the year before that which we have reached—by dissolving the Friars' houses at Oxford, and then visiting with a body of followers the neighbouring nunnery of Godstow, with a commission, as he said, to suppress it. The Abbess, though promoted by Cromwell himself, did not like his ways and refused to surrender the house to him, as he was an old enemy of hers ; on which he not

Surrenders of monasteries taken by Dr. London.

---

[1] *L. P.*, XIV. ii. 42.

[2] His name occurs in a list given by Foxe (iv. 585) of "such as were forced to abjure in King Henry's days."

only used threats, but tried to inveigle her and her sisters one by one in a way she had never heard of. Cromwell was obliged to listen to her complaint, and Dr. London was ordered to withdraw.[1] Yet, when the work of suppressing monasteries began again, after the pause, in July 1539, not only did Dr. London take the lead, but nunneries seem to have been committed to him as a principal charge; for in Lincolnshire, the Midlands, Bedfordshire, and Buckinghamshire he took surrenders of eleven houses, seven of which were nunneries. Indelicacy, it would seem, was no disqualification for such business.

Monasteries in general were going down. Evidently they were all to be got rid of. In the summer it seems to have been suspected that the abbots of three great houses were encouraging each other by secret messages not to surrender. Needless to recount in detail what took place with regard to them. We may learn it from Cromwell's memoranda written beforehand :—

"The Abbot [of] Reading to be sent down *to be tried and executed* at Reading with his complices.

"Item, the Abbot of Glaston *to be tried at Glaston, and also executed there* with his complices."

And so Richard Whiting, Abbot of Glastonbury, was hanged with two of his monks on Tor Hill in the immediate neighbourhood of his own monastery, while Hugh Cook, Abbot of Reading, suffered the like fate at the gate of his, with two priests of Reading. The third abbot was Thomas Beach or Marshall, Abbot of Colchester, whose execution took place, apparently at Colchester,[2] a very little later. Of course there was not much refusal to surrender after that, and in the spring of 1540 there were no more monasteries in England.

Three abbots hanged.

We must do justice, however, even to Henry VIII. An Act was passed in Parliament in the same session

---

[1] *L. P.*, XIII. ii. 758, 911.   [2] *L. P.*, XIV. ii. App. 45.

as that of the Six Articles, empowering the King
to make new bishoprics by letters patent out of the
confiscated property of the monasteries, and a draft
scheme of new bishoprics, with alteration of the staffs
of old ones, remains to this day among the records of
the realm. The cathedral of Christchurch, Canterbury, was to be altered, the monks being replaced by
a provost and twelve prebendaries, with six preachers
and various readers and students. Rochester was
to undergo similar changes. A new see of Westminster was to be created, and one at Waltham for
Essex. Winchester and Worcester were to have
secular chapters. Gloucester, St. Albans, Oxford,
and Peterborough were to become bishoprics. The
monks of Ely were to give place to a college with
a provost, ten prebendaries, a reader and ten
students of divinity, forty scholars in Greek and
Latin, and a fixed staff of canons, choristers, and
the like. Burton-upon-Trent was to be a college
likewise, and so was Chester. Shrewsbury was to
have a bishop, six prebendaries, a reader of divinity,
six divinity students (three to be found at Oxford
and three at Cambridge), a schoolmaster and thirty
scholars, an usher, eight petty canons, and so forth.
Carlisle and Durham were to become colleges.[1] These
projects in a few years were somewhat modified. In
the end six new bishoprics were created, and they
all exist to this day except Westminster, which
endured only for about ten years, and was abolished
by Edward VI.

Thus Henry's good intentions in this matter
took their time, and were only partly fulfilled after
all. His real objects in passing the Act of the Six
Articles were accomplished at once. It was popular.
It served the Emperor as a pretext for not treating
the King of England as an enemy to Christianity.

---

[1] Henry VIII.'s *Scheme of the Bishoprics*, privately printed by Henry Cole
in 1838 ; *L. P.*, xiv. ii. 429.

Politically, its only drawback was that it offended his German friends whom he was so anxious to cultivate in order to keep the Emperor in check.   But the worst that even Melancthon had heard of its effects when he wrote to Henry on the 1st November to remonstrate against it, was that Latimer, Shaxton, Crome, and others, doubtless of excellent learning, whose names he had not heard, had been committed to custody.[1] Still, his disappointment was serious seeing that, in the spring of that same year, he had been expressing ardent hopes that the King would come to an agreement with himself and Luther in doctrine, and complete the work of reformation by throwing off the superstitious rites and beliefs of Rome, as he had already done her jurisdiction.[2]   And Dr. Barnes, who had been busy on the Continent trying to promote a league between England and the German Protestants—what became of him now?   He returned home soon after the passing of the Act, and the King refused to see him—or else he had not the courage to seek an audience.[3]

Barnes out of favour.

He had been Henry's agent, at least, in establishing a friendly understanding with Christian III. of Denmark.   But the King was shut out of the Protestant ' League by the terms of the truce of Frankfort; and even the bright prospects held out to the Duke of Cleves failed for a time to meet with the response that might have been expected.   For though the Duke was not himself an avowed Protestant, his eldest sister Sibylla was married to John Frederic, Elector of Saxony, who had a contingent reversion in Cleves and required to be consulted as to the marriage of any of his wife's sisters, which he was bound, by his own marriage settlement, to assist.[4] But after the Frankfort truce, when the Duke of Cleves wanted his advice, the Elector took himself

[1] L. P., xiv. ii. 444.   [2] L. P., xiv. i. 613, 666, 737.
[3] L. P., xiv. ii. 400, pp. 139, 140.   [4] L. P., xiv. ii. 220.

out of the way. He had, no doubt, other reasons, and weighty ones, for repairing to his own country, especially the death of his cousin, Duke George of Saxony (of the Albertine branch), which materially strengthened the Protestant interest in Germany;[1] but it may also be surmised that he was not anxious at that time to promote a match of somewhat doubtful bearings on German tranquillity. A few months later, however, the Pope urged the Emperor not to confirm but to annul the Frankfort truce, as it was intended to pave the way for a religious settlement apart from him;[2] and it was soon apparent that England and the Protestants, however little the latter believed in Henry's religious sincerity, might have as much need of each other's help as ever. For Charles V. was in Spain, most anxious to reach the Low Countries to quell a dangerous outbreak at Ghent, of which Francis I. had not only refused to take advantage, but had even given the Emperor notice, and had invited him to pass through France in order to subdue it. This invitation he gladly accepted, and the French and Imperial ambassadors in England went together to the King to inform him of the proposed Imperial journey.[3]

Observers were astonished and at first incredulous. The two rivals seemed completely to have forgotten old grudges, the Emperor trusting himself unreservedly to the loyalty and good faith of Francis in passing through his country, while Paris was making great preparations to receive the Imperial guest with all possible honour. Not only had Ghent good reason to fear his resentment as soon as he should reach the Low Countries, but the Duke of Cleves might well expect to be driven from his new acquisition of Gueldres, and Henry VIII. might have to face even yet a combination of the Emperor and

Unwonted friendship of Francis I. and Charles V.

---

[1] *L. P.*, xiv. i. 920. [2] *L. P.*, xiv. ii. 69 (2).
[3] *L. P.*, xiv. ii. 508.

Francis to execute the papal sentence against him and turn him out of his kingdom. Henry, however, was not at all dismayed. The tempting bait held before Cleves was working. Even on the 29th July the Elector of Saxony had written to the Duke promising to send him some of his Council expressly for the King's matter;[1] and on the 4th September the Duke sent ambassadors to England to conclude the match. The treaty was actually concluded in London on the 4th October.[2]

Anne of Cleves crossed from Calais to Deal in the very end of December. On the last day of the year she reached Rochester, where the King visited her *incognito*, returning afterwards to Greenwich. On the 3rd January 1540 he received her in procession at Blackheath, and conducted her through Greenwich Park to the Palace. On the 6th they were married, while the Emperor was in Paris receiving the splendid hospitality of Francis. *The marriage with Anne of Cleves;*

The marriage, of course, irritated the Emperor extremely; but it served its purpose—the only purpose really for which it was contracted. It gave England the support, not only of the Duke of Cleves but of all his Protestant kinsmen and allies against any attempt to give effect to the papal excommunication. It also gave secret satisfaction to Francis, as he found in the course of time that his generosity towards the Emperor had been entirely misplaced. If he hesitated at first to renew old intrigues with German princes, England had now done all that was needful to strengthen them against their superior lord. All the trouble that Charles V. and Maximilian before him had ever experienced from Charles, Duke of Gueldres, who, in alliance with France, had frequently invaded the lands of the House of Austria, might now be expected from William, Duke of Cleves, the claimant of Gueldres, supported by his brother-

---

[1] *L. P.*, XIV. ii. 33.   [2] *L. P.*, XIV. ii. 127-8, 286.

in-law, Henry VIII. of England. And William, Duke of Cleves, would be further supported by the Elector of Saxony, the Landgrave of Hesse, and the King of Denmark.

So it seemed. But neither princes and statesmen abroad nor his own subjects at home could read the secrets of Henry's heart. He did, indeed, reveal to Cromwell, and in the most disgusting fashion, the secrets of his own bed-chamber; but the world was none the wiser. That he was disappointed with his wife as regards her beauty at the very first sight of her, is a statement that rests only on his own authority, and may or may not be true. What is true, or may be pretty distinctly read through all those shameful private revelations, is that he was determined from the first to keep it in his power to make out a case of nullity, which he might get his Parliament and the clergy, if needful, to endorse.

a marriage by which Henry VIII. never intended to be bound. The marriage was to be declared a sham marriage whenever it had served its purpose—whenever, that is to say, the King was of opinion that the alliance of the German princes might be safely dropped, for the sake of more comfortable relations with the Emperor. And time gradually brought the matter about. For months Cromwell's policy and the Anne of Cleves marriage remained suspended in the balance. For months it was uncertain whether they would be maintained or condemned together. Strange vacillations were noted from day to day. Cromwell was made Earl of Essex in April, but Bishop Gardiner, who had been long excluded from the Council, was taken again into favour. Sampson, Bishop of Chichester, was one morning nominated as the first Bishop of Westminster; two hours later he was disgraced and imprisoned. Ambassadors came from the Duke of Cleves to demand help from the King to secure Gueldres, but they received only a cold answer. At last, on the 10th June, Cromwell

was arrested on the ground that he had been counter-
working the King's endeavour to procure a settlement
of religion.   On the 6th July a Commission was
issued requiring the clergy of England, in General
Synod assembled (in accordance with a request
from Parliament, passed at a secret meeting), to
inquire as to the validity of the King's marriage.
The Synod met next day in the Westminster Chapter-
house, and, with all forms duly observed, pronounced
the marriage invalid.   The evidence had been obtained from Cromwell in writings under his own
hand, after his committal to the Tower.   Then, on
the 28th, Cromwell was beheaded.   Two days
later Dr. Barnes, with two other divines of the new
school, went to the fire in Smithfield, where, on the
same day, Powell, Abell, and Fetherstone, three
notable adherents of the Pope, were hanged for
denying the King's Supremacy.

The repudiation of Anne of Cleves was a thing
for which even Henry's previous matrimonial vagaries
had not prepared the world.   Imperial statesmen
were amused.   Covos, the Emperor's secretary in
Spain, remarked that it was not without a reason
that the King of England claimed spiritual authority
to judge of the validity of marriages after his own
will; but the result could not but be good for the
Emperor in his dispute with Cleves.   The same
consideration, however, told very differently upon
Francis I., to whom Sir Edward Carne had to report
that the question of the validity of Henry's marriage
was committed to the clergy.   " What ! " said Francis,
" the matrimony with the Queen that now is ? "
" Yea," replied Carne.   " Then he fetched a great
sigh, and so spake no more." [1]

---

[1] *L. P.,* xv. 870.

BOOK IV
THE REIGN OF THE ENGLISH BIBLE

CHAPTER I

THE STORY OF THE ENGLISH BIBLE

THE fall of Cromwell did not end the religious despotism which Royal Supremacy had set up, but made it for a while less arbitrary. The need of a religious settlement was felt more and more. The Act of the Six Articles, even before Cromwell fell, was one great effort to steady matters upon the old lines. But it was not to be expected that when the power of bishops and clergy had already been broken by one Act of Parliament, the state of religion could be effectually mended by another. That Act, no doubt, was fairly effective at first against most of the things at which it was aimed; its stringency, indeed, had to be relaxed by a new enactment taking away the capital penalty for priestly incontinence.[1] It completely shut the mouths of Calvinists and Sacramentaries, one of whom, writing to Bullinger at Zurich, attributes the result to their depending too much on the support of influential persons. "We did not consider," he wrote, "that it was the Lord's teaching. But as soon as He had destroyed the hopes we had reposed in one individual, we raised up to ourselves another in whom we placed our confidence; until at last God has taken them all away from us, and has inflicted upon us such a want of sincere ministers of the Word, that a man may now travel from the East of England to the West, and

---

[1] Stat. 32 Hen. VIII. c. 10.

from the North to the South, without being able to discover a single preacher, who out of a pure heart and faith unfeigned is seeking the glory of God. He has taken them all away. And here I mean Queen Anne who was beheaded, together with her brother; also the Lord Cromwell, with Latimer and the other bishops." [1]

There could hardly be more convincing evidence than this, that the kind of religion favoured by the writer was not popular in England, and had only received factitious support from Anne Boleyn and Cromwell, and such of the bishops as had owed their advancement to Anne Boleyn's influence over the King. But if further evidence be required, it is to be found in an account transmitted to Cromwell by the notorious heretic, George Constantine, of his conversations, just after the passing of the Act of the Six Articles, with John Barlow, Dean of Westbury, a brother of Bishop Barlow, and Thomas Barlow, prebendary there, another brother, while they were all three on a journey from Westbury-on-Trym in Gloucestershire to Slebech in South Wales. They had conversed about the resignations of the two bishops, Latimer and Shaxton; about the return of Dr. Barnes from the Continent; and, finally, about the new Act, with regard to which they were all agreed it was well that there was no commission yet issued to put it in force;—and the Dean blamed Archbishop Cranmer for allowing it to pass, believing that he might have effectually opposed it. But Constantine showed that opposition would have been useless, and that my Lord Privy Seal (that is to say, Cromwell) was fully persuaded that the Act was right. "It is marvel if it so be," remarked the Dean. In reply to which Constantine observed: "Wonderful are the ways of the Lord! Kings' hearts are in the hand of God. He turneth them as He lusteth. How merci-

[1] *Original Letters* (Parker Soc.), pp. 203, 204.

fully, how plentifully and purely hath God sent His Word to us here in England! Again, how unthankfully, how rebelliously, how carnally, and unwillingly, too, we receive it! Who is there, almost, that will have a Bible, but he must be compelled thereto? How loth be our priests to teach the commandments, the Articles of the Faith, and the *Paternoster* in English! Again, how unwilling be the people to learn it! Yea, they jest at it, calling it the new *Paternoster* and New Learning; so that, as help me God, if we amend not, I fear we shall be in more bondage and blindness than ever we were. I pray you, was not one of the best preachers in Christendom the Bishop of Worcester (meaning Latimer)? And now there is one made [1] that never preached that I heard, except it were the Pope's law. But, alas! beside our naughtiness, cowardness and covetousness is the occasion of much of this. The cowardness of our bishops to tell truth and stand by it while they might be heard, and the covetousness of our visitors; for in all our visitations we have nothing reformed but our purses."

The New Learning unpopular.

"By God's mercy," the Dean rejoined, "thou sayest truth." [2]

There were many extremely interesting things in the conversation besides this, which it is hardly possible to pass by altogether without notice; for never was there reported at length in King Henry's days a conversation of such high significance in reference to so large a number of subjects. They went on to talk of the prospect of the King's marrying again. The Dean understood that both the Duchess of Milan and Anne of Cleves were spoken of; and there was good hope of the latter match, for the King's painter (Holbein) had been sent over to take her likeness. Moreover, the Duke of Cleves favoured God's

---

[1] John Bell, Latimer's successor in the bishopric.
[2] *Archæologia*, xxiii. 56-9.

Word, and was a mighty prince now, having possession of Gueldres against the Emperor's will. The match with the Duchess of Milan was really broken off because she would have the King accept the Pope's dispensation. Moreover, she required pledges. "Why pledges?" asked the Dean. "Marry," replied Constantine; "she sayeth that the King's Majesty was in so little space rid of the Queen's, that she dare not trust his Council, though she durst trust his Majesty. For her Council suspecteth that her great aunt (Katharine of Aragon) was poisoned; that the second (Anne Boleyn) was innocently put to death, and the third lost for lack of keeping in her childbed." [1]

I must break off here, though there was much else on subjects of first-rate importance, especially as to the circumstances leading up to the execution of Anne Boleyn and her supposed paramours—a matter about which Constantine could tell something, as he was then servant to Henry Norris, one of the victims. What we have to consider at present is the evidence these documents afford, in harmony with the testimony of Marillac, the French ambassador, that the repressive legislation of the Act of the Six Articles, instead of being disliked, was popular; that the people did not love the Bible and the Paternoster in English, which were really forced upon them against their will; and that they thought it no more than right to punish married priests or men who introduced new sacramental doctrine. The only thing wonderful was that legislation to that effect should have passed with the approbation of the King and Cromwell, when the influence of authority had so long been turned in the contrary direction. Wonderful, indeed, Constantine might well consider it, how God turned the hearts of kings! For few indeed knew all about the Frankfort truce and its effect on the King's policy; but it was an effect for

[1] *Archæologia*, xxiii. 60, 61.

which almost every one was thankful. And, of course, when they censured the irreverence and profanity of past years they laid the blame on the King's minister, not on the King. On Cromwell's fall, next year, they could speak their minds freely. The Act of his attainder[1] declared, among other things, that being a detestable heretic, determined to sow sedition and variance among the King's subjects, he had secretly set forth and dispersed into all the shires numbers of false and erroneous books, many of which were printed beyond seas, to alienate men from "the true and sincere faith" of the Blessed Sacrament of the Altar and other Articles of Religion declared by the King by the authority of Parliament. He had also caused parts of the said books to be translated into English; and, even on the report made by the translator thereof that the matter was expressly against the Sacrament of the Altar, he had, after reading the translation, affirmed the heresy so translated to be good. He had also "obstinately holden opinion and said" that every Christian might be a minister of the Sacrament as well as a priest, and, abusing his authority, as the King's Vicegerent, to reform errors and direct ecclesiastical causes, he had, without the King's knowledge, licensed heretics to preach and teach. Nay, he had written to the sheriffs of sundry shires, as if it were the King's pleasure, to set at large many false heretics, and had defended such persons and rebuked their accusers. He had defended the preaching of Barnes, then in the Tower, declaring that even if the King turned against it, he would fight for it, and, holding up his dagger, added, "Or else this dagger thrust me to the heart; and I trust if I live one year or two, it shall not lie in the King's power to resist or let it if he would"— affirming the words by a great oath.[2]

How Cromwell's rule was hated.

---

[1] Stat. 31 Hen. VIII. c. 62.
[2] Burnet, iv. 417-9.   The Act is 32 Hen. VIII. c. 62.

Of course we do not expect to find justice in an Act of Attainder. The old fiction that the minister acted "without the privity of the King" was always ready, however glaringly untrue. But that Cromwell's great influence had been used in promoting heresy such as was generally abhorred by honest people there is really no doubt whatever. Yet his acts stood for the acts of the nation, and gave England a bad name among the nations. On his fall Richard Pate, who was then at Bruges ambassador to the Emperor, wrote to the Duke of Norfolk, that while Cromwell ruled, England had always been ill spoken of abroad, people saying that in that country the Sacrament of the Altar was abolished, and all piety and religion banished. When people visited England they said they would take their chaplains with them to say mass in their chambers, expecting that they would have no opportunity in church.[1] Now, he hoped, foreigners would think better of the country. And doubtless there was some improvement.

At the same time, it is to be noted that the Act of the Six Articles, severe as it was against sacramental heresies and married priests, gave no kind of security against an English Bible or against the spread of that "New Learning" which was founded on its literal interpretation. The English Bible, in fact, as we have seen, was actually forced upon a reluctant Progress of people, and though the New Learning was not "the New Learning." yet by any means popular, it was a growing force. But how this came about, or what led up to it, deserves some further consideration than we have yet bestowed on the subject. And for this purpose we must go back to the history of past years.

To translate Scripture into English as a matter of private enterprise and circulate it in any diocese

[1] *L. P.*, xv. 876.

without the approval of the bishop, had always been accounted, as we have already had occasion to observe, conduct distinctly heretical and opposed to the good order of the Church, whether the translation was good or bad.   But there was always a good deal of heretical feeling in places, and especially among city merchants like Hunne, who hated spiritual courts and spiritual parade.   Now Tyndale, who led the way at this time in translating and printing the Bible, was encouraged by at least one city merchant —possibly by more.   He had gone abroad in 1524, *Tyndale's* assured of remittances from one Humphrey Mon- *activity.* mouth, to pursue a work which he could not safely prosecute at home.   He took counsel in the matter with Luther at Wittenberg, where, it would rather seem, he printed, as early as the beginning of 1525, an English translation of the two first gospels on the model of Luther's New Testament of 1522.   This translation was quite distinct from his edition of the whole New Testament—a work which he began a little later at Cologne, where, as is well known, he was interrupted in the printing of it, and obliged to remove to Worms.   There it was completed, and it appears to have been smuggled into England in the early part of 1526.   But of the 3000 quarto and 3000 octavo copies printed at Worms only one imperfect quarto and two octavo copies are known now to exist.   For as soon as it was discovered that such a work was disseminated in England the bishops took pains to get it suppressed.   Tunstall, who was then Bishop of London, denounced it in a sermon at Paul's Cross, declaring, as it would appear by Roye's satire, that he found 3000 errors in it ; and after the sermon a bonfire was made of the volumes.   On the 3rd November 1526 a mandate was issued by the Archbishop of Canterbury to his suffragans to search for this and other prohibited books ; but the Archbishop was anticipated by Tunstall, who on the

24th October,[1] without attributing the work to Tyndale (could he have been at that date ignorant of its authorship?), notified his Archdeacon of London that "many children of iniquity, maintainers of Luther's sect, blinded through extreme wickedness and wandering from the way of truth and the Catholic faith, craftily have translated the New Testament into our English tongue, intermeddling therewith many heretical articles and erroneous opinions, pernicious and offensive, seducing the simple people, attempting by their wicked and perverse interpretations to profanate the majesty of the Scripture which hitherto hath remained undefiled, and craftily to abuse the most holy Word of God and the true sense of the same; of which translation there are many books imprinted, some with glosses and some without, containing in the English tongue that pestiferous and most pernicious poison dispersed throughout all our diocese of London in great numbers."[2] The city merchants who had encouraged Tyndale in his labours, and sent him remittances from England, of course knew how to import and disseminate his books.

Tunstall's words no doubt strike the modern reader as strangely vehement. Yet he was really one of the mildest of the whole bench of bishops, and his words are not more severe than those of Sir Thomas More, who was not a bishop at all. Nor were these the only men of the day who saw clearly that Tyndale's Testament, like his other works, was intended to produce an ecclesiastical and social revolution, of a highly dangerous character, aided by mistranslations of Holy Writ and sophistical glosses in the margin. For us who live long after such a revolution has been actually accomplished, who do not

[1] It was known in London even on the 3rd September that the English Testaments were to be put down and burned. *L. P.*, IV. 4693, 4694.

[2] Foxe, iv. 666-7. In the general account of Tyndale I have followed Demaus's Life of him (Lovett's ed.).

realise the agony of the crisis, and to whom even such of the mistranslations as remain do not vitiate the general sense of writings which we feel to be inspired, it is difficult to realise the causes of alarm. Yet, looking back, we ought to be aware that the great shipwreck of the old system really did produce disastrous and demoralising results ; that it set men afloat in tempestuous seas on rafts made of the broken timbers of what had once been St. Peter's ship ; that the attempt to preserve the unity and independence of a national Church only led to cruelty and repression ; and that at last we have found peace—if we have found it even now—in what might almost be called the principle of an agnostic State trying to hold the balance even between contending denominations.   But one thing is certain—that the pre-Reformation system is dead and cannot possibly be revived.

Archbishop Warham not only took active steps to suppress the new translation, but believed presently that he had succeeded in purchasing the whole impression of each edition with a view to its destruction. The following letter from Richard Nix, the aged Bishop of Norwich, shows how warmly he was seconded in this enterprise :— *Efforts to suppress his New Testament.*

BISHOP NIX TO ARCHBISHOP WARHAM

In right humble manner I commend me unto your good Lordship, doing the same to understand that I lately received your letters dated at your Manor of Lambeth the 26th day of the month of May, by the which I do perceive that your Grace hath lately gotten into your hands all the books of the New Testatment translated into English, and printed beyond the sea,—as well those with the glosses joined unto them, as the other without the glosses, by means of exchange by you made therefor, to the sum of £66 : 9 : 4.

Surely, in mine opinion, you have done therein a gracious and a blessed deed, and God, I doubt not, shall highly reward you therefor !   And where in your said letters ye write that in so much as this matter and the danger thereof, if

remedy had not been provided, should not only have touched
you, but all the bishops within your province; and that it
is no reason that the whole charge and cost thereof should
rest only in you, but that they and every of them for their
part, should advance and contribute certain sums of money
toward the same; and for that intent desire me to certify
you what convenient sum I, for my part, will be contented
to advance in this behalf, and to make payment thereof unto
Master William Potkyn, your servant; pleaseth it you to
understand that I am right well contented to give and
advance in this behalf ten marks, and shall cause the same
to be delivered unto the said Master Potkyn shortly; the
which sum I think sufficient for my part, if every bishop
within your said province make like contribution and
advancement, after the rate and substance of their benefices.
Nevertheless, if your Grace think this sum of ten marks not
sufficient for my part in this matter, your further pleasure
known I shall be as glad to conform myself thereunto, in
this or any other matter concerning the Church as any your
subject within your province; as know Almighty God, who
long preserve you to his most pleasure and your heart's
desire.   At Hoxne in Suffolk, the 14th day of June 1527.
Your humble obediencer and bondman,

R. Norvicen.[1]

Addressed: To my Lord of Canterbury's good Lordship.[2]

It is strange that Archbishop Warham should
have imagined that he had succeeded in getting
into his hands the whole impression of two separate
editions of a work like Tyndale's New Testament.
Apparently he and the bishops were quite mistaken
in thinking so; but, stranger still is it, if we may
trust a story to be presently related, that the discovery
of their error did not prevent a repetition of the
same expensive and futile policy by Tunstall two
years later. Not less notable, however, is the self-
denying zeal of the bishops, who were willing to tax
themselves so highly in order completely to eradicate

---

[1] The signature of this letter is in a very shaky, irregular hand, the poor
old bishop no doubt at that very time getting blind, as he afterwards became.
I have omitted to quote a short *P.S.* regretting his inability to come up and
"do his duty" to Warham that summer.

[2] MS. Cott., Vitellius B. ix. 117.*

what they regarded as a source of pestilent error. Bishop Nix's offered contribution of ten marks, or £6 : 13 : 4—rather more than a tenth of the whole sum laid out by the Primate, but Norwich undoubtedly was a rich diocese,—corresponded probably to ten or twelve times that nominal value in our day; and on the same scale we may reckon that the whole sum laid out by the Primate was equivalent to at least £700 or £800 of modern currency. But the literature read in their dioceses was still a subject of anxious consideration for conscientious bishops; and until the King himself became a patron of heresy, they could mark as contraband and get the aid of the civil power to suppress, alike in England and in foreign countries, all that was considered really dangerous. The invention of printing, however, had already begun to make such measures exceedingly difficult. Merchants and tradesmen in London had been sending orders abroad for copies of Tyndale's New Testament, and some of their correspondence on the subject was discovered in 1528 in the house of one Richard Harman at Antwerp, which was searched by authority procured from the Margrave in order to seize his books and papers.[1]

In February 1528 Garret's escape from Oxford created much disturbance in the University, and led to the disclosure of a large underhand sale of Lutheran books partly, at least, procured from Harman.[2] But that story is not specially connected with the New Testament. Tyndale is said to have been at that time at Marburg, where, it is supposed, he got Hans Luft to print for him his *Parable of the Wicked Mammon* and his *Obedience of a Christian Man*. In 1529 it would seem that he must have paid a visit to Antwerp, and been

[1] *L. P.*, IV. 4693, 4694.
[2] *L. P.*, IV. 4030. For the story of Garret and Farman, pastor of Honeylane, see their names in the index to that volume; also Dalaber's narrative in Foxe, which, however, is written much later.

there in August, when Bishop Tunstall was there also on his return from Cambray, where he and Sir Thomas More were present on behalf of England at the negotiations between the Emperor and Francis I. Here some very remarkable proceedings took place, which are told with great gusto by Hall the chronicler as follows :—

Here it is to be remembered that at this present time William Tyndale had newly translated and imprinted the New Testament in English; and the Bishop of London, not pleased with the translation thereof, debated with himself how he might compass and devise to destroy that false and erroneous translation (as he said). And so it happened that one Augustine Packington, a mercer and merchant of London, and of a great honesty, the same time was in Antwerp where the Bishop then was; and this Packington was a man that highly favored William Tyndale, but to the Bishop utterly showed himself to the contrary. The Bishop, desirous to have his purpose brought to pass, commoned of the New Testaments and how gladly he would buy them. Packington then hearing that [which] he wished for, said unto the Bishop "My Lord, if it be your pleasure, I can in this matter do more, I daresay, than most of the merchants of England that are here; for I know the Dutchmen and strangers that have bought them of Tyndale and have them here to sell. So that, if it be your Lordship's pleasure to pay for them, for otherwise I cannot come by them but I must disburse money for them, I will then assure you to have every book of them that is imprinted and is here unsold." The Bishop, thinking that he had God by the toe, when, indeed, he had (as after he thought) the Devil by the fist, said "Gentle Master Packington, do your diligence and get them, and with all my heart I will pay for them whatsoever they cost you, for the books are erroneous and nought, and I intend surely to destroy them all, and to burn them at Paul's Cross." Augustine Packington came to William Tyndale, and said "William, I know thou art a poor man, and hast a heap of New Testaments and books by thee, for the which thou hast both endangered thy friends and beggared thyself; and I have now gotten thee a merchant which with ready money shall despatch thee of all that thou hast, if you think it so profitable for yourself." "Who is the merchant?" said Tyndale. "The Bishop of London," said Packington. "Oh,

How it was bought up by Tunstall.

that is because he will burn them," said Tyndale. "Yea, marry," quod Packington. "I am the gladder," said Tyndale, "for these two benefits shall come thereof: I shall get money of him for these books to bring myself out of debt, and the whole world shall cry out upon the burning of God's Word. And the overplus of the money that shall remain to me shall make me more studious to correct the said New Testament, and so newly to imprint the same once again, and I trust the second will much better like you than ever did the first." And so, forward went the bargain. The Bishop had the books, Packington had the thanks, and Tyndale had the money.[1]

A capital story this, which, it need hardly be suggested, has lost nothing in the telling. Yet, doubtless, it is a true story in the main, for there are evidences that go some way to establish it, while there are certainly points which are wrong in detail. Hall, it will be seen, relates it in connection with the events of 1529, just as if there had been no other buying and burning of the books before. And further, he caps it with a sequel which is all that is required to make it still more effective :—

Afterward, when mo New Testaments were imprinted, they came thick and threefold into England. The Bishop of London, hearing that still there were so many New Testaments abroad, sent for Augustine Packington, and said unto him " Sir, how cometh this, that there are so many New Testaments abroad, and you promised and assured me that you had bought all?" Then said Packington "I promise you I bought all that then was to be had, but I perceive they have made more since; and it will never be better as long as they have the letters and stamps. Therefore it were best for your Lordship to buy the stamps too, and then are you sure." The Bishop smiled at him and said "Well, Packington, well," and so ended this matter.

Shortly after, it fortuned one George Constantine to be apprehended by Sir Thomas More, which then was Lord Chancellor of England, of suspicion of certain heresies. And this Constantine being with More, after divers examinations of divers things, among other Master More said in

---

[1] Hall's *Chronicle*, pp. 762, 763.

this wise to Constantine : "Constantine, I would have thee plain with me in one thing that I will ask of thee, and I promise thee I will show thee favor in all the other things whereof thou art accused to me. There is beyond the sea Tyndale, Joye, and a great many mo of you. I know they cannot live without help. Some sendeth them money and succoureth them ; and thyself, being one of them, hadst part thereof, and therefore knowest from whence it came. I pray thee, who be they that thus help them ?" "My Lord," quod Constantine, "will you that I shall tell you the truth ?" "Yea, I pray thee," quod my Lord. "Marry, I will," quod Constantyne. "Truly," quod he, "it is the Bishop of London that hath holpen us ; for he hath bestowed among us a great deal of money in New Testaments to burn them ; and that hath [been], and yet is, our only succour and comfort." "Now, by my troth," quod More, "I think even the same, and I said so much to the Bishop when he went about to buy them."

It may be remarked, however, that Bishop Tunstall could scarcely have been such a simpleton as to have no misgivings as to the effect of his policy, even if Sir Thomas More had not suggested to him how it would probably turn out. It was his duty, he conceived, to suppress the edition, even at considerable expense to himself, if he could possibly do so. It may or may not be the case that he was at first deceived as to the character of Augustine Packington, that merchant "of a great honesty," who, according to Hall, "highly favored William Tyndale, but to the Bishop utterly showed himself to the contrary" (Hall's notions of "great honesty" seem to have been quite compatible with double dealing); but it is evident, even in the narrative, that when Packington wished to lead him on to get "the letters and stamps," meaning, apparently, the types and presses, the Bishop had no mind to trust him further. The smile with which he said "Well, Packington, well !" is exceedingly significant.[1]

[1] The notices of Augustine Packington in records and State papers are a little curious. On the 12th October 1525 we meet with a grant to John and

The difficulties bishops had to contend with in doing what had always been esteemed their duty—that is to say, suppressing literature which was considered poisonous—were becoming simply insuperable when the printing press, from various hidden quarters, diffused such literature in numerous and multiplied copies, and nothing but strong government at home, aided by the friendly efforts of continental governments as well, could be expected effectually to put down this contraband industry and traffic. But now on the Continent there were places of refuge like Wittenberg, or Marburg in the land of Hesse, fully protected by Protestant princes; and at home, even while the old *régime* continued, Henry VIII., with a view to getting married to Anne Boleyn, was secretly encouraging heresy while openly putting forth proclamations against it. The bishops were beginning to feel the altered nature of the ground, and " Well, Packington, well," was all that could be said.

The bishops thwarted by the printing press.

In truth, it may reasonably be suspected that the joke of compelling bishops to contribute to the commercial success of a publication which they detested was a part of the speculation of Monmouth and Tyndale from the first. Once the book was published, they knew well enough that the bishops must endeavour to buy it up, and that if they bought only a considerable number it would help to pay expenses. A good many had already been bought and burned at Paul's Cross in the autumn of 1526, and Warham believed that he had secured the whole impression in May 1527. But in the autumn of 1528 we find Hermann Rinck, a senator of Cologne, whom Cochlæus had persuaded to suppress the printing begun there

Austin Pakyngton (brothers, perhaps) of the office of chirographer of the Common Pleas, to be held in survivorship (*L. P.*, IV. 1736). A year or more afterwards we find a petition to the King by John ap Howell of London, mercer, complaining that on the 8th October 1526, during his absence beyond sea, his house and shop were broken into and goods to the value of £2400 taken away by a company of whom Augustine Packington was one. Presumably, however, this was under some legal process.

three years before, commissioned by Wolsey to arrest Tyndale and Roye, and also to buy up their books. Rinck received Wolsey's letters at Frankfort, whither they had been despatched from Cologne with the utmost haste, so that they were transmitted in two days; and in reply he wrote that the men had not been seen at Frankfort Fair since Easter, and their printer, a John Schott of Strasburg, did not know where they had gone to. But he had been inquiring about their vile books three weeks before receiving Wolsey's letter, and found that some had been pawned to the Jews of Frankfort for ready money. He hoped he had secured the whole of these. There were two books also of which copies were to have been smuggled into England and Scotland covered with paper in ten packages tied up with packthread. But he had stopped all that, and he would endeavour to arrest both Roye and Tyndale and all other mischievous Englishmen, as he had been in past times an important political agent both of the King and of his father. He had compelled John Schott to take oath before the authorities at Frankfort as to the numbers of English books he had printed for Roye and Tyndale, who, he said, had no money to pay for them, and he had purchased the whole stock and had them at his house at Cologne, awaiting Wolsey's instructions what to do with them. Thus it is clear there was a good deal of buying and burning of books before the year 1529,[1] though these, indeed, were not New Testaments.

In connection with Hall's anecdote, however, it may not be amiss to set before the reader what Sir Thomas More himself says three years later about this George Constantine whom he interrogated in the manner above reported. In the Preface to his

---

[1] *L. P.*, IV. 4810. The whole text of Rinck's letter is given with a translation (not quite accurate, however) in Arber's reprint of Tyndale's New Testament, pp. 32-6.

Confutation of Tyndale's Answer, made in 1532, More states that Constantine had been arrested for heresy and escaped. Before his escape he "was ready to have, in word at the least wise, abjured all the whole doctrine." It was intended to show him the more favour "in that he seemed very penitent of his misusing himself in falling to Tyndale's heresies again; for which he acknowledged himself worthy to be hanged that he had so falsely abused the King's gracious remission and pardon given him before, and had for all that in the while both bought and sold of those heretical books and secretly set forth those heresies. Whereof he showed himself so repentant that he uttered and disclosed divers of his companions, of whom there are some abjured since and some that he wist well were abjured before, namely Richard Necton, which was by Constantine's detection taken and committed to Newgate, where, except he hap to die before in prison, he standeth in great peril to be, ere it be long, for his falling again to Tyndale's heresies, burned." [1]

More follows this up with some other instances of the duplicity of Constantine and his allies; and he adds that Constantine not only disclosed his own heresies, but studied how "those devilish books" that he and his fellows had brought and shipped might come to the Bishop's hands to be burned, and gave the shipman's name "and the marks of the fardels," by which More got them into his hands. [2]

The burning of the books took place in St. Paul's Churchyard in May 1530 by Tunstall's order, [3] though he was no longer Bishop of London at that time, having been translated to Durham in March; but his successor, Stokesley, was then upon the Continent on a special

The burning of Tyndale's Testaments.

---

[1] More's *Works*, p. 346. Necton's real Christian name was Robert, not Richard, and he does not appear to have incurred the fate which More anticipated for him. He was one of those, doubtless, whom the influence of Anne Boleyn protected.

[2] *Ibid.*, p. 347.   [3] Hall's *Chronicle*, p. 771.

mission from the King. Tyndale, however, does not seem to have applied the funds with which the Bishop had indirectly supplied him to a revised edition of his New Testament; for such an edition, apparently, was not published till five years later. It is suggested, however, with something more than plausibility, by Demaus, the biographer of Tyndale, that he applied them to biblical work of the same character; for he had just completed his translation of the Pentateuch from the Hebrew, which issued from the press of Hans Luft at Marburg (if we may trust the printed date) on the 17th January 1530.[1] And this work was illustrated by woodcuts which had been used by Vorstermann in the Dutch Bible which he printed at Antwerp in 1528. They were changed when he reprinted that bible four years later; so that it would appear the blocks were purchased from him by Tyndale at Antwerp in 1529 and carried off to Marburg,[2] or to the place where the Pentateuch was printed. This fact is of some value as confirmatory of Hall's statement that Tyndale actually was at Antwerp that year, which otherwise, as we shall see by and by, might possibly have been open to question.

The bishops were doing their utmost to suppress heretical literature, and the King as he had always done, affected to second their efforts. Yet in that very month of May 1530, in which Tyndale's books were burned in St. Paul's Churchyard, it seems to have become notorious that the King was really encouraging their distribution. For thus writes again Bishop Nix to Archbishop Warham on the 14th May in that year :—

The King encourages heresy underhand ;

After most humble recommendation, I do your Grace to understand that I am accumbered with such as keepeth and

---

[1] There is no doubt, it should be added, that in this instance January 1530 means of the historical year beginning on the 1st January. There is doubt, as we shall see hereafter, whether " Marburg " be not a fictitious date.

[2] Demaus's *Tyndale*, p. 217.

readeth these erroneous books in English, and believe and give credence to the same, and teacheth others that they should so do. My Lord, I have done that lieth in me for the suppression of such persons; but it passeth my power, or any spiritual man for to do it. For divers saith openly in my diocese that the King's Grace *would* that they should have the said erroneous books, and so maintaineth themselves of the King. Whereupon I desired my Lord Abbot of Hyde to show this to the King's Grace, beseeching him to send his honorable letters under his Seal down to whom he pleases in my diocese, that they may show and publish that it is *not* his pleasure that such books should be had or read, and also punish such as saith so. I trust before this letter shall come unto you my lord Abbot hath done so. The said Abbot hath the names of some that cracketh in the King's name that their false opinions should go forth, and will die in the quarrel that their ungracious opinions be true, and trusteth by Michaelmas day there shall be more that shall believe of their opinions than they that believeth the contrary. If I had known that your Grace had been at London, I would have commanded the said Abbot to have spoken with you. But your Grace may send for him when you please, and he shall show you my whole mind in this matter, and how I thought best for the suppression of such as holdeth these erroneous opinions; for if they continue any time, I think they shall undo us all.

The said Abbot departed from me on Monday last; and sith that time I have had much trouble and business with others in like matter; and they say that wheresomever they go, they hear say that the King's pleasure is, the New Testament in English should go forth, and men should have it and read it. And from that opinion I can no wise induce them but [*i.e.* unless] I had greater authority to punish them than I have. Wherefore I beseech your good Lordship to advertise the King's Grace, as I trust the said Abbot hath done before this letter shall come unto your Grace, that a remedy may be had.

For now it may be done well in my diocese, for the gentlemen and the commonality be not greatly infected, but merchants and such that hath their abiding not far from the sea. The said Abbot of Hyde can show you of a curate, and well learned, in my diocese, that exhorted his parishioners to believe contrary to the Catholical faith. There is a college in Cambridge called Gunwell Hall, of

the foundation of a bishop of Norwich. I hear of no clerk
that hath come out lately of that college but savoureth of
the frying pan, though he speak never so holily.

I beseech your Grace to pardon me of my rude and
tedious writing to you. The zeal and love I owe to
Almighty God cause me this to do. And thus Almighty
God long preserve your Grace in good prosperity and health.
At Hoxne, the 14th day of May 1530.

Your obedienciary and daily orator,
RI. NORWICENSIS.[1]

Never was the beginning of a great change of times
more distinctly indicated. The King patronising
heresy! For his own security it was the last thing
any king had done hitherto; and Henry VIII., the
Defender of the Faith against Luther, how could he
do so? It could not be true; and yet men were
bold enough to say it was so. If the King could
encourage a religious literature distinctly disapproved
by the Church, how could the Church successfully
maintain the war for truth against falsehood? Bishop
Nix must have positive assurance on the subject,
and the Abbot of Hyde (John Salcot, a man agreeable
to the Court, who was four years later made Bishop of
Bangor for his obsequiousness) must learn the exact
truth. Things were very serious when a whole college
at Cambridge was full of heresy, and there was an
incumbent in the Bishop's own diocese—evidently
Bilney,[2] who, as we have seen, had exceptional favour
shown him,—a "well learned" man, who openly
exhorted his parishioners to believe things contrary
to the Catholic Faith. Whether bishops had or had
not the power to stop all this depended mainly on
the support they received from the temporal power.
And what did the King do about it? For

---

[1] MS. Cott., Cleop. E v. 366. The flyleaf with the address of this letter is
lost, but there is no doubt it was addressed to Warham, though in *L. P.* IV.
6385 it has been supposed to be addressed to the Duke of Norfolk.

[2] Bilney was Dean of Foston in Norwich diocese, collated to that benefice
in 1518.—Blomefield's *Norfolk*, vii. 364.

an answer we may again refer to Hall, who begins his record of the twenty-second year of the reign (which dates from 22nd April 1530) as follows :—

In the beginning of this two and twentieth year, the King, like a politic and prudent prince, perceived that his subjects and other persons had, divers times within four years last past, brought into his realm great number of printed books of the New Testament, translated into the English tongue by Tyndale, Joye, and others, which books the common people used and daily read privily; which the clergy would not admit, for they punished such persons as had read, studied or taught the same, with great extremity; but, because the multitude was so great, it was not in their power to redress their grief.   Wherefore they made complaint to the Chancellor [Sir Thomas More], which leaned much to the spiritual men's part in all causes; whereupon he imprisoned and punished a great number; so that for this cause a great rumor and controversy rose daily amongst the people.   Wherefore the King, considering what good might come of reading of the New Testament with reverence and following the same, and what evil might come of the reading of the same if it were evil translated, and not followed; came into the Star Chamber the five and twentieth day of May, and there commoned with his Council and the Prelates concerning this cause; and, after long debating, it was alleged that the translation[s] of Tyndale and Joye were not truly translated, and also that in them were prologues and prefaces which sounded to heresy and railed against the Bishops uncharitably.   Wherefore all such books were prohibited, and commandment given by the King to the Bishops that they, calling to them the best learned men of the universities, should cause a new translation to be made, so that the people should not be ignorant in the law of God.   And notwithstanding this commandment, the Bishops did nothing at all to set forth a new translation; which caused the people to study Tyndale's translation; by reason whereof many things came to light, as you shall see hereafter.[1]

yet holds a Council to put it down.

The last sentence of this extract is entirely unjust, as *we* shall see hereafter.   But the whole extract

----
[1] Hall's *Chronicle*, p. 771.

deserves careful attention. For, in the first place, the writer was a well-informed contemporary. Secondly, he was a lawyer and very careful of his statements, though a sad special pleader in favour of the King. And thus we have the advantage of viewing from the other side the very same facts that are shown in Bishop Nix's letter last quoted—the importation of Tyndale's books and the impossibility of suppressing them on account of their number, notwithstanding the willing aid given by Sir Thomas More, as Chancellor, to the bishops in arresting and punishing those guilty of the illicit traffic. Not a word, of course, is told us by Hall about the King's connivance at their diffusion — that would have been showing up the King's hypocrisy. We are only told of the measures taken by the King to meet an acknowledged evil— how he conferred upon the matter with his Council and the prelates, how he graciously listened to the complaints that the translations made by Tyndale and by Joye (Tyndale's fellow-labourer, as he was at first, though by this time he had become a troublesome rival, publishing unauthorised revisions),—and how he (the King) had consequently prohibited the circulation of such books, but had at the same time, with unquestionable wisdom or cleverness, laid upon the bishops the duty of making a new and wholesome translation, to counteract the mischief done by such works as Tyndale's. Thus ingeniously did the King meet a crisis which he had certainly done something to render more acute; and the very proclamation itself—as thus reported, at least—showed that there was some ground for current rumours, when the King virtually confessed that he wished the people to have, if not "erroneous books," at least a translation of the New Testament in English. But we shall get a more exact account of this proclamation presently.

I have already spoken of the character of Tyndale's New Testament. Yet the substantial benefit we have gained by a vernacular translation from the Greek very naturally hides from our view, after the lapse of ages, the indications of a perverse and bitter spirit running through the whole design. The marginal glosses have long ago been dropped, and the most offensive mistranslations have long ago been corrected. But the spirit of the author was visible in many little turns of expression which look harmless now. If the modern reader, however, be disposed to think the censure passed upon Tyndale and his handling of Scripture altogether unjustifiable, it is worth while to consider in what a reverent frame of mind he prepared for press and annotated his English version of the Pentateuch—a work which he had completed only four months before in Germany, and which had already come to be known in England. It had *Tyndale's* numerous marginal annotations of a biting and *bitterness.* sarcastic character. "Not a single passage is overlooked," says Demaus, "from which any comment could be drawn against the doctrines and practices of the Pope and clergy." And the following are given as illustrations: "How shall I curse whom God curseth not?" asks Balaam in Tyndale's version (Numb. xxiii. 8), and a marginal note makes answer, "The Pope can tell how." Even on the text (Genesis xxiv. 60), "They blessed Rebekah," is a sarcastic observation, "To bless a man's neighbour is to pray for him and to wish him good, *and not to wag two fingers over him*"; and with reference to Genesis ix. 6 ("Whoso sheddeth man's blood," etc.), the bishops in a somewhat lengthy note are spoken of as "the Pope's Cains," whom kings should not allow to shed blood without requiring their own in return. So Tyndale in translating Scripture wished to hold up bishops to opprobrium as murderers, though he knew well that heretics were burned only by order of the civil power. He had not proceeded quite to these lengths in defiling the New Testament with partisan glosses, but his general intent, even there, was obvious enough to his contemporaries.

Hall's account of the King's consultation in the Star Chamber seems to be just one day wrong in the date. It took place, not on the 25th, but on the 24th of May; for a long official record of it is entered on Archbishop Warham's register, in which it is stated that his Highness was "in person in the chapel called the Old Chapel, which sometime was called St. Edward's chamber, set on the East side of the Parliament chamber within his Grace's palace at Westminster, upon the 24th day of May in the year of our Lord God Jesus Christ 1530, and in the twenty-second year of his reign," where he called notaries to make authentic instruments of his decree.[1] The document itself begins with an open address to the faithful in time to come by the Archbishop, relating how the King, as Defender of the Faith, in order to counteract the influence of pernicious books, had called a Council of his chief prelates and clerks and learned men of each university, and had taken their judgments on such of those books as he had read; and how this Council had "found in them many heresies, both detestable and damnable," likely to corrupt a great part of the people if suffered to remain in their hands. Then followed a list of heresies found in each of the books referred to, viz. in the *Wicked Mammon* and *The Obedience of a Christian Man* (both books of Tyndale), *The Revelation of Antichrist, The Sum of Scripture, The Book of Beggars,* and so forth. All which errors are denounced with the books containing the same, and also "the translation of Scripture corrupted by William Tyndale, as well in the Old Testament as in the New."

Order given to preachers.
After this was entered a "bill in English to be published by the preachers," how to warn their flocks of the decision that had been come to, notifying that

[1] Wilkins's *Concilia,* iii. 736, 737.

it had been unanimous, although perfect freedom was granted to every man in the assembly " to say as his conscience and learning served him." The preacher then is to bid his hearers, if they possess such books, " detest them, abhor them, keep them not in your hands, deliver them to the superiors, such as call for them ; and if by reading of them heretofore anything remains in your breasts of that teaching, either forget it, or by information of the truth expel it and purge it, to the intent that ye, so purified and cleansed of that contagious doctrine and pestiferous traditions, may be fit and apt to receive and retain the true doctrine and understanding of Christ's laws, to the comfort and edification of your souls. Thus I move and exhort you in God to do ; this is your duty to do ; this ye ought to do ; and, being obstinate and denying or refusing this to do, the prelates of the Church, having the cure and charge of your souls, ought to compel you, and your prince to punish and correct you not doing of the same : unto whom, as St. Paul saith, the sword is given by God's ordinance for that purpose."

How far the King was to be relied on in this matter perhaps the clergy did not feel very well assured, but they were quite assured as to what was his duty. Then follows this passage which bears most upon our subject :—

Ye shall also further understand that the King's Highness, forasmuch as it was reported unto him that there is engendered an opinion in divers of his subjects, that it is his duty to cause the Scripture of God to be translated into the English tongue, to be communicate unto the people ; and that the prelates and also his Highness do wrong in letting or denying of the same ; his Highness, therefore, willed every man there present in that assembly, freely and frankly to show and open unto him what might be approved and confirmed by Scripture and holy doctors in that behalf, to the intent that his Highness, as he then openly protested, might conform himself thereunto, minding to do his duty towards his people as he would that they should do their duties towards him. In which matter,—after Scriptures declared, holy doctors and authors alleged and read, and all things said [that] might be, on both sides and for both parties, spoken, deduced and brought forth,—finally it appeared that the having the whole Scripture in English is not necessary to Christian men, but that without having any such Scripture, endeavouring themselves to do well, and to apply their minds to take and follow such lessons as the preacher teacheth them, and so learn by his mouth, may as well edify spiritually in their souls, as if they had the same Scripture in English. And like as the having of Scripture in the vulgar tongue, and in the common people's hands, hath been by the Holy Fathers of the Church heretofore in some times thought meet and convenient, so at another time it hath been thought to holy Fathers not expedient to be communicate amongst them; wherein, for as much as the King's Highness, by the advice and deliberation of his Council and the agreement of great learned men, thinketh in his conscience that the divulging of this Scripture at this time in English tongue to be committed to the people, considering such pestilent books and so evil opinions as be now spread among them, should rather be to their further confusion and destruction than the edification of their souls; and that as holy doctors testify, upon such like considerations, the semblable hath been done in times past;—it was thought there in that assembly to all and singular in that congregation, that the King's Highness and the prelates in so doing, not suffering the Scripture to be divulged and communicate in the English tongue unto the people at this time, doth well. And I also think and judge the same; exhorting and moving you that,—in consideration his Highness did there openly say and protest, that he would cause the New Testament to be by learned men faithfully and purely translated into the English tongue, to the intent he might have it in his hands ready to be given to his people, as he might see their manners and behaviour meet, apt and convenient to receive the same, —that you will so detest these pernicious books, so abhor these heresies and new opinions, so decline from arrogancy of knowledge and understanding of Scripture after your phantasies; and show yourselves in commoning and reasoning so sober, quiet, meek, temperate, as, all fear of misusing the gift of Scripture taken away, ye may appear such, in your prince's eyes and the eyes of your prelates, as they shall have no just cause to fear any such danger; persuading unto your-

Determination come to about translating the Bible.

selves in the mean time without grudging or murmuring, the very truth, which is this : that you cannot require or demand Scripture to be divulged in the English tongue, otherwise than upon the discretions of the superiors ; so as whensoever they think in their conscience it may do you good, they may, and do well to, give it unto you.   And whensoever it shall seem otherwise unto them, they do amiss in suffering you to have it.[1]

Thus it will be seen that while Hall's account of this proclamation is correct so far as it goes, it lays a little too much stress on the King's order to the bishops to get a new translation made.   That was, in any case, a work which would have occupied some time, and the bishops, in point of fact, did not lose sight of it.   But Hall carefully avoids informing the reader of what is so explicitly stated above, that the bishops and learned men whom the King consulted upon the matter, were decidedly of opinion that it was a mere question of expediency whether it was advisable that the common people should possess the Scriptures in the vulgar tongue or not, and that the bishops themselves were the rightful judges of that expediency ; moreover that the King, too, though he wished a careful translation to be made, quite agreed in the judgment of those whom he consulted, that it was not at all advisable, at that time, to place such a translation in the hands of the public.   He meant the bishops to get the translation made, but he would keep it in his own hands, ready to be given to the people when they seemed fit to make good use of it. We may think what we will of this method of dealing with an English Bible, but it clearly commended itself to the most pious and learned men of the day, and it was the policy that the King himself solemnly declared that he would adopt at the very time that irrepressible rumours declared that he meant to sanc-

---

[1] Wilkins's *Concilia*, iii. 728-36, from Warham's register ; also in Collier's *Ecclesiastical History*, iv. 140-49.

tion not only the New Testament in English, but all
sorts of heretical publications besides. What are we
to think ? Was the King's solemn promise sincere,
or did rumour interpret his intentions truly ? I am
afraid we must say the latter. In accordance, however, with what had been determined in the Council,
a proclamation was issued in June, forbidding the use,
or even the keeping, of the heretical books denounced,
and declaring that it was not expedient at that time
to have the Scriptures in English.[1]

Here it may be desirable to interrupt the story of
Tyndale and his Bible for a while, in order to follow
that of another biblical translator. There is a great
difference, certainly, between the work of Tyndale and
Origin of
Coverdale's
Bible. that of Coverdale ; for Tyndale translated the New
Testament and the Pentateuch from the original
languages, while Coverdale translated them only from
the Vulgate and some modern translations. Tyndale's
work, moreover, was of his own prompting, while
Coverdale's was done at the solicitation of some one
else, and there can be no doubt that that some one
was Thomas Cromwell. Coverdale himself writes
humbly enough about his task, saying that it was one
which he had not sought for his own part, and that
he had made his version from the Latin and some
other translations, especially " Dutch," by which he
meant German, and no doubt Luther's in particular.
The following are his own words upon the subject :—

And to help me herein I have had sundry translations, not
only in Latin, but also of the Dutch interpreters, whom,
because of their singular gifts and special diligence in the
Bible, I have been the more glad to follow for the most part,
according as I was required. But, to say the truth before
God, it was neither my labor nor desire to have this work
put in my hand ; nevertheless it grieved me that other nations
should be more plenteously provided for with the Scripture in
their mother tongue than we. Therefore, when I was instantly

---

[1] *L. P.*, IV. 6487 ; Wilkins's *Concilia*, iii. 740.

required, though I could not do so well as I would, I thought it yet my duty to do my best, and that with a good will.[1]

It would be interesting if we could find the date at which he was so commissioned, but it seems uncertain. The following letter, however, if we could assign it to the precise year in which it was written, would be a very considerable assistance.

MILES COVERDALE TO THOMAS CROMWELL

Most singular good master, with due humility I beseech unto your mastership all godly comfort, grace, and prosperous health. Forsomuch as your goodness is so great toward me, your poor child, only through the plenteousness of your favor and benevolence, I am the bolder of your goodness in this my rude style, if it like your favor to revocate to your memory the godly communication which your mastership had with me, your orator, in Master Moore's house upon Easter Eve, among many and divers fruitful exhortations, specially of your singular favor; and by your most comfortable words I perceive your gracious mind toward me. Wherefore, most honourable master, for the tender love of God, and for the fervent zeal that you have to virtue and godly study, *cordis genibus provolutus,* I humbly desire and beseech your goodness of your gracious help. Now I begin to taste of Holy Scriptures; now, honor be to God, I am set to the most sweet smell of holy letters, with the godly savour of holy and ancient doctors, unto whose knowledge I cannot attain without diversity of books, as is not unknown to your most excellent wisdom. Nothing in the world I desire but books, as concerning my learning. They once had, I do not doubt but Almighty God shall perform that in me, which He of His most plentiful favor and grace hath begun. Moreover, as touching my behaviour, your mastership's mind once known, with all lowliness I offer myself, not only to be ordered in all things as shall please your wisdom, but also as concerning the education and instruction of other, alonely to ensue your prudent counsel; *nam quicquid est in te concilii, nihil non politicum, nihil non divinum est. Quicquid enim ages nihil inconsulte agis ; nusquam te primum*

---

[1] Coverdale's *Remains,* p. 12 (Prologue to the Bible).

philosophum præbes. De rore autem cœli summam, more Jacob, surrepuisti benedictionem. De tuo ipso torrente maxime potare exopto, teque coram alloqui non mediocriter cupio. Vale, decus literarum, conciliorum, omnium denique probitatum. From the Augustines, this May day.

Your child and bedeman in Jesu Christ,
FRERE MYLES COVERDALE.

Addressed: Unto the Right Worshipful and his most singular good master, Master Cromwell, this be delivered with due manner.

It is pretty clear that in whatever year this letter was written it was just about the time that the writer was beginning to consider the undertaking on which he had embarked, and that it was Cromwell who engaged him in the task. As the work was completed in October 1535, we cannot but allow some time—a year or two is little enough—for its accomplishment; and the address of the letter is further evidence on that point, for from April 1534 till June 1536 Cromwell was commonly addressed as secretary to the King's Grace. Moreover, he was a Privy Councillor pretty early in the year 1531, and though the title was not invariably given him in the letters he received at that period, it is not likely that it would have been omitted by so devoted a servant, as we may really call him, as this Friar Miles Coverdale. Besides, I must add that though Anderson in his *Annals of the English Bible* is inclined to date the letter 1531 on the ground that "the style proves that Cromwell had already much in his power,"[1] there is rather a material fact to be considered in favour of a still earlier date. For in 1528 one Thomas Topley, an Augustinian friar like Coverdale himself, was cited before Bishop Tunstall for heresy, and confessed that his faith had been disturbed by reading the book called *Wycliffe's*

---

[1] Anderson, i. 556-7. This book is still valuable for many things, though published so long ago as 1845.

Wicket, though he did not agree with it " till," he says, " I heard Sir Miles Coverdale preach, and then my mind was sore withdrawn from the Blessed Sacrament, insomuch that I took it then but for the remembrance of Christ's body." " Furthermore," the deposition goes on, " he said and confessed that in the Lent last past, as he was walking in the field at Bumpstead with Sir Miles Coverdale, *late* friar of the same Order, going in the habit of a secular priest, who had preached the Fourth Sunday in Lent [29th March 1528] at Bumpstead, they did commune together of Erasmus's works, and also upon Confession. This Sir Miles said and did hold, that it was sufficient for a man to be contrite for his sins, betwixt God and his conscience, without confession made to a priest; which opinion this respondent thought to be true, and did affirm and hold the same at that time. Also he saith that at the said sermon by the said Sir Miles Coverdale, at Bumpstead, he heard him preach against worshipping of images in the church, saying that men in no wise should honour or worship them; which likewise he thought to be true, because he had no learning to defend it." [1]

Thus it would appear that Miles Coverdale had preached in March 1528 in an Essex village, a sermon that must have been considered distinctly heretical according to conventional standards, and that, about that time, assuming a secular priest's habit, he apostatised from his Order, and was no longer considered as a friar. What was to become of such a man in the nature of things? Of course, he would have to flee the country; for England would have been no longer safe for him. And that he did so there is not only a strong presumption, but something very like positive evidence, of which presently. But first as to the strong presumption, which does not rest entirely on his declared heresy,

(margin note: Coverdale a runaway friar.)

---

[1] Anderson, i. 185, from the Episcopal Register; also Foxe, v. 40.

for he might have been caught or have lain hid for a while. It has been remarked as not a little striking that in all Sir Thomas More's diatribes against heresy, in which he seems to mention by name every man who had troubled the peace of England with heretical books, the name of Coverdale is entirely absent.[1] But till More's dying day Coverdale had not issued any heretical books, so far as is known; and even if More had heard, as he possibly might have heard, that a friar, named Coverdale, had turned heretic and fled the country, there was no reason why he should have taken notice of him. There is, however, another fact much more remarkable. Unless the letter just quoted be an exception, not one single letter of Coverdale's, written to his patron Cromwell after 1527, has been preserved until we come to the year 1536 — a blank of eight whole years, covering, no doubt, the whole time when the translator was engaged on his arduous labours. And the correspondence of Cromwell, preserved to this day, is so full and so well kept, that we can hardly imagine that very much of it is missing.

Could the above letter, then, written on May Day, be as early as the year 1527? Well, we have a letter from Coverdale to Cromwell, written in that year, which it may be as well to examine before we proceed further. It is in these words :—

Right honorable Master, in my most lowly manner I commend me unto you, evermore desiring to hear of the preservation of your prosperity. So it is, I was required by Mr. George Lawson to deliver this writing to your mastership mine own self. Notwithstanding, such an impediment hath chanced that I must desire favor on your behalf for my excusation. For Master Moore's kinsman is not all well at ease; *nam e febribus laborat. Opinandum est sane febris esse speciem; nam in alimentis lunatico more solet diflectere. Sed jam compertum est pene exolevisse.* Wherefore

---

[1] Anderson, i. 555.

I beseech you to have me excused; and if I knew that my coming to London might stand with your favor, truly the bird was never gladder of day than I would be to come. But, briefly, I am ready at your commandment, *nam restat tibi facultas apud tuum Milonem mandandi quæ voles.*

Cæterum nihil apud nos promulgatum est novi, nisi quod rumor est apud nostrates (cum unus nostratium magistrorum homicidii sit accusatus, alius criminis hæreseos sit dilatus) quod tertius jam magister sit furtivi criminis deferendus,— nempe Magister ille Stookes junior ; cujus rei subinde manifestius te certiorem faciemus. Denique, præter istuc nullum mihi scribendi argumentum relictum est, nisi quod tu tuique rectissime valeatis. Quod faxit Christus Optimus Maximus, cui sit honor et imperium in æternum. Amen. Ex Cantabrigia, 27 die mensis Augusti, Anno Domini 27 supra sesquimilesimum.

Tuus quantus quantus,

MILO COVERDALUS.

Addressed : Unto the Right Worshipful Master Cromwell this be delivered with speed.

In this letter, at least, we have the advantage of a very exact and positive date, and we note first that it was written from Cambridge (of course from the house of Austin friars there, of which Dr. Barnes was prior), the year before the writer preached that heretical sermon at Bumpstead, and apostatised (as the act was called), that is to say, abandoned his Order. And we have one earlier notice of Coverdale, the year before this letter was written, which we ought to keep in mind. For, in 1526 he acted as secretary to his prior, Dr. Barnes, when examined on a charge of heresy. It is well known that there was at this time considerable sympathy with Luther among scholars at Cambridge, and among the Austin friars (Luther's own Order) there were several who were so affected. But what we have to note at present is that we have some sure record of Coverdale in three successive years. In 1526 he assists his prior, Dr. Barnes, when called up before Wolsey and other bishops. In 1527 he writes the letter just quoted, and in 1528 he preaches a heretical sermon in Essex and abandons his Order. Now observe that in the May-day letter he is still a friar, and actually calls himself so; and that the tone and address of that letter are very similar to those of the letter last quoted. Further, although it is a minor point for our purpose, there is a certain Mr. Moore mentioned in both letters, though it is his kinsman, not himself, that is spoken of in this latter one. I must mention, however, by the way, that it is quite a mistake to suppose, as some writers have done, that the man so named is Sir Thomas More;[1] for the idea that Thomas Cromwell and Coverdale once met in Sir Thomas More's house, and had what they called "godly communication" there, is absolutely incredible. For what those of Coverdale's school called "godly communication" would never have been tolerated by Sir Thomas.

It seems, therefore, as if 1527 were the latest possible date for the May-day letter, though it has unfortunately been arranged with State papers of a much later year. To this, however, a very plausible objection might be raised; and if it were not for the fact that Coverdale had unfrocked himself in 1528, we should have been disposed to agree with Anderson, who places the May-day letter in 1531, as the earliest year in which Cromwell seemed to have the requisite authority to set a man on such work with a prospect of his labour being suitably recognised. But though Cromwell was not a Privy Councillor in 1527, as he was four years later, he was in the way of possessing

---

[1] The name in both these letters is given in the possessive case—in the May-day letter as "Moorys" (in the original spelling), in the August letter as "Moores." The double o can hardly be called important evidence that the name was not More, but it is well to note the exact form here for the sake of accuracy. The apostrophe used in later times for a possessive case is the representative of a vowel which was formerly written. If the o had not been double, "Morys" might have stood pretty well in the spelling of the times, either for "More's" or "Morris's."

considerable influence otherwise, as a well-to-do man and a devoted servant of the great Cardinal. Two and a half years later, indeed, his master's fall would have involved him in utter ruin, but that he managed to push his way into the Court and win the favour of the King himself. But in 1527 he was a wealthy man of business, of whose transactions we have a number of evidences in the State papers, and of whose worldly goods we have an interesting cata- logue drawn up in June of that very year.[1] Already he possessed a sumptuous house opposite the gate of the Austin friars in London—indeed, we find him there as early as March 1524;[2] he was very frequently there later in Wolsey's time;[3] and it was his prin- cipal residence afterwards when he was Henry VIII.'s sole minister. He had been specially useful to Wolsey in suppressing the small monasteries, whose endow- ments the Cardinal was authorised to use in the foundation of his two colleges; he was called one of my Lord Cardinal's Council;[4] and being a man of decided literary taste, with plenty of wealth at command, why should he not have engaged, even on his own responsibility, a promising scholar among those Austin friars, who, though their home might not be in the London house adjoining his own resi- dence, no doubt frequently visited London and were lodged there during the times of their sojourn?

Again, might not his influence with Wolsey have appeared a considerable inducement to an assiduous scholar to rely on Cromwell's patronage in attempting an English version of the Bible? Tyndale's version, indeed, was already abroad, and was denounced by the clergy; but that was because it was considered corrupt and scandalous. There would be no real objection if such a work could get episcopal sanction,

[1] *L. P.*, IV. 3197.   [2] *L. P.*, IV. 166.
[3] *L. P.*, IV. 3675, 3742, 4433, 4837, 4843, 4906, 5034, 5069, 5268, 5285, etc.
[4] *L. P.*, IV. 5492.

to an English version made with care from the Vulgate, even if the translator collated it with modern versions in other languages. Such a work might be valued by the learned in the Cardinal's splendid college at Oxford, and so long as the translator was not one who was visibly at war with the Church, it would not matter much, to Wolsey at least, to what particular theological school he might attach himself. On this subject I may quote the words of the late Professor Brewer :—

Before the year 1528 he (Wolsey) had been indifferent, in a much greater degree than More, to the advance of Lutheran opinions. His selection of scholars and lecturers for his new colleges at Oxford and Ipswich had been chiefly made from those who were infected with the New Learning, as it was called; at all events from the rising young men of ability in both universities, whose Lutheran tendencies were scarcely considered by him as any disqualification. He was much less concerned than any other statesman or prelate of the time to suppress diversities of religious opinion by the secular arm, rightly judging that the most effectual way of meeting the evil would be the diffusion of education; and that societies of scholars, supplied with ample endowments and means of study, as in his college at Christ Church, would prove a more effectual support of the faith than violent repression or monastic institutions, which had now fallen far behind the necessities of the age.[1]

But with the alarm created by the sale of Tyndale's New Testament and Garret's escape from Oxford in 1528, Wolsey himself felt compelled to be more rigorous in his attitude towards heresy. At the same time men like Coverdale, if they persevered in their unpopular theology, had to declare themselves and fly if they could from impending fate. And so, as I have Coverdale's said, it would seem that Coverdale fled abroad, and exile. the next thing we hear about him definitely is that he, and Tyndale also, were at Hamburg together

---

[1] *Reign of Henry VIII.*, ii. 267 ; from Introduction to *L. P.*, IV. p. ccclxvi.

for a time in 1529. So Foxe tells us in these words :—

> At what time Tyndale had translated the fifth book of Moses called Deuteronomy, minding to print the same at Hamburg, he sailed thitherward ; where by the way upon the coast of Holland he suffered shipwreck, by which he lost all his books, writings, and copies, and so was compelled to begin all again anew, to his hindrance and doubling of his labors. Thus, having lost by that ship both money, his copies, and his time, he came in another ship to Hamburg, where, at his appointment, Master Coverdale tarried for him and helped him in the translating of the whole five books of Moses, from Easter to December, in the house of a worshipful widow, Mistress Margaret Van Emmerson, A.D. 1529,—a great sweating sickness being at the same time in the town. So, having despatched his business at Hamburg, he returned afterwards to Antwerp again.[1]

It is true that this story in all its details is difficult to reconcile with accepted facts ; so that while some investigators declare it " fully charged with inaccuracy," others have gone the length of treating it as an absolute fiction. Of course, if it is altogether true, the story of Packington's negotiation with Tyndale at Antwerp must be given up. Again, the idea of Coverdale assisting Tyndale in his translation, unless it were as a mere amanuensis, is scarcely plausible, as it is very questionable whether Coverdale knew anything of Hebrew. And further, the intention to print the Pentateuch at Hamburg is not likely, for there is some doubt whether Hamburg had a press at this time, although there is notice of one solitary work printed there as early as 1491. On the other hand, evidence has been found in other quarters that the sweating sickness was really prevalent in Hamburg in 1529, and that the widow of a senator named Van Emmerson was then resident in the town.[2] Moreover, the printing of Tyndale's Pentateuch was completed

---

[1] Foxe, v. 120.   [2] Demaus's *Tyndale*, pp. 220-21.

on the 17th January 1530, avowedly from the press of Hans Luft at Marburg.

"If theory may be admitted on the question," says Demaus, "it seems allowable to suppose that Foxe was mistaken as to the duration of Tyndale's visit to Hamburg. He may have returned from that city to Antwerp about the end of August, in time to allow of the interview with Packington; or the interview may have taken place in that immediate return to Antwerp which seems to have followed his shipwreck." Some such conjecture seems fairly admissible; and one more, perhaps, might clear up the whole difficulty. In reporting some information that he had received, Foxe might very well have mixed up the names of two places, Hamburg and Marburg, which were both in the story. Tyndale might have gone to Hamburg meaning to print at Marburg; and Coverdale, who does not seem to have looked on the enterprise of other translators as any bar to his own project,[1] might have assisted, even in his absence, in transcribing his work (might not some of his manuscripts have been recovered after his shipwreck damaged by sea-water ?), and in arranging for its conveyance when printed from Hamburg into England.

Thus the story in Foxe may possibly be accounted for without the suggestion of any unnatural mistakes. But it must be owned that speculation is dangerous, and even arguments that seem to be well grounded sometimes miscarry. On this very subject evidences that once seemed conclusive have been produced to show that the name of Marburg or " Marlborough in

---

[1] Coverdale seems to have had the most generous appreciation of Tyndale's work, regarding his own Bible as a mere stopgap till Tyndale should have completed his. In his "Prologue" addressed to the reader he writes: " Though Scripture be not worthily ministered unto thee in this translation by reason of my rudeness, yet if thou be fervent in thy prayer, God shall not only send it thee in a better shape by the ministration of other that began it afore, but shall also move the hearts of them which as yet meddled not withal to take it in hand, and to bestow the gift of their understanding thereon, as well in our language as other famous interpreters do in other languages."—Coverdale's *Remains*, p. 20 (Parker Soc.).

the land of Hesse," which appears in the date of this and other English publications professedly printed there by Hans Luft, was a fictitious place-name intended to mislead. This view, I regret to say, was treated as proved in the first impression of this work ; but I find it is now discredited, and as there is little doubt that Hans Luft had really a branch press at Marburg, we must presume that the ostensible date and place of publication of Tyndale's Pentateuch were the real ones.[1]

At this time, therefore, the evidences seem to show that both Tyndale and Coverdale remained abroad, the one as a heretic and the other as a runaway friar, neither of whom would have been safe in England.[2] What was Coverdale, the quondam friar, about during the next five years and a half ? The answer is clear. He was engaged in translating the Bible and getting it printed *somewhere*. The locality, however, has been a matter of speculation. He had the advantage of Tyndale in one respect, but in one respect only : he was allowed to complete, apparently undisturbed, a translation of the whole Scriptures. This must have been the work of years, and could only have been done abroad. He was lying hid, and nobody Where was knew what he was about all the while. He was he hid ? forgotten in England, and he was not even corresponding with Cromwell, so far as we know. In fact, if he wrote to him at all during this period, his letters, one would think, must have been systematically burned—a thing which is by no means inconceivable, as Cromwell could not have wished, after

---

[1] See on the one side Mombert's *English Versions of the Bible*, pp. 108-15, where the evidences for his view are fully given. They are also repeated in the same writer's " Biographical Notice of Tyndale " prefixed to his edition of Tyndale's Pentateuch (1884). On the other side, see Darlow and Moule's Historical Catalogue of printed editions of Holy Scripture in the Library of the British and Foreign Bible Society, i. 3 (Introd.), and the *Athenæum* for 18th April 1885.

[2] It seems that one "dominus Coverdale" took the degree of Bachelor of Laws at Cambridge during the year 1530 or 1531 (Grace Book B, part ii. 164, Luard Memorial Series). But though the name is almost unique, this could hardly be Miles Coverdale.

the year 1528, to be found in correspondence with a heretical friar who had fled abroad. But as Coverdale himself must have fully appreciated that fact, he most probably did not write to his former patron at all till times were considerably changed. That he ventured while abroad on the task of translating the whole Bible into English, and that he managed to get it printed abroad by October 1535, are matters which are past dispute ; but it could not very well have been under the encouragement of his first patron. How he did it we shall inquire presently.

Meanwhile let us consider what was going on in England while he was patiently and secretly pursuing this great labour. It was in 1530 that Tyndale's books generally were burned at St. Paul's, and that the King, having consulted his clergy, gave it to be understood that a new translation of Scripture was not then considered desirable, though it might be expedient later when there was a less violent spirit of Lollardy among the people. Hall's statement that the King at that time commanded the bishops to get a new translation made by learned men of the universities is not strictly accurate ; for all that Henry intimated then was that he would have a careful translation made of the New Testament, to be published at a more propitious time. He did not even promise that he would at once call upon the bishops to prepare one ; and to all appearance he did not. For four years later, in December 1534, the bishops themselves, together with the abbots and priors in the Convocation of Canterbury,

Proposal to petitioned the King to allow a new translation to be authorise made and delivered to the people. Their feeling, an English translation. indeed, remained as strong as ever against heretical books, especially in English, whether printed in England or beyond the seas, and they desired the King at the same time to command every one to deliver up such things under a penalty. They hoped also that he would forbid, under a penalty, quarrelsome disputations by laymen on articles of the Catholic Faith or on Holy Scripture.[1]   But the fact that they sought the King's leave to have a new translation made is surely sufficient proof that the King had not commanded them to make one.

No doubt, just as the King could get his faithful Commons to petition him to do anything he particularly wished to do, it may be urged that even the bishops in 1534 were subjected to some pressure, as indeed they were, far more than they had ever been till a few years before.   But there is no reason to believe that in petitioning the King for leave to get a translation made of the Bible they were acting at his instigation, for the appearances are quite otherwise.   The considerations which would naturally weigh with the bishops were evidently these.   Notwithstanding all their self-sacrifice they had found that the art of printing, the industry of Tyndale, and the enterprise of merchants in importing forbidden literature had made it really impossible to stop the circulation of translations which they considered objectionable, without setting forth a better.   The heretics, moreover, had been emboldened to keep up, even from the first, an agitation in favour of an English Bible—no doubt that they might be able to sell more freely Tyndale's Testament and Pentateuch ; and only half a year after the Council at Westminster and the proclamation against heretical books, when it was declared inexpedient to have the Scriptures in English, we find a nameless writer (who has been erroneously identified with Latimer) addressing a long letter to the King to destroy the effect of that proclamation, and urge him to let the Scriptures in English have the freest possible circulation.   This letter, which is distinctly dated at the end, of December 1530, begins with a long argument to show

[1] Wilkins, iii. 776.

that the greed and ambition of the clergy prove them to be no true followers of Christ, and that rather than have their wealth diminished "they will set debate between king and king, realm and realm, yea between the King and his subjects, and cause rebellion against the temporal power." Persecution, on the other hand, was what Christ promised to his followers, and where the Word of God was truly preached there was always persecution. The pretences on which the clergy wished the reading of Scripture in English forbidden were merely selfish.

"But as concerning this matter," the writer goes on, "other men have showed your Grace their minds how necessary it is to have the Scripture in English. The which thing also your Grace hath promised by your last proclamation ; the which promise I pray God that your gracious Highness may shortly perform even to-day, before to-morrow. Nor let the wickedness of these worldly men detain you from your godly purpose and promise. . . .

The King is urged to do so at once.

"But peradventure they will lay this against me, and say that experience doth show how that such men as call themselves followers of the Gospel regard not your Grace's commandment, neither set by your proclamation, and that was well proved by those persons which of late were punished in London for keeping such books as your Grace had prohibited by proclamation ; and so, like as they regarded not this, so they will not regard or esteem other your Grace's laws, statutes or ordinances. But this is but a crafty persuasion ; for your Grace knoweth that there is no man living, specially that loveth worldly promotion, that is so foolish to set forth, promote, or enhance his enemy, whereby he should be let of his worldly pleasures and fleshly desires ; but rather he will seek all the ways possible that he can, utterly to confound, destroy, and put him out of the way. And so, as concerning your last proclamation, prohibiting such books, the very true cause of it and chief counsellors (as men say, and of likelihood it should be) were they whose evil living and cloaked hypocrisy these books uttered and disclosed. And howbeit that there were three or four that would have had the Scripture to go forth in English, yet it happened there, as it is evermore seen, that the most part overcometh the better. And so it might be that these men did not take this proclamation as yours, but as theirs set forth in your name, as they have done many times more, which hath put this your realm in great hindrance and trouble and brought it in great penury, and more would have done if God had not mercifully provided to bring your Grace to knowledge of the falsehood and privy treason which their head and captain was about." [1]

It was decidedly prudent in the writer of this letter not to put his name to it, but it was very rash on the part of Foxe, who first printed it, to attribute it to Latimer. Latimer was not the man thus to fly in the face of a royal proclamation to the passing of which he had himself been accessary.[2] Indeed, just before that proclamation he had been selected by the Vice-Chancellor of Cambridge as one of the twelve divines who were to meet an equal number of divines from Oxford to examine the mischievous English books commonly read among the people;[3] and if before the end of that year he had changed his tune so completely, it would undoubtedly have been made an additional article to those preferred against him for heresy in 1531. No, this letter to the King, which vilifies the clergy so much, may, indeed, have been written by a clergyman; but its object was to encourage prejudice against the clergy as a body, and to impute

---

[1] The whole letter may be read, reprinted from Foxe, in Latimer's *Remains*, pp. 297-309.   See Foxe, vii. 506-11.
[2] *L. P.*, IV. 6402.   [3] *L. P.*, IV. 6367.

to them interested motives in doing what was generally regarded as their duty. The last sentence, moreover, is an ignoble thrust at the fallen Cardinal Wolsey, dated the very day after his death. And the writer not only suggests that the clergy as a body are dangerous to the peace of kingdoms, but even insinuates that the men punished for disobeying the King's proclamation were more loyal than those who procured it; for he presumes that the proclamation had not really the King's approval, as it professed to have, and that the King had been misdirected by others to give his assent to it.

Now, all this was a bold thing to insinuate in the reign of Henry VIII. if it had not been the fact, as we have seen already, that the King was by no means unwilling, for purposes of his own at this time, to encourage complaints against the clergy, and even to have his own past policy in defence of their order discredited. If the writer was not Tyndale himself, who was abroad beyond reach of the English bishops, he was probably an intelligent layman in England who had a tolerable notion how the wind blew.[1] And it was quite agreeable to the King's secret purpose that some irresponsible persons should clamour for an English Bible just to give the clergy trouble. So whether the author were Tyndale or Cromwell, or some one else, there is no difficulty in understanding how such a letter was actually addressed to the King himself in 1530, and how a copy of it exists among the State Papers at this day.[2]

---

[1] I hesitate to suggest that it was Cromwell, for the case is by no means clear, and the reflection on his dead master, Wolsey, would be extremely discreditable to him. But Cromwell, though not called as yet to the King's Council, had already gained the King's ear, and, if we are to believe Pole, had already suggested to him Royal Supremacy over the Church, for which this reviling of the clergy and encouragement of heresy was the actual preparation.

[2] This copy was, unfortunately, overlooked in *L. P.*, IV.; and Professor Brewer, who knew the document only as printed in Foxe, suspected the date to be erroneous, which it must have been if Latimer had been the author. But the copy in the Record Office is dated as in Foxe.

But the clergy showed no intention to yield to such influences, and it does not appear that even the King had declared himself more in favour of having the Scriptures in English in 1534 than in 1530. Much else had taken place in those four years, and in no years certainly was the lesson more severely brought home to the clergy that they lay helpless under the heel of a ruthless despot who was resolved to turn ecclesiastical authority to his own purposes. I need not again remind the reader of the *præmunire*, the extortionate contribution, the acknowledgment of a qualified Supremacy (now to be treated as unqualified by Parliament), and the famous "Submission of the Clergy." These things, except the Statute of Supremacy, had cleared the way for the marriage with Anne Boleyn in 1533, and for the King's defiance of that papal excommunication which was sure to follow. And now, in the spring of 1534, the Lower House of Convocation had been got to vote, by a majority of thirty-four to four, and one vote doubtful, that the Bishop of Rome had not a higher authority than any other foreign bishop ;[1] after which Convocation was prorogued to November. In that and the following month, however, the divines were much occupied with the question how to check the circulation of those mischievous English books which found so much favour at Court. A number of them were handed in for examination, including one attributed to Tyndale—probably the work of that " nameless heretic " whom More had already answered, on " the Supper of the Lord." On the 19th December

---

[1] The question was astutely worded to answer the King's purpose :—
" Whether the Roman Pontiff had a greater jurisdiction conferred upon him by God *in Holy Writ* than any other foreign bishop." This way of putting it virtually forbade any one to say "Aye" who did not maintain that papal authority was founded on the text *Tu es Petrus*. Those who regarded it as of merely ecclesiastical origin, however highly they valued it, were bound to vote for the negative. That only thirty-nine of the clergy gave any vote at all, either for, against, or doubtful, is really pretty strong evidence how much they disliked the question being raised.

a writ was received in Convocation for its prorogation to the 4th November next year. But before reading it the Prolocutor communicated to the Archbishop and the bishops in the Upper House the censures of the Lower House on the books submitted to them. Then it was that the two resolutions were taken which have been already referred to. The bishops, abbots, and priors of the Upper House agreed that the Archbishop (Cranmer) should petition the King that all who possessed books of suspected doctrine, especially in English, printed on either side of the sea, should give them up within three months after warning to persons appointed by the King ; and further, that His Majesty would deign to allow Holy Scripture to be translated by good men to be named by him, and forbid, under a penalty, any layman among his subjects to dispute on articles of the Faith, or on Holy Scripture.[1]

Convoca-
tion and
the Bible.

It may possibly be, though there is no evidence of the fact, that the bishops and clergy were by this time aware of the last thing Tyndale had done abroad. In November he had just completed a revised edition of his New Testament, so that a translation by authority in England was all the more requisite to correct the poison of what was certainly considered a heretical and objectionable version. But whether aware of this or not, the bishops certainly thought it time to set to work upon an English version, and it is not true, as we are often told, that they did nothing, and cared to do nothing, in the matter. It is true, indeed, that the result of their labours appears to have been lost, and the constant sneer of followers of the New Learning that the bishops did nothing has acquired plausibility from the fact that what they did does not appear to be extant.

---

[1] Wilkins, iii. 769-70 ; cp. p. 776. The former entry is taken from Heylin's excerpts from the Convocation Records ; the latter from an extant MS. of the time in the Cottonian Library.

But one bishop, at least, was deeply interested in the project, and, notwithstanding many other calls upon him, which were certainly increased by the multiplicity of royal commands at this period, Stephen Gardiner completed, by his own labour, an English version of two of the Gospels.

Gardiner translates two of the Gospels.

This fact, which is incidentally mentioned by Gardiner himself in a letter to Cromwell, seems to be regarded by one of our biblical historians as an excellent joke,[1] though why we should disbelieve Gardiner's own statement in black and white, which Cromwell, to whom it was addressed, apparently never challenged, is not apparent. It is believed, of course, that Gardiner was the very last man in the world to think of translating the Bible. That the reader may form his own opinion, however, I quote the whole passage in which the statement occurs, premising only that the beginning of the letter relates to the execution of some commands laid upon the bishops by the King, the nature of which is not expressed.[2] Then comes another matter which has an interest of its own, though our information about it is imperfect :—

As touching children, I have delivered these verses herein enclosed, to be learned, to the scholars of Winchester. To other petty teachers I give commandment in general. This is done onward, and more shall be if ye think necessary; whereof I pray you take the pain to advertise me. And although, as I have devised the words to be spoken, I preach the matter upon Sunday next in every man's mouth, yet will I preach also, omitting all other respects of myself, rather than I should be otherwise taken than I am,—that is to say, openly to swear one thing and privily to work, say, or do otherwise; whereof I was never guilty. Nevertheless I have as great cause as any man to desire rest and quiet for the health of my body; whereunto I thought to have intended, and to abstain from books and writing, having finished the trans-

[1] Anderson, i. 453.
[2] Probably it had to do with the valuation of benefices. See Gardiner's letter a month earlier. *L. P.*, VIII. 654.

lation of St. Luke and St. John, wherein I have spent a great labor.[1]

It will be observed that Gardiner mentions his biblical labours only incidentally. His letter was about other things. The matter to be preached was no doubt the King's Supremacy, and children at school were to be taught the new doctrine in verses which they were to repeat by rote. But as regards the translation of the two Gospels, surely nothing is less like a joke or a statement that could have been intended to mislead. There was one bishop, however, it seems, not so compliant as Gardiner. On this subject I may as well quote a passage in Strype, familiar enough to students of the early English Bible, the information in which is derived from Foxe's MSS. The general ordering of the translation was naturally committed to Archbishop Cranmer, and the mode in which it was done was as follows :—

How Cranmer arranged for an English translation of the New Testament.

First, he began with the translation of the New Testament, taking an old English translation thereof, which he divided into nine or ten parts, causing each part to be written at large in a paper book, and then to be sent to the best learned bishops and others, to the intent they should make a perfect correction thereof. And when they had done, he required them to send back their parts, so corrected, unto him at Lambeth by a day limited for that purpose. And the same course, no question, he took with the Old Testament. It chanced that the Acts of the Apostles were sent to Bishop Stokesley [of London] to oversee and correct. When the day came, every man had sent to Lambeth their parts corrected; only Stokesley's portion was wanting. My lord of Canterbury wrote to the Bishop a letter for his part, requiring him to deliver them unto the bringer, his Secretary. He received the Archbishop's letter at Fulham, unto which he made this answer :— " I marvel what my lord of Canterbury meaneth, that thus abuseth the people, in giving them liberty to read the Scriptures, which doth nothing else but infect them with heresy. I have bestowed never an hour upon my portion, nor never

---

[1] State Papers, i. 430.

will. And therefore my lord shall have his book again, for I will never be guilty of bringing the simple people into error." My lord of Canterbury's servant took the book and brought the same to Lambeth unto my Lord, declaring my Lord of London's answer. When the Archbishop had perceived that the Bishop had done nothing therein, " I marvel," said he, " that my Lord of London is so froward that he will not do as other men do." One Mr. Thomas Lawney stood by; and hearing my Lord speak so much of the Bishop's untoward-ness, said " I can tell your Grace why my Lord of London will not bestow any labor or pains this way. Your Grace knoweth well that his portion is a piece of New Testament. But he being persuaded that Christ had bequeathed him nothing in his Testament, thought it mere madness to bestow any labor or pain where no gain was to be gotten. And, besides this, it is the Acts of the Apostles; which were simple poor fellows, and therefore my Lord of London dis-dained to have to do with any of them." Whereat my lord of Canterbury and others that stood by could not forbear from laughter.[1]

The authority for this story is a very good one, for the MS. which Strype followed was a writing of Cranmer's own secretary, Ralph Morice—in fact, of the very secretary whom the Archbishop despatched on this matter to Bishop Stokesley. Moreover, Strype has followed his authority closely, for except at the beginning he has simply transcribed every word with the least possible alteration to adapt it to his own narrative; and the flavour of the original telling by Morice is preserved. But as to the first sentence it is to be remarked that Morice does not speak of the Archbishop having made use of " an old English translation " of the New Testament as a basis, and he says nothing whatever, of course, of what Strype himself only mentions as a presumption, that the like was done with the Old Testament. The words of Morice are simply :—

My Lord Cranmer, minding to have the New Testament thoroughly corrected, divided the same into nine or ten parts

---

[1] Strype's *Cranmer*, i. 48, 49.

and caused it to be written at large in paper books, and sent unto the best learned bishops, etc.[1]

If Strype's version of the story here had been fully vouched for by his authority, we should have thought the "old English translation" which Cranmer took must have been a Wycliffite one, or perhaps an earlier still; for Tyndale's was a very modern one, besides being such as the bishops would most likely have declined even to use as a basis. Yet, strange to say, Anderson, who had no other authority than Strype to go by, quietly observes that "Cranmer took an existing translation—Tyndale's, of course, for as yet there was no other."[2] There certainly were others in existence, and though we do not know positively that it was an "old" version, I am rather inclined to think it was.

But the main thing to be noted in this well-authenticated story is that it confirms one statement that I have made above. Not only did the bishops generally in 1534 petition the King to let them get a new translation made, but they really co-operated to produce one. Every bishop did his part, with the single exception, it would seem, of Stokesley, who, we see, disapproved of the attempt, thinking it would do more harm than good, and lead the laity into heresy by encouraging every man to interpret the sacred text for himself without reference to the well-considered opinions of great divines and scholars. If this be so, a question arises whether Bishop Stokesley was present in the Convocation of 1534, where the wording of the record rather seems to imply that the resolution in favour of a new translation was passed by the bishops unanimously. But possibly the words of the record really mean that only the resolution touching heretical books was passed unanimously, and that the resolution which followed it, touching a new

The bishops, with one exception, co-operate.

---

[1] See Nichols's *Narratives of the Reformation* (Camden Society), p. 277.
[2] *Annals of the Bible*, i. 453.

translation, was passed by the bishops generally.[1]
Anyhow, we are given to understand that the bishops,
one and all, except Stokesley, sent in to the Archbishop at Lambeth the portions allotted to them, so
that a number of MSS., forming together a nearly
complete English New Testament of episcopal origin,
were among the treasures of Lambeth in the year
1535. What has become of them?

On the 4th October Coverdale completed his great
labour, and for the first time there existed a printed
edition of the whole Bible in English. Where had it
been printed? Scholars for a long time could not
answer the question. But more than forty years ago
Dr. Ginsburg produced what seems quite conclusive
evidence that it issued from the press of Froschover
at Zurich.[2] We must not, however, suppose that
Coverdale at once betook himself to Zurich when he
left England in 1528; for it was not likely that he
should have gone so far in the first instance, and we
have seen already that he was with Tyndale at Hamburg in 1529. Possibly—indeed I think, probably—
before he went to Hamburg he had gone to the
Netherlands, the country from which the largest
amount of heretical literature was imported into
England, and where English heretics, until particularly sought after, could often rest for a time tolerably secure. This, it is true, is only surmise, but we
have a piece of testimony of a later date which goes
far to confirm it.

In the life of Emanuel van Meteren, prefixed to his
Nederlandtsche Historie, in 1614, and written by his
friend the Reverend Symeon Ruytinck, it is stated
that he was born at Antwerp in 1535, and that he

Coverdale's Bible printed at Zurich,

---

[1] I think this must be the true meaning of the words, for we have no
record of any illness of Bishop Stokesley that could have kept him out of
Convocation in December 1534. Whether he attended the Parliament at
that date cannot be ascertained as the Roll of the year is wanting.

[2] See Kitto's *Cyclopædia of Biblical Literature* (1862), i. 567-9; also Dr.
Ginsburg's *Ecclesiastes*, App. ii.

was the son of Jacob van Meteren of Breda, who
"displayed his especial zeal in defraying the cost of
though the translating and printing the English Bible in Antwerp,
translation employing for that purpose the services of a learned
was helped student, Miles Coverdale by name, to the great
by advancement of the kingdom of Jesus Christ in
Meteren. England." Moreover, we are informed by Mr. Moens,
the editor of the *Register of the Dutch Church* at
Austin Friars, that the Reverend Symeon Ruytinck
was the senior minister of that church, and Emanuel
van Meteren was "one of the oldest members of the
congregation and the leading member of the merchant
strangers, as the Netherland Consul," so that there
must have been constant communication between
them.[1] Thus the information, though by no means
contemporary, must be considered of high importance.
Mr. Moens adds : "The whole history of the English
Bible of 1535 must have been well known to both;
to Van Meteren from his parents and to Ruytinck as
conservator of the archives of the church." But surely
some allowance as regards detail must be made for the
lapse of time, and Mr. Moens himself sees reason to
suspect that the words "and printing" in Ruytinck's
statement are inaccurate ; for they are not warranted
by a document which he presumes Ruytinck intended
to follow, but cited only from memory. This was
an affidavit of Emanuel Meteren, discovered by Mr.
Moens himself among the archives of the Dutch
Church, which is so important that I reproduce it
here :—

Emanuel Demetrius, marchant of Andwarp, aged about
74 yeares, doth witnes and can depose that he was brought in
England Anno 1550, in King Edward's the 6 dayes by his
father, a furtherer of reformed religion, and he that caused
the first Bible at his costes to be Englissled (*sic*) by Mr. Myles
Coverdal in Andwarp, the which his father, with Mr. Edward
Whytchurch, printed both in Paris and London ; by which

---

[1] *The Dutch Church Registers*, London, Historical Introduction, p. xiv.

meanes he, wel acquaynted, was one of the Suters for the erection of a Dutche Church at the Augustin Fryers, and made this Deponent a member of the same Anno 1552.

And he doth wel remember that the Churchyeard and houses on bothe sydes of the West dore of the Church were inhabited and possessed by the Members of the Church, and harde his father and others of the Elders of the Churche often tymes consel of buylding there, and making of another dore for the Churche at the Cestern to receyve the raynwater of the Churche to the vse of washing or bleaching.

But the sayd Church, Anno 1553, in Queen Mary's time was left, and the Members dispersed, and for a time was vsed for the Queen's storehouse for provision of a navy that went to Conquet in Brittaine, and afterwards vsed by the Florentyns marchants to say masse in, the Dutche pulpet always remayning in it.

At the Queen Elizabeth's coming to the Crowne, the former gift of King Edward was fully confirmed to the Strangers agayne, which bestowed great reparations, but the Churchyeard was then occupied by the then lord Tresuror, Marquis of Winchester, and his heyres, who plucked down the lead of the Quyre and covered it with tyles that was in their possession, and the vse of the churchyeard was differred and, lest to offend, neglected, yet often interpellation made. Thus much I can depose, in London, 28 of May 1609.

(*Signed*) EMANUEL DEMETRIUS.[1]

Interesting as this document is throughout, we are of course only concerned with the first paragraph here, which, it will be seen, fully bears out the statement that Coverdale translated the Bible at the expense of the elder Meteren. And this explains just what we were seeking to understand—how, having for the time lost Cromwell's patronage, he was enabled to go on with the great work that Cromwell had originally set him on, by the zeal and liberality, perhaps we might also say by the enterprise, of a flourishing trader abroad. But this deposition, it must be remembered, is far from being contemporary. In fact, it is only a conscientious state-

[1] Van Meteren or Demetrius ; according to the custom of the day, learned and eminent men gave a Latin rendering to their names.

ment made by one who was born in the very year
when Coverdale's Bible first appeared; and though it
fully warrants us in believing that his father bore
Coverdale's expenses in translating the Bible into
English, it does not follow that his father printed the
first edition. It was another Bible, though mostly
made up from Coverdale's, that "his father with Mr.
Edward Whytchurch printed in Paris and London"
three years later.

That Jacob van Meteren, who had enabled Coverdale to live while translating the Bible, would willingly
have printed the first edition of it may be taken for
granted; but it seems from what has been already
said that it was printed at Zurich. And it is further
shown by Dr. Ginsburg that not only does the typo-
graphy declare unmistakably that it emanated from
the press of Froschover, but the translation itself
follows closely, even in the headings of the chapters,
that of the German Swiss Bible printed by him in
1531. It seems, therefore, that whatever progress he
may have made with the work at Antwerp with the
assistance he had received from Meteren, it could
only have been in manuscript. Probably he found it
unsafe to remain at Antwerp and was obliged to shift
his quarters; or, it may be, Meteren found it unsafe
to print for him. At Zurich, no doubt, he not only
enjoyed greater security but also met with the same
zealous and liberal assistance that had been given
him by Meteren at Antwerp; for Froschover was a
warm friend to scholars, especially to Reformers. And
when the great enterprise was at length completed,
there was no doubt good reason to believe that it
could be made to pay its expenses; for Coverdale's old
patron, Cromwell, was no longer in fear of the Church,
but was the Church's master, and so was in a
position to turn his biblical labours to considerable
account. For he was by this time the King's Vicar-
General in spiritual matters, and probably would have

little difficulty in imposing an English Bible on the clergy, even by his own authority. Doubtless Meteren and the Flemish traders had been able to get him spoken to on the subject, even before the book arrived in England.

There had been for some years before this a large influx into England of books printed abroad, even English books, many of them. This was counted a grievance, and by an Act of the 25th of Henry VIII.,[1] passed to encourage English industries, it was forbidden under a penalty of six shillings and eightpence a volume to buy books printed abroad, ready bound in leather or parchment, for sale in England, after Christmas 1534; or to buy any books printed abroad, of aliens, except wholesale. This Act was naturally an obstacle to the commercial success of the new Bible, but a device was found to disarm suspicions, as well as, perhaps, to remove other objections. The first sheet, with the title-page and preliminary matter, was removed and a new sheet substituted, which was undoubtedly printed by James Nycolson of Southwark. No complete copy of the original sheet and title-page now exists, and only one copy is known of two leaves of that sheet, including the original title-page printed by Froschover. The new title-page contained a change in the wording, for it omitted a statement honestly made on the face of the work that it was " translated out of Douche " (that is to say, German) " and Latyn." Evidently such a confession was not thought to be a recommendation.[2] So a new title-page and a new sheet of preliminary matter were inserted, with which the volume was issued and reissued in three successive years, as there are dated editions of 1535, 1536, and 1537, all bearing the same corrected title-page. The first two

It was published in England with a new title-page.

[1] Stat. 25 Hen. VIII. c. 15.
[2] A strangely different inference was drawn by Mr. Fry, but surely the object of the suppression is obvious.

mentioned Queen Anne, that is to say, Anne Boleyn, in the dedication to the King; the last Queen Jane, that is to say, Jane Seymour.[1]

That Cromwell sought to recommend this Bible for political reasons in the days of Anne Boleyn there cannot be a doubt. On the 20th February 1536 Chapuys writes about it to Granvelle (under the mistaken impression which, we have seen, it was an object to promote, that the whole book was printed in England):—"A Bible has been printed here in England in which the texts that favour the Queen [*i.e.* the late Queen Katharine], especially Deuteronomy xix., have been translated in the opposite sense."[2] The reference, Deut. xix., is evidently a mistake, for there is nothing in that chapter about marriage with a deceased brother's wife. The passage intended was undoubtedly Deut. xxv. 5, in which Coverdale, advised, as we may suppose, by some scholars of the day, substituted, "hir kynsman" for "her husband's brother." Elsewhere, as in Leviticus xviii. 16, this Bible might be quoted in justification of the marriage with Anne Boleyn, so long as that was an object. But Anne was brought to the block, and her marriage declared null, in May of the same year. Still, the King adhered to the view that his

---

[1] See *The Bible by Coverdale,* MDXXXV. By Francis Fry, F.S.A., London, 1867. This brief and careful treatise, with facsimiles from the different issues, is most valuable for the information which it gives, but some of the inferences seem to have been made in ignorance that Dr. Ginsburg had already proved decisively that the book was printed by Froschover at Zurich, and also that Coverdale could not have translated it from the Hebrew (see authorities cited at p. 271, note 2). It is strange also that not only Mr. Fry, but other commentators before him, should have discredited Coverdale's own words that the work was "translated out of Douche and Latyn," and supposed that they were withdrawn by Coverdale himself because he had really examined the Hebrew text! The only written evidence that might suggest a knowledge of Hebrew on his part is his joint letter with Grafton to Cromwell in 1538 (State Papers, i. 576); but the words do not necessarily bear this meaning, for the Bible to which they refer was partly Tyndale's. And Coverdale further says in his dedication to the King that he translated "out of five sundry interpreters." He clearly never claimed originality as a translator. At the same time he very likely took the opinion of some Hebrew scholar about one or two passages like Deut. xxv. 5, to which I am about to refer. [2] *L. P.,* x. 352.

first marriage was unlawful; and, apart from its exposition of the Levitical law, the value of a whole printed Bible in English required little argument to set it forth.

In August of the same year Cromwell, as the King's Vicegerent (now also Lord Privy Seal), issued a set of injunctions to the clergy, one article of which required the incumbent of every parish to procure, before the feast of St. Peter ad Vincula next coming—that is to say, the 1st August in the following year—a whole Bible in Latin and also one in English, to be placed in the choir for the use of any who chose to read them. The only printed English Bible procurable at that time was Coverdale's, and it would seem that Cromwell was bent on turning the project, which he had so long ago encouraged Coverdale to undertake, into a good mercantile speculation. It may be doubted, indeed, whether the pecuniary aid which he had given to Coverdale before his flight from England was on a very liberal scale, for at that time the translator could not have made much progress with the work, and Cromwell was not the man to invest money in a scheme from which there was little hope of profit. In Wolsey's time, moreover, he could never have expected to be able greatly to promote the sale of the book by his own personal influence. But now he had much in his power. He believed that he could compel every parish clergyman in England to purchase a copy before August 1537. But apparently some obstacles presented themselves, and this clause, though included in the injunctions of 1536 as printed by Bertholet, was omitted in the copy in Cranmer's Register.[1] There was, moreover, inserted in the other set of injunctions issued two years later, in September 1538, a similar order to

Ordered to be placed in churches.

---

[1] Pocock, in his edition of Burnet, says that it is found in Bonner's Register, though not in Cranmer's; which is curious, as Bonner was not a bishop in 1536.

provide for each church a "whole Bible of the largest volume" in English, nothing being there said about a Latin one, and there seems every reason to believe that the order of 1536 about Bibles could not have been generally enforced.

The question whether the Bible were the only rule of faith, assumed an acute form in the year 1537. A "book of Articles" had been published the year before by royal authority, setting forth some cardinal principles of the Church, including Transubstantiation and the three Sacraments of Baptism, of Penance, and of the Altar, nothing being said about the other four generally recognised. This seems to have been intended as a kind of compromise, for it contained nothing at variance with old beliefs, and could only be considered unsatisfactory on points on which it was silent. But since then had occurred the great Northern Rebellion, or series of rebellions rather, largely occasioned by the putting down of the minor monasteries, and the belief that religion was being tampered with by Cromwell as the King's Vicegerent, aided by bishops who had owed their promotion to their approval of the marriage with Anne Boleyn. Anne Boleyn was now gone, but her bishops remained, and the hope generally entertained at first that with the unhappy Queen's fall the King and kingdom would return to their old spiritual allegiance had been rudely dissipated. The King, however, evidently felt it necessary to show that he was meditating no unjustifiable changes ; and no sooner had the rebellions in the North been repressed, the failure of which men even then imprudently regretted, than he caused his bishops and divines to assemble at Westminster to consider the terms of a new and more complete religious settlement. The bishops began to meet in February 1537, and continued their sittings till the middle of July ; when, among other satisfactory results, it was given out that the four Sacraments omitted in last year's formulary were " found again." [1] The final issue of their deliberations was the little treatise called *The Institution of a Christian Man,* more popularly named " the Bishops' Book."

"The Bishops' Book."

During these deliberations, one day when Cromwell presided in the Assembly as the King's Vicar-General, he introduced to the bishops the Scotsman, John Alane, better known by his Latinised name of Alesius,[2] as the King's scholar, for whom he desired a respectful and indifferent hearing. Alesius thereupon spoke in support of Cranmer against the proposition maintained by most of the other bishops that there were seven Sacraments, and when answered by Bishop Stokesley, who ventured to maintain it by what Alesius himself, describing the discussion, elegantly calls " certain stinking glosses and old lousy writers," replied again, offering to prove next day that the Christian faith rested only on what was written in the Bible. His intrusion in the debate was naturally resented, and Cranmer himself felt compelled to warn him, as even Cromwell did also,

---

[1] *L. P.,* XII. i. 789 (p. 346).

[2] I must here correct, I fear, more than one error of my own on this matter. The explicit date, 1537, given by Alesius himself to this incident had been questioned by others (see Hardwick's *Reformation,* p. 182, *n.* 5), and in my *English Church in the Sixteenth Century,* p. 175, I followed Canon Dixon in referring it to the discussion in Convocation on the Ten Articles in 1536. But the presumption founded on the fact that Bishop Foxe is described as having newly come out of Germany ought scarcely, I think, to discredit the date given by the author himself, seeing that all else agrees just as well with the spring of the following year, and, indeed, even better ; for the articles agreed to in 1536 could not have occasioned much, if any, controversy, whereas in 1537 the question was about a fuller statement of doctrine. Moreover, the book in which this date is given ("Of the Auctorite of the Word of God ") would seem to have been published in 1538—not within five years of the arrival of its author, Alesius, in England, as I have stated in *L. P.,* XII. i. 790 (p. 346 *n.*), but five years after his *Epistola contra decretum quoddam Episcoporum in Scotia quod prohibet legere Novi Testamenti libros lingua vernacula.* This book, of which there is a copy in the Grenville Library in the British Museum, is distinctly dated 1533, and it was written and published when he was in Germany. His book on the "Word of God," therefore, was presumably published in 1538, the year after the incident had taken place, and is not likely to have been wrong about the date.

not to appear again, though Cromwell had, not long before, for his own part, rebuked Bishop Stokesley for defending "unwritten verities." In short, it is evident that it had been Cromwell's policy, by the aid of Alesius and of the Anne Boleyn bishops, to lower the received standard of the Church's teaching, but he had found it expedient to forbear.

But the policy of forcing an English Bible upon the use of the Church was, as we have seen, by no means given up, for it was enforced again by the second set of royal injunctions issued in 1538. Meanwhile, in the August of the same year, 1537, a
A new
English
Bible.
new English Bible makes its appearance quite suddenly, in very remarkable circumstances. The bishops had completed their "Book" in the middle of July, and had been glad to escape from London, where there was great mortality from a visitation of the plague.[1] Archbishop Cranmer had got down to Ford in Kent, when he wrote to Cromwell in praise of this new translation, of which he sent him a copy by the bearer of his letter. He liked it better than any previous translation. It might, no doubt, have faults which could be from time to time amended; but he begged Cromwell to show it to the King, to whom it was dedicated, and obtain his licence, if possible, that it might be sold, and that every one might read it freely, "until such time," he writes, "that we, the Bishops, shall set forth a better translation, which I think will not be till a day after Doomsday!"[2]

Cromwell did present it to the King and obtained the licence required.[3] But whence did this Bible come, of which we have no earlier notice? Did the translator bring it down to Cranmer in Kent, or could the Archbishop have brought it with him from London? And were Cromwell and the King wholly

---

[1] *L. P.*, XII. ii. 293.   [2] *L. P.*, XII. ii. 434; State Papers, i. 561.
[3] *L. P.*, XII. ii. 512.

unprepared for its appearance ?   The last supposition
is scarcely probable.   Yet the origin of the book was
certainly mysterious.   On the title-page it professed
to contain "the Old and New Testament, truly and
purely translated into English by Thomas Matthew."
The name was a fiction.   In fact, the title-page itself
was a fiction, intended to convey the impression of
being, what Cranmer distinctly calls it, a new translation.[1]   For it was no new translation at all, but a
compound of two which had already appeared.   The
first books of the Old Testament to the end of the
Second Book of Chronicles, and the whole of the New
Testament, were actually Tyndale's—the very translation which had been all along denounced ; the rest
was Coverdale's, only subjected to some revision.
The name Thomas Matthew itself was apparently an
alias of John Rogers, who became the first of the
long catalogue of martyrs under Queen Mary.   And
yet the part taken by Rogers was not that of a translator, but only a reviser and annotator of the work
of others.   He had been chaplain to the Merchants
Adventurers at Antwerp, where he had been familiar
with Tyndale ; and it was there, no doubt, after Tyndale's death, that he got printed off the first part of
this composite Bible as far as the beginning of Isaiah.
From this point the printing was continued by Richard

---

[1] Foxe, himself, is wonderfully candid on this subject, for he tells us (v.
410) : "In the translation of this Bible the greatest doer was indeed William
Tyndale, who with the help of Miles Coverdale, had translated all the books
thereof, except only the Apocrypha, and certain notes in the margin, which
were added after.   But because the said William Tyndale, in the mean-
time, was apprehended before this Bible was fully perfected, it was thought
good to them that had the doing thereof to change the name of William
Tyndale, *because that name was odious, and to father it by a strange name
of Thomas Matthewe* ; John Rogers, at the same time, being corrector to the
print, who had then translated the residue of the Apocrypha, and added
also certain notes thereto in the margin ; and thereof came it to be called
'Thomas Matthewes Bible.' "   Foxe here overestimates the amount of the
work done by Tyndale, and is wrong in saying that Coverdale co-operated
with him in the translation, the truth being that what was not Tyndale's in
this version was supplemented from Coverdale's.   But he is certainly right
in saying that the name of Thomas Matthew was a mere blind, to cheat the
public, and, if possible, even the bishops, with the acceptance of Tyndale's
work.

Grafton, a member of the Grocers' Company of London, and his partner, Edward Whitchurch,[1] the half-printed work having been, no doubt, smuggled into England by the agency of the Merchants Adventurers. The printing was completed in secret, and the work was not referred either to the bishops or to Convocation. But the Archbishop's approval shut the mouths of all objectors, and while Cromwell reigned, at least, no one ventured to criticise the shortcomings of the book.

In expressing his thanks to Cromwell for obtaining the King's licence for the free sale of the work, Cranmer wrote, "You have showed me more pleasure herein than if you had given me a thousand pound."[2] But Grafton, the printer, writing to Cromwell shortly afterwards, was naturally still more interested. In asking his acceptance of six copies of the book as a present, he said it was for his "most godly pains, for which the Heavenly Father is bound, even of His justice, to reward you with the everlasting Kingdom of God." Such incense was not too gross to be offered to the all-powerful minister, especially when the writer had a practical object in respect of his own interests. In spite of what Cromwell had done, there were some, it seemed, who would not believe the King meant to authorise the publication, and he begged that it might be licensed under the Privy Seal, of which Cromwell was the Keeper. As this was for the maintenance of the Lord's Word, no doubt Cromwell would be earnest therein, and Archbishop Cranmer and Bishops Latimer and Shaxton would also thank him.[3] Cromwell, however, did not think the Privy Seal authorisation necessary, and Grafton wrote to him next, desiring him to consider the great expense he had incurred. For he had printed 1500 complete copies, and it had cost him over £500 ; and

[1] Anderson's *Annals*, i. 568-9 ; Chester's *Rogers*, p. 29.
[2] *L. P.*, XII. ii. 512; Cranmer's *Remains* (Parker Soc.), pp. 345-6.
[3] *L. P.*, XII. ii. 593 ; Cranmer's *Remains, ib.*

now that the work was commended, other printers
were going to reissue it in cheaper editions in a
smaller type.   It was pure covetousness on their
part, and they would be sure to falsify the text, for
they did not seek to set it out "for God's glory."
Some Dutchmen dwelling in England, who could
neither speak nor write good English, were actually
going to undertake the printing, and would not give
£20 or £40 to a learned man to see it well done.
But, in truth, if any other printed it before he had
sold his copies (which, he believed, would take three
years at least), Grafton considered himself utterly
undone.   So he begged that he might either have
the sole privilege meanwhile, or else, as an excellent
means to take away "blindness and superstition,"
that Cromwell would command, in the King's name,
that every beneficed clergyman should procure a copy, How
"that they may learn to know God and to instruct Grafton
their parishioners."   Also that every abbey should sale to be
procure six, to be laid in six several places for the pushed.
use of the convent and visitors (at this time the
larger abbeys still remained, though the smaller had
been suppressed).   "Yea," he adds, "I would none
other but they of the papistical sort should be compelled to have them, and then I know there should
be enough found in my lord of London's diocese to
spend away a great part of them ; and so should this
be a godly act worthy to be had in remembrance
while the world doth stand." [1]
    This combination of oily hypocrisy and self-interest
was addressed to a minister who understood business.   Indeed, we have seen already that in 1536
Cromwell himself had thought of compelling every
parish clergyman to purchase a copy of Coverdale's
translation, and though he forbore to carry out the
idea at that time, the same policy was revived two
years later, that is to say, in September 1538, the

[1] *L. P.*, XII. ii. App. 35 ; Strype's *Cranmer*, App. xx.

year after Grafton had thus written to him. In the injunctions of that date we read as follows :—

Item, that you shall provide, on this side the feast of Easter next coming, one book of the whole Bible of the largest volume, in English, and the same set up in some convenient place within the said church that you have cure of, where as your parishioners may most commodiously resort to the same and read it; the charges of which book shall be rateably borne between you, the parson, and the parishioners aforesaid, that is to say, the one-half by you and the other half by them.

Item, that you shall discourage no man, privily or apertly, from the reading or hearing of the said Bible, but shall expressly provoke, stir, and exhort every person to read the same as that which is the very lively word of God that every Christian man is bound to embrace, believe and follow if he look to be saved; admonishing them, nevertheless, to avoid all contention and altercation therein, and to use an honest sobriety in the inquisition of the true sense of the same, and refer the explication of obscure places to men of higher judgment in Scripture.

Injunctions like these may seem very plausible as a means of promoting general knowledge of the Scriptures ; but they were absolutely at variance with the methods by which, as we have seen, the Church had hitherto sought to guard the special sanctity of Holy Writ from careless interpretations and profane and vulgar use. The latter clauses, indeed, containing an admonition to avoid altercations and to use " sobriety," were added apparently merely to meet objections on the score of decency. Parsons were to be compelled to place Bibles in their churches and bear half the expense of doing so, in order that the exposition of Scripture might be, as much as possible, taken out of their hands, so as to please men of the new school. Of course a great many parsons considered obedience to such an injunction, not as a duty, but as a violation of duty, and obedience, consequently, could not be pressed effectually.

But before these latter injunctions were issued Cromwell's thoughts had taken a wider range, and he had determined to employ both Grafton and Coverdale on a more luxurious work. In fact, they were both engaged upon it at that very time in Paris, where the "Bible of the largest volume" was even then passing through the press under their supervision and that of William Gray, the ballad-maker who had contributed so much ribald verse to the great cause of putting down superstition. Grafton's fears of being under-sold were doubtless easily dissipated. Cromwell's authority would have checked that without any special ordinance. Except a revision of Matthew's Bible by Richard Taverner, who had been one of the "New Learning" canons in Wolsey's College at Oxford, there seems to have been no reprinting of that work by other printers, and Taverner's was virtually a different Bible, favoured by authority and dedicated to the King. Its influence, indeed, though published in two editions, folio and quarto, was but slight and transient. Such emendations as it introduced, though made by a competent Greek scholar, were sometimes whimsical, and were not followed in subsequent translations. The book, in short, very soon became, what it remains to this day, a mere curiosity. But Matthew's Bible kept its place and became the basis of all further authoritative editions; and Coverdale was now seeing what was afterwards known as "the Great Bible" through the press at Paris, where finer paper could be had, and where the art of printing had been carried to greater perfection than in England. A licence had been obtained from Francis I.[1] not only to print the work but to convey the printed copies into England, with merely a saving clause that the printers should do their work honestly, without making it the vehicle of private or illegitimate opinions. A more unqualified

The "Great Bible" printed at Paris.

---

[1] *L. P.*, XIII. ii. 973. See the text in Strype's *Cranmer*, App. No. xxx.

licence could not have been expected in that day in any Christian country.

Francis, no doubt, was willing to oblige Henry, even by protecting his agents against the Inquisition to some extent, if he could only have done so decently. But he could not have done more in this case without recognising and protecting what was accounted heresy. So Coverdale and Grafton had not long got to work before they were threatened with interference;[1] but they remained unmolested for nearly six months more. They were complained of, however, by Englishmen at Paris. In the middle of December they confided as much of the work as was then ready to Bonner, at that time Bishop of Hereford and ambassador in France, to be conveyed into England.[2] Four days later a second citation (we do not know the date of the first) was out against them and Francis Regnault, the bookseller under whom they worked.[3] Coverdale and Grafton escaped from Paris, leaving behind them the copies still remaining, which were to be destroyed in the Place Maulbert. Foxe says the number was 2500, which perhaps was the whole impression, and Bonner had certainly been able to get a good number sent off. But they recovered "four great dryfats of them" by purchase afterwards from a haberdasher to whom "the lieutenant-criminal," in his covetousness, had sold this quantity.[4] As for the rest, neither Bonner's remonstrances, which were very earnest, nor Cromwell's own complaints on the matter to the French ambassador Marillac, seem to have had much effect.[5] The work, however, was completed in England in April, for means were found to get away from Paris the printing presses, types, and even workmen; and a copy on vellum is now in St. John's College, Cambridge, containing the statement at the end that it

[1] *L. P.*, XIII. i. 1249 (State Papers, i. 575).   [2] *L. P.*, XIII. ii. 1043.
[3] *L. P.*, XIII. ii. 1085, 1086.   [4] Foxe, v. 411.
[5] *L. P.*, XIV. i. 371 (1, 2), 908 (p. 425), 934, 989, 1208.

was " fynished in Apryll, anno 1539." [1] It was completed in haste for use in the churches as required by the injunctions, without an intended commentary to which notes of reference were printed throughout the volume. [2]

Thus the " Bible of the largest volume " was not in the hands of the public until more than half a year after the proclamation which enjoined the use of it in churches ; and the proclamation, even by the very nature of things, could not be generally obeyed—as we actually know it was not even two years later. [3] But in that same month of April 1539 Parliament assembled, and the King, being in great dread of invasion by a possible combination against him to give effect to papal excommunication, was intending " to extinguish diversities of opinion " by law, so as to show himself as good a Christian as any continental sovereign. Even at the beginning of the session, in anticipation of the passing of the Act of the Six Articles, he had drawn up a proclamation to correct the abuses which had sprung up from such diversities. These, he found, had been fostered by disputes over the Scriptures, the use of which in English he had sanctioned : some arguing from them in a manner to subvert the sacraments, and others for the restoration of the Bishop of Rome, of pilgrimages, of idolatry, and of other old superstitions. He therefore ordered that no one, under a penalty, should call another heretic or Papist unless he was prepared to prove it ; that none except beneficed clergymen, or graduates of Oxford or Cambridge, should be admitted to preach or expound the Bible, and that none should read it in church in a high voice so as to create disturbances. [4]

On the 14th November following, Cromwell, though he could get no reimbursement from France of the

The Act against diversities of opinion.

---

[1] Anderson, ii. 31, 79. [2] Westcott's *History of the English Bible.*
[3] See *L. P.*, XVI. 783, 803 (Burnet, iv. 507).
[4] *L. P.*, XIV. i. 868. Printed in Strype, *Eccl. Mem.* I. ii. 434 ; also (but under a wrong date) in Wilkins, iii. 810-11.

expenses which he told Marillac he himself had laid out in the printing of this Bible, obtained from his own King a commission to prevent any one printing it without his leave for five years, on the ground that otherwise it might lead to inconveniences, " as when wilful and heady folks shall confer upon the diversity of the said translations." [1]   Curiously enough, on that very day Cranmer had written to Cromwell about the price to be charged for the " Great Bibles," for which he had composed a Preface and submitted it to the King's judgment.   The King's printer, Bartelett (or Berthelet), and Edward Whitchurch, the partner of Grafton who was actually employed on the work, had been with him, and by Bartelett's advice he had arranged that the volumes should be sold for thirteen shillings and fourpence a piece.   But he understood from Whitchurch that Cromwell wanted them sold at ten shillings, and though Whitchurch thought this too low, he and Grafton were content, provided they had a monopoly of the sale. [2]

The book came out with Cranmer's Preface in April 1540 ; and very shortly afterwards, on the 7th May, we find John Uvedale writing to Cromwell in further-ance of advice which he had already given to him personally, to enjoin the bishops, each to set up in his cathedral "two or three Bibles, as seemly and ornately as they can deck them, with seats and forms for men of all ages to read and study on them." This, he considered, would be the godliest monument they could leave in their churches. [3]   It was meant to be, apparently, an invitation for laymen as well as clergy-men to read and expound the Scriptures in cathedrals to separate congregations, occupying seats and forms round the reader, whether the clergy in charge approved of it or not.

But Cromwell was now scarcely in a position to

[1] L. P., xiv. ii. 516 (Rymer, xiv. 649).
[2] L. P., xiv. ii. 517 (State Papers, i. 589).   [3] L. P., xv. 648.

take such a step. Although just made Earl of Essex Cromwell's
his fall was really impending; and he was doubtless position
precarious.
pretty well aware how precarious the King's favour
was. It was uncertain, indeed, from day to day
whether the religious policy of which he had been the
instrument would be maintained or reversed. One
morning Sampson, Bishop of Chichester, was desig-
nated for the proposed new bishopric of Westminster.
Two hours later he was committed to the Tower on a
charge of treason,[1] and the bishopric was afterwards
given to Thirlby. That Sampson's preferment would
have meant a return to ancient ways in many things
is perfectly certain; and no less certain is it that his
arrest meant a change to the very opposite policy, as
Dr. Nicholas Wilson, a leading divine of the old
school, was arrested along with him. And so the
fitful changes went on till Anne of Cleves was divorced
and Cromwell himself was sacrificed. Yet even then
the nation was made fully aware that there was to be
no return to Popery. For two days after Cromwell's
execution, while three Lutherans were burned in
Smithfield—Dr. Barnes, William Jerome, and Thomas
Garrard, or Garret,—three Papists, Abell, Fetherstone, and Dr. Edward Powell, were butchered at the
same place as traitors by the horrible death then
awarded for treason.

Luther perfectly understood the situation when in
that very year he wrote, in reference to the death of
Dr. Barnes, who had been with him in Germany,
"What Squire Harry wills must be an article of the
faith for Englishmen, for life or death." [2]

After Cromwell's fall, Gardiner, who had been
excluded from the Council during his ascendancy,
had much more influence. But in spite of the Act
and Proclamation of 1539, the question who was a

---

[1] *L. P.*, xv. 737, 758. That Marillac means Bishop of Westminster by
"de Valmaister" is certain. See *L. P.*, xiv. ii. 429 (p. 152).

[2] *L. P.*, xvi. 106.

heretic and who was a Papist became more embittered than ever; only the contentious factions discharged their arrows at each other through the Press. There was a regular war of ballad-makers, some denouncing the fallen minister as a traitor and rejoicing at his overthrow, others rebuking the first set for want of charity, and accusing them of being popish and reactionary. Among the other poetasters one Thomas Smith, clerk of the Council to Queen Katharine Howard, was bitterly answered by William Gray, the ribald versifier who, as Cromwell's underling, had railed alike at such things as the Rood of Grace and at Friar Forest's martyrdom. Grafton printed Gray's ballads, and, to shield himself, issued them as "printed at London by Richard Bankes." But Richard Bankes denied before the Council that they had proceeded from his press, and Grafton was compelled to confess that he was the real printer, not only of these effusions, but also of an English translation of Melancthon's letter to Henry VIII. remonstrating against the Act of the Six Articles.[1] One Thomas Walpole had already been arrested for seditiously setting forth this epistle in reprobation of "the King's acts of Christian religion";[2] and the Council at once took pains to stop its circulation.

A war of ballad-makers.

Grafton was committed to the Fleet, as were also Thomas Smith, William Gray, and others. Grafton, however, had other things to answer for as well, which were probably brought against him after his committal. Foxe, who is our sole authority here, is certainly wrong in making them the cause of his committal, which the Privy Council records show to have been as above stated. But we may allow Foxe to state the matter in his own way :—

After this the bishops, bringing their purpose to pass, brought the lord Cromwell out of favor, and shortly to his

---

[1] *L. P.*, xvi. 366, 422-4.   [2] *L. P.*, xvi. 349, 351, 420, 424.

death; and, not long after, great complaint was made to the King of the translation of the Bible, and of the preface of the same; and then was the sale of the Bible commanded to be stayed, the bishops promising to amend and correct it, but never performing the same.   Then Grafton was called, and first charged with the printing of Matthew's Bible; but he being fearful of trouble, made excuses for himself in all things.   Then was he examined of the Great Bible, and what notes he was purposed to make; to which he answered that he knew none.   For his purpose was to have retained learned men to have made the notes; but when he perceived the King's Majesty and his Clergy not willing to have any, he proceeded no further.   But, for all these excuses, Grafton was sent to the Fleet, and there remained six weeks, and before he came out was bound, in three hundred pounds, that he should neither sell nor imprint, nor cause to be imprinted, any more bibles, until the King and the Clergy should agree upon a translation.   And thus was the Bible from that time stayed during the reign of King Henry VIII.[1]

What is said here of the conduct of the bishops is, of course, one-sided, and, moreover, not exactly true. That the bishops brought Cromwell out of favour is only a way of saying that old principles were recovering lost ground, for Cromwell's whole government had been one continual war upon their authority, and consequently on the peace and order of the Church. This had served the King's policy for a long time, but even he was not comfortable about it now. What the bishops actually did about the Scriptures we shall see presently. But there are some statements in the above extract which apparently require chronological adjustment—a thing not very wonderful, when they were written so many years after the events. For Grafton's committal to the Fleet was on the 4th January 1541, and the complaints of the bishops—at least those which stand on record—about the translation of the Bible were made in Convocation in February 1542. Nor is it true that the Bible was even from that date

---

[1] *Acts and Monuments*, v. 413.

"stayed, during the reign of Henry VIII." But though we have no actual record of the fact, it may conceivably have been stayed for a time after Grafton's imprisonment, or perhaps even before that event, soon after Cromwell's fall; for there seems indirect evidence to that effect, to be noticed further on. In that case the stay may have been due to the simple action of the bishops in their several dioceses, since they had to some extent recovered their authority by Cromwell's fall; and they were probably justified in saying that the King no longer insisted on the use of that English Bible required by Cromwell's injunctions.

Meanwhile we must take note of what was done after Grafton's committal to the Fleet. He does not appear to have lost, except, perhaps, for a few weeks, his position as the King's printer;[1] but on the 25th April 1541, nearly four months later, the privilege of selling the bibles "of the great volume" was given to Anthony Marler of London, merchant (who apparently had bought the stock from Grafton), the prices which he was permitted to charge being ten shillings for an unbound copy, and twelve shillings for a bound one "trimmed with bullions."[2] Marler, however, required conditions similar to those that Grafton had obtained. On the 1st May a petition from him was read in Council for the issue of a fresh

Every church to procure a bible. proclamation requiring that every church not yet provided with a bible should procure one according to the injunctions.[3] This was agreed to, and the new proclamation was issued on the 6th, setting forth that as many towns and parishes had neglected to comply with the King's injunctions in this matter, they were required to supply the books by All Saints' Day following, upon penalty of forty shillings for

---

[1] His name actually appears in conjunction with that of Whitchurch on the proclamation of 6th May 1541. See Ames's *Typographical Antiquities,* by Herbert and Dibdin, iii. 444.

[2] *L. P.,* XVI. 756.

[3] *L. P.,* XVI. 783.

every month's further delay.   It was also declared
that the King intended these bibles to be read humbly
and reverently.   People were not to read them aloud
in time of mass or other divine service, and, if
laymen, they were not to argue thereupon.[1]

Of the effect of this proclamation it may be well
to read what the French ambassador, Marillac, says in
writing to his own sovereign, Francis I., on the 11th
May 1541, just five days after it was issued:—

> What they are now in the way to do is to make new
> ordinances and decrees in matters of religion; wherein they
> change purposes so often that I cannot well think what will
> be the end of it all, as last year they put to death those whom
> they had used as instruments to put out the monks and apply
> the revenue of their foundations to this King's profit.   Several
> decrees were also made about bibles in their vernacular
> speech which they keep in all the churches, in such wise
> that the people dare no longer read them.   Now within
> these eight days they have made a contrary decree, giving
> permission to read the said bibles, which a few days before
> they wanted to take away entirely, with a very express com-
> mandment to all the bishops and their commissaries to
> preach to the people purely and simply the text of the bible
> without admitting any opinion of doctors.   Which thing,
> Sire, one knows not how to interpret, whether it be to
> discover thereby those who have any opinion contrary to
> what has been ordered, or if it be to enter further than
> ever into the new doctrines of the Germans.[2]

The struggle was evidently still going on between
the bishops and the innovators, and if the former had
succeeded for a while they were depressed again.
Vested interests were evidently against them.   Marler
must sell his bibles some way, just as Grafton had
done; and he had now got compulsory powers to
force the sale.   But the bishops, who had no longer
a Cromwell riding rough-shod over them, might hope
to plead their cause with the King himself, who was

[1] *L. P.*, XVI. 803, 819.
[2] Kaulek, *Corresp. politique de MM. de Castillon et de Marillac*, pp. 301-
302.

really both a reasonable and a very judicious sovereign in all that did not affect his own particular interests; and no doubt both Gardiner and other members of the episcopate had been making representations to him on the subject of these different bibles, which were, one and all of them, as they considered, corrupt, and calculated to do much mischief among the people. In fact, we know from Foxe himself that the very first of them, Matthew's Bible, with which Cranmer was so greatly pleased, had appeared to them exceedingly objectionable, and Foxe himself shall tell us why :—

The setting forth of this book did not a little offend the clergy, namely the bishops aforesaid, both for the prologues, and especially because in the same book was one special table collected of the common places in the Bible, and the Scriptures for the approbation of the same; and chiefly about the supper of the Lord, and marriage of priests, and the mass, which there was said not to be found in the Scripture.[1]

A few extracts from this "table of common places" will perhaps assist the reader to understand why the book seemed so objectionable. The subjects are arranged alphabetically, and the first article is " Abhomynacyon," under which we read :—

Offensive character of Matthew's Bible.

Abhomynacyon before God are idoles and images before whom the people do bow themselves.

This, of course, was intended as a direct rebuke to the time-honoured mode of worship observed in all the churches in the land.

Abuses.—The abuses that be in the Churche ought to be corrected by the Prynces.
Cursynge.—God doth curse the blessynges of the preastes and blesseth their curssyngz. Mala. ii. *a.*

And, to come to the special examples pointed at by Foxe himself:—

---

[1] *Acts and Monuments*, v. 412.

Maryage.—Maryage is institute of God, gen. ij. *d*; fro which none shulde be refused, for to avoyed fornycacyon j Cor. vij. *a*; for it is honorable.   Hebre xiij. *a*; the prayse wherof is Prover xviij. *d*.   The forbyddinge of mariage then is the doctryne of dyuels.   j Tim. *a*.

Masse.—The worde masse is not in the Byble, translated by S. Jerom, nor in none other that we have.   And therfore could I not tell what to note therof, but to sende the reader to the Souper of our Lorde Jesus Christ.   i Corin. xi. Act. xx. *b, c*.

Supper.—The supper of our Lord is a holy memorye & geuyng of thankes for the deth of Christ.   Mat. xxvj. *c*. Mar. xiiij. *c*.   Luke xxij.   i Cor. xi. *e*, x. *d*.

Is it extraordinary that, however Cranmer may have been pleased with it, the bishops generally objected to a Bible being thrust upon them containing prefatory matter of this description? How could those who had taken vows of celibacy, and considered them sacred, have allowed their people to read, even in their very churches, that what was called the "forbidding of marriage" was the doctrine of devils? Or how could honest clergy of the old school have tolerated statements suggesting that the mass was not authorised by the Bible, and that the Lord's Supper was only a memorial and giving of thanks? In spite of Cranmer's approbation of the book, the objections raised by the bishops evidently had some effect, for the Great Bible of 1539 had no such offensive "table of common places," nor the Bible of 1540 either, to which Cranmer supplied a Preface. But the translation itself did not please them, and when Convocation met in the beginning of 1542 a thorough examination of the whole book was called for. The King knew what was said about it, and on the 27th January Cranmer himself conveyed to the assembled clergy and prelates a royal message desiring them to consult among themselves what things needed reformation, as there was no doubt that there was much that required correction in the English Bible, both in the Old and in the New Testament. On the 3rd February the message was taken into consideration, and the Archbishop asked every one separately whether they could, without scandal and open offence to faithful souls, retain the Great Bible as translated in English. The

The Great Bible condemned by Convocation. majority declared that it could not be retained without careful revision and comparison with the Vulgate, and some other matters were put aside till this could be discussed. On the 13th, after a conference between the Houses about the mode of procedure, the Prolocutor of the Lower House entered the Upper House and presented a book of annotations made by the clergy, which he submitted to the judgment of the bishops. Select committees of the divines of both Houses were appointed to examine the New Testament and the Old; and on the 17th, when the Prolocutor again appeared in the Upper House, Gardiner read out a list of Latin words and phrases [1] which, on account of their

---

[1] These were : " Ecclesia, pænitentia, pontifex, ancilla, contritus, olocausta, justitia, justificare, idiota, elementa, baptizare, martyr, adorare, dignus, sandalium, simplex, tetrarcha, sacramentum, simulachrum, gloria, conflictationes, ceremonia, mysterium, religio, Spiritus Sanctus, spiritus, merces, Confiteor tibi Pater, Panis propositionis, communio, perseverare, dilectus, sapientia, pietas, presbyter, lites, servus, opera, sacrificium, benedictio, humilis, humilitas, scientia, Gentilis, synagoga, ejicere, misericordia, complacui, increpare, distribueretur, orbis, inculpatus, senior, Apocalypsis, satisfactio, contentio, conscientia, peccatum, peccator, idolum, prudentia, prudenter, parabola, magnifico, Oriens, subditus, didragma, hospitalitas, episcopus, gratia, charitas, tyrannus, concupiscentia, cisera, Apostolus, Apostolatus, egenus, stater, societas, zizania, Christus, conversari, profiteor, impositio manuum, idololatria, Dominus, Sanctus, confessio, imitator, Pascha, innumerabilis, inenarrabilis, infidelis, paganus, commilito, virtutes, dominationes, throni, potestates, hostia." The list was copied by Fuller from the records of Convocation, which are now lost, with the note, "Take faults and all, as in the original." It contains, certainly, as Fuller copied it, several manifest errors, which are partly corrected by Wilkins, whose corrections I have followed for the most part. But apparently some errors remain, *e.g.* "distribueretur orbis" (a single phrase wrongly treated as two separate words in Wilkins) seems to be a misreading of *distribueretur fabris* in 4 (2) Kings xxii. 9, where the English translation is really not quite so clear as the Latin. It is curious that when two accidental repetitions, *conflictationes* and *mysterium* have been struck out of the list printed by Fuller, the number of the words and separate headings handed in by Gardiner appears to have been exactly one hundred.

special significance, he wished to see retained, as far as possible, in their Latin form, or rendered into English as suitable as could be found,—meaning, apparently, by words etymologically similar.[1] His object, manifestly, was to maintain reverence for the sacred text, even at the cost of leaving it, possibly, a little mysterious at times. But it was the object of an opposite school to popularise the Scripture, even at the almost certain cost of many misapprehensions ; and that opposite school carried the day. It is true that an English Bible was not yet in everybody's hands, and, as it was soon felt, some abuses required to be checked. But the movement to popularise the language of Scripture, and, so far as may be, the deep thoughts of Scripture, has never abated from that day to this. It has, of course, given rise to much crude thinking, and even to a great deal of misapplied scholarship. But it is better in every way that there should be no cause of suspicion given to the multitude of anything that savours of an attempt to shut the gates of knowledge to the unlearned.

Yet Gardiner's protest in favour of preserving the Latin form of certain words was by no means uncalled for. It was doubtless framed with a view to the recognition of certain general principles of translation rather than to impugn any particular terms used in the Great Bible. In fact, the Great Bible itself had conformed to Gardiner's principle in many things where Wycliffe's and Coverdale's Bibles had adopted more familiar expressions—as in the use of the word " regeneration," where Wycliffe had translated it " again begetting," and Coverdale and " Matthew " " the new birth." So also Wycliffe had made Redeemer " again buyer," and Resurrection " rising

---

[1] " Publice legebat verba Latina in sacro volumine contenta, quae voluit pro eorum germano et nativo intellectu et rei majestate, quoad poterit vel in sua natura retineri, vel, quam accommodatissime fieri possit, in Anglicum sermonem verti."

again." And though it may be that no one desired to revive antiquated language, there was no less objection felt to mere commonplace phraseology. It would doubtless have been a shock, even to that generation, to have reproduced Wycliffe's version of our Lord's words in John xx. 17—"I have not yet styed to my Father."

But while the Old and New Testament committees were pursuing their work, although it could not have been left in more competent hands—for the men who served on them were undoubtedly the best Greek and Hebrew scholars then in England,—a new royal message came to the Houses, delivered through Cranmer as before. It is to be feared that Cranmer himself was a not unwilling counsellor in this, though the main object, doubtless, was to satisfy vested interests. The message was to the effect that Convocation were to proceed no further in the matter, as the King proposed to refer the translation of the Bible to the two Universities. The bishops not unnaturally resented this, and with only three exceptions (namely, Cranmer, Goodrich of Ely, and Barlow of St. David's) united in protesting that the business was one which was far more suitable to the Synod than to the Universities.[1] But Cranmer had the King's orders, and the work was put aside.[2] The real object was simply to stop the business of revision altogether, for two days later (on the 12th March) Anthony Marler obtained a patent giving him sole authority to print the Bible during the next four years.[3]

In short, the combined work of Tyndale and Coverdale was actually forced upon the clergy in

The revision stopped.

---

[1] According to Fuller, who had seen the original records of Convocation, the bishops affirmed that "the universities were much decayed of late, wherein all things were carried by young men, whose judgments were not to be relied on, so that the learning of the land was chiefly in this Convocation" (*Church History*, ed. Brewer, iii. 201).

[2] Wilkins, iii. 860-2.   [3] *L. P.*, XVII. 45 (Rymer, xiv. 745).

spite of all remonstrances. They had positively condemned the book in Convocation as unfit to be used
without very large revision, and they were proceeding
to revise it,[1] even in obedience to the King's own
message, when they were stopped and told to forbear
on a pretext which was a positive falsehood. The sale
of the faulty work was simply to be forced on as before.
The government of the Church was absolutely paralysed, and there was nothing left for bishops or clergy
but to pursue the policy of the importunate widow,
who had her just claims listened to at length by the
judge who feared not God, neither regarded man.[2]

The large bibles which had been set up in churches
were certainly not an unmixed blessing to the people.
Seats and forms may not have been provided to hear
them read, as Uvedale had suggested to Cromwell; but
we have seen already that disputes over the Scriptures had been seriously animadverted on by the King
himself, and that among other provisions against
abuses it was strictly forbidden to read those bibles
with a high voice so as to create disturbances. As
this was forbidden by proclamation, we may not
unreasonably suspect that it had been already practised ; and the fact that it was so comes out very
distinctly from the words of one who considered the
practice praiseworthy. In accordance with the injunctions, Bishop Bonner had placed six large bibles
in St. Paul's ; and this is how Foxe tells us that they
were used :—

The Bibles thus standing in Paul's, by the commandment
of the King and the appointment of Bonner the bishop, many

---

[1] Drs. Wotton and Leighton had laid before Gardiner in Convocation a
translation made by themselves of St. Paul's Epistles to the Corinthians, in
the session to which the royal message was announced. (Wilkins, iii. 862.)
The Dr. Leighton here mentioned seems to have been Dr. Edward Leighton,
who later in this year was made a prebendary of the new foundation at
Westminster.

[2] Just before this, on the 14th February, the bishops in this Synod had
urged a supplication to the King that the public plays and comedies which
were acted in London "in great dishonor and contempt of the word of God"
should be corrected.

well disposed people used much to resort to the hearing thereof, *especially when they could get any that had an audible voice to read unto them,* misdoubting therein no danger towards them; and no more there was, so long as the days of Cromwell lasted. After he was gone, it happened amongst divers and sundry godly-disposed persons which frequented therein the reading of the aforesaid Bible, that one John Porter used sometimes to be occupied in that godly exercise, to the edifying as well of himself as of other. This Porter was a fresh young man and of a big stature; who by diligent reading of the Scripture, and by hearing of such sermons as then were preached by them that were setters-forth of God's truth, became very expert. The Bible being then set up by Bonner's commandment, upon divers pillars in Paul's church, fixed unto the same with chains for all men to read in them that would, *great multitudes would resort thither* to hear this Porter, because he could read well, and had an audible voice. Bonner and his chaplain being grieved withal (and the world beginning then to frown upon the gospellers) sent for the said Porter, and rebuked him very sharply for his reading. But Porter answered him that he trusted he had done nothing contrary to the law, neither contrary to his advertisements, which he had fixed in print over every Bible.[1]

John Porter's Bible readings.

We are then informed that the Bishop charged him with making expositions upon the text (which laymen had been forbidden to do) and gathering multitudes about him to make tumults. " He answered, he trusted that should not be proved by him," though what else we are to infer does not appear. The Bishop sent him to Newgate prison, where it appears he severely expiated his offence. " He was miserably fettered in irons, both legs and arms, with a collar of iron about his neck fastened to the wall in the dungeon," and when a kinsman got him released from this painful constraint, he was placed among prisoners committed for felony and murder :—

Where Porter, being amongst them, hearing and seeing their wickedness and blasphemy, exhorted them to amendment of life, and gave unto them such instructions as he had

---

[1] Foxe, *A. and M.* v. 451-2.

learned of the Scriptures; for which his so doing he was complained on, and so carried down, and laid in the lower dungeon of all, oppressed with bolts and irons, where, within six or eight days after, he was found dead.

It seems only right thus to give the conclusion of the story from the only authority from which we know anything of the case at all. But though the harshness and cruelty of prison treatment in that age is indisputable, we can hardly persuade ourselves that there was nothing more in the case of this man of lawless piety and noisy Bible-reading than Foxe chooses to let us know.

How much disorder in connection with Bible-reading took place under Cromwell's protection we are left to imagine for ourselves. Porter's case occurred in 1541, the year after his death, and the effort of Convocation to get the Great Bible amended was in the early part of 1542. The clergy were snubbed; but next year the abuse of noisy readings came under the cognisance of Parliament. An Act was passed " for the advancement of true Religion and for the abolishment of the contrary," in which many regulations were made as to the proper use of the Bible, and, among other things, practices like that of Porter were distinctly made penal. For one clause enacts :—

That no manner of person or persons, after the first day of October next ensuing, shall take upon him or them to read, preach, or teach openly to other[s] in any church or open assembly within any the King's dominions, the Bible or any part of Scripture in English; or by any other person or persons cause it or any part thereof openly to be read, preached, or taught to other in any church or open assembly as is aforesaid, unless he be so appointed thereunto by the King's Majesty or by any ordinary, or by such as have rule, government and authority to make deputation or assignment of the same, upon pain that every such offender . . . shall suffer imprisonment of one month.

This was really a provision for the keeping of good order in church, to prevent agitators, however full of biblical zeal, from disturbing congregations. But the general scope of the Act was far wider. It forbade the printing or sale of prohibited books, the playing of interludes or singing or rhyming any matter contrary to the doctrines laid down since the year 1540—the punishment even for the first offence of such a character being three months' imprisonment and a fine of £10 for every illicit book. For the keeping of any English books against the Sacrament of the Altar or in favour of the doctrines of the Anabaptists, or any other English books that had been prohibited, the penalty was £5. But Bibles and New Testaments in English which were not of Tyndale's translation were not to come under the Act unless they contained annotations or preambles; if they did, the owners were to cut or blot them out before the 1st October following under a penalty of forty shillings. Noblemen and gentlemen householders might read the Bible or allow it to be read quietly in their own families, and even merchants who were householders might read it privately. But the liberty granted by the King to his subjects generally to read it had been so much abused by a great multitude of them, especially "of the lower sort," that women, artificers, prentices, and others under the degree of yeomen were henceforth forbidden to do so, either privately or openly, under pain of a month's imprisonment for each offence, unless the King, perceiving their lives to be amended by the doctrines he had set forth, thought fit to give them liberty to read. Other persons not of those lower grades might read the Bible to themselves; and every noblewoman or gentlewoman might read it to herself, but not to others.[1]

An Act regulating the use of bibles.

Such was the last legislation of Henry VIII. on

[1] Stat. 34 & 35 Hen. VIII. c. 1.

the subject of bibles, and such later utterances and proclamations of his as referred to it were conceived in the same spirit. He had no natural desire that "the Word of God" and questions of doctrine should be made a cause of noisy discussions in church and "jangled in every ale house." But his own past policy was greatly answerable for results so unseemly; and truly it was scarcely consistent on his part to punish irreverent use of a Bible which he himself had caused to be set up in churches, though his bishops, with few exceptions, had declared it to be a book of mischievous tendency.

CHAPTER II

In our last chapter we have traced the story of the different English translations of the Bible during Henry VIII.'s reign, and shown some of the influences which promoted their sale or controlled their use. But the same period which saw the issue of these different English translations witnessed also the publication of three authorised formularies of faith; and the influences under which these formularies were produced have a most important bearing, not only on the subject of the Bible itself, but also on certain matters of very great significance, for the full understanding of which it is necessary to devote a special chapter to the subject, notwithstanding that some part of the ground has been traversed already.

Of these three authorised formularies published in this reign, the first two have already been slightly referred to. And my purpose now is not so much to examine their contents as to inquire into the history of their formation. But it may be as well at the outset for the reader to take notice of the dates at which they were issued, that he may consider their relation to preceding and subsequent events. They were as follows :—

I. "Articles devised by the Kinges Hignes Majestie to stablyshe Christen quietnes and unitie amonge us and to avoyde contentious opinions; which articles be also approved by the consent and determination of the hole clergie of this Realme, Anno MDXXXVI." This "Book of Articles," as it was called at first, is commonly spoken of by historians as "the Ten Articles," as that was the number of headings under which the vital principles of the faith were summed up. It was published in July 1536, two months after the fall of Anne Boleyn.

II. "The Institution of a Christian Man." Published in 1537, just about a year after the preceding.

III. "A Necessary Doctrine and Erudition for any Christian Man." Published at the end of May 1543.

All three were printed by Berthelet, the King's printer. What was it that called for their publication?

The King was now "Supreme Head" of the Church of England. He had excluded all reference to Rome on matters of faith and doctrine, as well as of Church discipline. He had taken the Pope's place, and with it he had taken upon himself responsibilities which no King of England had ever undertaken before. The bishops and clergy were still the spiritual rulers of the people, and their authority was generally accepted as it had been in the past. But there was always a possibility of individual directors of the conscience being themselves misled, and if even bishops disagreed and there was to be no reference to Rome, who was to decide disputes in the last instance except the "Supreme Head" himself? It is true that, just as in Acts of State he guarded himself against personal responsibility by that high constitutional doctrine that the King can do no wrong and only ministers can be made accountable, so also he intended to exercise his new Supremacy in Church matters. He would throw the responsibility of everything, as much as possible, on the official guardians of religion, the bishops. If they disagreed,

How Henry exercised his Supremacy

his Vicegerent in spiritual things was Thomas Cromwell, and he could lay the responsibility upon his shoulders. If, finally, the tyranny of his Vicegerent became insupportable and threatened to produce dangerous consequences, he could be got rid of, as he ultimately was. Meanwhile the true principles, which alone could make for peace and order, would gradually reassert themselves; and the King would still take care to show that he had never sanctioned, and never would sanction, anything that was not truly orthodox. This clue must be carefully preserved by any one who would hope to understand either the religious or the political complexities of Henry's reign.

But, however much the King would divest himself of responsibility, he could not divest himself of the anxieties due to a position which he had actually created for himself. In throwing off spiritual subjection to Rome he had not only intimidated the clergy, but had naturally filled up vacancies among the bishops by a new set of prelates, who easily accepted Royal Supremacy, and took no oath of obedience to the Pope in respect of their bishoprics. Such men were only to be found among those whose minds were more or less affected by the principles of Lollardy; and a new school of bishops thus arose who, from the very nature of the case, were bound to differ considerably on some points from their brother bishops, and whose disputes in Convocation might have led to serious difficulties had they not all been bound, willingly or unwillingly, by the new allegiance. At the time of the making of the Ten Articles, bishops of the new school had only been appointed during the previous three years; for even when the King was still prosecuting his divorce, and knew well enough that he must ultimately break with Rome in order to marry Anne Boleyn, he appointed to important bishoprics men like Edward

Lee, Stokesley, and Gardiner, whose ideas were entirely formed on the old system of the Church. And though these men might accept and even write in favour of the new Supremacy, as all bishops were required to do, they did not like the doctrinal tendencies of those who became bishops shortly after them. For during those three years what men had been promoted? First, Cranmer, who while in Bishops of the new school. embassy in Germany had cultivated relations with the Protestants, and married a niece of Osiander. The marriage, of course, was in itself uncanonical and therefore unrecognised by the Church, like a good many other clerical marriages; but the Protestant connection looked ill. Then there were Roland Lee promoted to Coventry and Lichfield, Goodrich to Ely, and Capon to Bangor, in 1534 — all mere serviceable tools. Then foreigners were deprived of bishoprics by Act of Parliament, and in the places of two Italian absentees Shaxton was made Bishop of Salisbury, and Latimer Bishop of Worcester—both favourable specimens of the new school, but both a little subservient. These two promotions were in 1535, as was also that of Foxe, Bishop of Hereford, who had assisted Gardiner in promoting the King's policy at Rome, and more recently had been trying to find a basis of religious concord with the Protestants in Germany. Finally, there was William Barlow, made Bishop of St. Asaph first while on an embassy to Scotland, and, three months later, of St. David's, a very unscrupulous man. Eight bishops in all promoted under the Anne Boleyn influence, or more than one-third of the entire bench. Since her fall, the balance had been slightly redressed by the preferment of Abbot Repps, or Rugge, one of the mitred abbots, to Norwich, and of Sampson, Dean of the Chapel Royal, to Chichester. These, indeed, were not men given to heresy; and they had been promoted not long before the promulgation of the Ten

Articles, to which their signatures as bishops were appended along with those of the others.

These Ten Articles, then, were formulated and approved in a Convocation which met at St. Paul's on the 9th June, the month after Anne Boleyn's fall. This was a special Convocation, in which the clergy of the Northern province sat along with those of the Southern. A new Parliament had opened just the day before, having been called principally to pass a new Succession Act and also a final Act "for extinguishing the authority of the Bishop of Rome," which subjected all who acknowledged that authority to the penalties of *præmunire*, and compelled justices everywhere to make inquiry as to any persons who upheld it.[1] This measure was, undoubtedly, drawn up in expectation of the issue of a bull for a General Council, in preparation for which the Pope was now summoning divines to Rome—among them the Englishman, Reginald Pole, not yet made Cardinal. And one thing which was expected of this English Convocation was a thing in which it easily concurred, when bishops and clergy united in setting their signatures to an opinion that General Councils should be summoned by princes, and not by the sole authority of "the Bishops of Rome."[2]

The Convocation of June 1536. In truth, this special Convocation was expected to do the King's work; which, indeed, was not very wonderful, for Convocations had always been summoned for the King's business—by archbishops, no doubt, but by virtue of the King's writ to each archbishop to call his clergy together. So that it was always for the King's sake and to assist him in promoting what was held to be the public weal that Convocation met at all, though when it did meet it was always free to discuss spiritual matters as well as the King's secular needs. But now there was no doubt

[1] Stat. 28 Hen. VIII. c. 10.   [2] *L. P.*, XI. 80, 124.

that the King's needs were spiritual as well as secular in character. And Convocation was to be made to feel that it had not even the privilege allowed in that day to the House of Commons of deliberating by itself, without being continually under the eye of the King's ministers. After listening to Latimer's arrogant sermon at the opening, of which an account has already been given,[1] the bishops were visited on the second day, the 16th June, by Dr. William Petre, who said that as the King was Supreme Head of the Church of England, and a chief place in the Synod should be set apart for him, which the Lord Cromwell, his Vicar-General in ecclesiastical causes, had a right to occupy, he himself desired that place as Cromwell's deputy; and it was assigned to him accordingly. At the third sitting, on the 21st June, Cromwell himself appeared, while the Archbishop produced the sentence of nullity of the marriage of the King and Anne Boleyn, which was signed a week later by the prelates and the Prolocutor. But at the fourth sitting on 23rd June, something of a different character took place, which showed that the Church had still a good deal of independence left.

The Prolocutor brought up from the Lower House and laid before the Archbishop a book of protest against sixty-seven *mala dogmata*, which were openly preached by various clergymen in the province of Canterbury. Some of these dogmas were simply Lollard, and one or two smacked of Lutheranism. Moreover, the Lower House complained that the bishops had not expressly condemned various heretical books which they had already pointed at, some of which had even got abroad *cum privilegio*, although not formally sanctioned by the King. And, whereas Latimer in his sermon had spoken in favour of curtailing the number of holidays, the Lower House

The Lower House denounces various heresies.

---

[1] See pp. 90, 91, *ante.*

distinctly reproved, among other things, the opposition
to their observance. It was owing, of course, to the
leaven of heresy among the Anne Boleyn bishops
that action was not taken altogether as the Lower
House desired.

On the 11th July Foxe, Bishop of Hereford, produced a Book of Articles of faith and ceremonies
which was signed by Cromwell, the Archbishop, and
other prelates, and the clergy of the Lower House.
This was the Book of Articles above referred to :
and I shall not dwell upon the proceedings of this
Convocation longer except briefly to say that, on
the 19th, ordinances were agreed to by Cromwell
and both Houses for the observance of feast days
throughout the year ; and that on the 20th, Bishop
Foxe produced a bill of reasons why the King
should not appear in the General Council now
summoned by "the Bishop of Rome." Which bill
being signed by Cromwell and the members of
both Houses, the Convocation was dissolved in the
afternoon.[1]

Such was the way in which the Ten Articles were
authorised. What was their origin ? Some writers
have not untruly found for them a German origin ;
for there is no doubt a good deal of their language
was derived from Lutheran documents, and the fact
that Bishop Foxe, who presented them, had just returned from Germany, where he had been in communication with German divines, no doubt explains
a good deal. But these Articles were by no means
completely Lutheran. On the contrary, they contained very little, except in the way of omission,
to which the most orthodox Romanist could object.
Indeed, Reginald Pole, who was then at Venice,
ardently hoped, when he received a copy, that they
indicated a design on the King's part to restore true
principles of religion, if not even to return to the

[1] Wilkins, iii. 803-807.

unity of the Church.[1]   For their contents were briefly as follows :—

First, they set forth the authority of the three Contents of Creeds ; the Sacraments of Baptism, Penance, and the the Ten Articles. Altar ; the doctrine of Justification (which was to be attained "by contrition and faith joined with charity "); the right use of images, the honouring of saints, praying to saints, rites and ceremonies, and purgatory,—as to which last article preachers were to urge that "no man ought to be grieved with the continuance " of the practice of praying for souls departed, but abuses were condemned which had been advanced under the name of purgatory, suggesting that souls might be delivered thence by " the Bishop of Rome's pardon," or " masses said at *Scala Cœli*."

In the preamble the King declared that he had always considered it the most weighty of all the responsibilities of his " princely office " to see that God's word should be truly believed and kept, and unity of opinions in religion should be fostered, so as to extinguish a number of discords that had un- happily sprung up.   For this purpose he had caused the bishops and clergy of the whole realm to assemble in Convocation, where, after mature discussion, they had agreed not only as to what matters were com- manded by God and necessary to salvation, but also as to " honest ceremonies and good and politic order."

How, then, it will be asked, if there was Lutheran language in these Articles, could the Articles them- selves have struck minds like that of Reginald Pole as tending to favour orthodoxy ?   At home they did not give general satisfaction, as was very soon apparent.   But this was partly because the authority under which they were issued, being avowedly the King's, even though they were the result of synodical

---

[1] *L. P.*, XI. 1197.   The date " Festo S. Joannis Baptistæ " cannot well mean 24th June, under which Pole's letter is noticed.   That is, indeed, the day dedicated to the Nativity of St. John the Baptist ; but the feast intended was probably his " Decollation," 29th August.

action, was not felt to be the right authority in such matters. A more serious grievance, however, was found in the omissions. The Articles set forth only three sacraments out of the recognised seven, and said nothing about the other four, just as if they had never been heard of. This was certainly the chief objection felt to them, especially by the King's Northern subjects, who were less under the shadow of direct royal influence than those in the home counties. The positive statements in the Articles seem nowhere to have been impugned; but sacraments passed over seemed to be discredited, and the minds of the people were disquieted. In spite, however, of an apparently Lutheran origin and of Lutheran turns of expression in this remarkable document, we may fairly consider it orthodox so far as it went; and how it should have been so, under the circumstances of the case, certainly deserves attentive consideration.

Of one thing there is no doubt. The heading prefixed to the Ten Articles themselves implies that there was at this time a mass of "contentious opinions" in the community; and the pronouncement of the Lower House of Convocation on the sixty-seven evil dogmas preached by some only emphasises the same fact. That these dogmas were really a sign of a progressive theology beneficial in its effects among the public, is a view rather difficult to maintain. Good, honest Fuller, writing a century later, frankly admits, as every one must do, that many of them were both extravagant and profane, containing, to use his own words, "many vile and distempered expressions." He nevertheless found in a few of them "the Protestant religion in ore"— that is to say, what he considered wholesome truth imbedded in much corruption. And in this, perhaps, we might agree with him if the negations of Protestantism were valuable in themselves and not merely as a protest against too much dogmatism by a Church professing to be Catholic. But was it not right, before the old traditions of authority had been given up, before even any new theology had been imposed by any recognised authority whatever, that the Church should rebuke men who freely spoke about sacred things in the way which that catalogue of sixty-seven evil dogmas showed had become common? "Why should I see the sacring of the high mass?" some would say. "Is it anything else but a piece of bread, or a little pretty round robin?" Was the Sacred Synod of the Church not even to protest against the denial of extreme unction as a sacrament? Was it right to be silent when men said that priests had no more authority to administer sacraments than the laity? or even—against old practice, though in agreement with modern feeling—"that children ought not to be confirmed by the bishop till they come to years of discretion"? These are the first four dogmas reprehended, and not the most extreme. The sea makes inroads on the land in places and washes away the standing ground of past generations. But they who value the firm land of faith will defend it vigorously; and nothing that is valuable there can ever be really lost.

We see, however, that in 1536—the year of Anne Boleyn's fall—there was much ventilation of novel doctrines, whether good or bad. And we also see that a few of these were of Lutheran origin. But German theology, as a whole, was not popular in England— indeed, we may freely say it never has been; for the minds of average Englishmen are never very receptive of ideas essentially scholastic in their origin, as Lutheran ideas were. Lutheranism had got some hold at the universities, but not among the people. Luther confessed a debt to Wycliffe, but Wycliffe's countrymen were slow, even at this time, to accept their own wares back again. Still, there were scholastic as well as popular errors in the *mala dogmata*. But the use of Lutheran language in the Ten Articles was due to another cause.

Early in the year 1535 the King had despatched Dr. Barnes to Germany on a mission which did not come to much. It was to get the opinions of Lutheran divines on that matrimonial question in which he was so much personally interested.[1] As to the doctrinal matters in which the Lutherans themselves were interested, Barnes had little to say. The King apparently did not care much for them. But no cruelty, Barnes assured them, was used in England towards those of a better way of thinking; and Melancthon wrote to the King a letter full of high praise for his encouragement of learning, hoping that he would use his great influence to remedy abuses in the Church. Not very long afterwards it would seem that he received through Barnes an invitation to visit the King in England, which he was preparing to obey.[2] In the autumn Edward Foxe, Bishop-elect of Hereford, was also despatched to Germany, with letters to the Elector, John Frederic of Saxony and the other Protestant princes with a view to an alliance between the King and them for mutual protection against the Pope and the Emperor. This would naturally be a religious league, with a view to which Foxe was to ascertain on what points the Lutheran divines had so fully made up their minds that they could not be persuaded otherwise.[3] Of course it was desirable for both parties to avoid insisting on anything that could not be maintained, lest they should suffer a defeat in the coming Council; and Foxe was to suggest that the Elector should send an ambassador to the King to discuss matters, not only to make sure of their common ground,

The King and the German Lutherans.

[1] *L. P.*, VIII. 375, 384.   [2] *L. P.*, VIII. 630.
[3] *L. P.*, IX. 213, the date of which would seem to be a little later than it has been placed, as Foxe's credentials were dated 30th September. See Mentz's *Die Wittenberger Artikel von 1536*, p. 3, n. 2.

but to enable them to insist that the Council should be held in a free and indifferent place, not merely in a place that the Pope and Emperor were agreed upon. After expatiating on these matters he might propose some articles, such as upon free will, the power of the Church, or the like, merely to open the way for fuller discussion, and also to put forward the King's own special grievance against the Pope for giving sentence in favour of the Emperor's aunt (Katharine of Aragon) against him. But he must not make the determination of the King's matrimonial question a principal cause of his coming. With Foxe there was also despatched on the same mission Dr. Nicholas Heath.[1]

The Protestants were highly pleased, and sent the King an answer about their union and steadfastness in the faith, and their attitude with regard to the Council, and how they rejoiced that the King sought an agreement with them in doctrine, promising to cause their councillors to confer with the King's ambassadors on the subject.[2] The first result of the King's overtures appears to be set forth in a document called the " Petition " of the Elector of Saxony and the Landgrave of Hesse to the King of England, which was laid before his ambassadors at Schmalkalden on Christmas Day.[3] In this the political basis of the alliance was set forth for the King's approval. Neither party was to agree to a General Council without mutual consent, and if they could not agree both were to do their utmost to oppose its meeting. Conditions of pecuniary aid from the King in defence of the league were also laid down. The ambassadors then withdrew to Wittenberg to pave the way for a further agreement as to the doctrines both sides were to support, and there they continued in conference with the Lutheran divines till April 1536. Foxe had, no doubt, brought with him from England, as Barnes expected,

---

[1] See *L. P.*, IX. 213 (4), 217-9, 1018.   [2] Mentz, pp. 5, 6.
[3] *L. P.*, IX. 1016, 1018.

certain Articles " for the stablishing of Christendom
and the stopping of adversaries' mouths " ;[1] but how
far the purport of these Articles served as a basis in
their conferences we cannot tell, for their tenor does
not appear to be preserved. Even these were probably founded to some extent on the Confession of
Augsburg, of which Cranmer could have imparted the
contents before they were drawn up. In any case, the
general drift of the agreement could not be doubtful
when the English were in constant communication
with Luther, Melancthon, Bugenhagen, Justus Jonas,
and Cruciger.[2]

In point of fact, though Luther undoubtedly agreed,
it is Melancthon's pen that seems to have drawn
up " the Wittenberg Articles of 1536," which have
long been known to Church historians, and which
Seckendorff [3] describes as a *repetitio et exegesis* of the
Augsburg Confession. To these Articles, sixteen in
number, Henry's agents believed that he would make
no serious opposition, and we may surmise that they
were transmitted to England in April by Dr. Barnes,
who went over about that time.[4] But some of them,
certainly, were not likely to find favour in England,
and others the King would probably not accept without
material alteration. Even in ordinary diplomacy he
was not accustomed simply to adopt the projects of
others, and what he was engaged in now was really
religious diplomacy. He knew something of divinity
himself ; for that matter, enough to secure himself
plausibly in every position he took up. But he did
not mean to commit himself in any way without the
advice of his bishops.

How " the Ten Articles " for English use were
elaborated out of the sixteen Articles of Wittenberg

The Wit-
tenberg
Articles of
1536.

---

[1] *L. P.*, IX. 543.
[2] See Mentz, pp. 9, 10.   Dr. Mentz's Introduction is founded partly
on unpublished matter in the Weimar archives.
[3] *Commentarius de Lutheranismo*, lib. iii. 111 ; Mentz, p. 11.
[4] Mentz, p. 13.

we cannot trace in detail.   But certain it is that the
bishops did something, and that the King himself
" put his own pen to the book," as he afterwards said.
There was no doubt a good deal of discussion among
the bishops, especially between those of the old school
and the new.   In the end a set of Articles were agreed
upon, differing altogether from the German set, though
retaining in some passages a good deal of the same
phraseology.   No notice was taken in the new Articles
of the proposals for communion in both kinds and
marriage of the clergy ; and the sum total was, in
Melancthon's opinion, a most confused production—
confusissime compositum was his expression.[1]   Whether
it would have been very different if Melancthon
himself had come to England, as he was invited to do,
may perhaps be doubted.   But, when the news of
Anne Boleyn's fall and execution reached Germany,
matters were so greatly changed that he felt no longer
called upon to comply.[2]   The result of the English
deliberations was no doubt what Henry aimed at—a
formula which the Germans could not entirely disown
and the Orthodox could not heartily denounce.

That Convocation itself would not willingly have
omitted all mention of four out of the seven accepted
sacraments we may take for granted from what we
have just seen of their disposition.   The Ten Articles
themselves, assuredly, did nothing to abate religious
discontent.   On the contrary, those who stood upon
the ancient ways considered it an abuse of the King's
proper functions that, even when backed by a weight
of episcopal authority, he should set his name to a
manual for the teaching of religion ; it was an offence
to God and a degradation both of King and realm.
So Henry himself interpreted their murmurings in a
very remarkable document, issued a few months later.
Evidently many of the clergy had refused to read the
Articles, and when the Lincolnshire rebellion broke

Unpopularity of the Ten Articles in England.

[1] Quoted by Mentz, p. 12.   [2] *L. P.*, x. 885, 1106.

out in October following, the Ten Articles were a particular rock of offence. This is noted in Hall's *Chronicle*, where the writer, a strong supporter of royal authority, says: " In this book is specially mentioned but three Sacraments, with the which the Lincolnshire men (I mean their ignorant priests) were offended, and of that occasion depraved the King's Highness." Then in November, after the Lincolnshire rebellion, barely quieted, had been followed by further disturbances in the North, the King addressed a circular letter to his bishops, blaming them severely for not having carried out his instructions more effectually. For it was chiefly owing to these murmurs, he considered, that the insurrections were due ; and he required each bishop, personally, on every holiday to read the Articles in his cathedral or in the church of the parish where he happened to be staying, and to make a "collation" at the same time, declaring the obedience due by God's law to the Sovereign, and always to compel all his clergy and the governors of religious houses to obey the same order, and not allow it to be treated with disrespect.[1]

However orthodox, therefore, they might be in tone, the Ten Articles were not calculated to win the affections of the English people, and what effect they had upon the German mind we have seen already by the words of Melancthon. Yet the Germans could not but take the document as an attempt towards union with them, and if they were so persuaded it served its purpose in that quarter. They were ready, meanwhile, to send an embassy to England ; and John Frederic of Saxony wrote to the King on the 1st September anxious to know if he approved the Wittenberg Articles, seeing that the Pope had promised the Emperor to call a General Council, about which prompt measures must be taken.[2] Evidently the Germans had not even then received the Ten Articles, of which

[1] *L. P.*, XI. 1110.   [2] *L. P.*, XI. 388.

Alesius had despatched a translation to Germany on the 31st July.[1] When they received them they must assuredly have felt that the prospects of a theological agreement with Henry were not quite such as the King's envoys had led them to suppose. But Henry was still a friend whom they must not lose sight of.

He certainly did not wish for a General Council more than they did. But early next year (1537) when one was actually summoned to meet at Mantua on the 23rd May,[2] their anxiety was far greater than his. Henry himself, in the beginning of the year, was straining every nerve to stamp out disaffection among his Northern subjects, and fear of the Council must have been a minor matter to him. But to the Germans it was a matter of urgency. On the 3rd March, John Frederick of Saxony and the Landgrave of Hesse declared at Schmalkalden to the Imperial ambassador, Matthias Held, in the name of all their confederates, their objections to the Council; and on the 26th they wrote to the King of England in the same fashion, pointing out that it appeared from the bull itself that the Pope would never allow the restoration of true doctrine or the correction of abuses.[3] The danger, however, soon passed away, as the Duke of Mantua could not make suitable arrangements; and Henry had received a warning that he would do best to leave matters of faith in his own kingdom more evidently to the keeping of the clergy. For reproaches addressed to his bishops for not giving fuller effect to the Ten Articles had not turned out of great utility, seeing that, scarcely a fortnight afterwards, amid an insurgent population, the Northern clergy met at Pomfret in an informal Convocation to deny Royal Supremacy, uphold the old clerical immunities, and demand restoration of the suppressed

---

[1] *L. P.*, XI. 185.　　　　[2] *L. P.*, XII. i. 432-3.
[3] *L. P.*, XII. ii. 564, 745.

abbeys, and also of those clergymen who had suffered for opposing the King's superiority over the Church.[1]

Very early, accordingly, in the year 1537—though the last thing Henry VIII. ever thought of conceding was a reversal of his own past acts—he seems virtually to have admitted that the Ten Articles might not be altogether a satisfactory exposition of Christian faith and duty. In the examinations taken after the Lincolnshire rebellion, it was stated among other things, that " every one grudged at the new erroneous opinions touching Our Lady and Purgatory." [2] Some time, it would seem, in the latter half of February, though on what precise day we cannot tell,[3] an assembly of bishops and divines met at Westminster to consider the affairs of religion. It was said that Bishop Foxe would be President ; but Cromwell, of course, was the King's Vicegerent, and it was he that delivered the King's message to the Convocation. He told them they were summoned to determine certain controversies in religion, which were disturbing not only England, but all nations throughout the world. " For the King," he said, " studieth day and night to set a quietness in the Church ; and he cannot rest until all such controversies be finally debated and ended through the determination of you, and of his whole Parliament. For, although his special desire is to set a stay for the unlearned people whose consciences are in doubt what they may believe—and he himself by his excellent learning, knoweth these controversies well enough,—yet he will suffer no common alteration but by the consent of you and his whole Parliament." He added that they were further desired to conclude all matters by the Word of God without brawling or scolding ; neither would His Majesty " suffer Scripture to be wrested or defaced

A new special Convocation.

---

[1] *L. P.*, xi. 1245-46. [2] *L. P.*, xii. i. 70 i.
[3] On the 18th, John Husee writes to Lord Lisle : " Most part of the bishops have come, but nobody knows what is to be done." *L. P.*, xii. i. 457.

by any glosses, any papistical laws, or by authority of doctors and Councils." Much less would he admit any articles or doctrines not contained in Scripture and approved only by old custom, or by "unwritten verities," which they were so fond of alleging. He trusted, however, that they would "conclude a godly and a perfect unity."[1]

On the conclusion of this speech the bishops all rose up and thanked His Majesty for his zeal, as in duty bound. Then began a discussion led by Stokesley, Bishop of London, who, in spite of the warning not to rest upon "unwritten verities" and the authority of Fathers and Councils, insisted on maintaining the Seven Sacraments, and was supported in doing so by Archbishop Lee of York, and by Bishops Longland of Lincoln, Clerk of Bath, Sampson of Chichester, and Rugge of Norwich; who, on the other hand, were opposed by the Anne Boleyn bishops, Cranmer, Shaxton, Goodrich, Foxe, and Latimer. Cranmer urged that it was, after all, but a question of "bare words," about which it was unseemly for men of learning "to make much babbling and brawling." But would the bishops venture to maintain that the ceremonies of confirmation, of orders, of annealing, and so forth, which could not be proved to have been instituted by Christ, and which contained no word to assure remission of sins, deserved to be called Sacraments, as compared with Baptism and the Lord's Supper?

Cromwell had brought with him, to hear the discussion, a Scotsman named Alexander Alane, whose surname for scholastic use was made into Alesius,[2] a scholar of St. Andrews who had been driven abroad

[1] Foxe, v. 379. His account, however, is derived from that of Alexander Alesius, referred to later on.

[2] I regret that in a former work of mine I have followed the opinion of those who, in spite of the positive date, 1537, assigned to this occurrence in the book of Alesius himself, suppose it to have reference to the formation of the Ten Articles in 1536. Even internal probability is in favour of the year 1537.

for religion, but had come over to England in 1535 the bearer of a book from Melancthon to the King.[1] He had been invited to England, in fact, by Cromwell and Archbishop Cranmer, but, being then sent to read a lecture at Cambridge, he excited so much opposition that he withdrew and for a while took to the practice of physic in London. According to his own account, he met Cromwell by chance in the street, and was taken by him to this assembly of divines; and, after Cranmer had spoken, Cromwell called on him to speak also. He took up the same line as the Archbishop, that the first question was as to the meaning of the word Sacrament, citing some definitions, and leading on to the conclusion that there were but two Sacraments instituted by Christ, the others being of mere human origin. He was interrupted by Bishop Stokesley, who denied vehemently that all Sacraments must have been instituted by Christ or must signify remission of sins. Alesius would have replied, but gave place first to Bishop Foxe, who made "a pithy speech" about the doings of the Germans; and then, after a rejoinder from Stokesley, Alesius continued the debate till twelve o'clock, and offered to prove next day that the Christian faith rested only on the Bible. But he received a message from Cranmer in the morning, warning him that great offence had been taken at his intrusion, as a mere stranger, into the debate; and Cromwell, whom he consulted on the subject, also counselled him to abstain from another appearance, and to deliver the paper he had written to him. In it he had railed at Cochlæus and other opponents, and accused the Bishop of London of "impudent blasphemy."[2]

The bishops, however, were not to be put down;

Alesius takes part in the debate.

---

[1] *L. P.*, IX. 224-5.

[2] All this comes from Alesius's own account in his tract "Of the Auctorite of the Word of God," of which an abstract will be found in *L. P.*, XII. i. 790.

and in the course of the spring Archbishop Lee informed one Dr. Dakyn, that those four Sacraments omitted in the Ten Articles were "found again," and that "the book" would be printed anew.[1] On what day this decision was come to does not appear. For Palm Sunday, which this year fell upon Lady-day (25th March), a discussion was arranged on the Invocation of Saints, on Purgatory, on Clerical Celibacy, and on "Satisfaction."[2] But even on the 12th May, though the bishops were said to be "at a point," it was still unknown what was to be the approved doctrine in England.[3] And their labours had only come near an end on Tuesday, the 17th July, when they all "subscribed their books," and had agreed upon certain notes about the Creed. A new and more elaborate formulary called *The Institution of a Christian Man* was ready to go to press; and Bishop Foxe undertook to correct the proofs.[4] But even yet there was some further delay.

Result of the Convocation.

When issued at last, the work appeared with a Preface which was in form and effect an address to the King, signed by the assembled divines, stating that they presented to His Majesty the result of a commission he had imposed upon them with a view to the removal of "errors, doubts, and superstitions," and "the perfect establishing" of his subjects "in good unity and concord." They had begun with an exposition of the Apostles' Creed, then treated of the institution and right use of the Seven Sacraments; thirdly, they had discussed the Ten Commandments, and fourthly, the interpretation of the *Paternoster* and of the *Ave Maria*. Finally, to omit nothing contained in "the Book of Articles" of the year preceding, they had subjoined the two Articles on Justification and Purgatory, just as they stood in

---

[1] *L. P.*, XII. i. 789 (p. 346).   [2] *L. P.*, XII. i. 708.
[3] *L. P.*, XII. i. 1187.   [4] *L. P.*, XII. ii. 289.

that formulary. So the whole might really be regarded as the Ten Articles enlarged and with omissions supplied. And they ended by petitioning the King, if he approved, to have it printed and set forth with his sanction, "without the which power and licence of your Majesty," they say, "we acknowledge and confess that we have none authority, either to assemble ourselves together for any pretence or purpose, or to publish anything that might be by us agreed on and compiled." They were all agreed, indeed, "that the said treatise was in all points concordant and agreeable to Holy Scripture," yet they humbly submitted it to his correction. There was evidently now quite a new sense of a King's authority no less in spiritual matters than in temporal.

In truth, though the bishops might be unanimous that the book was in complete conformity with Scripture, they were not so well agreed about other things, and it seemed as if there still remained at the end some little questions to be referred to the King's decision. For even when Foxe wrote to Cromwell, on the 20th July, that the bishops had signed their books on the previous Tuesday (the 17th) and were ready to go to press with the King's permission, they still awaited orders about the Preface, and whether the book was to go forth in the King's name or that of the bishops.[1] There were also some notes to be supplied upon the Creed, about which they were agreed. Next day both Cranmer and Latimer wrote to Cromwell that these also would be signed on the following Monday, to complete the body of the work. Poor Latimer, who was certainly no theologian, only hoped that when it was done it would be well done. "For verily," he wrote, "for my part I had liever be poor parson of Kinton again than to continue thus bishop of Worcester; not for anything that I have had to do therein, or can do,

[1] *L. P.*, XIII. ii. 289.

but yet, forsooth, it is a troublous thing to agree upon a doctrine in things of such controversy, with judgments of such diversity, every man (I trust) meaning well, and yet not all meaning one way. But I doubt not but now in the end we shall agree both one with another, and all with the truth, though some will then marvel. And yet, if there be any- thing either uncertain or unpure, I have good hope that the King's Highness will *expurgare quicquid est veteris fermenti*; at least wise give it some note that it may appear he perceiveth it, though he do tolerate it for a time, so giving place for a season to the frailty and gross capacity of his subjects." [1]

A little of the old leaven, it seems, was to be tolerated for a time, notwithstanding Cromwell's not too scrupulous attempt to purge it out by the intru- sion of a stranger into the Convocation. The old bishops, in truth, had gained the day on the most important points when they got the four omitted sacraments restored and purgatory acknowledged. On the other hand, justification by faith, the cardinal doctrine of the Reformation, was admitted also. But it was a doctrine so distinctly scriptural that no divines of the old school could have opposed it. Luther had only brought it into greater prominence ; and it was quite impossible to overlook its importance now. Four years later, at the Diet of Ratisbon, almost complete agreement was come to about this doctrine, and the Lutheran view was not without zealous advo- cates even at the Council of Trent.

Of the mode in which the four lately discredited sacraments came to be restored we have only partial glimpses ; but they are interesting. Comparatively little difficulty, apparently, was found about the Sacrament of Holy Orders, on which a declaration was signed by the bishops and divines, with instruc-

Delibera- tions on the Sacra- ments.

---

[1] Latimer's *Remains*, pp. 379, 380.

tions how it was to be taught.[1] This declaration was embodied in the new book, with only a few verbal alterations. But a very large addition was made : first, to guard against the old error of the Donatists, who regarded a sacrament as losing its efficacy when administered by a priest of vicious living ; and secondly, to set forth the " power and authority belonging unto priests and bishops." This was threefold : first, to rebuke and excommunicate obstinate sinners—a power which was only exercised by word and not by violence or constraint, and the discretion to be used in its exercise is likewise indicated ; second, to admit fit persons to the office of preaching and cure of souls in parishes when nominated by the King or other patrons ; and third, to make rules for the observance of holy days and fasting days. But as no special injunctions are given in Scripture as to the mode in which these powers are to be exercised, a good deal is added about the relations of priests and bishops to the civil power, and the falsehood of the claims of " the Bishop of Rome, not only to be head and governor of all priests and bishops," but even to have power to depose kings.

As to confirmation three questions were submitted to the divines, to which they individually gave different answers. They were :—

1. " Whether this sacrament be a sacrament of the New Testament instituted by Christ or not ? "

2. " What is the outward sign and invisible grace that is conferred in the same ? "

---

[1] *L. P.*, XI. 60 (Burnet, iv. 336). This document has unfortunately been catalogued in the year 1536, as if it was the work of the Convocation of that year ; and I regret to say I was still under that delusion when I wrote my Church History volume. The original MS. is in the Cottonian collection (Cleop. E v. 45), and one line omitted by the clerk has been supplied in Cranmer's own handwriting. With one or two verbal alterations the whole text is embodied in *The Institution*, in the article on the Sacrament of Orders. But a very large addition was made to it, beginning with the words "Thirdly, for as much," and filling nearly eight pages (pp. 105-123) in Lloyd's *Formularies*.

3. "What promises be made that the said graces shall be received by this sacrament?"

I give a few of the answers to the first question, to exhibit the different points of view.

Archbishop Lee considered that confirmation was instituted by Christ because the apostles used it, as appeared in Acts, chapters viii. and xix., and gave the tradition to the Church—an opinion which he confirmed by citations from St. Clement, St. Dionysius, St. Augustine, and others. Bishop Goodrich of Ely, on the other hand, found no express mention of its institution by Christ in the New Testament, but the Fathers had taken it for a sacrament of the New Testament. Bishop Hilsey of Rochester used rather an involved argument, to show that, though not exactly instituted by Christ (except, as St. Thomas said, by promise), it was begun by Holy Fathers to confirm the faith of baptized infants when they came to years of discretion. Bishop Longland of Lincoln was clear that it was a sacrament of the New Law instituted by Christ; Capon (or Salcot) of Bangor said it was a sacrament of the New Testament, not instituted by Christ, so far as appeared in Scripture, but by the Fathers. Stokesley of London affirmed simply that it was a sacrament of the New Testament. Cranmer found no place in Scripture which declared it to be so. The supposed evidence of institution in the New Testament was only "acts and deeds of the apostles," and these were done by a special gift which did not now remain.

Such were, in substance, the answers of the first four bishops, whose opinions were taken, to the first question. I need not epitomise those of the other bishops and divines, which the curious may study at leisure, along with the opinions of all upon the second and third questions.[1] But it evidently appeared that even those who were most with Cranmer in his nega-

[1] Strype's *Ecclesiastical Memorials*, I. ii. 340-63.

tions still admitted a high authority for the rite, and their opinion could not overrule that of those who held it to be a sacrament of divine institution. There are also fragments of other portions of "the Bishops' Book," as it was called, with earlier drafts of some parts, extant among the MSS. in the Record Office, which may perhaps not be unworthy of minute examination by some closer student of the history of doctrine.[1]

But, after all the labours of his bishops, the King made a rather curious answer to their request that he would sanction the publication. He wrote that he had found no sufficient time to give it a careful perusal and weigh such things as they had written, but, trusting that men of such learning had accomplished what they professed, he had caused it to be printed and conveyed to all parts of the realm. His object, which they said they had endeavoured to fulfil, was "to have a sure and certain kind of doctrine, not as made by men but by them searched out of the Holy Scripture," in matters "meetest to be observed of men that profess Christ and his religion." Not-

The King allows "the Bishops' Book" to be published.

withstanding his occupations, he had taken "a taste" of the book and found nothing that was not praiseworthy; and he desired them to set it forth, expelling for ever, if possible, "all manner of idolatry, superstition, and hypocrisy." They were to order some part of it, at least, to be read every Sunday and festival day in every parish church for three years, that the people might be thoroughly familiarised with its contents.[2]

So the book was published in this curious manner, without being expressly adopted by the King, and indeed without the royal *imprimatur* being printed in the book itself, though the petition for royal sanction by the joint Convocation of the two pro-

---

[1] *L. P.*, XII. ii. 401.
[2] Cranmer's *Remains*, pp. 469, 470 (Parker Soc.).

vinces, with their signatures attached, was allowed to
do duty as a Preface. And it is impossible not to
feel that, as Henry was a master of statecraft, this
three years' licence, so given but not published, had a
very distinct and politic end in view—or rather two
or three distinct and politic ends. For, in the first
place, he avoided objections raised by his own subjects
—that royal authority in matters of faith and doctrine
was a thing out of place, as the King was no more
competent to lay down principles in such things
than to alter the rules of grammar. The *Institution* was the fruit of pure synodical action by the
bishops and divines in Convocation. Secondly, he
had thus fortified himself against any objections that
might be raised by the Germans, for he still looked
to them for further co-operation. If their theologians
found anything wrong they might come and discuss
it with English theologians, and no doubt further
agreement ought to be the result. The King had
made nothing unalterable. And thirdly, he had
emancipated himself to a great extent from responsibility for the acts of his Vicegerent Cromwell, who
had been trying hard to carry out a religious revolution on a Lollard basis, discrediting many of the old
sacraments and observances as having no foundation
in Scripture. But while the sufficiency of Scripture
as a foundation was still maintained (even in "the
article of Purgatory," prayer for souls departed was
justified from the book of Maccabees), the publication
of the *Institution* was, on the whole, a great victory
for the bishops of the old school over those who had
been so vehement against Church traditions, and so
disrespectful even to the authority of ancient Fathers.

For it was in August of the year preceding (1536) Cromwell's
that Cromwell, as the King's Vicegerent, had issued first In-
those first Injunctions to the clergy, mentioned in the August,
last chapter in connection with the order contained in 1536.
them about English and Latin Bibles. But this was

only one of the things enjoined. The principal matters were—first, observance of the Acts abolishing the jurisdiction of the "Bishop of Rome" and confirming the King's Supremacy; and secondly, the clergy were to set forth—but with discrimination between essential matters of faith and mere ceremonies—the Ten Articles and those abolishing superfluous holidays. They were also warned that images were not to be extolled, and that pilgrimages ought to be discouraged. They were to teach the Lord's Prayer, the Articles of the Faith, and the Ten Commandments in English. Then came the article by which every incumbent was to provide, before the 1st August 1537, "a book of the whole Bible, both in Latin and also in English." Then, priests were not to haunt alehouses, and certain charges were laid on non-resident parsons for the poor of their parishes, and on the richer incumbents for the support of scholars at the universities.[1] These articles were certainly in advance of the time; but their worst fault, no doubt, was that they were manifestly forced on the Church by lay authority, and the unpopularity of their enforcement fell upon Cromwell. The order about the Bible seems to have been a job, and apparently was not persevered in. But the Ten Articles really received a higher sanction—although with a certain qualification—as soon as *The Institution of a Christian Man* was published. Nor were images and pilgrimages here quite so much discouraged as in the Injunctions. The exposition of the Second Commandment expressly admits that there is a good use for images in churches, which is not prohibited; but it reproves the fashion of "putting difference between image and image, trusting more in one than another," and of going on pilgrimages "even to the images," and "calling upon the same images for aid and help."

[1] Burnet, iv. 308-313; Wilkins, iii. 813-15. A copy of these Injunctions in the Record Office is dated August 1536. *L. P.*, xi. 377.

In fact, the Church still gave her sanction to old observances in the abstract as much as ever, but clearly admitted that they were liable to abuse and that the people should be warned against misusing them.

Now when the King saw that his bishops at home were coming to something like a religious settlement, he was ready enough to declare himself, as his German allies had done, on the subject of the threatened General Council. But it was evidently not quite so early in the year as has been suggested that he published that little book against it by which they were so delighted.[1] On the 1st June it must have been still unpublished when Bonner wrote to Cromwell suggesting its immediate issue; for "whatever some men may think," he says—which, no doubt, means that Gardiner, at least, was against it,—he considers that, as others have declared their opinion on this subject, the King ought not to withhold his, especially as he was at liberty to add or withdraw at pleasure.[2] So it was clearly at least in June, if not in July, that the little book was published, which was at once reprinted at Wittenberg and afterwards disseminated throughout Germany in different German translations during the years 1537 and 1538.[3]

The publication of the *Institution* bears date 1537. It took place, it seems, "at Bartholomew-tide," that is to say in August;[4] and a good number of copies had certainly been issued that year by the beginning of October.[5] Yet on the 10th of that month Wriothesley writes to Sir Thomas Wyatt in Spain that he refrains from sending him a copy, as it was to be amended in many points.[6] And in January following (1538) we find that the King made corrections which Cranmer partly agreed to

The King's book against the Council.

---

[1] See Book II., chap. ix.
[2] *L. P.*, XII. ii. 7.   See the text in State Papers, i. 550.
[3] *L. P.*, XII. i. 1310.
[4] *L. P.*, XIII. i. 686.
[5] *L. P.*, XII. ii. 818, 834, 846.
[6] *L. P.*, XII. ii. 871.

and partly criticised.[1] The King certainly felt that it was incumbent on him as Head of the Church, who had taken the Pope's place, to decide, ultimately, for England at least, what was right or wrong in matters of theology ; and though he shielded himself, to some extent, from responsibility by letting the book go forth merely as the work of his bishops, they, at least, had been taught by this time the full meaning of Supremacy, and knew that nothing was finally settled without his sanction. Of this we shall see some further evidence presently. Meanwhile the book went forth in the name of the bishops, though authorised, at least for temporary use, by the King. It was sometimes, indeed, called "the King's Book,"[2] but more correctly it was spoken of as "the Bishops' Book" ; and a few years later "the King's Book" became the more appropriate designation of the third formulary, of which we have still to speak.

"The Bishops' Book" not everywhere well received. Yet even with Episcopal authorisation, enforced, no doubt, by each separate bishop in his diocese, as it clearly was by Voysey, Bishop of Exeter,[3] it was not always well received. One Mr. Inolde, or Enold, curate of Rye, was complained of by some of his parishioners for not having "preached down" the Bishop of Rome since his bishop's last visitation. He had not even preached at all, or read the Gospel or Epistle in English for a whole twelvemonth, and when he read "the Bishops' Book" he read "scant a piece of a title," which apparently was unintelligible without what they called "the rhetoric words." This man, indeed, was terribly insubordinate, keeping abrogated holidays, and allowing a friar to do daily service in the church in his friar's apparel, which Cromwell was just then insisting that they should all abandon. Moreover, the vicar, one Dr. Snede, who, as it appears by other evidences, leased the

---

[1] L. P., XIII. i. 78, 141-2. [2] L. P., XIII. i. 1199, 1291.
[3] L. P., XIII. i. 1106.

profits and duties of the living to Inolde for a term of years,[1] had been an absentee for four years and neglected everything.[2] Such a case naturally called for Cromwell's interference—not, indeed, because the living was leased, a point of which nothing was said —and he commissioned two of the parishioners, Alexander Wells and John Raynolde, to search Parson Inolde's house, and send up to him all books and bills found in it. The parson seems to have been suspended, and one Alexander Wells took the services in the parish church under his control. Wells, apparently, would have taken a new course, going a little further than any ordinances or injunctions yet issued ; but either he was complained of to the Bishop of Chichester, or he wisely forebore from innovation till he had laid the case before him. He wrote to Bishop Sampson on the 26th July (this was seven weeks, all but a day, after Mr. Inolde's house had been searched) ; and the Bishop wrote to him in reply on the 21st August, expressing satisfaction that he had not " enterprised " to sing any service in English, and hoped, for the common quietness, that he would forbear such novelties till it pleased the King to declare his pleasure on matters of ritual.[3]

There can hardly be a doubt that in this case Wells, who acted under a commission from the King's Vicegerent, was prepared, with Cromwell's connivance, to carry a lawless policy as far as he could be allowed. Indeed, we find that Bishop Sampson, shortly afterwards, was not in favour with Cromwell, no doubt because he did his duty.[4] So long as it was not a conservative lawlessness, or insubordination to new commands from a seemingly new authority, a good deal, doubtless, might be tolerated. Cromwell was at this very time preparing a new set of Injunctions for the clergy, which came out on the

Cromwell's new Injunctions, 5th Sept. 1538.

---

[1] *Valor Ecclesiasticus*, i. 345.　　[2] *L. P.*, XIII. i. 1150.
[3] *L. P.*, XIII. ii. 147.　　[4] *L. P.*, XIII. ii. 339.

5th September. One of the first points contained in them was the article already quoted about providing in every church a Bible of the largest volume, and allowing it to be read. Other articles, too, had a plausible justification. It was an old complaint, which doubtless had not quite lost its force since the days of "Piers Plowman's Creed," that friars or clergy were not always so attentive to expound the Christian faith to the laity as they were eager about other things ; and now all the clergy were enjoined, every Sunday and holy day throughout the year, plainly to recite to their parishioners "twice or thrice together, or oftener, if need require, one article or sentence of the Paternoster or Creed in English, to the intent that they may learn the same by heart; and so, from day to day, to give them one like lesson or sentence of the same, till they have learned the whole Paternoster and Creed in English by rote." They were also to expound the meaning of these great documents and exhort all parents and house-holders to teach them to their children and servants. And, further, they were to teach and expound the Ten Commandments, one by one, every Sunday and holy day. Then there was an order for sermons to be made every quarter of a year to declare " purely and sincerely the very Gospel of Christ," and not to repose their trust in "men's fantasies besides Scripture." "Wandering to pilgrimages, offering of money, candles or tapers to feigned relics or images, or kissing or licking the same, saying over a number of beads not understood or minded on, or such like superstition," was denounced as tending to idolatry. Then the clergy were forthwith to take down such images as they knew to be " abused with pilgrimages or offerings of anything made thereunto." If they had ever extolled such practices they were now to recant and show that they had done so on no ground of Scripture, but had been misled by a common error.

These Injunctions further ordered, for the first time, the keeping of parish registers, and forbade the withdrawal of tithes on the plea that clergymen neglected their duties (a plea on which Wycliffe would have justified it); they also forbade " the commemoration of Thomas Becket," and recommended the omission of the *Ora pro nobis* addressed to saints in litanies.[1]

These Injunctions to the clergy, issued on the 5th September, were followed up on the 16th November —the day of Lambert's trial—by a lengthy royal proclamation, which has already been given in substance,[2] laying down orders on the following matters : —The printing and licensing of books were henceforth to be more strictly regulated.   The circulation of the poisonous literature of Sacramentaries and Anabaptists[3] must by all means be put down.   Disputing about the Sacrament of the Altar was not to be allowed except to learned divines in the schools, and a number of interesting ceremonies were to be observed till the King was pleased to change them.   Married priests were to be deprived.   Orders were given for the bishops and clergy to set forth distinctly in sermons the difference between things commanded by God and ceremonies used in the church.   Becket was unsainted, his images were to be put down, and his festival no longer to be kept.

Of course, the explicit orders of a royal proclamation like this were generally obeyed through fear. The article about Becket was only a natural sequel to what the King had already done, and most of the earlier articles were such as would be sure to meet with general approbation.   But the two which concern ceremonies and preaching are particularly inter-

A royal proclamation, 16th Nov.

---

[1] Burnet, iv. 341-6 ; Wilkins, iii. 815-17.
[2] See pp. 154-5 *ante.*
[3] "Sacramentaries" were those who denied Transubstantiation and understood "This is my body," etc., in a merely figurative sense.   "Anabaptists" held that those who were baptized in infancy required to be baptized anew.

esting. The first expressly sanctioned, till further orders, the continuance of a number of time-honoured usages till the King saw fit to change them; the second, no doubt, gratified men of the new school, by inculcating the difference between things resting on divine and things resting on mere ecclesiastical authority. By this it might be seen, not altogether obscurely, that usages, for the present sanctioned or tolerated, might ere long be abolished when the King saw fit to do so; and it is to be noted that the ceremonies mentioned are now, with one exception, altogether disused, one or two of them even in Roman Catholic countries. Women are still "purified" in our churches after child-birth, though the rite is now differently named; and it was the practice to offer a "chrisom"[1] on that occasion even in the following reign, when there was a positive direction to that effect in the First Prayer-Book of Edward VI. As for the other observances we cannot now, perhaps, enter into the spirit of them all; but surely the practice of creeping to the Cross on Good Friday could only have a chastening influence, most fitting to the day when it becomes us, more than any day, to think of human frailty and of the Infinite Love that died for us.

The main thing to be observed, however, as regards this part of the proclamation is, that ceremonies were now made to rest on royal sanction. This, of course, was simply carrying the principle of Royal Supremacy one step further; for, just as ceremonies which are not ecclesiastical maintain their hold by custom and

[1] The "chrisom" was a white robe put upon an infant at baptism by the priest. It was offered up by the mother when she came to be churched; but if the child died previously it was buried in the chrisom as a shroud. Hence "a chrisom child" was not really an unbaptized child as many have supposed, but a baptized one which died within a month. The word "chrisom" seems to have been a corruption of "chrism," which was properly the unction used at baptism; and secondarily, a fillet bound on the forehead to preserve the holy oil. Then it was applied to the white robe received by the newly baptized.

not by decree, so in the Church also custom was a fairly sufficient warrant for them, except that their validity or expediency could always have been referred to the decision of a papal authority which was now abolished. But the practical result of this proclamation in making ceremonies depend on royal authority appears to have been to lessen the respect in which many of them were held, and to raise up a very considerable crop of disputes during the next three or four years. Nor was a supplementary proclamation, issued on the 26th February following (1539),[1] calculated to obviate such consequences; for it enjoined the bishops and clergy every Sunday to instruct the people as to the " right use and effect " of the ceremonies used on that particular day, whether it were only the significance of holy bread and holy water, or the reason for such an observance as carrying candles on Candlemas Day. It seemed as if the intention were to make people rationalists, whether they were so disposed or not, and to encourage them to demand a reason for everything, without yielding, as heretofore, simply to authority or custom when there was no substantial objection to it.

But another matter contained in this supplementary proclamation was that it declared the King's pardon to all persons, whether his subjects or aliens, who had been seduced by Anabaptists or Sacramentaries coming from abroad, and who desired to return to the Catholic Church. The King's Church was still the Catholic Church, for there was no breach of communion recognised in England.

Thus it will be seen that since the publication of " the Bishops' Book " in 1537 there had been issued within a year and a half, first, a second set of injunctions from the King's Vicegerent, and then two royal proclamations for the control of various matters in the Church. What a multiplicity of orders! And was it

[1] *L. P.*, XIV. i. 374.

safe to trust them all equally? "The Bishops' Book" was only half authorised, and was, in fact, allowed to remain on trial for three years. The injunctions were Cromwell's, but as he was the King's Vicegerent, they apparently had full authority from the Head of the Church himself. The royal proclamations were past dispute; but apart from the injury they did to old traditional feeling on the subject of Becket and his "pictures," they contained nothing worse than the mere foreshadowing of a possibility of future change. Still, on the whole, "the Bishops' Book" and the proclamations were better obeyed than the injunctions, being, indeed, far less unpopular.

Unpopularity of the injunctions.

For of the unpopularity of the injunctions we have very special evidence. In December 1538, just three months after they were issued, a circular was sent out to the Justices of the Peace throughout the kingdom, in which the King, first of all, commends their zeal in the discharge of their duty, especially against the maintainers of the Bishop of Rome's authority. Their exertions in this matter had kept the country quiet for some time. But now, it goes on to show, there were sundry parsons who "read so confusely, hemming and hacking the Word of God and such our injunctions as we have lately set forth, that almost no man can understand the true meaning of the said injunctions." They had also got up rumours positively to misrepresent their meaning, and had made people think that the keeping of parish registers was ordered with a view to the taxation of christenings, weddings, and burials; which was very far from the King's mind. This had raised an outcry that the King was going to take away the liberties of the realm, for the conservation of which, as they said, St. Thomas—that is to say, Becket— died. The justices were therefore to find out and punish such seditious tale-tellers, and also such "cankered parsons" as would only mumble the injunctions, saying they were compelled to read them, and would then tell their parishioners to do as they liked.[1] A document like this requires no comment.

In fact, it is clear that the injunctions were very largely evaded. In Warwickshire Sir Robert Mawde, parson of Whatcott, read them in his church on Sunday, 2nd March 1539, using some very derisive and unseemly language if the witnesses against him reported truly. "This must needs be conned," he said, "for by God's bones I have read this unto you a hundred thousand times, and yet ye be never the better. And it is a matter that is as light to learn as a boy or a wench should learn a ballad or a song, and by God's flesh here is an hundred words in these injunctions where two would serve, for I know what it meaneth as well as they that made it; for, lo, it cometh in like a rhyme, a jest, or a ballad." We are not surprised to hear that there were other things against this parson. He received "valiant beggars" in his house, and played cards with them. He had never read the Gospel nor the Epistle in English. He had only once recited the Bishop's injunctions and the King's commandments for the abolition of the Bishop of Rome's power; he said the former were too hard to learn, and as to the latter, there was never a man in Westminster Hall that would read so much for twenty nobles.[2]

This man's bishop was Latimer, but he was examined before three local gentlemen under a commission from Cromwell, and committed to Warwick gaol. No doubt, he was but a specimen of a class of rollicking, irreverent parsons, whose ways went far to excuse the Lollardy (or Puritanism,[3] as

---

[1] *L. P.*, XIII. ii. 1171.   [2] *L. P.*, XIV. i. 542.
[3] Puritanism, as perhaps we shall find hereafter, was but a development of the earlier Lollardy, founding itself in the same appeal to Scripture and the same disregard of antiquity in any other form ; endeavouring also to make saints of Sir John Oldcastle and other insubordinate personages ; curtailing the people's holidays, and insisting merely on the observance of one day in the week as of Scriptural obligation ; calling Sunday Sabbath and

we might call it) which was now again gaining strength.

In Salisbury Cathedral, on the afternoon of Easter Day, an awkward incident occurred. The people were kneeling and kissing an image of Christ standing on an altar on the north side of the choir, when John Goodall, the vice-bailiff, appeared and ordered one of the priests to take it away. The King had commanded that no such kissing of images was to be allowed but only creeping to the cross and kissing it on Good Friday and Easter morning, both of which were now past, for it was three o'clock afternoon. The priest hesitated to obey, knowing, what Goodall did not know, that the consecrated host was within the image; and Goodall then ordered his servant to take it down. On this the mayor and aldermen wrote to complain of Goodall, denouncing him as a heretic who dishonoured the Sacrament and despised the King's proclamation for the observance of all laudable ceremonies till further orders. But Bishop Shaxton wrote in his defence to Cromwell, assuring him that no man was more zealous in promoting obedience, both to the injunctions and the King's proclamation; and he could answer for it the man had no heretical opinion of the Sacrament, but detested Sacramentaries.[1] A little later John Goodall flattered himself that though he had sustained displeasure "for declaring the manifest enormity of the clergy in the Close of Sarum," he had done some good; for now the residentiaries not only preached, but had a chapter of the New or Old Testament
They are
little
obeyed.
read at dinner time. But from Sarum westward, he said, the injunctions were not observed, and would

turning that Sabbath into a day of gloom. It has made religion, even to our own times, far too much a mere Sunday matter. But its faults arose out of its very merits; for it was at least marked by a strong sense of principle, of which there is always, unfortunately, too great a lack in established or conventional religion.

[1] *L. P.*, XIV. i. 777-8.

never be until Cromwell sent down a commission of inquiry.[1]

Then we find justices in various places reporting that many of the clergy had not bibles in their churches as required, and did not preach as they were directed by the injunctions;[2] or that some particular parson has left the word *Papa* in his mass-book, and the name of Thomas Becket and whole legends about him in his breviary and other books.[3]   Even in Kent the injunctions were ill obeyed, and, as Dr. Henry Goderick complained, no sermons were " sincerely " preached except by Arch-bishop Cranmer and his chaplains.   At Ashford, on the proclamation about Becket, " they transposed his image in the church, took the cross out of his hands and put in a woolcomb, till they saw that Mr. Gold-well caused all Becket's images in his parish church to be broken and put down."   This was intended to be a compromise, but Dr. Goderick told them that transposing would not serve.[4]

The open Bible in church was a subject of trouble in Calais, as we have seen that at another time it was in London.   On a Saturday, apparently the 12th April,[5] one Tornaye or Torner, a soldier of the garrison at Calais, was reading the Bible kept for general use in Our Lady church to all who cared to listen.   Gregory Botolf, one of the Calais clergy, after evensong in the choir, came into the circle of listeners, and found that he read first the Epistle to the Romans and then turned to the translator's introduction to that Epistle (Tyndale's too cele-brated prologue, which was founded upon Luther's), returning afterwards to the text.   Botolf went

A soldier reads the Bible with a com-mentary in church.

---

[1] *L. P.*, xiv. i. 894.

[2] *L. P.*, xiv. ii. App. 6.

[3] *L. P.*, xiv. i. 821.

[4] *L. P.*, xiv. i. 1053-54.

[5] Gregory Botolf's letter, *L. P.*, xiv. i. 1351, is clearly much earlier than July, the date in which it has been placed.   If "the 12th inst." was really a Saturday, that would suit April as well as July, and letter 1009 certainly suggests that Cromwell had been written to on the subject some time before the 15th May.

up to him and said aloud, but not with unseemly loudness, that he ought to inform his hearers when he was reading Scripture and when an exposition. Torner resented the remark, and was disposed to argue ; and at last, Botolf, having a Testament "of large volume" in his hand, spoke aloud to the congregation, saying, "Friends, I shall read unto you the same thing wherein he left, whereby ye shall, according to the translator's meaning, the better understand the Epistle of St. Paul to the Romans at all times hereafter," and he continued for nearly an hour.[1] The dispute was awkward, and to prevent similar disturbances, the deputy, Lord Lisle, gave orders that the Bible should be read no more during mass or service time. But this only raised a murmur among those who "favoured God's Word" that there should be any time forbidden for such an exercise ; and Cromwell was informed about it.[2] To put a stop to religious altercations at Calais, Cranmer wrote to Lord Lisle promising to do his best to find a discreet parish priest and send him thither as his commissary, with instructions to suffer none to preach out of his cure without authority either from the King or the Archbishop. "As concerning such persons," he added, "as in time of divine service do read the Bible, they do much abuse the King's Grace's intent and meaning in his Grace's injunctions and proclamations ; which permitteth the Bible to be read, not to allure great multitudes of people together, nor thereby to interrupt the time of prayer, meditation and thanks to be given unto Almighty God, which, specially in divine service, is, and of congruence ought to be, used ; but that the same be done and read in time convenient, privately, for the condition and amendment of the lives both of the readers and of such hearers as cannot themselves read, and not in contempt and hindrance of any

---

[1] *L. P.*, xiv. i. 1351. [2] *L. P.*, xiv. i. 1009.

divine service or laudable ceremony used in the Church; nor that any such reading should be used in the Church as in a common school, expounding and interpreting Scriptures, unless it be by such as shall have authority to preach and read." [1]

Thus it would seem that the effects of Cromwell's injunctions had not been greatly favourable to religious peace. As for "the Bishops' Book," it seems to have been generally obeyed as being the work of the bishops, though some, here and there, may have done like Heliar, parson of Warblington in Hampshire, who "left out the declaration of purpose" when he read it.[2] But the three years' licence for the book expired in 1540; and in June of that year preparations were made for the composition of a more authoritative formulary. Seventeen questions were disseminated by the King's authority among bishops and divines as to the nature of a Sacrament, first according to Scripture, and secondly according to ancient authors; then how many there were by Scripture or by ancient authors; whether the term Sacrament should be applied only to the Seven, and whether the Seven Sacraments were found in any old authors or not. And so on, some of the questions touching upon the particular powers of bishops, priests, and kings. The answers to these questions are preserved in MS. at Lambeth, and as they have been printed by Burnet,[3] I need not discuss them in detail. But we must again note the effect of the new royal papacy in the answer given by the most responsible of all the bishops—the Primate of all England. Cranmer wrote his answer to each of the questions *seriatim*, and appended at the foot not only his signature, "T. Cantuarien.," but also

Preparation for a new formulary.

---

[1] Cranmer's *Letters* (Parker Soc.), 391; *L. P.*, XIV. i. 1264.
[2] *L. P.*, XIII. ii. 817 (p. 326).
[3] *History of the Reformation*, iv. 443 *sq.*, and vi. 241 *sq.* (Pocock's ed.); or (for any edition), *Records*, Pt. I., Book III., No. xxi., and Pt. III., Book III., No. lxix.

these words in his own handwriting: "This is mine opinion and sentence at this present, which I do not temerariously define, and do remit the judgment thereof wholly unto your Majesty." [1]

There is something in this humility that belongs neither to an earlier nor to a later age. Nor, indeed, was it shared, or at least avowed so plainly, by very many contemporaries; so that one is almost inclined to call it Cranmer's own. But the feeling of the great body of the nation seems certainly to have been that if the King of England was disposed to take upon himself the spiritual rule of his kingdom as well as the temporal, he must be allowed to do so; the responsibility lay with him and not with his subjects. Even his bishops had yielded the point, and there was generally nothing more to be said. But Cranmer, who was a real theologian, forced against his will into a position of the highest responsibility, had clearly thought out the whole question in his own mind; and Royal Supremacy was a doctrine which he fervently believed all his days, till at the last, driven from point to point to make fuller recantations before his end, he for one brief interval repudiated it and some other doctrines, only to make amends at the stake by confessing sadly that he had belied his conscience to save his life.

Cranmer's view of authority.

Royal Supremacy was, indeed, to him what Papal Supremacy was to others. A kingdom could not stand if not founded in righteousness; and, fearful as the acts of Henry VIII. undoubtedly were, there was this, at least, in him, that in spite of his self-will and ferocity, he always felt some foundation in sound principles necessary even for his own safety. So, too, Cranmer felt that obedience to this high power was a duty; and even if his king had been like the unjust judge who feared not God, neither regarded

[1] Cranmer's *Miscellaneous Writings*, p. 117 (Parker Soc.).

man, yet the clamour of the importunate widow and the respectful submission of the Church would establish truth and justice in the end. But Henry after all was not altogether an unjust judge. He had always acknowledged high principles ; he thought somewhat himself about theology, and could form his own opinion—at least in things put forward by his divines—what beliefs seemed to have a sure resting-place in men's hearts and what others were less firmly held. He was not going to frame a new theology for his subjects, or define old principles anew without full consultation with those whose business it was to advise him. Very far from it. And to the ultimate judicial opinion of such an authority even the Primate of all England was prepared to bow.

Bishop Bonner's opinion was given with exactly the same deference, although, just because he was not Primate, there was no necessity in his case to refer to the ultimate control of royal authority. What he wrote at the foot of his answers was : "*Ita mihi, Londoniensi episcopo, pro hoc tempore dicendum videtur, salvo judicio melioris sentenciæ, cui me prompte et humiliter subjicio.*" [1] The same thing is implied in the answer of Dr. George Day, Provost of King's College, Cambridge, who wrote underneath it, "*Opiniones non assertiones.*" The questions raised were in great part new, and divines naturally gave their opinions with some deference. But that Cranmer could hold his own with the King is clearly enough shown by the criticisms which he made on a number of the textual emendations proposed by the King in *The Institution of a Christian Man* ; for, while he passed many things as unobjectionable, he declared many others to be superfluous, and it appears that his objections were listened to.[2]

But even while these answers were being returned

---

[1] *L. P.*, xv. 826 (6).
[2] See Cranmer's *Miscellaneous Writings*, pp. 83-114.

Change on
Cromwell's
death.
a great change was taking place. Cromwell's career
as the King's Vicegerent was at an end, and he was
lying a prisoner within the Tower, soon to meet the
fate of an attainted traitor. After he was gone the
King was not altogether comfortable about events
abroad. There was amity between the Emperor and
France; and there was some fear that the Lutherans
of Germany, whom the Emperor had been endeavouring to conciliate by repeated Diets, might at length
come to agreement with the Catholics. This would
have been disastrous to Henry, and it was apparently
to prevent this, quite as much as to preserve the
Emperor's friendship to himself, that he sent over
Gardiner's
mission to
Ratisbon.
Gardiner, a firm adherent of the old theology, as
his ambassador to Charles V., with instructions to
follow him to Ratisbon, where the Diet was to be
held. The German Protestants had by this time
ceased to expect any good from the King of England.
The Act of the Six Articles and the burning of
Robert Barnes showed clearly that he was no real
friend of their religion, so they could no longer
be used as confederates against the Emperor. But
Germany might still be kept in a turmoil if the
Catholics were strongly urged not to compromise
matters with them; and this was an object which
Gardiner could most conscientiously promote—though
not from any desire on his part to keep Germany in
a turmoil. The Emperor, in truth, was not at that
time particularly anxious for the visit of such an
able English diplomatist, but could not avoid seeing
him at Namur just after Christmas, and letting him
follow to Ratisbon in the beginning of 1541.

Gardiner's despatches home seem to have had a
very sensible effect on the King's policy, and the men
who had been Cromwell's agents were more out of
favour than ever. Diplomatists in Flanders and in
Germany were at first doubtful how to meet this
emissary of a heretical king; and when he came

to an interview with Granvelle and complained of the Emperor's coldness towards Henry, the Imperial minister in reply told him that the Emperor had treated his master even better than he deserved. Had not the King divorced the Emperor's aunt (Katharine of Aragon), even in contempt of that papal authority to which all Christian princes were bound to show deference? Yet the Emperor had several times offered, if he would only agree once more to be obedient to the Holy See, to sue to the Pope for his pardon; and he was willing even now to intercede for him with the Holy Father, especially as that wicked minister, Cromwell, had been removed, who was the chief cause of evil. How could Gardiner tax the Emperor with coldness to his master?[1]

Gardiner was perplexed how to answer. He could not deny that Cromwell's influence had been very bad, and he seemed to admit that there was a great deal of truth in what Granvelle had said; but it was treason in England even to suggest such a thing as the King's reconciliation to Rome. Granvelle had quite turned the tables on the ambassador, and made it appear, as was really the fact at this time, that the Emperor's friendship was even more valuable to Henry than Henry's was to the Emperor. So he wrote to Chapuys, the Imperial ambassador in England, to do what Gardiner could not do, that is to say, exhort the King to let the Emperor plead for him and make his peace with the Pope. And this Chapuys undoubtedly did, not without good diplomatic results at least. For within six weeks Gardiner had a reply from the King, instructing him to thank Granvelle for his offer to get the Emperor to intercede for Henry with the Pope, and Granvelle told the nuncio Morone that he hoped good would come of it.[2] Two months later, when some approach

Granvelle offers to procure the Emperor's intercession for Henry at Rome.

---

[1] *L. P.*, XVI. 548.   [2] *L. P.*, XVI. 676.

seemed to be making in the Diet of Ratisbon towards religious peace, he even told another papal messenger that, if only the Protestants could be got to concede some points, he was informed by the English ambassadors (for besides Gardiner, whose mission was temporary, there was Sir Henry Knyvet, who was to be resident) that their King would permit the Emperor to undertake his reconciliation to the Pope; and if England returned to the Church, the Lutherans would probably be entirely submissive.[1]

So, at least, the papal messenger understood matters, and he was not altogether wrong. But he should not have spoken of the English ambassadors in the plural number; for it was only from Gardiner, not from Knyvet, as we shall see presently, that Granvelle could have got any such impression as that Henry would allow the Emperor to undertake his reconciliation at Rome. Still the fact appears indisputable that at this time the King was positively thinking—not, perhaps, that he would of himself go so far (for the chapter of accidents might probably save him from such humiliation)—but that he might, perhaps, be compelled, as a matter of policy, to retrace his past steps and seek peace once more with the Holy See; and he was glad to know that if he should be driven to such a course, he might rely on the Emperor's good offices to smooth his way. At least, by suggesting such a possibility he enabled Gardiner the more easily to lay the foundation of a closer political alliance between him and the Emperor; and as soon as he had done so Gardiner was recalled.[2]

There is no doubt that Henry greatly appreciated the value of Gardiner's services, yet apparently Gardiner himself was not without grave apprehensions as to the reception he might meet with on his

---

[1] *L. P.*, xvi. 870. See Baronius, xxxii. 577-8.
[2] *L. P.*, xvi. 910, 941 (p. 454).

return. " The Bishop of Winchester is recalled,"
wrote Morone from Ratisbon to Cardinal Farnese,
" and fears for his life for persuading the King to
return to the Church." [1] This could not have been
exactly the case, as we have seen already how
cautious Gardiner was about the matter. But an
awkward incident had occurred, the true nature of
which we can understand perfectly from the pages
of Foxe. It is needless to say that what passed
between Gardiner and Granvelle on the subject of
reconciliation with Rome was of a very confidential
character indeed, and how far Gardiner himself dared
to report it to his Sovereign we do not know. It
was through Granvelle's writing to Chapuys, and
Chapuys's exhortations, that the matter was really
moved to the King himself; after which Gardiner,
of course in the strictest privacy, was commissioned
to thank Granvelle as already mentioned. Out of
this, it appears, came other private communications ;
and one day an Italian banker named Lodovico was
charged by the Legate Contarini, then on the point
of leaving Ratisbon, to go to the English ambassador
and ask him for an answer to the Pope's letters
which the legate had delivered to him. The man,
unfortunately, communicated the request to William
Wolfe, Sir Henry Knyvet's steward, to convey to his
master. Of course the ambassador intended was not
Knyvet, but his colleague, and the message ought
to have been delivered to Gardiner himself in the
strictest secrecy. But Lodovico, not being an Englishman, could not imagine how dangerous the matter
was, and he was under the impression that Wolfe was
Gardiner's servant. Knyvet thus learned that his
colleague was receiving communications from Rome,
and he could not but feel bound to inform against
him. The matter naturally gave rise to a great deal
of gossip, and it is not wonderful that Foxe, with his

*An awk-
ward
incident.*

[1] *L. P.*, xvi. 968.

invariable animus against Gardiner, records it as one of the "causes that moved the King to suspect his fidelity towards his godly proceedings in religion."[1]

Gardiner well received on his return home.

But, it need hardly be said, there was never any real doubt about Gardiner's feeling in religious matters, and if anybody misunderstood his conduct it was certainly not the King,[2] from whom, on his return, he met with a very good reception. He took his place again at the Council table, and even the painful disclosures about Katharine Howard, whom he examined on the subject of her misdemeanours, only proved how high he stood in the King's confidence. It was next year, 1542, that Convocation condemned "the Great Bible," and Gardiner read out his catalogue of words and phrases from the Vulgate, which he desired to see retained as nearly as possible in their Latin forms. But "the Great Bible," as we have seen, was retained in use in spite of Convocation.

Convocation in 1543.

In the year following, 1543, the Convocation of Canterbury met on the 16th February, and, after the two Houses had voted a heavy subsidy to the King, the Prolocutor exhibited some homilies composed by certain prelates, which were intended as an aid and stay to ignorant preachers; but their use was not then authorised. On the 21st the Archbishop intimated that it was the King's pleasure " that all mass books, antiphoners, portuises in the Church of England should be newly examined, corrected, reformed, and castigated from all manner of mention of the Bishop of Rome's name, from all apocryphas, feigned legends, superstitious orations, collects, versicles, and responses; that the names and

---

[1] *Acts and Monuments*, vi. 165-8; vii. 588-91.
[2] According to the deposition of Sir Thomas Chaloner some years later, serious disputes arose about this matter between Sir Henry Knyvet and Gardiner at the Emperor's Court for about a fortnight or twenty days, "till, at last, by letters from the King's Majesty, both the Bishop and Sir Henry were commanded to lay all things underfoot, and to cease that matter, joining together in service as before."—Foxe, vi. 168.

memories of all saints which be not mentioned in the
Scripture or authentical doctors should be abolished
and put out of the same books and calendars; and
that the services should be made out of the Scriptures and other authentic doctors." Also that, to
prevent further negligence in the matter, "the
examination and correction of the said books of service" were to be committed to the Bishops of Sarum
and Ely (Capon and Goodrich) "taking to each of
them three of the Lower House such as should be
appointed for that purpose. But this," it is added,
"the Lower House released."[1]   They were not
anxious, apparently, to assist the two subservient
bishops in defacing a number of ancient MSS., which
are disfigured to this day with the word "Pope"
crossed out wherever it occurs, and the title "Bishop
of Rome" interlined in place of it.

It was further ordered "that every Sunday and
holy day throughout the year, the curate of every
parish church, after the *Te Deum* and *Magnificat*,
should openly read unto the people one chapter of
the New Testament in English without exposition,
and when the New Testament was read over, then to
begin the Old." We have heard in later times of the
principle of reading the Bible "without note or comment," as, indeed, the practice itself is common
enough without any orders on the subject. But
whenever such orders are made, surely the question,
"Understandest thou what thou readest?" should
also be prohibited.

The Synod then, after passing the Bill of Subsidy,
put forward, for presentation to the King, four
petitions, as follows:—

"1. For the Ecclesiastical laws of this realm to
be made, according to the Statute made in the fifth
(error for 25th[2]) year of his most gracious reign.

[1] Wilkins, iii. 863.
[2] The Act 25 Hen. VIII. c. 19, passed after the Submission of the Clergy,
forbade their making ordinances or canons in time coming without the King's

" 2. For remedy to be provided by his Highness for the ungodly and unlawful solemnisation of marriages frequently used, or abused, in the chapel or hospital of Bethlehem without Bishopsgate.

" 3. For an Act of Parliament to be made this session for the union and corporation of small and exile benefices through this realm, which for smallness of fruits be not able to find a priest, and so rest untaken by parson, vicar, or curate.

" 4. For some good order and provision to be made by his Majesty and established by Parliament for due and true payment of tithes, both predial and personal, throughout this realm, for quietness of all persons and discharge of consciences of the laymen," etc.[1]

Thus we see that the Church under bondage was still striving to do its best. On the 17th [March ? —*ejusdem mensis* in the record, but apparently some passages have been left out] the Synod was adjourned till the 4th April. But nothing important was done till the 20th, when steps were taken in the preparation of the third Formulary. That day there were laid before the prelates the Lord's Prayer and the Angelic Salutation with the English Commentary or interpretation contained in the *Institution*; and after these had been examined by the Archbishop and by Bishops Gardiner, Heath, and Thirlby, the Prolocutor entered, and they were delivered to him for the consideration of the Lower House. Next day the first five Commandments of the Decalogue, with the English Commentary, were in like manner considered and delivered to the Prolocutor. On the 24th the remaining five Commandments were dealt with, and likewise delivered to the Prolocutor, together with the articles on Baptism and the

Revision of the Institution.

assent, but allowed the King to nominate, when he was so pleased, thirty-two persons, one-half lay and one-half clerical, to examine the canons already enacted, so that those approved by them and the King should still be enforced.   [1] Wilkins, *u.s.*

Eucharist. So, at least, it stands on the record; but the Eucharist, certainly, was not fully considered that day. The whole of these articles had been examined by the Archbishop and by Bishops Thirlby, Heath, Salcot, and Skipp. Thirlby, who in 1540 had been made Bishop of the new See of Westminster, and Heath, Bishop of Rochester, were the only two of these who were really of the old school, though even they, of course, had accepted the Supremacy. Of the subservient Salcot, or Capon, as Bishop of Bangor, I have already spoken; he had been since translated to Salisbury in Shaxton's room. Skipp had been Queen Anne Boleyn's almoner, but was not made a bishop till after her fall, and he now filled the See of Hereford. So there was a large infusion of the "New Learning" in the Committee by which the matter was decided. Next day the same bishops examined and revised the articles on the Sacraments of the Eucharist, Matrimony, Penance, Orders, Confirmation, and Extreme Unction, and delivered them to the Prolocutor, desiring to have the judgment of the Lower House upon them on Friday following, the 27th April.

On that day the Archbishop and the Bishops of Winchester, Rochester, and Westminster, examined and approved an English exposition of the word "Faith" (probably Cranmer's own composition), and of the twelve articles of the Creed. In the afternoon were read tracts upon Justification, Good Works, and Prayer for the Dead, which were all delivered to the Prolocutor and brought back on the Monday following (30th April). On which day, after an article on Free Will had been read and discussed by the bishops, it also was delivered to the Prolocutor to be read by him to the Lower House; and the Lower House returned the whole treatise, with expressions of cordial approval and great thanks to the bishops for all the labours and pains they had bestowed upon the subject. The Convocation was then prorogued.[1]

The book of *Necessary Doctrine.*

The final result of all these deliberations was given to the world on the 29th May in the printed treatise entitled, "A Necessary Doctrine and Erudition for any Christian Man; set forth by the King's Majesty of England." It was essentially "the Bishops' Book" remodelled, and might fairly now be called, as it was called, "the King's Book," not only because it was "set forth" by him, but because, if not the substance, at least the turns of expression, were in many cases modified more or less in accordance with the King's own suggestion. Henry was quite at home in theology—at least in its verbal implements; and he had already shown, even in dealing with the compositions of German divines, how he could alter and modify phraseology as well as argue, which all his own divines knew that he could do very well.[2]

Accordingly, like a true Defender of the Faith, he prefaced the new Manual with an address to his faithful and loving subjects, stating that he, in the time of darkness and ignorance, had striven to purge his realm of hypocrisy and superstition; but as now, in the time of knowledge, the Devil had attempted to return into the house purged and cleansed, with seven worse spirits, and people's hearts were inclined "to sinister understanding of the Scripture, presumption, arrogancy, carnal liberty, and contention," he was constrained, in order to avoid diversity in opinions, to set forth, with the advice of his clergy, "such a doctrine and declaration of the true knowledge of God and His Word" as would teach men what was necessary for every Christian to know. And as we only know God perfectly by faith, the

---

[1] Wilkins, iii. 868.
[2] *L. P.*, xiii. i. 1307 (3); for the text of which, and the corrections in the King's hand, see Pocock's *Burnet*, iv. 408.

article in explanation of faith occupied the first place in the treatise.   Then followed the explanation of the articles of the Creed, of the Seven Sacraments, of the Ten Commandments, and of the *Ave Maria*. Further, as people had been much " embusied " about the understanding of free will, justification, good works, and praying for souls departed, the plain truth on these subjects also was set forth without ambiguity.   And he exhorted all his people " both to read and print in their hearts the doctrine of this book."

The book is certainly a more finished production than its predecessor, yet there is no marked difference of tone.   Some of the articles are substantially and almost verbally the same in both books.   The exposition of the Creed is more condensed than in the *Institution*, the form also being altered from that of a personal confession of faith to a simple statement of doctrine ; and " the Notes and Observations of the Creed," which were appended to the exposition of it in the earlier book were got rid of in the later. Some readers may be disposed to regret the omission of special passages in the *Institution*.   Certainly the heart may well be touched with the warm language in the interpretation of the second article : " And I believe also and profess that Jesu Christ is not only Jesus, and lord of all men that believe in him, but also that he is my Jesus, my God and my Lord." Yet the somewhat extreme and Calvinistic statement of the doctrine of Original Sin to which these words are a prelude was very well left out.   In the Sacraments much of the matter is recast, especially in Baptism, Penance, and the Sacrament of the Altar. As to the last, it is to be noted that the *Institution* merely set forth in one single paragraph the doctrine of the Real Presence and the necessity of self-examination before reception—a teaching which would not have repelled the Lutherans ; but the *Necessary*

Doctrine declared very explicitly, and at considerable length, the doctrine of Transubstantiation, as a truth which was infallible, the sufficiency of receiving in one kind, and the propriety of a fasting reception, while those who attended should forbear to talk or walk up and down. A higher view was taken on the subject of Orders; and on the whole it is sufficiently clear that the ancient teaching of the Church was on most subjects more explicitly defined than it had been in the previous Formulary. Just as the *Institution* itself supplied the omissions of the Ten Articles, the *Necessary Doctrine* supplied still more fully what was thought wanting in the *Institution*. Men were not prepared yet to forego many things, even of the nature of doctrine, which had been rooted in the hearts of humble souls by the tradition of ages. And the rude violence with which these things had been assailed was now, in spite of despotic and other influences which had all along tended to irreverence, rebuked alike by episcopal and by royal authority itself.

CHAPTER III

It might be said, no doubt, and with perfect truth, that the bishops and divines whose advice the King was obliged to take in order to vindicate his own position before the world, had now triumphed over a mass of irreverence, unbelief, and blasphemy which the King had been sedulously fomenting in an underhand manner ever since he first recognised Rome as his enemy in seeking a divorce from his first wife. But it must not be supposed that the enemy he had stirred up was altogether vanquished. Very far from it. The Six Articles had made some forms of heresy and irreverence dangerous; but there were many others far more subtle than a denial of Transubstantiation. The *Necessary Doctrine* had done what its name implied: it had formulated almost everything really necessary to the faith of Christians—in fact, everything absolutely necessary. And there is no doubt that these successive definitions had done much to free a time-honoured faith from persecution. But what are formularies and definitions after all? They are like treaties between great powers, valuable and binding so long as powerful interests find it more advisable to keep them than to break them. Unhappily, there is no other guarantee for their maintenance. For there is always ample margin for evasion and subtlety; and there is not always an absolute guarantee against positive breach of faith.

357

Conflict
between
the Old
and the
New
Learning.

But in these matters relating to the Christian faith there was little need of overt acts of rebellion. The world was already divided into two schools of thought, the Old Learning and the New. The Old Learning had been gradually built up upon the decisions of a Church believed to be infallible; the New rested really upon private interpretations of a book believed to be infallible also. The authority of the book, of course, was not in question; it was acknowledged by all. The only question was about its interpretation—whether such and such translations were good and wholesome, whether such and such commentaries were not mischievous, and whether such and such sectarian and novel views ought to be licensed, with full power to decry and to rail at the teachings of learned divines in past ages confirmed by a long course of traditional acceptance. The mind of the sixteenth century could not endure such a conflict of authorities. Men felt that there could be but one truth, and the one truth only could be wholesome. Even the Bible-men tried to make themselves and the world believe that they were in perfect harmony with each other as possessed of superior enlightenment. They, moreover, did study the Bible more than others, whether in wholesome or corrupt translations; and if the Great Bible was a corrupt translation, as Convocation had declared it to be, the King had taken very good care that it should not be amended. The vested interests of printers, stationers, and jobbers were of vastly superior importance in his eyes to the rectification of errors and misapprehensions connected with the sacred text. To discredit and supersede a version already before the world could only produce unsettlement. So the Bible-lovers had their way, and had an authorised translation to appeal to — not authorised by the Church, indeed, but solely by the King; while those who were content with old Church teaching went to mass as they had always done, without troubling themselves much either with the English Bible or with the clear elocutionists who read it out aloud in St. Paul's and other churches, to the disturbance generally of the peaceful, religious atmosphere of a place that was meant for devotion.

Moreover, the new school had the immense advantage of the well-known sympathy of the Primate of all England ; and when, like some other cathedrals, that of Canterbury underwent a constitutional change, the old cathedral convent of Christchurch being replaced by a dean and canons, Cranmer had a special opportunity for advancing that New Learning which was dear to his heart. The great change took place on the 8th April 1541, two years before the publication of the book of *Necessary Doctrine*. The Prior of Christchurch and twenty-six of his monks were pensioned off; seven others were made prebendaries on the new foundation ; a gospeller and epistoler were named in the patent, who may perhaps have filled those offices before ; and the remaining monks were provided for as petty canons or scholars. Five other prebendaries were appointed, making the number of those dignitaries twelve, among whom was one Dr. Nicholas Ridley, vicar of Herne, and already master of Pembroke Hall, Cambridge. Six preachers were also appointed on the staff of the Cathedral, of whom one was a Dr. Lancelot Ridley, Nicholas Ridley's cousin-german. Archbishop Cranmer himself then visited Canterbury, and on Trinity Sunday, 12th June, having called before him all the prebendaries and preachers, he told them in the course of his address that " the Bishops' Book " had been put forth without his consent, as the King very well knew.[1] This was clearly a hint that preaching of a different character would not be severely censured by the Primate, though it is very doubtful whether

Cranmer at Canter-
bury.

[1] *L. P.*, XVIII. ii. 546 (p. 368).

"the King's Book," which he was obliged to sanction two years later, was really much more to his mind. In this year, 1541, he gladly assisted the King in carrying further his war against superstition. For in spite of past orders to take away the images and bones of saints to whose shrines the people had resorted to make offerings, the King intimated to him by letters missive (probably drawn up by himself beforehand) that he understood that many shrines with their coverings still remained, and therefore enjoined him at once to search his cathedral to get rid of any that were still found there, and command the clergy of his diocese to do the like.[1]

Of the way in which this order was carried out we have an interesting glimpse in depositions taken two years later. The parson of St. George's in Canterbury, whose name was John Tofer, at once wrote from London to his curate, John Paris, and his churchwardens, Mr. Rand and Mr. Bartilmewe, to take down the image of St. George, as directed by Mr. Commissary. If it were not done before his coming home, he said, he would do it himself; and he and the churchwardens actually did take it down accordingly. But this was not enough; for on Friday following Cranmer's Commissary came and inquired whether they had also cut it in pieces. "No," was the reply. Then said the Commissary, "It is not only the King's Majesty's pleasure to have such images abused to be pulled down, but also to be disfigured, and nothing of such images to remain, with the tabernacle." Rand pleaded that surely it was not the King's pleasure to pull down such "pictures" (images were often called pictures) when there was no common offering at the shrine, especially a "picture" of the patron saint of England, to whom, moreover, the church was dedicated? "Why not?" said the Commissary, who undoubtedly breathed the

---

[1] *L. P.*, xvi. 1262; or Cranmer's *Works*, p. 490 (Parker Soc.).

spirit of his master, Cranmer : " why not, as well as
the crucifix ?   We have no patron but Christ."   A
churchwarden could not be expected to hear this with
equanimity.   " If you pull down the crucifix," said
Rand, " then pull down all."   The Commissary
did not stick at this, but, " for the more surety,"
ordered it to be done, and bade his sumner, John
Briggs, see it done.   This was surely rude treatment
of old associations, especially at a time when images in
churches were held to be in themselves legitimate ;
for even " the Bishops' Book," in expounding the
Second Commandment, had expressly admitted that
they were valuable to promote piety, instancing
especially the crucifix, which Cranmer's Commissary
now insisted on getting rid of.   Formularies, apparently, had no binding force when Cranmer or his Cranmer
master wished to go beyond them.   Yet the King's goes
general order only applied to images and relics to beyond
which offerings were made, on the ground that they express
were the cause of superstition.   And here nothing orders.
worse could be alleged than that once a year—on St.
George's Day—the image of the Saint was taken down
and borne through the streets " in the honor of God
and the King, with Mr. Mayor, the Aldermen and
their wives, with all the commons of the same going
in procession." [1]   To all appearance, it was more of a
popular holiday than a superstitious observance.

Now, considering that the old orthodox position
about images, as well as about some other things,
was again revindicated two years after this in the
third of our formularies (the *Necessary Doctrine*)
even more strongly than it was in " the Bishops'
Book," and that the King himself then found it
necessary to authorise this third Formulary, we may
feel some surprise that an archbishop of Canterbury should meanwhile deliberately set himself to
contravene that teaching which had already been laid

[1] *L. P.*, XVIII. ii. p. 309.

down by his brother bishops, and which was afterwards to receive the highest sanction now acknowledged in the Church of England. But so it was.
For two years and more before the publication of the
Necessary Doctrine, Cranmer had been actively help-
ing on the war against images and carrying it further.
The utmost that had been yet ordained by any
external authority whatever was, that a particular
class of images should be taken down to avoid the
danger of idolatry; and the very injunctions by
which this was decreed—the injunctions, that is to
say, of Cromwell, whose authority, it might have
been supposed, did not deserve increased respect
after his fall—distinctly indicated that images in
themselves had their legitimate use. To make this
fully apparent, let us see the precise words of
Cromwell's injunctions of 1538 which bear upon the
subject.[1] After enjoining sermons against superstition and things tending to idolatry, they go on :—

Item, that such images [2] as ye know in any of your cures
to be so abused with pilgrimages or offerings of anything
made thereunto, ye shall for avoiding of that most detestable
offence of idolatry, forthwith take down and deley ; [3] and
shall suffer from henceforth no candles, tapers, or images of
wax to be set afore any image or picture, but only the light
that commonly goeth across the church by the rood loft, the
light before the sacrament of the altar, and the light about
the sepulchre ; [4] which for the adorning of the church and

---

[1] I print this paragraph as it stands in the original injunctions issued by
Berthelet, of which there is a copy in the British Museum—not a perfect copy,
indeed, but containing the whole of this paragraph. There appear to be
some verbal differences in the copy entered in the Archbishop's register as
printed by Burnet and Wilkins, and these, for the sake of accuracy, I have
noticed in footnotes.

[2] The copy in Cranmer's register reads " feigned images."

[3] So the word is spelt in the printed original, and also in a MS. copy signed
by Cromwell in the Record Office. The register apparently reads "delaye,"
as in Wilkins (iii. 816), and Murray's great Dictionary gives "deley" as
simply an obsolete form of "delay," but the sense seems rather to suggest
"delete" or destroy.

[4] A "sepulchre" was a niche in the church wall in which the sacrament
was placed after the mass of Maundy Thursday till the morning of Easter
Day. Many "sepulchres" still remain in English churches, especially in
Lincolnshire.

divine service, ye shall suffer to remain still,[1] admonishing
your parishioners that images serve for no other purpose but
as to be books of unlearned men that can no letters, whereby
they might be otherwise admonished of the lives and conversation of them that the said images do represent; which
images if they abuse for any other intent than for such
remembrances, they commit idolatry in the same, to the
great danger of their souls. And therefore the King's
Highness, graciously tendering the weal of his subjects'
souls, hath in part already, and more will hereafter, travail
for the abolishing of such images as might be occasion [2] of so
great an offence to God, and so great danger [3] to the souls of
his loving subjects.

" In part already, and more will hereafter." There
was no doubt an indication here of things to come,
which might be taken differently by different people.
The party which had set its face against all images
whatever no doubt saw here a vision of a future
policy very much in accordance with their wishes.
But there was no distinct implication that further
ordinances were to be made, and the words might be
read merely to imply that further steps would be
taken to enforce principles already laid down. That
the ambiguity was intentional there can hardly be a
question; for it would have been bad policy to state
expressly that measures were in contemplation which
might create still further disturbance and call for
remonstrance from the bishops generally. But even
if the ordinance was only to be understood as temporary, it ought surely not to have been pressed further
than the language distinctly warranted; and we see
that the order itself indicates that there was a use of
images—as books for the unlearned—which was not
only unobjectionable but wholesome. And to add
to all this, it may be reasonably presumed that, as

---

[1] There is no punctuation here in the printed original, which leaves it
doubtful whether a stop should be made after "remain" or after "still."
But the MS. copy signed by Cromwell has the comma after "still."

[2] The register reads "an occasion."

[3] The register reads "a danger."

Cromwell was no particular theologian, Cranmer himself had been taken into consultation about the language of this injunction. In fact, we can read here what Cranmer's secret policy undoubtedly was. He would tolerate images at present just so far as he must. They were, at the best, books for unlearned folk, which would be needless if everybody could read; and though School Boards were not even thought of in his day, sermons might bring home to the ignorant all such truths as were of any real value, about saints or about any other subject which could be considered edifying. That being so, what was the harm of going a little further than even ordinances and proclamations warranted? Cranmer had a convenient instrument in his Commissary, just as the King had in Cromwell. The name of this official was Christopher Nevinson, and he was related by marriage to the Archbishop, for his wife was Cranmer's niece. Her mother, who was Cranmer's own sister, had been a miller's wife; and, strange to say, during her husband's life she had married another man of the name of Bingham. The fact was attested by two different witnesses in the course of some voluminous depositions taken before Cranmer himself, of which an account will be given presently, and though he cross-questioned them and others about many other matters he seems never to have contradicted this.

Cranmer's Commissary favours heretics.

There were also serious complaints of the Commissary as a man who actually favoured heretics, connived at irregular practices, and had resigned a benefice under a bond that his successors should pay him for many years the greater part of its value. Yet this man had been elected by Cranmer's influence as one of the proctors in Convocation of Canterbury Cathedral.[1]

What wonder, then, that in spite of episcopal formularies "the New Learning," and the new irreverence shown to old usages, made steady pro-

[1] *L. P.*, xviii. ii. pp. 291, 329, 330, 359.

gress, at least in the diocese of Canterbury? When
Bishop Gardiner returned home from Germany in
the autumn of 1541, he naturally heard mass
in Canterbury Cathedral.   Among the prebendaries
on the new foundation, which had not been quite
half a year in existence, he found a namesake of
his own, William Gardiner, also known by another
surname, Sandwich.   After mass he inquired of this
namesake as to the condition of religious matters
among them, and was told, as he indeed had heard
already, that the preachers did not agree with each
other.   In reply to further questions, William Gardiner
told him about the preaching of Dr. Lancelot Ridley
and of Master Scory, another of Cranmer's six
preachers, afterwards an Edwardine and Elizabethan
bishop.   The Bishop listened quietly till the prebendary spoke of an objection, raised by one or
other of these, to prayer in an unknown tongue,
which he had said was only babbling.   "There he
missed," said the Bishop, "for the Germans themselves are now against that saying."   Bishop Gardiner
added that my Lord of Canterbury must correct such
preaching, and he believed he would.   But it was
not mere erroneous preaching that disturbed Canon
Gardiner.   His own preaching was marked by others,
and he feared they were anxious to catch him tripping.   He asked the Bishop's advice what to do.
The Bishop advised him to write his sermon beforehand in a book, every word as he would preach it,
and ask the best man that could read among the
audience to take the book and read it as he preached.
If he took care not to say more than he had written,
that would be his safeguard; and as to others, if
they preached amiss, he had better say nothing.[1]

It had come to this, then, that in the chief
metropolitan diocese of England, and especially in
and about Canterbury itself, it was dangerous to

Orthodox preachers intimidated at Canterbury.

[1] *L. P.*, XVIII. ii. p. 339.

say too much, even in favour of things hitherto
approved, although no acknowledged authority had
yet openly denounced them. So strange a revolution deserves careful study; and the materials for
studying it have recently been made available. The
reader, of course, has often heard of certain alleged
"conspiracies" against Cranmer on account of the
doctrine taught by him and his chaplains in Kent;[1]
the chief of which "conspiracies" was a complaint
made against him by the prebendaries of his own
cathedral, backed by some of the local gentry and
country justices. This complaint, we can tell, was
laid before the King in 1543, the year of the publication of the book of *Necessary Doctrine.* That
no such complaint had been laid before the King
earlier was due merely to the manifest favour in
which Archbishop Cranmer was regarded by the
Supreme Head of the Church of England. In fact,
efforts had been made to complain before, but the
petitions had been quashed and refused consideration. Henry, however, must have been ruminating
in private over Granvelle's communications, and the
possibility that one day, even to have some friend
or other upon the Continent, he might, perhaps, be
driven to reconciliation with Rome. These thoughts,
at least, may have had their influence in his allowing
Convocation to settle the terms of his third formulary
of faith in a sense more congenial than before to
ancient doctrine, as there was now no use in holding
a door open to conciliate the Lutherans. At all
events, it is sufficiently clear that in 1543 the
adherents of the ancient faith were beginning to
entertain hopes that their protests against new-
fangled doctrines would meet with a more hearty
response from the King himself.

How the professors of such teaching had been
encouraged in previous years appears distinctly from

[1] Nichols's *Narratives of the Reformation,* p. 251.

documents of unquestionable authority. On that same Trinity Sunday above referred to, in 1541, Cranmer intimated to his clergy at Canterbury "that he had set in Christchurch six preachers, three of the Old Learning and three of the New." "My Lord," said Canon Gardiner, "that is a mean to set us at variance!" But the Archbishop at once silenced him with the reply, "The King's pleasure is to have it so." In August following "about the Assumption of Our Lady (the 15th) the Archbishop spoke about the matter again in the consistory, when, as Cox, one of the petty canons, reported, he said that the six preachers had been appointed, three of Oxford and three of Cambridge, "to the intent that they might between them try out the truth of doctrine." Cox, when interrogated upon the subject two years afterwards, could not be sure whether the Archbishop's words implied that the King had made the appointments, or the Archbishop himself; but the Archbishop clearly was anxious to shelter himself under the King's authority. It certainly would appear both by Canon Gardiner's statement and by that of several other canons, that Cranmer did at first convey the impression that he had made the appointments himself and then shown the King what he had done, when the King expressed his approbation. Canon Gardiner, too, on being further questioned, stood by this statement, saying, "of his conscience," that the Archbishop had used such words; but ultimately he was brought to acknowledge—without revoking what he had said otherwise—that the Archbishop had announced, even at the first, that it was the King's pleasure to have three of the Old Learning and three of the New.[1]

One might have supposed that the point mattered little. Cranmer had the King's authority for what

[1] *L. P.*, xviii. ii. pp. 323, 333 (Interr. 5, answered affirmatively by Mills, p. 366), 345 (same interr.), 348, 353, 361, 363, 364, 376.

he did, whether given before or after; and he certainly would not have ventured beforehand on an innovation which the King was at all likely to disapprove. But it was none the less an awkward innovation, tending distinctly, as Canon Gardiner had said, to foster religious differences and disputes. Moreover, if the preaching of opposite schools was to be addressed to popular audiences, it was a novelty that was hard to justify. But Cranmer was anxious to explain it otherwise. A diversity of preachers had been appointed, one of his friends declared, "to the intent that they might between them try out the truth of doctrine"; or, as another put it, "that matters then in controversy might be reasoned among themselves, and not preached among the people to engender strife."[1] The apology, however, was but a lame one. To try out the truth of doctrine by disputation was a mere scholastic function, and scholars at the universities might raise questions with the greatest freedom. They might even discuss, as they had done in past times, whether God existed or not. But this was not the function of preaching; and discussion, if it did not edify the people on matters on which the mind of the whole Church had sufficiently declared itself, could hardly edify scholars either, if the pulpit was to be the vehicle of disputation.

There is no doubt, unfortunately, that these appointments did actually tend to engender strife, as Canon Gardiner had foretold. Conspicuous among the new preachers were Dr. Lancelot Ridley and Dr. John Scory. In 1541 they were both accused of evil preaching during Rogation week[2] (before the middle of April); and on Ascension Day, Scory had given further offence in a sermon delivered at St. Alphege's church in Canterbury.[3] In this sermon

[1] L. P., xviii. ii. pp. 323, 364. [2] L. P., xviii. ii. p. 363.
[3] L. P., xviii. ii. pp. 304, 317, 347, 352.

he had said, "There is none in Heaven but Christ only"; and also, "Ye have a saying, the child which is born between man and wife, it is born in original sin; and so it is. And ye say that the sin is taken away by the water of baptism, but it is not so. But look how the wife that occupieth the fire all the day and at night covereth it with ashes to preserve the fire; so doth the sin remain under the Sacrament." [1] Four witnesses vouched for the charges against both him and Ridley; but they were never called to recant, and nothing was done to them. [2] No doubt, if freedom of the pulpit be a very desirable principle, this was just as it should be; but such freedom, in that case, should have been given impartially. In this same year Robert Serles, vicar of Lenham, another of the six preachers of Canterbury, but of the Old Learning, was sued in the Archbishop's consistory court for his preaching, and had to give a bond that he would appear before Cranmer on the 10th October, and abide his judgment. He did so, and was then committed to prison. Another of these Cathedral preachers, Edmund Shether, was also imprisoned for his preaching, apparently about the same time; and we do not know precisely for what they were censured. Canon Gardiner was of opinion that the preaching of both was perfectly innocent; and indeed it was popular, both in the city and in the country round about. [3]

But Cranmer was reported to have said in private that he could defend the positions taken up by Ridley and Scory if they had an indifferent judge; only he would have that judge out of Germany. [4] He was

Cranmer's German leanings.

[1] *L. P.*, XVIII. ii. pp. 314-15. In this deposition "Ascension day was twelvemonth" seems clearly to be a mistake, the Ascension day referred to being no doubt the same as in the other deposition, that is, two years before these depositions were taken. In each case the sermon is preached in St. Alphege's church, and Cranmer said he would uphold the doctrines of which both Ridley and Scory were accused in the *first* presentment against them; that is in 1541 (see p. 304).   [2] *Ib.*, pp. 304, 321, 337, 350, 354, 365.
[3] Nicolas's *Privy Council Proceedings*, vii. 244; *L. P.*, XVIII. ii. pp. 346, 348.
[4] *L. P.*, XVIII. ii. pp. 298, 334, 341, 356-7 (22nd interrogatory in p. 356, and answer to it p. 357).

even now maintaining a constant correspondence with the German reformers;[1] and he evidently regarded Germany as the land of judicial impartiality in matters theological. But his own impartiality between the two opposite schools in his own cathedral city is not manifest. Canon Gardiner had good reason to sympathise with Shether; for he and Shether were both out of favour, and both, as they felt, for simply doing their duty. In obedience to a letter to them from the Archbishop himself, they had felt bound to inform against one Humphrey Chirden or Cherdian, parson of St. Alphege's, Canterbury, who was accordingly examined before Cranmer at Lambeth. His preaching had been pointed enough —against the Confessional, for one thing. For on the first Sunday in Lent he had told his congregation : " If Judas had gone to God and confessed his fault, saying *Peccavi*, as he went unto the priests, he had not been damned."[2] Chirden, however, had good friends in Mr. Battersté of Canterbury, and Mr. Salter, "one of the King's beadsmen," who got men to sign a bill drawn up by them for his exculpation ; and Battersté was known to have said in private "that Mr. Gardiner and Mr. Shether should quail for the troubling of the said Sir Humphrey."[3]

Another thing is recorded of that conference on Trinity Sunday, 1541, between Cranmer and his Cathedral staff. Serles had certainly upheld strongly in his sermons the use of images. Whether he had transgressed limits imposed in the *Institution* or Injunctions does not appear ; but he had said there could be no idolatry in the case of an image of Our Lady, for all images were but representatives of saints and were not idols. The Archbishop told him, on the contrary, that all images were idols. Serles objected to this, and the Archbishop asked

---

[1] *L. P.*, XVIII. ii. p. 329. [2] *L. P.*, XVIII. ii. p. 299.
[3] *L. P.*, XVIII. ii. pp. 309, 310, 342, 346, 351-2, 357, 359, 365.

him, "What is *idolum*?" He replied readily from
Scripture, *Idolum nihil est.* Cranmer told him that
idolum and *imago* meant the very same thing. On
this Canon Gardiner broke in with a protest of his
own; he could not think that an image and an idol
were quite the same thing, but that an image to
which undue honour was paid was an idol. "You
know not the Greek," said Cranmer authoritatively;
"*idolum* and *imago* are all one." Canon Gardiner
could not take this quite submissively. "My Lord,"
he said, "although I know not the Greek, yet I trust
I know the truth, and that by St. Paul," referring
to Romans i.; and his argument, surely, was none
the worse because the Vulgate here does not use
the word *idolum*, but in verse 23 has the expression
similitudinem imaginis.[1]

If all images were idols, which was just what the
old Lollard party considered them, all images, of
course, were objectionable, whether "abused" with
offerings and pilgrimages or not. But as yet images
were supposed to be tolerated; and it really seems
that in this, as in other things, the adherents of the
Old Learning scarcely met with fair play.

Meanwhile, Scory and Dr. Lancelot Ridley were in
no fear. On the fourth Sunday in Lent, "1541"
(which in our computation means 1542, the day being
19th March), Scory preached the doctrine that faith
alone justifies, which Cranmer, doubtless, would have
upheld also, especially by the aid of "a judge out of
Germany"; and he afterwards maintained from the
pulpit "that the Supper of the Lord, which is *sacrificium et hostia* is not *hostia pro peccatis* but *hostia
laudis.*[2] Dr. Lancelot Ridley, about the same time (on

Cranmer
considers
an image
the same
thing as an
idol.

[1] *L. P.*, XVIII. ii. pp. 321, 348, 352, 355, 361, 366-8. Shether evidently
made a slip in his deposition on this subject at p. 352, where he dates the
occurrence "on Trinity Sunday was twelvemonths," which would be 1542.
The date is absolutely fixed in Hunt's deposition, p. 368, and identified with
the time when Cranmer said that "the Bishops' Book" had been published
without his consent.
[2] *L. P.*, XVIII. ii. pp. 304-305, 317, 363, 366, 367.

Passion Monday), preached at Ash "that prayer for souls departed availed nothing."[1] This gave great offence, as it was not only opposed to all hitherto received teaching, but was in express contradiction even to "the Bishops' Book," the last issued formulary; while that third formulary still to come, the *Necessary Doctrine*, commended not only prayers but masses for the deceased, "trusting that these things do not only profit and avail them but also declare us to be charitable folk." But some of Scory's further utterances even Cranmer could not defend. At Christmas, when there was a general procession ordered by the King, he preached in Canterbury Cathedral, and said, "Every country hath a custom to choose a patron, as England hath chosen St. George, Scotland St. Andrew, thinking rather by intercession of Saints to obtain the victory of their enemies. But, good people, forasmuch as Saints be circumscript, it is not possible for that Saint that is in the North to hear the prayer that is made in the South, nor that Saint that is in the South to hear the prayer that is made in the North."[2] If preaching like this was intended as an antidote to superstition, it certainly seems an odd one. No wonder, then, that when complaints against new-fangled doctrines were raised a little more loudly in 1543, even Scory found himself for a time in prison. The matter which caused his arrest seems to have been a sermon delivered shortly after Easter in that year.[3]

It is clear that up to this time Cranmer and his Commissary had protected some heretics, even of a rather extreme type, against the rigour of the law; for such was certainly Joan Baron of Canterbury, otherwise named Joan Bocher, apparently a butcher's wife, who was at last burned in the reign of Edward VI. She was already notorious, and her immunity was denounced as positively scandalous by men like

Marginal notes:
Freedom of the new preachers.

Joan Bocher.

[1] *L. P.*, xviii. ii. p. 349.   [2] *Ib.*, pp. 305, 308.   [3] *Ib.*, p. 329.

Prebendary Milles, another dignitary on the new establishment of Canterbury Cathedral. Indeed, it is rather extraordinary, considering the extreme severity of the Act of the Six Articles, and what we are commonly told of the relentless manner in which it was pressed, to find unquestionable evidence that a woman who had "denied the Sacrament of the Altar with many slanderous words," and whose written confession of the fact was in the hands of Cranmer's officers, was protected by Cranmer's Commissary from the punishment due by the law. She began, apparently, to disturb the world at Colchester, which was in Bishop Bonner's diocese, but there she was abjured. This was, however, before Bonner was bishop, and before the Act was passed in 1539; for abjuration was no protection from the death penalty under the Act when the leading doctrine of the Sacrament was denied. Moreover, she had the benefit of the King's pardon issued under a proclamation of 26th February 1539, four months before the Act was passed, in favour of those who had been seduced by Anabaptists and Sacramentaries, and were willing to return to the Church.[1] This document she carefully preserved for her security; yet occasionally she seems to have defended her old opinions in a way that provoked comment.

Meanwhile she had removed, or been removed, to Canterbury—the story at this point is not clear. In 1542 she had gone over from Canterbury to Calais, where she was again accused of heresy, but acquitted by a jury. The Council of Calais, however, remanded her to prison as there was another information against her at Canterbury, and she was sent back to England.[2] In about two years, which probably included the time she was at Calais, she was imprisoned in England also, without any evidence being brought against her, it was alleged—that is to say,

[1] *L. P.*, xiv. i. 374.   [2] *L. P.*, xvii. 829.

apparently, without any judicial process; for there was sufficient evidence of her heresy in a written confession of her own. She had been brought at first before some temporal judge, who delivered her into the hands of the Archbishop's officers. Cranmer's Commissary then proposed to set her free under the proclamation, but Prebendary Milles objected, saying that her own confession condemned her—a statement in which, apparently, he was supported by several others. "Be you all able to prove that you have spoken?" said the Commissary; and he called upon them to justify it. "Sir," said the Prebendary, "her confession is in your registry." The Commissary said he had not been able to find it, but would inquire further. This, however, was a mere excuse; and he caused a number of witnesses to come on the week of Palm Sunday. Prebendary Milles said he had taken much unnecessary trouble, and undertook himself to find her confession in the registry if the Commissary would despatch his servant thither along with him. The result was that the confession was found. So the next court day the Commissary declared her to be a heretic both by her own confession and by witnesses, and told her she could not deny it. "But," he said, "you have a thing to stick to, which may do you good. I advise you to stick to it." On this she brought out the King's pardon for penitent Anabaptists and Sacramentaries.[1]

This was probably in the spring of 1543. Heresy had been running riot till then in spite of the Six Articles, for "the whip with six strings," as the heretics called it, was not very frequently laid on; and, if report spoke truly, Cranmer himself once,

Cranmer declares the Sacrament only a similitude. "booted and spurred, read a lecture on the Sacrament of the Altar, saying it was but a similitude." We can well imagine that such a declaration " troubled

<hr>

[1] *L. P.*, xviii. ii. pp. 291, 313, 314, 331, 353-4, 359, 366.

the hearers' hearts much,"[1] and we almost wonder whether they had heard him truly, seeing that the legal penalty for such an utterance was, at that time, nothing less than death.   But such we know were Cranmer's avowed opinions at a later date, when the Act was repealed, and the incident was put on record four years before its repeal.   What are we to think ? It seems as if the Primate might take liberties with the law which another man would not dare to venture upon.

But early in 1543 matters were taking a new turn.   Even before Convocation had addressed itself to the task of revising the *Institution* and turning it into the third formulary of *Necessary Doctrine*, the King appears to have been convinced that it was desirable to do something to check the spread of heresy ; and the chief agent whom he employed was, as might have been expected, not a man of over-refined feeling or over-scrupulous conscience.   Dr. London was the man.   He had been made a prebendary of Windsor in the autumn of 1540, when he was appalled at the hold heresy had got in St. George's Chapel.   But apparently it was no use stirring in the matter till the spring of 1543, when he succeeded in calling the King's attention to the subject, who expressed great astonishment and indignation.   So it appeared that a heresy hunt was now beginning, and no one was to be afraid to accuse even the most exalted persons.

In the Advent season of the preceding year Robert Serles had preached at Chilham in Kent, where the vicar, Dr. Willoughby, was a King's chaplain ; and he took the opportunity, when there, of urging Willoughby to " put up articles to the King," seeing that his relations with royalty imposed on him a special duty to inform against heresy.   Serles said that he himself had previously endeavoured to put up

Reaction towards orthodoxy in 1543.

---

[1] *L. P.,* xviii. ii. p. 331.

articles, "but they were so cloaked that the King never saw them, and on his return he was laid in prison." This, as we have seen, had occurred just a year before, late in 1541; and Serles evidently considered that orthodoxy was treated as heresy, while heresy received special protection. Dr. Willoughby said he was quite willing to "put up articles," provided they were such as could be proved; and, Serles having preached at his church again on Passion Sunday (11th March 1543), they both rode up to London together on the Friday following. Dr. Willoughby had an object of his own which required him to see the City Chamberlain, and on the Saturday Serles, apart from Dr. Willoughby, presented some articles to Dr. London. Next day, Palm Sunday, Serles brought Dr. Willoughby to Dr. London, saying that he would present the articles. But Dr. Willoughby asked to hear them first, as he had never yet seen them, and then declined to present them, as they rested only on hearsay. This led to a scene. Dr. London had already reported the articles to some of the Council, and he told Serles he would declare who brought them; then, turning to Willoughby, told him that it was his duty to reveal such shameful articles now that he had seen them. "Fear not," he added, "for I have set such a spectacle before you at Windsor in bringing to light abominable heresies, at the which the King's Majesty was astonied and wonder angry, both with the doers and bearers." On this Dr. Willoughby gave his assent, and Dr. London wrote the articles anew, but with additions of his own, "to bring the matter into the justices' hands and certain of the spiritualty." This was not fair either to Dr. Willoughby or to Serles, and they were both vexed.[1]

Much heresy hunting.

At this time the King's Council were busy with matters of heresy to the exclusion of every other

[1] *L. P.*, XVIII. ii. pp. 324-6.

subject. They were sitting at Westminster from day to day, and the following is the exact record of their business :—

March 15*th.*—" Letters were sent for Dr. Haynes " (this was the Dean of Exeter) " to repair unto the court and to present himself before the Council the morrow after at 2 of the clock at afternoon."

March 16*th.*—" Dr. Haynes appearing before the Council, after certain things objected against him touching his own evil opinions, and the maintaining also of sundry persons in the like, was committed to the Fleet."

March 17*th.* — " Thomas Weldon, one of the masters of the Household, sent for to appear before the Council, being found culpable in the maintaining of one Sir Thomas Parson, clerk, who was known to be a man of evil opinions touching the Sacrament of the Altar, was committed to the Fleet."

March 18*th* (this was Palm Sunday).—" —— Sternall, for like causes objected and proved against him, was committed likewise unto the Fleet.

" The same day Philip Hobby, one of the gentlemen ushers of the King's Privy Chamber, for the maintaining of the above named Sir Thomas Parson, etc., was also committed unto the Fleet.

" Letters were sent to Windsor to call up Testwood, Morbecke and Benett, inhabitants of the same, to appear before the Council."

The above is the whole record of the acts of the Privy Council for four successive days. What follows is only two items extracted from the business of the day following :—

March 19*th.*—" —— Morbacke, inhabitant of the town of Windsor, for certain seditious opinions and other his misbehaviours in defence and maintenance of the same, was committed to the Marshalsea.

" A letter was sent, signed by the stamp, to the Bishop and Chapter of Exeter to certify what

they knew touching the evil opinions of Dr.
Haynes." [1]

Thus it will be seen that so important a dignitary
as the Dean of Exeter had by this time got into
trouble for heresy, and also some persons about the
Court, and some persons of Windsor. We can see
something of Dr. London's doings here, who had
" set such a spectacle at Windsor," as he said himself.
But the reader may be interested to know a little
more about these Windsor men than the mere names.
"Morbacke," as his name is spelt on the record, was
no other than the famous musician, John Marbeck,
who was organist of St. George's Chapel. Testwood
was a singer in the choir there. Robert Benett, a
lawyer, was not a man of importance. " Sternall,"
who is not named as a Windsor man, and probably
had no particular connection with Windsor, was a
gentleman of the King's Chamber, known to posterity
as Thomas Sternhold, the author of a metrical version
of the Psalms. Lollard piety had evidently taken a
poetical and a musical turn with some people, just as
the kindred spirit of Calvinism had awakened the
muse of Clement Marot in France.

Dr. Willoughby and Dr. Serles were both uncomfortable. Dr. London insisted on dragging Willoughby
before the Council to declare everything upon his
allegiance; and Willoughby, if he had been compelled
to go before them, would have been obliged to say
that he could not vouch for the articles except by
hearsay. But after being kept three days in suspense
he told Dr. London he would go home on the Wednesday afternoon. He remained, however, till Thursday
morning, when he endeavoured to see Bishop Gardiner
in his house at St. Mary Overy's. Unluckily in the
parlour he found Dr. London, who was angry that he
was not gone, and bade him go at once and tell the
prebendaries that they should have a commission

The
Windsor
heretics.

---

[1] Dasent's *Acts of the Privy Council*, i. 96-98.

within a week. He might also tell the Justices of the Peace that the Council were not at all well pleased at their negligence in allowing such heresies to be preached in the country unchecked. Dr. Willoughby got home on Good Friday, ill at ease about the articles to which he was committed. On Easter Eve he came to Canterbury, where, after dinner, Canon Gardiner called him into his garden and showed him articles drawn up against the Archbishop himself, asking him if they might trust him to let Dr. London see them privately, and deliver them to the Bishop of Winchester. This he agreed to do, and he made a second journey up to London in Easter week. Dr. London "made much joy" when he saw the articles. A deputation from Canterbury came at the same time to complain of Humphrey Chirden, and received much encouragement when they went before the Council. Dr. Willoughby also was comforted by Bishop Gardiner, who told him he should not be made responsible for the articles which he had been induced to put up; he had done his duty if they were true, and if they were false the blame should rest with the promoters.[1]

Heresy was getting rebuked. On the 14th May one Robert Wisdom, clerk, whom the Council had committed to the custody of Richard Cloney, apparitor - general to the Bishop of London, was obliged to find surety of £40 that he would remain "true and faithful prisoner" without attempting to escape, and pay for his meat and drink, bedding and other comforts until discharged of his imprisonment. Three friends, a scrivener, a mercer, and a stainer of London, all well-to-do citizens no doubt, the last of whom, John Wisdom, was presumably a near relation, agreed to stand surety for him;[2] and he remained in what must have been comparatively easy

---

[1] *L. P.*, XVIII. ii. pp. 326-8.
[2] Foxe, vol. v., App. No. 12. (Extract from Bonner's Register, f. 44.)

durance for some weeks. On Relic Sunday, 8th July,[1] he and two other clergymen, the one named Thomas Becon, otherwise Theodore Basil, the other Robert Singleton, recanted their heresies at Paul's Cross; "and the said Thomas Becon cut in pieces at his said recanting eleven books which he had made and caused to be printed, wherein was contained heresies."[2]

Recantations at Paul's Cross.

Who were these men? Robert Wisdom was, according to Foxe, "parish priest of St. Margaret's Lothbury," but according to Wriothesley, "curate of Aldermary under Dr. Cromer" (meaning Dr. Crome). As a matter of fact, he held no London benefice, and "parish priest" evidently does not mean incumbent. He may have assisted at times in the services of St. Margaret Lothbury, and also been curate at St. Mary's Aldermary to the very popular Dr. Crome, who himself had a considerable tendency at times to get into hot water. We shall hear of him again before the end of the reign. Later, under Edward VI. he got promotion, and after a sojourn abroad in Mary's time, he came back and was made Archdeacon of Ely under Queen Elizabeth. But his recantation at this time at Paul's Cross seems to have been as full as could have been expected. He began: "Worshipful audience, I am placed this day in the midst of these two penitents, as one who professes himself earnestly sorry that with my earnest countenance, gestures, behaviour, and speech I have, under the name of God's Word and pretence of Christian charity, so much slandered the true doctrine of our religion and defamed the charity of the public ministers of common justice." He goes on to say that he had preached against Free Will and against praying to Saints, and he regretted that he had

---

[1] Relic Sunday, according to the Sarum Missal, was the first Sunday after the Translation of St. Thomas "the Martyr," which was on the 7th July. Nicolas's *Chronology* is misleading on this point.

[2] Wriothesley's *Chronicle*, i. 142-3.

therein spoken untruly. He wished those whose
ways he had followed would recant likewise, and
ignorant people would soon be content to accept
"the most perfect Christian doctrine now set forth
by the King's Majesty" (the book of *Necessary
Doctrine* had by this time been published). He had
preached against charity that men could not live
well in Christ, but they were persecuted and imprisoned for the truth's sake; but in this he had
slandered common justice, for he had known no man
in particular to have been persecuted for the truth,
but several justly executed for their false doctrine
—such as Lambert, Barnes, Garret, and Jerome.
"This," he added, "is a realm of justice and of no
persecution of them that be good"; and he denounced
as untrue what his companion, Thomas Becon, had
said in his book of *David's Harp* "that persecution
is a token of the true Gospel."

Becon was a man of about thirty-one years of age,
who had been five years in Orders. His abjuration
was quite as humble. He acknowledged having
during the past three years preached false doctrine
in Norfolk and Suffolk, which he recanted there. He
had then removed into Kent, where he lay hid for
a time under the apparel of a layman, calling himself
Theodore Basile, and under that counterfeit name
had written mischievous books and got them printed.
He deplored his own pride and folly in the books
that he had written, of which he gave particular
instances; and he had given special offence before
his first recantation by preaching against praying to
Saints, against the continency of priests, against
prayer for the dead, and against the Sacrament of
the Altar. He had also preached in derogation
of the Sacraments of Confirmation and Extreme
Unction. He then recanted a number of specific
errors contained in individual books that he had
written, and in token that he completely disowned

them he cut each book to pieces. After this, being released, he withdrew into the Midlands and rejoined Wisdom for a time in Staffordshire. Under Edward VI. he soon got a city living, became Archbishop Cranmer's chaplain and a prebendary of Canterbury Cathedral. Under Mary he was committed to the Tower, but, being released, escaped abroad; then, returning after her death, he was restored to his benefices, and he lived some years into the reign of Elizabeth as a rather notable preacher.

Robert Singleton had been a chaplain of Anne Boleyn's, but very little is known of him—little, certainly, that is to his credit.[1] His recantation was so brief that it may well be given in his own words unabbreviated :—

"Worshipful audience," he said, "my companions here present have spoken unto you many words for declaration of themselves. I shall conclude in a few, which be these. I am an unlearned fantastical fool. Such hath been my preaching, and such hath been my writing, which I here before you all tear in pieces. And to the intent no man should misreport

---

[1] He was suspected, Foxe tells us, though unjustly, of the murder of Robert Packington, mercer of London, who was shot by a gun on a misty morning, 13th November 1536, on his way from his house at Soper Lane to St. Thomas of Acres to hear mass (see Wriothesley's *Chronicle*, i. 59); Foxe, v. 600. In the spring of that year we find him at Dover, where he had been apparently to secure the arrest of one Friar Patrick, who was sent up to Cromwell (*L. P.*, x. 612, 640). Two years later he reported to Cromwell what he called "a sinister and seditious sermon," preached by Dr. Cotes at Sheen Charterhouse on Easter Day, in which the preacher had said no man was bound to do the King's commandment if it were against the law of God (*L. P.*, XIII. i. 819). After this recantation, it appears, he suffered as a traitor for stirring up sedition, though Foxe assures us, on his own testimony (!), that he was not guilty of this either. And he is mentioned by the Martyrologist at the end of his eighth book in a list of men "who all recanted in King Henry's time, and yet good soldiers after in the Church of Christ." Foxe, v. 600, 696. Gardiner, however, writing, even from prison, to the Protector Somerset in the first year of Edward VI., says : "Your Grace, I doubt not, remembereth Singleton's conspiracy" (Foxe, vi. 52); from which it may be inferred that Somerset himself had no doubt of his guilt in that matter.

As regards the murder of Packington, Foxe seems to be right in saying that Singleton was not guilty of it ; but his statement that Dean Incent had hired an Italian to do it, and confessed the fact on his death-bed, is a malicious scandal. See Nichols's *Narratives of the Reformation*, p. 297.

what I have said I have signed divers copies of that
I now rehearse with mine own hand, whereof each
man may have the copy that will." [1]

It was only four days after these recantations
(12th July 1543), and when everything seemed to
point to a revindication of old doctrines, that Henry
VIII. married his sixth and last wife, Katharine Parr, *The King marries Katharine Parr.*
at Hampton Court. She was a widow of about
thirty-one years of age, who had been twice married
already, and had buried her second husband, Lord
Latimer, not much more than half-a-year before.
She was certainly more than twenty years the King's
junior, and, no doubt, attractive. Learned she also
was, like some other distinguished ladies of that day,
and in her heart a friend of "the New Learning," as
the King surely must have known even then. Yet
little more than a fortnight after her union with the
King a beacon-fire was lighted at Windsor to warn
all England that the New Learning must be on its
guard.

The *Necessary Doctrine* had been given to the
world, and the bishops and clergy seemed to have
resumed their natural position as guardians of the
Faith. But, of course, there were always tares
among the wheat, and these had been multiplying
considerably since the first alarm from the Act of the
Six Articles had subsided. Moreover, there was
always Royal Supremacy; for Henry had not, after
all, been driven by political repentance to make his
peace with Rome, and if he felt perfectly safe he
might possibly encourage the tares even now, much
in the fashion he had done before; for he was
"Supreme Head" of the Church, with none to control him. But just for the present he was intent
on burning the tares. The Windsor men had to
expiate their offences.

One of them, indeed, was happily spared; for

[1] Foxe, vol. v., App. No. 12.

Marbeck, the organist, was pardoned; and of those not connected with Windsor, Dean Haynes was released on the 5th July "after a good lesson and exhortation, with a declaration of the King's mercy and goodness towards him," on a recognisance binding him to attend the Council any time that he might be summoned within the next five months, and answer all such things as might be laid against him.[1] There were also a few other notable persons in custody for heresy, who received their pardons later. But on the 28th July [2] Anthony Peerson, Robert Testwood, and Henry Filmer were publicly burned at Windsor.

Heretics burned at Windsor.

We have already seen how Testwood and one Benett, along with Marbeck, were summoned before the Council in March. Benett, it appears, was not sent to Windsor to suffer with the other three, because he fell ill in the Bishop of London's prison.[3] As to Anthony Peerson, whose name was sometimes written Parson, it may perhaps be suspected that he was the same man twice named "Sir Thomas Parson" in the Privy Council record. For Anthony Peerson seems to have been the most important of the three Windsor victims, the other heretics there apparently having been his followers. His story, derived from Foxe, is briefly as follows :—

Anthony Peerson.

He was a preacher who visited Windsor a good deal about 1540, and people flocked to his sermons both there and in the country. He seems to have been unmolested till Dr. London was made a prebendary of Windsor. But in that case the interval was probably not a long one; for Dr. London was made prebendary of Windsor in that very year, 1540, and was installed on the 30th September.[4] At this

---

[1] Dasent's *Acts of Privy Council*, i. 151.
[2] This is the date given by Wriothesley and Stow. Foxe, in the Almanack at the beginning of his works, makes the 18th the day of these "martyrdoms"; but he seems to be in error.
[3] See Foxe, v. 494.   [4] Le Neve's *Fasti*, iii. 393, ed. Hardy.

time, we are informed by our Puritan authority that
the clergy of St. George's Chapel, "for the most
part, favored the Gospel"; which, indeed, was just
what might be expected in a Chapel Royal after
Cromwell's long ascendancy, notwithstanding that the
King's quondam Vicegerent had been put to death just
two months before, attainted as a heretic and traitor.
At his first residence dinner Dr. London could not
help telling his fellow-prebendaries that ill reports
were spread of them, and some awkward conversation
arose. Afterwards he obtained fuller knowledge from
one William Simons, a lawyer, who showed him notes
of sermons preached by Anthony Peerson "against
the Sacrament of the Altar and their popish mass,"
which seemed to justify an indictment for heresy.
For whatever our sympathies may be, we must
remember that "the Sacrament of the Altar and
their popish mass" was at this time upheld by a very
stringent law (that is to say, if mass could be
"popish" without the Pope), and the wonder is,
not that the law was put in operation sometimes,
but that it was boldly defied or ignored by any
preacher at a seat of royalty like Windsor. This
immunity lasted, to all appearance, between two and
three years. Nay, Peerson, there seems no doubt,
was not only protected by Archbishop Cranmer's
Commissary, but was even commanded by him on
Palm Sunday, 1543, "to read and expound the bible
in All Hallows' Church, Canterbury."[1] It looks as
if the Commissary had been a little overbold; for
he ought to have known that by that time Dean
Haynes and others had already been sent for by the
Council, who were also much disturbed about the
"evil opinions" of "Sir Thomas Parson, clerk." But
perhaps, though the information against him is dated
in September 1543, the Palm Sunday referred to
may not have been of that year. In that year,

[1] *L. P.*, XVIII. ii. p. 313.

however, undoubtedly it was that Dr. London, with the aid of Simons, drew up an information against Peerson, and put it in the hands of Bishop Gardiner, who, by his influence with the King, got a privy search made in Windsor for such books and letters as Peerson had sent out.[1]

Marbeck. As to the other Windsor heretics, let us first say a word about Marbeck who escaped, but who was still in prison when his companions were burned, for he did not receive his pardon till October. This pardon cites part of the contents of his indictment, by which it appears that he wrote against the Sacrament of the Altar, affirming contemptuously "that the holy Mass, when the priest doth consecrate the body of Our Lord, is polluted, deformed, sinful and open robbery of the glory of God, from the which a Christian heart ought both to abhor and flee; and the elevation of the Sacrament is the similitude of the setting up of images of the calves in the Temple builded by Jeroboam, and that it is more abomination than the Sacrifice done by the Jews in Jeroboam's Temple to those calves; and that certain and sure it is that Christ himself is made in this Mass men's laughing stock." [2]

It must be acknowledged that this was pretty strong language, and presumably Marbeck had to declare his regret for it before he received his pardon; for the prosecution not only of himself but also of the three others who were burned, was in pursuance of the Act of the Six Articles. But surely he too, like Peerson, must have had some encouragement to believe that the Act was a dead letter when he ventured so plainly to defy it. He was also arraigned for having "with his own hand gathered out of divers men's writings certain things that were expressly against both the Mass and the Sacrament of the Altar." [3] From the information Foxe gives about his

[1] Foxe, v. 472-4.   [2] *L. P.*, XVIII. ii. 327 (9).   [3] Hall, p. 258.

five different examinations, it would indeed appear that he was very diligent with his pen, and, though not a Latin scholar, had half made an English concordance to the Bible on the model of an existing Latin one; he had also made extracts from the writings of Calvin, which he explained that he had copied before the Act of the Six Articles was passed. From these I imagine came the quotations given in his pardon, though I have not verified them.[1] He perhaps got his pardon the more easily on account of his musical talent; for many would have regretted the loss of the organist of St. George's Chapel.

Of the other two actual victims, Testwood was a singer in the same chapel, who had been many years there, and who seems on one occasion to have known some secrets of State before they were known to others. By Foxe's account, he had made himself obnoxious (it must have been in 1534), by railing at the Pope and denying that he was rightfully head of the Church, which, he said, every king ought to be in his own realm under Christ. The words were spoken at the common table, and created a commotion. Master Ely, one of the chantry priests, rose up from the table in disgust, and when Testwood followed him afterwards, " would not come nigh him but did spit at him, saying to others that walked by, ' Beware of this fellow, for he is the greatest heretic and schismatic that ever came into Windsor.' " Ely also complained to the Dean of Windsor's deputy, the Dean himself being then absent in London; but the Dean, at that time Dr. Sampson, who was afterwards Bishop of Chichester, came home suddenly at night a few days after, and, late as it was, sent his verger to all the canons and other officials, requiring their attendance in the chapter-house by eight o'clock next morning. When everybody was in his place, after commending their attendance in choir

Testwood.

[1] Foxe, v. 474-85.

and other duties, the Dean " began, contrary to every man's expectation, to inveigh against the Bishop of Rome's supremacy and usurped authority, confounding the same by manifest scriptures and probable reasons, so earnestly that it was a wonder to hear; and at length declared openly that by the whole consent of the Parliament House the Pope's supremacy was utterly abolished out of this realm of England for ever; and so commanded every man there, upon his allegiance, to call him Pope no more but Bishop of Rome; and whatsoever he were that would not so do, or did from that day forth maintain or favour his cause by any manner of means, he should not only lose the benefit of that house, but be reputed as an utter enemy to God and to the King. The canons, hearing this, were all stricken in a dump. Yet notwithstanding, Ely's heart was so great, that he would fain have uttered his cankered stomach against Testwood; but the dean, breaking his tale, called him old fool, and took him up so sharply that he was fain to hold his peace. Then the dean commanded all the Pope's pardons which hanged about the church to be brought into the chapter-house and cast into the chimney, and burned before all their faces; and so departed." [1]

A surprise at Windsor.

Such a graphic account of the manner in which Royal Supremacy was established in detail, could not but be quoted in the very words of the original informant; and no other words could so effectually bring before our eyes the angry feelings and state of spiritual disturbance created by this violent interference with an old system, with which the whole religious life of the nation had been hitherto bound up. The fact that the writer himself approves of the revolution gives additional point to his description. But we are concerned at present with Testwood, to whom, of course, the new turn of affairs was a

[1] Foxe, v. 465-6.

mighty triumph.   What wonder that he went on, as he now had been justified in doing, scoffing at old things with peculiar irreverence?   He scoffed at the candles and images of wax offered by pilgrims from the far western counties of Devonshire and Cornwall " to good King Henry of Windsor," thinking, perhaps with some reason, " how vainly the people had spent their goods in coming so far to kiss a spur, and to have an old hat set upon their heads."   He broke off the nose of an alabaster image of Our Lady, and trusted to Cromwell's protection to shield him from justice.   He made sport with St. Thomas à Becket's rochet and St. George's dagger.   Even in the choir of St. George's Chapel he answered a brother singer's " O Redemptrix et Salvatrix!" with " Non Redemptrix nec Salvatrix," the two " striving there with *O* and *Non* who should have the mastery," to the amusement of the profane and worldly minded. And though, at St. George's feast within a fortnight afterwards, he received a severe rebuke from the Duke of Norfolk, who " shook him up " for his profanity, nothing more, apparently, could be done to him at that time.[1]   The particular act for which he was indicted in 1543 was a jeering speech that he uttered at the elevation of the host: " What, wilt thou lift him up so high?   What, yet higher?   Take heed, let him not fall." [2]

Henry Filmer, the third victim, was a tailor who had been a churchwarden at Windsor, and had ventured to remonstrate with his vicar about two years before on some " fond and friarish tales " (the vicar having previously been a friar) that he had uttered in his sermon.   Perhaps they were foolish enough, even as figures of speech, and the vicar, it is said, took no offence, but promised " to reform himself."   But Simons, the lawyer, it seems, came in to make mischief here also, and spoke to the vicar about

Filmer.

---

[1] Foxe, v. 465-70.   [2] Hall's *Chronicle*, p. 358.

Filmer in such a way that at a later meeting the vicar said "he would bring him before the bishop to teach him to be so malapert." Though troubled with a sore leg, the vicar prepared to go with Simons to Salisbury to lay an information before Bishop Capon. The opposite party, however, determined to anticipate him with a charge of heretical preaching; and, as the vicar could not ride fast, Filmer and his company reached Salisbury before him, and had the advantage of speaking to the Bishop first. They laid their information against the vicar before he and Simons had arrived, and the Bishop told them they had done like honest men. The vicar and Simons then coming up, the former was shown the bill of complaint against him which he could not answer, and the latter received a severe rebuke.[1] But Bishop Capon, as we know well, favoured the new school, and was not over scrupulous in many things.

In this story we are not informed what it was that Simons told the vicar to make him alter his friendly feeling towards his churchwarden. But we are at no great loss for an explanation when we read the account of Filmer's indictment two years later, as given in the same work a little further on, as well as in Hall's *Chronicle*. It was couched in these words :—

That he should say that the Sacrament of the Altar is nothing else but a similitude and a ceremony; and also, if God be in the Sacrament of the Altar, I have eaten twenty Gods in my days.[2]

This, apparently, he said to his own brother to dissuade him from going to hear mass; and his brother was forced to give evidence against him. If Foxe's statement of the case be true, his brother was the only witness brought against him,[3] and the conviction ought to have been illegal, as even that

[1] Foxe, v. 470-72.   [2] *Ib.*, 488.   [3] *Ib.*, p. 489.

severe law required two witnesses. But it is clear,
at least, from the narrative, that the brother gave
unwilling evidence; and, whatever may have been
the case as to the administration of the law, surely
the offence itself was gross. Such ribaldry, no doubt,
had been going on for a very long time unchecked, in
spite of the severity of the statute. But this year
things were taking a new turn, and there was, for a
time at least, greater vigour shown in searching out
offenders.

In what spirit the victims met their terrible fate I
will not presume to judge. But the following incident is recorded, which is undoubtedly true as to the
essential fact, and which was repeated in later instances
during the Marian persecution :—

"Being all three bound to the post, a certain *Drinking*
young man of Filmer's acquaintance brought him a *at the*
pot of drink, asking if he would drink. 'Yea,' quoth *stake.*
Filmer, 'I thank you. And now, my brother,' quoth
he, 'I shall desire you, in the name of the living
Lord, to stand fast in the truth of the Gospel of
Jesus Christ which you have received.' And so,
taking the pot at his hand, he asked his brother
Anthony if he would drink. 'Yea, brother Filmer,'
quoth he, 'I pledge you in the Lord.'" [1]

Whatever the words spoken among themselves,
their friends, no doubt, sought to alleviate their
sufferings by strong drink. It may have been, perhaps, too much to say, as men did at the time, "that
they were all drunk and wist not what they said."
But can we honour men as martyrs simply because
their punishment was excessively severe? We may
feel for them; but if their acts were not good we
cannot honour them.

Burning for heresy is a repulsive thing, whatever
we may think of heresy itself. But these burnings at
Windsor, I take it, were regarded as a sign that now,

[1] Foxe, v. 493.

with the faith laid down in a new and orthodox
formulary approved by the King himself, a host of
irregularities, hitherto positively encouraged by the
Primate and his Commissary, would meet with an
effectual check, and that old devout usages, whether
superstitious or not, against which there was no
positive prohibition, might again be practised at
liberty. Thus Canon Gardiner "moved the people to
take again matins, evensong, their beads, and the
Seven Psalms, which of late they had cast away by
them that preached against all vocal prayer." The
vicar of Faversham also "moved in confession John
Tacknal to use his *paternoster* in English no more,
for he knew not how soon the world would change."[1]
So, indeed, many had long believed that old usages
must be permitted again. Thomas Bleane of North
Mongeham, when orders were received to deface
images, had commanded the priest and churchwardens
to let them alone, "saying that such ways should
continue but a while, and that they should see
shortly." And he had an image with three crowns
near his own seat still standing. Nay, in 1542, the
year after the order to take down images was issued,
Sir Thomas, curate of Sholden, and Thomas Sawyer
actually set up again four of them which had been
taken down by the King's command, "for abuses by
pilgrimages and offerings." And there was one
Vincent Ingeam, a gentleman of Sandwich, apparently
on the Commission of the Peace,[2] who went a little
further still; for he not only "repugned against the
doing of the Commissary in taking down the image
of St. John by the King's commandment," but on
Easter Monday, 1542, he forbade any man to read the
English Bible, or hear it read, on pain of imprisonment, and actually cast two men into prison, the

---

[1] *L. P.*, XVIII. ii. pp. 293, 294.
[2] *L. P.*, XVII. 285 (3) ; XIX. ii. 340 (54). The Commissions of the Peace
at this time are very negligently inrolled ; but his name is found in Commissions of Sewers for Kent a little later. *L. P.*, XX. i. pp. 315, 324.

one for speaking against what he had done, and the other for showing him the King's injunctions on the subject.[1]

But the friends of the New Learning were even more justified in believing that another change would take place in their favour. On the 31st August the King, being then at Ampthill, despatched a writ of privy seal to the Lord Chancellor for a pardon to a number of others implicated in these charges of heresy; which was accordingly passed under the Great Seal on the 5th September.[2] These were gentlemen and ladies about the Court, of whose pardon I shall have something more to say hereafter. The pardon given to Marbeck was despatched a little later —by privy seal from the King at Woodstock on the 24th September, and passed under the Great Seal on the 4th October.[3] So far, perhaps, this indication does not go for much, and may imply nothing but Court favour. But something certainly occurred about this time, or very shortly afterwards, which implied a good deal more.

I have already referred to the so-called "conspiracy" against Cranmer by his prebendaries, and have also given numerous pieces of information derived from the examinations which ensued. It will be seen that this "conspiracy" had been going on for some time, even before Dr. London had alarmed the King in the spring of this year about the prevalence of heresy at Windsor. It seemed to have come to a climax just after Easter, when Dr. London evidently believed that the net was closing round Cranmer himself. But summer came, and severe measures were taken only against inferior persons, of whom some were made to recant, some to burn, and some were by and by pardoned. Still, a complaint was actually lodged against the Arch-

[1] L. P., XVIII. ii. p. 299.   [2] L. P., XVIII. ii. 241 (6).
[3] L. P., XVIII. ii. 327 (9).

Cranmer
complained
of by the
preben-
daries of
Canter-
bury.

bishop, and presented to the King on behalf of the prebendaries of Canterbury and a number of the justices of Kent; for the Act of the Six Articles, it must be remembered, was to be administered by Justices of the Peace. And what came of this is graphically described in a well-known passage by Cranmer's secretary, Morice :—

The King on an evening rowing on the Thames in his barge came to Lambeth bridge, and there received my lord Cranmer into his barge, saying unto him merrily "Ah, my chaplain, I have news for you. I know now who is the greatest heretic in Kent!" And so pulled out of his sleeve a paper wherein was contained his accusation articled against him and his chaplains and other preachers in Kent, and sub-scribed with the hands of certain prebendaries and justices of the Shire. Whereunto my lord Cranmer made answer and besought his Highness to appoint such Commissioners as would effectually try out the truth of those articles, so that from the highest to the lowest they might be well punished in example of others if they had done otherwise than it became them. "Marry," said the King, "so I will do; for I have such affiance and confidence in your fidelity that I will commit the examination hereof wholly unto you, and such as you will appoint." Then said my lord Cranmer, "That will not (if it please your Grace) seem indifferent." "Well," said the King, "it shall be none otherwise, for I reckon that you will tell me truth,—yea, of yourself, if you have offended. And therefore make no more ado, but let a Commission be made out to you and such other as you shall name, whereby I may understand how this confederacy came to pass." And so a Commission was made out to my lord Cranmer, Dr. Coxe, his Chancellor, Dr. Bellasis, and to Mr. Hussey his registrar, who came immediately down to Canter-bury and sat there to inquire of these matters. By means whereof, every one that had meddled in those detections shrunk back and gave over their hold. And then his Chancellor and registrar were such fautours of the papists that nothing would be disclosed and espied, but everything colorably was hid.[1]

The last sentence comes upon us as a sort of

---

[1] Nichols's *Narratives of the Reformation*, pp. 252-3.

surprise. All that goes before it clearly implies (whatever the writer intended to convey) that not-withstanding the Archbishop's remonstrance—and how sincere that was we do not know—the King determined simply to make him judge in his own cause. And so he very effectually was made. He took the depositions of a large number of the wit-nesses in his own hand, and likewise made comments in his own hand, which may be seen to this day among the MS. treasures which Matthew Parker took such particular care should be consulted only in his own college—now called Corpus Christi College —in Cambridge.[1] But as to Cranmer's Chancellor Cox and his registrar Hussey, not to talk of Dr. Bellasis, a King's chaplain, recently made Archdeacon of Colchester,[2] it is certainly strange to be told that they were favourers of the Papists, when the character of Cox, at least, is well known as that of a pretty strong reformer, made Bishop of Ely in the days of Queen Elizabeth. Nor was there anything in this early part of his career at all inconsistent with his after-history; for the King, in fact, had just recently selected him as tutor to his little son, Edward.[3] Indeed, he was already, by recent pro-motions, Archdeacon and one of the prebendaries of Ely, and a prebendary of Lincoln as well.[4] How could such a man have been unduly favourable to Papists? But we must note what follows, in Morice's narrative :—

Insomuch that upon letters by me written unto Dr. Buttes and Mr. Denny, Dr. Lee was sent down, after they

The King makes Cranmer judge in his own cause ;

---

[1] See Masters's *History of Corpus Christi College*, p. 91.
[2] *L. P.*, xviii. i. 346 (62).
[3] Then, according to Edward himself at the commencement of his Journal, "at the sixth year of his age," which was completed in October 1543.
[4] He was made prebendary of Ely on its new foundation, 10th September 1541. He was archdeacon even earlier, on the promotion of Thirlby to the bishopric of Westminster in November 1540. See *L. P.*, xvi. 305 (48), 1226 (11). He had the prebend of Sutton-cum-Buckingham in Lincoln Cathedral given him in June 1542 (Le Neve's *Fasti*, ed. Hardy, ii. 217).

had sat six weeks, by the King. And he, by the King's advice, did appoint to the number of nine or ten of my lord's gentlemen, to search both the purses, chests, and houses of certain prebendaries and gentlemen, all in one moment; by means whereof such letters and writings were found, and that a great number, that all the confederacy was utterly known and disclosed, to the defacing of a great sort [*i.e.* company] of their dishonesties. And so, a parliament being at hand, great labor was made by their friends for general pardon, which wiped away all punishment and correction for the same, specially my lord Cranmer being a man that delighted not in revenging.[1]

This, no doubt, throws some light upon the matter. The secret inquiry, even in the hands of men like Dr. Cox and the Archbishop's registrar, Hussey, had dragged on for six weeks without results altogether sufficient. So, to quicken proceedings, Dr. Thomas Legh (or Lee), the quondam Visitor of monasteries, was sent down, and his very drastic methods broke up "the confederacy" completely. But by and by the confederates were received to mercy. All the secret records of this one-sided inquiry are now open to inspection, and have been transcribed and printed, for the most part *verbatim*. Archbishop Cranmer himself would hardly have liked the prospect of their publication, though we see that he did his best to investigate the charges against himself, and, if not to answer them, at least to shake the credit of the witnesses. He had even impounded and attached to this secret register a copy or draft of a letter written by one of the new preachers at Canterbury "to my Lord of N.," at a time when it was certainly thought that there must be a commission for heresies sent down into Kent, owing to the complaints against the Archbishop and his favourite preachers. There can be very little doubt that "my Lord of N." was Gardiner, Bishop of Winchester, and that the communication was very confidential. For among

and Cranmer investigates the complaints himself.

[1] Nichols's *Narratives*, p. 253.

various things that it contained were passages like
these :—

> Also, if my lord of Canterbury may know the witnesses'
> names of the articles, he will find some evasion by Dr.
> Gwent's counsel, his Commissary, and other, to prevent their
> deposition and make them insufficient.
>
> Also, if my lord of Canterbury be one of the Commis-
> sioners, it will stay many depositions.[1]

Thus it appears that Edmund Shether, one of the
six preachers placed by Cranmer himself at Canterbury (for he it was who wrote this letter), had no
confidence in his archbishop's fairness and impartiality if there were any investigation of the considerable increase of heresy in Kent. Nor were his
apprehensions at all unnatural, seeing that both he
and Serles had suffered imprisonment for their
preaching, though they knew that they had the
sympathy of most people in what they had preached.
And I fear, it must be owned, that a careful perusal
of the records of this secret examination goes far
to justify the suspicions that Shether entertained.
Indeed, we have seen already, from some of the
evidences elicited in this very inquiry, what became of
the information against Chirden ; and the inference
is a strong one from Batterste's words that Shether
and Gardiner were prosecuted in revenge for the
prosecution of Chirden. It was on St. George's Day
(23rd April 1543), as appears from a letter preserved
among these evidences,[2] that Batterste and Salter
procured signatures to the document for Chirden's
exculpation, and that the former declared that
Gardiner and Shether "should quail for the
troubling of the said Sir Humphrey." What else
could Shether do on hearing this but give secret
intimation to some powerful friend of the position
in which he found himself? And it is quite clear
that his confidential letter to "my Lord of N." above

[1] *L. P.*, XVIII. ii. p. 359.   [2] *L. P.*, XVIII. ii. p. 342, § v.

referred to was written at this very time; for the first part of it, which I shall now quote from the abstract in *Letters and Papers*, refers expressly to this subject :—

Reminds his Lordship that Thomas Batters of Canterbury and William Salter, one of the King's beadmen of Christchurch in the said city, have procured a testimonial for the honesty of Sir Humphrey Cherdayn "to the intent, as it is thought, to improve (*sic*) such witnesses as Mr. Gardener and Mr. Shether have brought in to depose in their articles objected against the said Humphrey; in the which testimonial many men's names be rehearsed, as it is thought, which were not consenting to it. By reason of the which fact many persons be discouraged from the disclosing of such enormities as they know. And for as much as the said Gardener and Shether be commonly noted to be accusers of men (which indeed did nothing but upon my lord of Canterbury's commandment), many fear greatly to speak, although they have like commandment given from like authority.

It would be a comfort to find, even in these secret records, anything to show that such suspicions were unjust. For whether we think heresy a deadly thing or not, impartiality in any investigation is of the utmost importance. But, unhappily, there is very little appearance even of this great virtue in the proceedings. For, while men of the one school were generally shielded from their accusers, their accusers themselves were sharply dealt with. It is true enough that the latter were brought to their knees, and some small admissions were wrung from one or two of them. But is it conceivable that they were fairly treated when such things passed between Cranmer and his clergy as these secret records reveal to us? "You and your company do hold me short," said the Archbishop to Canon Gardiner once in reply to a complaint: "I will hold you as short."[1] He had deeply resented Canon Gardiner's interference

Cranmer's peevishness.

[1] *L. P.*, xviii. ii. pp. 322, 375.

between him and Serles that Trinity Sunday about
idolum and *imago*, and he had told Shether at
Croydon that he would be even with Gardiner, "and
that shortly."[1]   Elsewhere he had likewise used
similar language.   After Palm Sunday he saw Prebendary St. Leger at Faversham, and asked him
if he had been at home that day.   St. Leger replied
that he had been at his benefice.   The Archbishop
then declared to him " the procession done that day
at Christchurch," and then said to him :   " Ye be
there knit in a band amongst you, which I will break."
He then added, " Ah, Mr. St. Leger, I had in you and
Mr. Parkhurst a good judgment, and especially in
you, but ye will not leave your old *mumpsimus*."[2]
Parkhurst gently replied: "I trust we use no *mumpsi-
muses* but those that be consonant to the laws of God
and our Prince," and he hoped Cranmer would be
good to them.[3]

It looks as if Cranmer was really frightened
when he resorted to threats against canons and
preachers of his own cathedral, for nothing apparently but for doing their duty.[4]   It was exactly the
time when, to all appearance, he himself was getting
into trouble ; and though, perhaps, he had great hopes
of the King's support, the date when the King gave
him personal assurance of it on taking him into his
barge must have been somewhat later.   His general
relations with the King, however, were such as to
inspire confidence ; for in most matters he could be
tolerably pliant, and the King could not easily have
found elsewhere a real divine so heartily devoted to
the all-important principle of Royal Supremacy.

Once the examination was set on foot the result

[1] *L. P.*, XVIII. ii. pp. 321-2, 349 (§ 14), 367.
[2] St. Leger writes it "mumpsimundes," which is a curious corruption.
The expression arose out of an old story of an illiterate clerk who had been
accustomed to misread the word "sumpsimus" as "mumpsimus," and
declared he would not give up his old *mumpsimus* for any new *sumpsimus*
that they might talk of.
[3] *L. P.*, XVIII. ii. pp. 349, 372, 378.   [4] See *L. P.*, *u.s.* p. 372.

His
opponents
are cowed.

was not doubtful. Dr. Willoughby had evaded responsibility from the first, and answered inquiries fully about others. Shether wrote a manly letter expressing regret if he had offended, but pleading that he had been desired by Sir John Baker, a leading member of Council, once Attorney-General, " to mark the chiefest fautors of new opinions." [1] Canon Gardiner expressed great penitence for not having borne to his archbishop so good a heart " as a true child ought to bear," and laid the blame on Dr. Willoughby for bringing his bills to Canterbury.[2] Prebendary Milles wrote from prison, suffering from cold and illness, acknowledging his unkindness in subscribing to certain articles, though it was done unadvisedly at the instigation of another.[3] All had tripped somehow or other, though not one of these seems to have been chargeable with more than indiscretion at the utmost. But there was one real mischief-maker in Dr. London, who in his zeal for hunting heretics had apparently stated more than he could justify, and was brought to condign punishment accordingly, as we shall see presently.

Of course people did not know the precise moment that the tide had turned, or that it was going to turn at all. But we can tell the time pretty well now, as the great martyrologist has preserved to us about this, as about other things, a vast amount of gossiping detail which we have only to read without his bias as simple matter of fact, and we shall not fail to understand what it all means, even better than he himself did. I therefore make no apology for a rather long extract, in which I have only inserted in brackets some slight rectifications and comments, mainly for the sake of chronological precision, and sometimes to bring the narrative back into the times of Henry VIII., getting rid of erroneous titles which belong to an

---

[1] *L. P., u.s.* p. 353. [2] *L. P., u.s.* pp. 338, 343.
[3] *L. P., u.s.* pp. 373, 378.

after date.   After describing the burnings at Windsor, Foxe goes on to tell us :—

Ye have heard before of one Robert Bennet,[1] how he was at the first apprehended with the other four persons aforesaid, and committed to the Bishop of London's prison; and about the time he should have gone to Windsor, he fell sick of the pestilence, by means whereof he remained still in prison.

This Bennet and Simons[2] (ye shall understand) were the greatest familiars and company keepers that were in all Windsor, and never lightly swerved the one from the other, saving in matters of religion, wherein they could never agree. For Bennet, the one lawyer, was an earnest gospeller, and Simons, the other lawyer, a cankered papist; but in all other worldly matters they cleaved together like burrs.

This Bennet had spoken certain words against their little round god [*i.e.* the consecrated host], for which he was as far in as the best, and had suffered death with the others if he had gone to Windsor when they went.   And now that the matter was all done and finished, it was determined by the Bishop of Salisbury [Dr. Capon], that Robert Ockam, on the Monday after the men were burned, should go to the Bishop of Winchester [Gardiner], with the whole process done at the sessions the Thursday before.   [This Thursday must have been 26th July, two days before the men were burned.]

Then Simons, at Bennet's wife's request, procured the Bishop of Salisbury's favorable letter to the Bishop of Winchester for Bennet's deliverance [on what plea he should have been delivered if the others were justly burned does not appear]; which letter Bennet's wife (forasmuch as her own man was not at home, who should have gone with the letter) desired Robert Ockam to deliver to the Bishop, and to bring her word again; who said he would.   So forth went Ockam toward the Bishop of Winchester with his budget full of writings, to declare and open all things unto him that were done at Windsor sessions.   But all their wicked intents, as God would have it, were soon cut off and their doings disclosed.   For one of the Queen's men named Fulk, who had lain at Windsor all the time of the business, and had got knowledge what a number were privily indicted, and of Ockam's going to the Bishop of Winchester, gat to the Court before   Ockam,   and   told   Sir   Thomas   Cardine   [Thomas

---

[1] See p. 384, *ante*.   [2] William Simons. See p. 385, *ante*.

VOL. II   2 D

Cawarden of Bletchingley, who, like Sir Philip Hoby, was knighted the next year at Boulogne] and others of the Privy Chamber how all the matter stood. Whereupon Ockam was laid for, and had by the back as soon as he came to the Court, and so kept from the Bishop.[1]

We interrupt the narrative here merely to note that already, within a week after the burnings at Windsor, the accused and the prosecutors seem almost to have changed places. Sharp execution had been done on the Windsor heretics; and Robert Ockam, the Clerk of the Peace before whom they had been indicted,[2] was hurrying to Bishop Gardiner to lay before him the whole procedure, when he was stopped on coming to the court, and not allowed to see the Bishop. To proceed:—

On the next morrow, very early, Bennet's wife sent her man to the Court after Ockam, to see how he sped with her husband's letter. And when he came there he found Sir Thomas Cardine walking with Ockam up and down the green before the Court gate; whereat he greatly marvelled, to see Ockam with him so early, mistrusting the matter. Whereupon he kept himself out of sight till they had broken off their communication.

And as soon as he saw Master Cardine gone (leaving Ockam behind), he went to Ockam and asked him if he had delivered his master's letter to the Bishop. "No," said Ockam, "the King removeth this day to Guildford, and I must go thither and will deliver it there." [The King had been at Woking from the 23rd to the 30th July, and was at Guildford on the 31st.[3] So this would seem to have been either on the 30th or 31st July.] "Marry," quoth he, "and I will go with you to see what answer you shall have, and to carry word to my mistress." And so they rode to Guildford together; when Bennet's man, being better acquainted in the town than Ockam was, got a lodging for them both in a kinsman's house of his.

That done he asked Ockam if he would go and deliver his mistress's letter to the Bishop. "Nay," said Ockam, "you

---

[1] Foxe, v. 494. [2] See p. 487; in Foxe, *u.s.*
[3] See *L. P.*, XVIII. i. 972; ii. 107 (1, 3-8, 13, 17, 23, 24, etc.).

shall go and deliver it yourself"; and took him the letter. And as they were going in the street together, and coming by the Earl of Bedford's lodging, then lord Privy Seal [Lord Russell, who was "then lord Privy Seal," but was not Earl of Bedford till the following reign], Ockam was pulled in by the sleeve, and no more seen of Bennet's man till he saw him in the Marshalsea. Then went Bennet's man to the Bishop's lodging and delivered his letter; and when the Bishop had read the contents thereof, he called for the man that brought it. "Come, Sirrah," quoth he, "you can tell me more by mouth than the letter specifieth"; and had him into a little garden. "Now," quoth the Bishop, "what say you to me?" "Forsooth, my lord," quoth he, "I have nothing to say unto your lordship; for I did not bring the letter to the town." "No!" quoth the Bishop, "where is he that brought it?" "Forsooth, my lord," quoth he, "I left him busy at his lodging." "Then he will come," quoth the Bishop; "bid him be with me betimes in the morning." "I will," quoth he, "do your lordship's commandment"; and so he departed home to his lodging. And when his kinsfolks saw him come in, "Alas, cousin," quoth they, "we are all undone!" "Why so," quoth he, "what is the matter?" "Oh," said they, "there hath been, since you went, Master Paget, the King's Secretary, with Sir Thomas Cardine of the Privy Chamber, and searched all our house for the one that should come to the town with Ockam; therefore make shift for yourself as soon as you can." "Is that all the matter?" quoth he; "then content yourselves, for I will never flee one foot, hap what hap will." As they were thus reasoning together, in came the aforesaid searchers again; and when Master Cardine saw Bennet's man, he knew him very well, and said, "Was it thou that came to the town with Ockam?" "Yea, sir," quoth he. "Now, who the devil," quoth Master Cardine, "brought thee in company with that false knave?" Then he told them his business, and the cause of his coming; which being known they were satisfied, and so departed. The next day had Bennet's man a discharge for his master (procured by certain of the Privy Chamber), and so went home.

Now was Ockam all this while at my lord Privy Seal's, where he was kept secret till certain of the Privy Council had perused all his writings; among which they found certain of the Privy Chamber indicted, with other the King's officers, with their wives; that is to say, Sir Thomas Cardine, Sir

A number of prosecutions stopped.

Philip Hoby, with both their ladies, Master Edmund Harman, Master Thomas Weldon, with Snowball and his wife. All these they had indicted by the force of the Six Articles as aiders helpers and maintainers of Anthony Peerson. And besides them they had indicted for heresy, some for one thing and some for another, a great number more of the King's true and faithful subjects; whereof the King's Majesty being certified, his Grace, of his special goodness, without the suit of any man, gave to the aforesaid gentlemen of his privy chamber, and other his servants, with their wives, his gracious pardon. And as God would have the matter further known unto his Majesty, as he rode one day a-hunting in Guildford Park, and saw the Sheriff with Sir Humphrey Foster sitting on their horsebacks together, he called them unto him, and asked of them how his laws were executed at Windsor. Then they, beseeching his Grace of pardon, told him plainly that in all their lives they never sat on matter under his Grace's authority that went so much against their consciences as the death of these men did; and up and told his Grace so pitiful a tale of the casting away of these poor men, that the King, turning his horse's head to depart from them, said "Alas, poor innocents!" [1]

"Alas, poor innocents!" So much pity His Majesty could afford them. Their offence had been merely this, that they had flagrantly violated a severe law passed, with the general approbation, only four years before, to protect from insult the Sacrament as it was then venerated by honest men, and some of the ordinances of the Church. The King had himself taken a marked interest in the enactment of that law, which he had manifestly urged; but the respect for things sacred, alike by King and Court, was perfectly hollow, and when there was no particular object in putting on extra virtue, the law was treated with contempt by men of the most exalted station. Bishop Gardiner was a man of the old school, somewhat more of a lawyer, indeed, than of a divine in Church matters; but he had been trying hard to believe that the old faith could be effectually protected under that

[1] Foxe, v. 494-6.

supremacy to which he and others were forced to bow, and he was now almost the only bishop left who was in earnest about the maintenance of that faith.   To him, accordingly, the sad spectacle at Windsor had its better aspect.   The Court, he supposed, was going to be purged of heresy.   The King himself had become alive to the danger of encouraging profanity and allowing things sacred to be treated with gross contempt, and Gardiner had been led to believe that informations would be followed up.   Unfortunately, his chief instrument overdid the matter. Dr. London was caught tripping, and the final result is disclosed in two more short paragraphs :—

After this the King withdrew his favour from the Bishop of Winchester, and being more and more informed of the conspiracy of Dr. London and Simons, he commanded certain of his Council to search out the ground thereof.   Whereupon Dr. London and Simons were apprehended and brought before the Council, and examined upon their oath of allegiance; and for denying their mischievous and traitorous purpose, which was manifestly proved to their faces, they were both perjured, and in fine adjudged, as perjured persons, to wear papers in Windsor; and Ockam to stand upon the pillory in the town of Newbury where he was born.

The judgment of all these three was, to ride about Windsor, Reading and Newbury, with papers on their heads, and their faces turned to the horse-tails, and so to stand upon the pillory in every of these towns, for false accusation of the aforenamed martyrs, and for perjury.[1]

There is no appearance that the accusations against " the aforenamed martyrs " were really false.   Foxe's own statements show clearly that they were transgressors of an existing law.   But there is evidence in the secret inquiry that Dr. London (though we know not what even he might have said in his defence before a fair tribunal) did some things for which he had apparently no good warrant at all, and aggravated

---

[1] Foxe, v. 496.

the case against persons to be impeached by statements which he wrongly imputed to some of the informants.[1] How he was led on to this is a matter of speculation. "The conspiracy," certainly, was a very bold one if the King was quite innocent of all that was going on, and only "withdrew his favour from the Bishop of Winchester" when more fully informed of it. But the discovery, it seems, was due to Ockam's arrest and the examination of his papers by the Council, who found several of their own members and their wives among those indicted as aiders and maintainers of Anthony Peerson. Among these were Philip Hoby, who had already been committed to the Fleet in March for this very offence,[2] and Thomas Cawarden (or Cardine, as he is called above), with the wives of both of these gentlemen. Yet Hoby had been released from the Fleet four days after his committal;[3] and Cawarden, as we have seen, maintained his place at Court, and was in no fear of Ockam, "that false knave" as he called him, who was arrested at that very time, and was having his papers searched with a result that Cawarden, no doubt, fully anticipated.

Hoby and Cawarden, however, had been indicted, along with a number of others who, it may be presumed, took the fact very comfortably; for they were all courtiers and knew well enough what was going to be the issue. They remained under indictment till the end of August, when, on the 31st, the King despatched from Ampthill a privy seal as a warrant for their pardon, and it was accordingly passed under the Great Seal by the Lord Chancellor at Walden on the 5th September. The persons named in the

---

[1] *L. P.*, xviii. ii. pp. 320, 326, 332. There is rather a significant interrogatory at p. 298 : " Whether you said that if every man was so handled as Dr. London was, there would be many papers worn ; and to what intent you said so ? "

[2] See p. 376, *ante*.

[3] *L. P.*, xviii. i. No. 314 ; Dasent's *Acts of the Privy Council*, i. 101.

document are Philip Hoby of Wraysbury, Bucks, and Lady (or Dame) Elizabeth Compton his wife; Thomas Welden of Bray, Berks; Thomas Carden or Caverden of Bletchingly, Surrey, and Elizabeth his wife; Edmund Harman of Langley, Bucks,[1] and Agnes his wife; Thomas Starnolde (Sternhold), gentleman of the King's Chamber; William Snowball, yeoman-cook for the King's Mouth, of New Windsor, and Margaret his wife; and John Westcote of New Windsor, yeoman.[2] The tide had certainly turned when the accused were pardoned, though impenitent, and the Clerk of the Peace who brought their indictments to Court was locked up in jail!

[margin note: Indictment of courtiers quashed.]

The state of matters during the course of the year is remarkably illustrated by a letter of Cranmer's secretary, Ralph Morice, written from Canterbury on the 2nd November to two influential men, Dr. Buttes (Sir William Buttes, as he afterwards became) and Anthony (afterwards Sir Anthony) Denny, the former of whom was the King's physician, the latter keeper of Westminster Palace, in behalf of a clergyman of the new school, Richard Turner, whom Morice himself, having the farm of Chartham[3] parsonage, had placed as "curate" there. As he was a stranger in the country (he was a Staffordshire man),[4] Morice writes that he had expected his teaching would have gained the greater credit. "But," he adds, "where malice once taketh fire against truth, no policy, I see, is able to quench it." Turner had been most assiduous on Sundays and holidays inveighing against the Bishop of Rome, and had made "innumerable people" change their opinions, so that his church, large as it was,

---

[1] The document gives Bray in Bucks and Langley in Berks by an accidental transposition.

[2] *L. P.*, XVIII. ii. 241 (6).

[3] "Chartham" might perhaps be taken to be a misprint in Foxe for "Chatham," as "Chatham" is mentioned in the latter part of the letter two or three times, and apparently the same place is meant. But Chatham does not fit the story.

[4] See *Dict. of Nat. Biography.*

could not always hold the audiences that came to
hear him. But "the Popish priests" went to the
justices with presents of capons and chickens and so
forth, and pressed their complaints even on "such
as were no small fools, as Sir John Baker, Sir
Christopher Hales, Sir Thomas Moyle, knights, with
other justices." The prebendaries of Canterbury
were made privy to the matter and lent their aid,
and the Archbishop with other commissioners was
appointed to sit at Lambeth on the examination of
these seditious preachers. But before Turner went
up to his examination, Morice obtained a favour of
Sir Thomas Moyle, who promised that he would in
Easter week hear Turner preach "a rehearsal sermon"
in his parish church at Westwell of all that he had
preached at Chartham. Turner accordingly preached,
both forenoon and afternoon, on the Wednesday in
Easter week, and gave Moyle so much satisfaction
that he dismissed him home to his cure with favourable words.

By this Morice hoped that he had made Turner's
appearance at Lambeth unnecessary, thinking that
Moyle would have answered for him; but such
a clamour was raised that he was sent for. He
defended himself, however, so well that he was sent
home merely "with a good exhortation," without
any recantation being enjoined. The "pope-catholic
clergy of Kent," however, raised a stir through Bishop
Gardiner, pretending that he went home in pompous
fashion and was met by 500 persons with banqueting
dishes to welcome him, whereas he came home above
eighteen miles on foot through the woods, avoiding
Rochester, and reached Chartham quite exhausted.
The King, misled by the malicious tale, sent for
Cranmer, wishing him to cause Turner to be whipped
out of the country. Cranmer accordingly sent for him
again. But Morice wrote vehemently to the Archbishop that it was mere malice, and the Archbishop

pacified the King's wrath.   Home came Turner once more without blot.

But the papists devised a new matter, that he had preached erroneous doctrines elsewhere before he came into Kent, had "translated the mass into English and said or ministered the same," and had preached against purgatory, praying for the dead, and so forth.   He was then convented before the whole Council by Bishop Gardiner, brought up to London bound (as Morice understood), and committed to prison for a time.   But now, while the Archbishop was in Kent investigating the conspiracy of the prebendaries and justices against himself, Turner was sent down to him to recant the doctrines that he preached elsewhere than in Kent.   Morice hoped that the King would not allow learned, honest men to be thus overcrowed by papists, who could not abide to hear his supremacy advanced.   Why should he recant to the overthrow of 500 men's consciences and more ?   All good subjects would lament it ; and yet it would not in effect be Turner but Henry VIII. himself who would " most odiously recant." [1]

Such was the general tenor of the letter ; but there was a sentence in this latter part which is worth quotation by itself for its special significance :—

What think your worships they would attempt, if his Majesty were at God's mercy (as God forefend that any of us should see that day, without better reformation), that can thus dally with his Highness, blinding his eyes with mists whilst he liveth and reigneth amongst us in most prosperity ? [2]

There were many who must have thought or feared that the exclusion of papal jurisdiction from England could hardly last after Henry VIII.'s day,

---

[1] Foxe, viii. 31-4.   The date "A.D. 1544" placed at the head of this letter by Foxe is erroneous.   See abstract of it in *L. P.*, XVIII. ii., at the end of Preface.   [2] *Ib.*, *u.s.* 34.

and that a hitherto unprecedented condition in Church and State must naturally pass away with him who was the author of it. Nay, Henry VIII. himself, as we may have occasion to notice further on, had his own misgivings as to the stability after his death of the peculiar edifice he had reared on the basis of Royal Supremacy.

Meanwhile one thing seemed to be settled. The Six Articles must not be allowed to be too much of a nuisance—especially to great people about the Court. Parliament met again, after prorogation, in January 1544, and one of its enactments (35 Hen. VIII. c. 5) was a modification of that famous Statute, requiring that none should be arraigned under the Act for offences more than a year old, nor even then except on presentments found by the oaths of twelve men before the commissioners. These provisions, even in themselves, must have gone far to make a number of prosecutions futile. Only two witnesses had been requisite, hitherto, for any prosecution. Now, a jury of twelve men must agree in an information; and, apart from the time limit, it would, no doubt, be difficult to get twelve jurors to impeach men of any considerable standing. But Parliament was theoretically as dead-set against heresy as ever; for it presently passed an Act of General Pardon (cap. 18)—this was the Act under which Cranmer's accusers found mercy — for offences committed before 14th January, the first day of the session, with express exception of all cases of heresy or high treason for which men had been imprisoned between that date and the 17th March.

The result of this exception was that three names more were added to the list of martyrs for Rome on the 7th March, and it was only owing to a recantation that the number was not four. One of the victims had been active in drawing up the indictment against Cranmer and his friends so lately. This

The Act of the Six Articles modified.

was Germain Gardiner, Bishop Gardiner's nephew,[1] whose account of Frith the reader will remember; and it seems as if his late ardour against heresy had been requited by an indictment for treason. The oath of Supremacy could always be pressed home if any had evaded it, or qualified it, as we have reason to know that many did; and this is the record of an indictment in which he was included :—

Sessions held at Westminster on Friday, 15 Feb. 35 Hen. VIII.

The Jury say upon their oath that John Heywood, late of London, gentleman, John Ireland late of Eltham in the county of Kent, clerk, John Larke, late of Chelsea in the county of Middlesex, clerk, and Germain Gardiner, late of Southwark in the county of Surrey, gentleman, not weighing the duties of their allegiance, nor keeping God Almighty before their eyes, but seduced by the instigation of-the Devil, falsely, maliciously, and traitorously, like false and wicked traitors against the most Serene and Christian Prince, our Lord Henry VIII., by the grace of God King of England France and Ireland, Defender of the Faith, and upon Earth Supreme Head of the English and Irish Church, choosing, wishing, desiring and cunningly machinating, inventing, practising and attempting—that is, each of them by himself falsely, maliciously, etc., choosing, wishing, etc., and attempting—together with many other false traitors unknown in confederacy with them—to deprive our said King, Henry VIII., of his royal dignity, title and state, that is to say, of his dignity, title and name of " Supreme Head of the English and Irish Church," which has been united and annexed to his Imperial Crown by the laws and proclamations of this his realm of England: [This they have attempted] falsely and traitorously by words, writings and deeds, which are notorious and public. Moreover, that falsely and traitorously, and contrary to the duty of their allegiance, [they attempted] to depose and deprive the same lord our King of his Majesty, state, power and royal dignity, and also, falsely and traitorously, with all their force and power, [endeavoured] to subvert, frustrate, and annihilate the good and praiseworthy statutes and ordinances of our aforesaid lord the King, made

[1] *L. P.*, XVIII. ii. pp. 325-6.

and provided for the estate, properties, government, and rule
of this his said realm of England.[1]

We naturally wonder what act it could have been,
on the part of any of the impeached,

> That roars so loud and thunders in the index.

Larke had been presented to a city living forty
years before, which he had retained, we are told,
till a few years before his death; though he had
meanwhile held the rectory of Woodford in Essex,
which he resigned for that of Chelsea, having been
nominated to the latter by Sir Thomas More in 1530.

Executions of opponents of Royal Supremacy. So that he was certainly a man in advanced years,
and he with Germain Gardiner and John Ireland (of
whom nothing more seems to be known than is above
stated) suffered at Tyburn on the 7th March. But
Heywood, after being placed upon the hurdle, recanted and received a pardon.[2]

Both Convocation and Parliament bestirred themselves at this time about that revision of the Canon
law, which had been always required since the submission of the clergy, but never could be carried into
effect. Two futile Acts of Parliament on the subject had already been passed, and now another was
added to the number.[3] But as regards heresy, after
that secret inquiry by Cranmer and those three
executions for treason, it is perhaps not wonderful
that we hear little or nothing said about it during
the year 1544. Henry's orthodoxy—not in theory,
it is true, but in practice—was governed not a little
by the political barometer. When there was any
serious danger of the Emperor and the Protestants

---

[1] Dom Bede Camm's *Lives of the English Martyrs*, i. 543-7. Note
correction of date in vol. ii. 655.

[2] *Ib.* Mention of Heywood occurs in Cranmer's secret inquiry. *L. P.*,
xviii. ii. pp. 297-8.

[3] Statutes 25 Hen. VIII. c. 19, 27 Hen. VIII. c. 15, 35 Hen. VIII.
c. 16. Cp. Wilkins, iii. 868: "Et mox" (after 1st Feb.) "habito inter eos
secreto tractatu de Regia Majestate adeunda pro legibus ecclesiasticis
condendis," etc.

coming to an agreement he was not unwilling that powerful friends should intercede for him with the Pope himself; and so long as the Emperor stood by him he was quite ready to listen to complaints against innovations not expressly authorised by himself. Early in 1543 he had pledged himself to aid the Emperor openly in his war against France, which he did in the following summer. So in 1544 he was for some time occupied preparing to invade France in person and then in the actual invasion. He besieged Boulogne, which surrendered to him in September. But his faithful ally the Emperor, who, just like himself, had his own special interests in view, at that very time arranged a separate peace with France. So now at the end of 1544 he had to continue the war alone ; and, what was still more serious, as the two continental rivals were reconciled, the Pope had good hopes at last of holding a General Council, which he summoned to meet at Trent in March following to put down heresy. Moreover, it was perfectly obvious that Francis had the Pope's sympathy, and might have the Pope's pecuniary aid, in the war he was carrying on against a schismatic and excommunicated King.

In view of these things, it may well have occurred, even to Henry's subjects, that Archbishop Cranmer's encouragement of heretical preachers was a positive danger to the kingdom. At all events, this was certainly the time when the second of the three attacks on Cranmer was made, as mentioned by Ralph Morice, the assailant in this case being Sir John Gostwick, "knight of Bedfordshire," who "accused him openly in a Parliament for his preaching and reading at Sandwich and at Canterbury." This statement requires some little correction, of which presently ; but let us consider the result in Morice's own words :— *Why Cranmer was complained of.*

As touching Mr. Gostwick's accusation, the King, perceiving that the same came of mere malice, for that he was a stranger in Kent, and had not heard my lord neither preach nor read there; knowing thereby that he was set on and made an instrument to serve other men's purposes, his Highness marvellously stormed at the matter, calling openly Gostwick *varlet*, and said he had plied a villainous part so to abuse in open parliament the Primate of the realm; specially being in favor with his prince as he was. "What will 'they (quod the King) do with him if I were gone?" Whereupon the King sent word unto Mr. Gostwick after this sort: "Tell that varlet Gostwick that if he do not acknowledge his fault unto my lord of Canterbury, and so reconcile himself towards him that he may become his good lord, I will sure both make him a poor Gostwick, and otherwise punish him to the example of others." Now Gostwick, hearing of this heinous threat from the King's Majesty, came with all possible speed unto Lambeth, and there submitted himself, in such sorrowful case that my lord, out of hand, not only forgave all the offence, but also went directly unto the King for the obtaining of the King's favor again, which he obtained very hardly upon condition that the King might hear no more of his meddling that way.[1]

Now it is certain that Sir John Gostwick was elected knight of the shire for Bedfordshire on the 22nd December 1544 for the Parliament summoned to meet on the 30th January 1545.[2] But it is almost equally certain that there was no session of Parliament held at that date.[3] Yet Gostwick seems never to have sat in any previous Parliament—at least, he was not returned for that of 1541-1542, and we need not go further back,—nor could he have sat in any later session, for he died on the 15th April following.[4] So there is evidently some great inaccuracy here. But the story, no doubt, is essentially true, and the truth, perhaps, is not difficult to surmise. Sir John Gostwick was elected for Bedfordshire, and feeling strongly, as many others did, the serious dangers that beset the country, traceable, in great part, to

[1] Nichols's *Narratives of the Reformation*, pp. 251, 253-4.
[2] See *Names of Members Returned to Parliament*, Part I. App. xxx.
[3] See *L. P.*, xx. ii. Pref. p. lvi.
[4] Inquis. p.m. 37 Hen. VIII. No. 1.

the heretical tendencies of the Archbishop of Canterbury, had said he was quite prepared to complain of
them in open Parliament. Then he met with the
severe rebuff recorded, and how far it accelerated his
death may be a matter of speculation. Perhaps the
fear lest others, like Gostwick, might speak their
minds a little too freely had something to do with the
action of the King in countermanding this Parliament. One thing, at least, is quite clear, that in this
case, as in the case of the prebendaries, Cranmer
was protected from disgrace by the King's personal
interference. And so he was also in the third case,
which is still better known, having been dramatised
by Shakespeare.

The date of that third case cannot be precisely
ascertained. But before inquiring as to any probable
date, let us get as near accuracy as we can, dismiss-
ing the Shakespearian version from our minds, and
taking the whole story from the original authority,
Morice, whose words, I am afraid, it will be impossible
to abridge without injury to the narrative :—

As to the third accusation, wherein the Council required
that the lord Cranmer might be committed unto the Tower
while he were examined, the King was very strait in grant-
ing thereof. Notwithstanding, when they told the King
that, the Archbishop being of the Privy Council, none man
must object matter against him unless he were first committed unto indurance, which being done, men would be bold
to tell the truth and say their consciences; upon this persuasion of theirs the King granted unto them that they
should call him the next day before them, and, as they saw
cause, so to commit him to the Tower. At night, about 11 of
the clock, the same night before the day he should appear
before the Council, the King sent Mr. Denny to my lord at
Lambeth, willing him incontinently to come unto Westminster to speak with him. My lord, being abed, rose straightway and went to the King into his gallery at Whitehall at
Westminster; and there the King declared unto him what
he had done in giving liberty unto the Council to commit
him to prison, for that they bare him in hand [*i.e.* tried to

*Proposal to
commit
Cranmer to
the Tower.*

persuade him] that he and his learned men had sown such doctrine in the realm that all men almost were infected with heresy, and that no man durst bring in matter against him, being at liberty and one of the Council, unless he were committed to prison. "And therefore I have granted to their request," quod the King; "but whether I have done well or no what say you, my lord?"

My lord answered, and most humbly thanked the King that it would please his Highness to give him that warning aforehand, saying that he was very well content to be committed to the Tower for the trial of his doctrine, so that he might be indifferently heard, as he doubted not but that his Majesty would see him so to be used. "Oh Lord God!" quod the King, "what fond simplicity have you, so to permit yourself to be imprisoned that every enemy of yours may take vantage against you. Do not you think that if they have you once in prison, three or four false knaves will be soon procured to witness against you and to condemn you, which else now, being at your liberty, dare not once open their lips or appear before your face? No, not so, my Lord," quod the King, "I have better regard unto you than to permit your enemies so to overthrow you. And therefore I will that you to-morrow come to the Council, who no doubt will send for you, and when they break this matter unto you, require them that, being one of them, you may have thus much favor as they would have themselves, that is, to have your accusers brought before you, and if they stand with you, withouten regard of your allegations and will in no condition condescend unto your requests, but will needs commit you to the Tower, then appeal you from them to our person, and give to them this ring" (which he delivered unto my lord Cranmer then), "by the which," said the King, "they shall well understand that I have taken your cause into my hand from them; which ring they well know that I use to none other purpose but to call matters from the Council into mine own hands to be ordered and determined." And with this good advice my lord Cranmer, after most humble thanks, departed from the King's Majesty.

The next morning, according to the King's monition and my lord Cranmer's expectation, the Council sent for him by 8 of the clock in the morning; and when he came to the Council Chamber door he was not permitted to enter into the Council Chamber, but stood without the door amongst serving-

men and lacqueys above three-quarters of an hour, many
Councillors and other men now and then going in and out.
The matter seemed strange, as I then thought, and therefore
I went to Dr. Buttes and told him the manner of the thing,
who by and by came and kept my lord company. And yet
or that he was called into the Council, Dr. Buttes went to
the King and told him that he had seen a strange sight.
"What is that?" quod the King. "Marry," said he, "my
lord of Canterbury is become a lacquey or a serving-man; *Cranmer*
for well I wot he hath stood amongst them this hour almost *forced to*
at the Council Chamber door, so that I was ashamed to keep *wait upon*
him company there any longer." "What," quod the King, *the Council;*
"standeth he without the Council Chamber door? Have
they served me so?" said the King. "It is well enough,"
said he, "I shall talk with them by and by."

Anon my lord Cranmer was called in to the Council, and
it was declared unto him that a great complaint was made of
him both to the King and to them, that he and other by his
permission had infected the whole realm with heresy, and
therefore it was the King's pleasure that they should commit
him to the Tower, and there for his trial to be examined.
My lord Cranmer required, as is before declared, with many
other both reasons and persuasions, that he might have his
accusers come there before him before they used any such
extremity against him. In fine, there was no entreaty could
serve but that he must needs depart to the Tower. "I am
sorry, my Lords," quod my lord Cranmer, "that you drive me
unto this exigent, to appeal from you to the King's Majesty,
who by this token hath resumed this matter into his own
hands, and dischargeth you thereof"; and so delivered the
King's ring unto them. By and by the Lord Russell sware a
great oath and said "Did not I tell you, my Lords, what
would come of this matter? I knew right well that the
King would never permit my lord of Canterbury to have
such a blemish as to be imprisoned, unless it were for high
treason." And as the manner was, when they had once
received that ring, they left off their matter and went all
unto the King's person both with his token and the cause.

When they came unto his Highness, the King said unto *for which*
them, "Ah! my lords, I had thought that I had had a *the Council*
discreet and wise Council, but now I perceive that I am *are re-*
deceived. How have ye handled here my lord of Canter- *buked.*
bury? What make ye of him a slave, shutting him out of
the Council Chamber amongst serving-men? Would ye be

so handled yourselves?" And after such taunting words said "I would you should well understand that I account my lord of Canterbury as faithful a man towards me as ever was prelate in this realm, and one to whom I am many ways beholden by the faith I owe unto God"—and so laid his hand upon his breast—"and therefore whoso loveth me," said he, "will regard him thereafter." And with these words all, and especially my lord of Norfolk, answered and said, "We meant no manner hurt unto my lord of Canterbury in that we requested to have him in durance; that we only did because he might after his trial be set at liberty to his more glory." "Well," said the King, "I pray you, use not my friends so. I perceive now well enough how the world goeth among you. There remaineth malice among you one to another. Let it be avoided out of hand, I would advise you." And so the King departed, and the lords shook hands every man with my lord Cranmer, against whom nevermore after no man durst spurn during the King Henry's life.[1]

Question as to the date of the incident.

If we attempt to find even a probable date for this occurrence, we should naturally presume that it must be placed some time after the Gostwick incident, the second attack on Cranmer related by Morice, as that incident itself occurred after the first-mentioned attack, viz. that of the prebendaries and justices. Next, we must note that the King was at Westminster and the Archbishop in residence at Lambeth. Dr. Buttes (Sir William Buttes), the King's physician, is very naturally attendant upon the King. Then, Lord Russell and the Duke of Norfolk are specially mentioned as taking part in the proceedings of the Council. Bishop Gardiner, whom Shakespeare brings in, has nothing to do with this matter, so far as we can learn from the original story.

But if the occurrence was later than the Gostwick incident, it must have been during the year 1545; and we have pretty accurate information of the King's movements during the whole of that year.[2] After spending the Christmas season at Greenwich,

[1] Nichols's *Narratives of the Reformation*, pp. 254-8.
[2] Collected from the dates of letters and privy seals for grants.

he was at Westminster from the 20th February to the 23rd May, when he removed to Greenwich again —if, indeed, he had not removed thither earlier, for Westminster is sometimes a mere formal date, and his Council had been sitting at Greenwich from the 17th April. But from the 23rd May we do not find either King or Council at Westminster till November, when both of them were there for a month continuously, that is to say, from the 22nd November to the 23rd December, except six days that the King spent at Hackney, from the 14th to the 19th December. In July the Court had moved to Portsmouth, where the *Mary Rose* foundered before the King's eyes, and the return journey was very gradual; while from August to the beginning of November the King rested chiefly at Woking, Oatlands, and Windsor. These considerations would lead us, almost inevitably, to November or December as the date of the Privy Council incident, and there are really points which seem to favour such a date. But, unfortunately, there is one thing which looks totally against it. Sir William Buttes died on the 22nd November [1]—and apparently after a long illness —the very day that the Council began to sit again at Westminster.

If, then, the name of "Dr. Buttes" in reference to it be not an error due to a slip of memory on Morice's part, this incident would seem, if not earlier than the Gostwick incident, to be at least not later than the middle of May. And so far as regards Cranmer himself, we have no positive evidence to the contrary. Moreover, there is a gap in the Privy Council records from July 1543 to the 10th May 1545, which will allow us to exercise our imaginations as to who were present in Council before the latter date; but the Duke of Norfolk did not attend the meetings recorded after it, which were pretty frequent, until the 6th

[1] See *Dict. of Nat. Biog.*

June at Greenwich, and Councils at Greenwich hardly seem to satisfy the requirements of the story. They may do so, indeed, as the Council, after being shown the ring by Cranmer, may have taken boat to White-hall to see the King. And it is not quite impossible that the incident may have occurred in the early spring, before the 10th May ; indeed, there seems no other time for it but the spring, unless we imagine— as we should not naturally do—that Morice was in error when he wrote, " I went to Dr. Buttes . . . and Dr. Buttes went to the King and told him."

Yet this is not altogether incredible. Sir William Buttes, indeed, was a very great friend of Morice and of Cranmer also. But so was another influential courtier ; and when anything urgent had to be done in behalf of the Archbishop, his faithful Morice, we find, was wont to write a letter to the Court, to be opened either by Buttes or by Sir Anthony Denny, which-ever of the two was first to be got at. Two such letters have already come under the reader's notice, and surely it is not inconceivable that, writing some years afterwards, Morice forgot that it was not Buttes but Denny to whom he resorted on this occasion, and who came to the Council door and saw the Archbishop ignominiously waiting outside. This, indeed, is a mere hypothesis ; but if we substitute the name of Denny for Buttes in the narrative, not only all the other conditions are satisfied, but some rather interesting light is thrown upon further matters, which we now proceed to consider.

On the 22nd November the Archbishop of Canter-bury was present in Council, and again on the 27th and 29th, but not on the intervening days, and never again till the 21st February following, when the Council sat at Greenwich. Yet Parliament had begun on the 23rd November, and he was present at every one of the frequent sittings of the House of Lords (which on some days had both forenoon and afternoon sittings during that session) from the opening day of the session till Christmas Eve, when it was dissolved. So, of course, he was resident at Lambeth all this time, as he must have been when the incident occurred; and the Council was sitting at Westminster—another of the conditions required to fit the story. Further, the Duke of Norfolk and Lord Russell (who was Lord Privy Seal) both continually attended the Council at this period till the 22nd December, after which Norfolk probably went home for Christmas, for he was absent on the 23rd.[1]

So Cranmer apparently felt that at this time his presence in the Council was a little embarrassing, and if it was in spring that he was so nearly committed to the Tower, even in November matters apparently were not at all comfortable. But suppose now that it was not in spring, but that squabbles having taken place in the Council on the 22nd November, it was *Probably November 1545.* that day—just before the opening of Parliament— that the King authorised his committal to the Tower. If so, he was fortified by the King's interference to meet the Council again on the 27th and the 29th, after which he was quite content to be absent from uncongenial society. Any way, there were reasons at this time which might well have made old Councillors of the King feel that it was no longer safe to play fast and loose with orthodoxy. For the Council of Trent was about to become a fact; indeed, it was formally opened on the 13th December. The Protestants of Germany were alarmed at the prospect. The authority of Rome was going to be upheld everywhere, and in France this year the poor Vaudois were persecuted wholesale with unheard-of cruelty, under a decree which had been left unexecuted for years. Henry himself had constantly maintained that, though papal authority was gone, the faith

---

[1] See Dasent's *Acts of Privy Council* and the *Journals of the House of Lords.*

remained in his kingdom inviolate, and his best friends thought that if this plea failed him, both he and the realm stood in imminent danger. He was not unwilling, for his part, that they should show themselves zealous to put down heresy, and I have no doubt he gave the Council leave, if they found it necessary, to send the Archbishop to the Tower. But he had always his own secret policy, which he did not communicate to any one else.

No doubt there was a general feeling that the tide was rising in favour of orthodoxy again ; and the very first Bill brought into Parliament that session Bill for the was one " for the abolition of heresies and of certain abolition of books infected with false opinions." But this Bill had heresies. a rather peculiar history. For on its first reading, on Friday the 27th November, it was committed for examination to the Archbishop of Canterbury, Lord Paulet (*i.e.* William Paulet, Lord St. John, Great Master of the Household since Suffolk's death), the Earls of Hertford and Shrewsbury, the Bishops of Ely, Salisbury, and Worcester (Goodrich, Capon, and Heath), and Lords Delawar, Morley, and Ferrers—a committee not at all likely to be too severe upon the New Learning, since Cranmer presided over it and the only bishop of the old school was Heath of Worcester. Of course, it was natural in any case (if there was to be a committee at all at this stage) that the Primate should preside, and Cranmer had not been deposed ; but the very composition of this committee suggests rather strongly that the object for which it was appointed was to enervate a Bill which was, no doubt, intended to propitiate a clamour against growing heresies. It was read a second time, however, next day, and after a long discussion (*post longam examinationem* are the words in the brief record), it was committed again to the same Lords as before. It was read a third time on Wednesday the 2nd December, and a fourth time on Thursday the 3rd, when it was committed to the King's Solicitor to be engrossed on parchment. Then it was read a fifth time, and passed without opposition, on Saturday the 5th; and on Monday the 7th it was one of four Bills sent down to the Commons.[1] But of what became of it there we have no record. It was evidently never passed. Moreover, we know pretty well that the King could obtain in most matters from the House of Commons almost any result he pleased.

Now, if there be anything in our surmise that it was just before the meeting of Parliament that the Privy Council had so nearly succeeded, as they thought, in committing Cranmer to the Tower, when he was again released from an inconvenient situation simply by the King's personal intervention, a not unnatural sequel to the incident may be found in the long discussion of this Heresy Bill in the Lords, and the fate which overtook it in the Commons after finally passing the Upper House, a climax being reached in the manner in which the session was wound up on Christmas Eve. And here there is nothing speculative, for the facts are very well known, and any doubts that it might once have been possible to entertain as to their having been coloured are now entirely removed by fuller documentary evidence. On the 24th December the King himself came to the House of Lords. The Speaker was summoned from the other Chamber, and, according to custom, addressed him in "an eloquent oration"; to which, instead of leaving the Lord Chancellor, as usual, to make answer, Henry himself thought best to reply with his own mouth, giving as his express reason for doing so, that his Chancellor could not set forth so plainly his "mind and meaning" and "the secrets of his heart." With this preamble he thanked the Speaker for what he had said, and hoped still to merit his praise. He

[1] *Journals of the Lords*, i. 269-72.

thanked him further for a subsidy voted by the Commons, and for an Act they had passed, placing all chantries, colleges, and hospitals in the kingdom at his disposal, which he hoped to order for the profit of the commonwealth. He would certainly not allow the ministries of the Church to decay, learning to be diminished, or the poor to be unrelieved. But he felt it necessary to utter some words of warning as follows :—

Henry VIII.'s speech on charity.

"Yet although I with you, and you with me, be in this perfect love and concord, this friendly amity cannot continue except both you, my lords temporal, and you, my lords spiritual, and you my loving subjects, study and take pain to amend one thing which surely is amiss and far out of order, to the which I most heartily require you, which is that charity and concord is not amongst you, but discord and dissension beareth the rule in every place. St. Paul esaieth to the Corinthians in the 13th chapter, 'Charity is gentle, charity is not envious, charity is not proud,' and so forth in the said chapter. Behold, then, what love and charity is amongst you when the one calleth the other heretic and anabaptist, and he calleth him again papist, hypocrite, and Pharisee. Be these tokens of charity amongst you? Are these the signs of fraternal love between you? No, no, I assure you that this lack of charity amongst yourselves will be the hindrance and assuaging of the fervent love between us, as I said before, except this wound be salved and clearly made whole. I must needs judge the fault and occasion of this discord to be partly by negligence of you, the fathers and preachers of the spiritualty. For if I know a man which liveth in adultery, I must judge him a lecherous and a carnal person. If I see a man boast and brag himself, I cannot but deem him a proud man. I see and hear daily that you of the Clergy preach one against another, teach one contrary to

another, inveigh one against another, without charity
or discretion.   Some be too stiff in their old mumpsimus,[1] others be too busy and curious in their new
sumpsimus.   Thus all men almost be in variety and
discord, and few or none preach truly and sincerely
the word of God, according as they ought to do.
Shall I now judge you charitable persons doing this?
No, no.   I cannot so do.   Alas, how can the poor
souls live in concord when you preachers sow amongst
them, in your sermons, debate and discord?   Of you
they look for light, and you bring them to darkness.
Amend these crimes, I exhort you, and set forth
God's word, both by true preaching and good example
giving, or else I, whom God hath appointed his Vicar
and high minister here, will see these divisions extinct,
and these enormities corrected according to my very
duty, or else I am an unprofitable servant and untrue
officer."[2]

We may well stand amazed at such a sermon
preached to his bishops and clergy by one who
claimed to be God's vicar in his own kingdom.   The
vicar of Christ recognised by other nations was at
Rome; but Henry had displaced him so far as his
dominions went, and had taken upon himself the full
responsibilities of the position.   And he went on to
rebuke the laity also for railing at bishops, and
speaking slanderously of priests, against good order
and Christian fraternity.   If they knew any bishop
or preacher to teach erroneous or perverse doctrine,
they ought to inform some of his Council, or himself,
whose business it was to reform such matters, and
not be judges themselves, for in such high causes
they might easily err.   "And although you be
permitted to read Holy Scripture," he added, "and
to have the Word of God in your mother tongue,
you must understand that it is licensed you so to
do only to inform your own consciences and to instruct

[1] See p. 399, ante.   [2] Hall's *Chronicle*, pp. 865-6.

your children and family, and not to dispute and make Scripture a railing and a taunting stock against priests and preachers, as many light persons do. I am very sorry to know and hear how unreverently that most precious jewel, the Word of God, is disputed, rhymed, sung, and jangled in every alehouse and tavern, contrary to the true meaning and doctrine of the same. And yet I am even as much sorry that the readers of the same follow it in doing so faintly and coldly ; for of this I am sure that charity was never so faint amongst you, and virtuous and godly living was never less used, nor God himself, amongst Christians, was never less reverenced, honoured, or served."[1]

Moral effects of Henry's "Reformation." From these words, proceeding as they do from the very highest authority, it does not seem that the Reformation of religion, initiated by Henry VIII., had hitherto produced very satisfactory fruit. Virtuous and godly living was never less used. But as to wrangling and jangling, though these are not agreeable signs in matters sacred, abuses call for protests, and it is not royal authority that will always still storms of that sort. This freedom to read the Scripture in English was already beginning to produce very remarkable results ; and a particularly interesting example of its effects had come to light in the previous month of March.

Story of Anne Askew. A young woman, by name Anne Askew, who came of a good family in Lincolnshire, had been married to one Thomas Kyme ; but the marriage, arranged by her father against her will, in the harsh feudal style, proved naturally unhappy. She was a devotee of the New School, and used to read the open Bible in Lincoln Cathedral. Her husband turned her out of doors, and she was in London early in this year, 1545, seeking a divorce, as it seems.[2] Here she was

---

[1] Hall, *u.s.*

[2] This must have been the time referred to in Louthe's narrative where he says that she "was lodged before her imprisonment at an house over

apprehended as a Sacramentary, and examined at Her first
Sadlers' Hall by commissioners under the Six Articles. examina-
Christopher Dare, one of the quest, asked her if she tion.
really believed the Sacrament of the Altar to be the
very Body of Christ.   She declined to reply unless
he would answer first a question proposed by herself:
"Wherefore was St. Stephen stoned?"   And her
examiner confessed that he could not tell.   Then
she was questioned about having said that "God was
not in temples made with hands"; which she justified
by pointing out the passages in Acts vii. and xvii.
She confessed to saying that she had rather read
five lines in the Bible than hear five masses, for the
one edified her and the other did not.   But she
denied other points imputed to her.   She was then
examined by a priest about the Sacrament, but
declined to answer as she "perceived him to be a
papist."   But when he asked her whether she did
not think that private masses helped souls departed,
she said it was great idolatry to believe more in
them than in the death of Christ.   She was then
taken before the Lord Mayor and questioned further.[1]
The Bishop's chancellor reproved her "for uttering
the Scriptures," saying St. Paul forbade women to
speak of the Word of God.   But she understood St.
Paul better, and said he only forbade women "to
speak in the congregation by the way of preaching."
In the end the Lord Mayor committed her to the
Counter, refusing to take sureties for her; and she
was not allowed to see any of her friends for eleven

against the Temple."   What Louthe says of her while she was lodged
opposite the Temple is interesting: "And one great papist of Wykeham
College, then called Wadloe, a cursitor of the Chancery, hot in his religion
and thinking not well of her life, got himself lodged hard by her at the next
house, for what purpose I need not open to the wise reader.   But the conclusion was that, where he came to speak evil of her, he gave her the praise
to Mr. Lionel Throckmorton for the devoutest and godliest woman that ever
he knew; 'for,' said he, 'at midnight she beginneth to pray, and ceaseth not
in many hours after, when I and others apply our sleep or do worse.'"—
Nichols's *Narratives of the Reformation*, p. 40.

[1] Her own account of her examination by the Lord Mayor is amplified by
Louthe, and it really seems to have been rather painfully ridiculous.

days. But Bishop Bonner sent a priest to examine her, to whom she expressed her willingness to be shriven, if it were by Dr. Crome, Sir Guilliam, or Huntington, that she might receive the Sacrament at Easter. At last, on the 23rd March (if the date she herself gives be not an error), she received a visit in prison from her cousin Brittayne, who afterwards went to the Mayor to induce him to bail her. The Mayor still refused without the consent of a spiritual officer. So her cousin applied to the Bishop's chancellor, and at length to the Bishop himself, who sent for her and, expressing much regret for her trouble, showed an evident desire to help her. After a lengthened interview he drew up a confession which he hoped she would agree to sign, and said she might thank others for the favour shown to her, as she came of a worshipful stock. Instead of simply signing it, however, she wrote underneath a declaration that she believed all things contained in the faith of the Catholic Church. The Bishop was greatly provoked, and turned away suddenly into his chamber; but after she had been remanded once more to prison, her friends succeeded, by and by, in getting him to accept bail for her.[1]

This is the substance of her own account of these, her first examinations—an account which was evidently quite honest, and, though it was written a year later, and was only published by Bale in Germany the year after her death, requires very little correction. But one point which seems to be erroneous is the date, 23rd March, given as the day her cousin Brittayne visited her in prison, as it is on record that Bishop Bonner extracted from her on the 20th[2]

_____

[1] Foxe, v. 538-43. Cp. Bale's account of her in the original publication; also Louthe's Reminiscences in Nichols's *Narratives of the Reformation.* Louthe speaks of this examination as if it had led to her execution, which it did not.

[2] If the 23rd were the true date of Brittayne's visit to her, then, according to the narrative, the Bishop could not have seen her and asked her signature to the confession before the 26th; and it is quite impossible that "the

a real recantation or explanatory confession to save her from condemnation on the points of which she was accused. This confession cannot be such a fabrication as Foxe insinuates; moreover, she herself gives the substance of it from memory. It was witnessed not only by Bishop Bonner himself, but by another bishop and eleven other persons named, others still being present in the room, and Bonner had read it over to her before asking her to sign it. He had first asked her if she agreed with it, and her reply was, "I believe so much thereof as the Holy Scripture doth agree unto; wherefore I desire you that ye will add that thereunto." He replied that she should not teach him what he should write. He then "went forth into his great chamber and read the same bill before the audience," who, according to her own saying, "inveigled and willed her" to set her hand to it. But when he placed it before her to sign, instead of a simple signature she wrote, "I, Anne Askew, do believe all manner things contained in the faith of the Catholic Church."

Such, at least, is her own story, by which it would appear that she was perversely bent on thwarting the Bishop's benevolent intentions towards herself. " So much as Scripture doth agree to "—" the faith of the Catholic Church!" The point for her was to clear herself of the imputation that she had brought herself under the Six Articles by questioning Transubstantiation, and to confess the change no less real whether the host was consecrated by a good or a bad priest, or whether it was then received or reserved in the pix. The form of words drawn up for her by Bonner was expressly intended to meet these points, and it seemed that she had really accepted the document, when she

twentieth " in the record can be an error for " the twenty-sixth " ; for it is added "in the year . . . after the computation of the Church of England 1544." That means the historic year 1545, for, by the computation of the Church of England, the number of the year of our Lord changed only on the 25th March.

wilfully added something of her own. The Bishop
" flung into his chamber in a great fury." But her
cousin, Brittayne, followed his lordship thither to
intercede for her. Dr. Weston also tried to explain
away her indiscretion, and though she was remanded
to prison, sureties were finally put in for her at St.
Paul's. But apparently she did at last actually sign
the confession required of her, though she may have
regretted it afterwards, for the document of the 20th
in Bonner's register gives the subscription : " By me
Anne Askew, otherwise called Anne Kime." Anyway,
she was liberated on bail ; and when, on the 13th
June following, she was arraigned with others at the
Guildhall, she was fully acquitted, as no witnesses
appeared against her.[1]

She is
arraigned
and
acquitted.

So for the remainder of that year she was at
liberty. But new and more serious trouble awaited
her in 1546. Not her only, however, for circumstances had been gradually leading the King to
consider how far he could safely go on with the old
game of playing fast and loose with heresy, and
preaching charity on both sides. The Council of
Trent had not only been formally opened on the 13th
December 1545, but had held its second session on the
7th January 1546. Even in expectation of its opening
the King had sought security against possible results,
first by luring to his aid the German Protestants, who
had a common interest with himself in endeavouring
to prevent it, and at the same time, as he strongly suspected that their efforts at prevention would fail, by
binding the Emperor in a closer alliance with himself
than ever, so that he could not be practically affected
by the fiery darts of excommunication. These two
different and opposite lines of policy he was carefully
pursuing at once, quite ready at any time to drop that
which proved to be the weaker as soon as it had served
its purpose. And though it is not my object in this

[1] Foxe, *u.s.*; Wriothesley's *Chronicle*, i. 155 ; Holinshed, iii. 968.

work to illuminate the crooked ways of diplomacy, a
word or two seem necessary at this particular juncture,
that the reader may take in the situation.

The treaty of Crépy, in 1544, between Charles V.
and Francis I. had given the Pope very great satisfaction, as making the Council appear at last a
possibility. He had seriously admonished the Emperor just before for being in league with a schismatic
king, and for endeavouring to settle matters of religion
in Germany by a Diet without reference to the Holy
See. And though Charles was not driven to peace
by mere theoretical considerations, he was beginning Religious
to feel that he had gone quite far enough in his and
efforts to conciliate the Protestants, and that he diplomacy
could not but pay some deference to the claims of before the
that spiritual authority which was acknowledged in Trent.
all his dominions except by some German princes.
Still, he could not easily afford to break off amity
with England, especially as there might yet be a
doubt of the durability of the new peace with France,
which, in point of fact, lost one great security for its
permanence by the death of the Duke of Orleans in
September 1545. Henry, on the other hand, had
been in communication with the Protestants, whom
he now encouraged to offer their services to mediate
between England and France, as these were the only
powers to which they could look for help if the Pope
and Emperor were united against them. Conferences accordingly took place at Calais between
Lutheran ambassadors and Henry's astute, confidential secretary, Paget, who understood his master's
mind very thoroughly; while Bishop Gardiner was in
the Low Countries, sent thither avowedly in the first
instance to meet the French Admiral, d'Annebaut,
with a view to a general pacification. Gardiner did
not like the notion of transactions going on with the
Protestants, but what was done at Calais was carefully concealed from him. The Protestants at Calais

were no less jealous of what Gardiner was doing at the Imperial Court, especially as he stayed long after d'Annebaut had left; but they, too, were mystified with ingenious excuses. By the end of the year it appeared that Protestant mediation was a failure, and the Lutheran envoys withdrew, while Gardiner, following out his instructions, drew the bonds of alliance closer between his master and the Emperor, the result being the treaty of Utrecht, which was signed in January 1546.

Now, of course, while the King was pursuing this double game abroad, he wished rival schools of theology to keep the peace at home, and it was quite natural that he should read them a lecture upon Christian charity. But as he became more and more hopeful of the Emperor's friendship, to protect him from the Pope and strengthen his hands against France, he knew that he must cast off his Lutheran friends, and show himself more plainly opposed to heresy within his own kingdom. Francis I. was fully committed to the Pope's cause, and the Pope was aiding him against England. Charles V., though he found it his interest now, as formerly, to maintain Henry's friendship, and give even stronger securities for it, was loyal to the Roman Pontiff, and could only keep friends with England if England showed some respect for the faith and practice of Christendom. And the King soon found it necessary to put some restraint upon Cranmer's reforming zeal in Church matters, which he had hitherto, as we have seen, supported against all kinds of criticism. For just at this time, while Gardiner was still at Utrecht, the Primate drew up a letter for the King's signature, to be addressed to himself, to give effect to a little reform on which he had apparently got the Bishops of Worcester and Chichester (Nicholas Heath and George Day) to agree with him. Though so many superstitions had been abolished, some still remained which the progressive party desired to get rid of. Bells were rung all night on the vigil of All Hallows (31st October); images in the churches were covered during the whole of Lent; the veil over the cross was lifted on Palm Sunday and the congregation knelt to it. Cranmer, Heath, and Day had been appointed "to peruse certain books of service," and as all other vigils had been for years abolished, except that the name of vigils still remained, they recommended that this should be abolished also. The King was further desired to forbid images to be covered henceforth; no veil was to be placed upon the cross, and no kneeling to it was to be allowed on Palm Sunday or any other time. But the letter drawn up for the King went even further than the suggestions of the Primate's coadjutors. "Creeping to the Cross" on Good Friday was a greater abuse than any, for it was accompanied by words and directions for the cross to be "adored," and this, by what the bishops themselves had set forth in the book of *Necessary Doctrine*, was against the Second Commandment. So this, too, must cease; and Cranmer was to intimate the abrogation of these abuses to all his suffragans.[1]

This reform was to have been set on foot along with the long suspended project for a revision of ecclesiastical laws.[2] Cranmer himself felt it very advisable that some good reasons should be set forth for the alterations, lest people should think that they involved dishonour to the Cross itself, or even to Christ. Perhaps, in conference with the King—for they had certainly been discussing the matter together at Hampton Court beforehand[3]—he may also have found out that there were prudential reasons for keeping reform within some limits; for, according to Foxe, the King had already been per-

---

[1] Cranmer's *Letters* (Parker Soc.), p. 414.
[2] *Ib.*, p. 415.
[3] This appears quite clearly both from what Foxe says, and from Cranmer's own letter to the King.

suaded to go still further than the Archbishop's letters suggest,—that it is, say, "to pull down the roods in every church," whereas the Archbishop's letters clearly contemplate that they should remain there. Nevertheless, even the more moderate programme had to be set aside. Cranmer sent the letters for the King's signature to the care of Sir Anthony Denny, but the King made answer :—

Further reforms stopped for politic reasons.

I am now otherwise resolved, for you shall send my lord of Canterbury word that, since I spake with him about these matters, I have received letters from my lord of Winchester, now being on the other side of the sea, about the conclusion of a league between us, the Emperor, and the French King, and he writeth plainly unto us that the league will not prosper nor go forward if we make any other innovation, change or alteration, either in religion or ceremonies, than heretofore hath been already commenced and done. Wherefore my lord of Canterbury must take patience herein, and forbear until we may espy a more apt and convenient time for that purpose.[1]

"Superstition" and "idolatry" were accordingly allowed to remain till a more convenient season could be found for getting rid of them. A progressive policy in Church matters might have been useful if it had come to a league with the German Protestants against the Pope and the Emperor; but, as a matter of fact, Protestant mediation with France had failed, and Gardiner had succeeded in securing the King's position otherwise, by a treaty with the Emperor. England now must be very orthodox that the Emperor might not be reproached as the ally of a heretical sovereign, and that France, exhausted by the war, might ultimately feel she also could make peace with Henry without apparent sacrifice of Catholic principles.

Pious souls and popular preachers, however, could not fully appreciate the reasons for moderation; and

[1] Foxe, v. 362.

in Lent Dr. Crome, preaching at the Mercers' Chapel, founded an argument against Purgatory upon what had just been done in Parliament. For an Act had been passed in the last session for the dissolution of chantries ; these foundations for the benefit of departed souls were to go the way of the monasteries. And it was not only natural, but surely quite justifiable, in Dr. Crome to tell his audience "that if trentals and chantry masses could avail the souls in Purgatory, then did the Parliament not well in giving away monasteries, colleges and chantries which served principally to that purpose. But if the Parliament did well (as no man could deny) in dissolving them, and bestowing the same upon the King, then it is a plain case that such chantries and private masses do nothing to confer (*sic*) and relieve them in Purgatory."[1]

That was very inconvenient reasoning, for it could not possibly be answered. Yet it was not even new, except that the Act was new by which he justified it, for he had said the same thing years before. In 1539 he had been in serious danger from the Act of the Six Articles, but went to the King and entreated him not to allow the law to be too severely administered ; and it was said to have been on his entreaty that prosecutions were stopped for a time. In 1540, just before Christmas, he had preached fervently on the insufficiency of works and on other subjects, denouncing masses for the dead as unprofitable, otherwise, he said, the King had done wrong in putting down the monasteries. At this the clergy took alarm, and Dr. Wilson was urged to apply a remedy by preaching of an opposite character, which he did. Such variance between preachers, however, was not to be endured ; so the King called both of them before him in January 1541, and delivered judgment that Crome should make a recantation at

Dr. Crome's sermon at the Mercers' Chapel.

He had been ordered to recant five years before ;

[1] Foxe, v. 537.

Paul's Cross in Lent, warning him that if he were accused again, the law must take its course against him. He was ordered expressly to declare, in opposition to what he had said, that " public and private masses were a profitable sacrifice, as well for the living as the dead. And although masses and other prayers and helps profit the departed, yet the King's Majesty and the Parliament have piously and justly abolished the monasteries in this realm." No reason, however, was given for this last opinion.[1]

How he fulfilled the mandate on that occasion is further related in the letter of Richard Hilles to Bullinger, from which the above information is derived :—

and read what he was told to read.

When the Sunday came on which he was to recant he preached a godly discourse, and at the end of it told the people that he had received a written document from the King's Majesty which he was ordered to read to them. And after he had read it, he committed the congregation to God in a short prayer, and so went away.

He had not altered his own doctrine apparently, nor said that he had altered it, but simply read what he was told to read ; but all that was done to him in consequence was an order not to preach any more. However dissatisfied the clergy may have been, the King apparently was not much offended at the evasion, and probably did not care even to shut permanently the mouth of a popular preacher who might yet be useful to him. So now, five years later, Crome was bold enough to repeat the offence, hoping that the Act against chantries might serve as his justification.

His sermon at the Mercers' Chapel had been delivered on Passion Sunday, the 11th April.[2] On

---

[1] *Original Letters* (Parker Soc.), pp. 211-15.

[2] The *Grey Friars' Chronicle* (Camden Soc.), p. 50, says it was preached "in his parish church," which would be that of St. Mary Aldermary ; and further, that "he preached against the Sacrament of the Altar." If so, the case was still more serious.

the 20th he was called to account, and this time
compelled to put his signature to certain articles,
with a view to a public recantation,[1] so that there
should be no new evasion.   This recantation he
was enjoined to make at Paul's Cross on the 9th
May, the second Sunday after Easter ; but again
he complied in a way that did not give satisfaction.
Bishops Bonner and Heath, with Richard Coxe (the
Prince's tutor), the Dean of St. Paul's, and other
notable divines were present to hear him, but
reported unfavourably of his sermon next day, when
he was called before the Council.   What had he said
this time ?

A report of the sermon exists which seems to con- His sermon
tain all the important points in it.   He took for his at Paul's
text John x. 11, "I am a good Shepherd" (as it was Cross.
translated in Coverdale's Bible, though the Greek
original has distinctly the definite article),[2] and after
enlarging on the opposite qualities of the good
Shepherd and the hireling, he gave thanks to God
for having laid aside many strange voices.   "For
my sheep, saith Christ, hear my voice, and the voice
of a stranger they know not."   Then he declared the
Bishop of Rome's usurped power to be a strange
voice,—his pardons, pilgrimages, purgatory, Peter-
pence, feigned religious foundations of monasteries
and chantries, to be strange voices.   "And in this
uttering," said he, "I have found my brethren the
priests wondrously offended with me, and that for
two causes.   One was, they say, because I speak
against their living ; the other cause is for because I
have spoken of late much against the Bishop of
Rome, calling him beggar, occasioned to do so by the

---

[1] Wriothesley's *Chronicle*, i. 167.
[2] In Matthew's Bible (1537) and in Cranmer's (1540) the definite article
was rightly used here, as it had been, before then, very naturally, by
Tyndale who translated from the Greek.   Yet, strange to say, not only the
Zurich Bible of Froschover but even Luther uses the indefinite : "Ich bin
ein guter Hirte."   And Coverdale, who had only the Latin and the German
translations before him, followed the latter here in their error.

Gospel that then I was in hand with, which is the
eighteenth chapter of St. Luke. To the first thus I
answer : I, for my part, would have my brethren to
have a living, even as I would myself to have a
living ; but that they should have it after the truth,
as God's word appointed it to them. Now to the
second, saith he, thus I answered : the Bishop of
Rome begging by his primacy, pardons, purgatory,
Peter-pence, pilgrimages, feigned religion, foundation of minsters and chantries, is a bold, valiant,
sturdy beggar. Well, the beggar is now gone, said
he. Yea, the King's Majesty, with his High Court
of Parliament, have taken this beggar by the head,
and hurled him quite out of the realm like an idle
beggar. But alack, this bold beggar's staff hath this
beggar of Rome left here behind him ; which staff
beateth both the bodies and souls of men. Now,
sayeth he, the Bishop of Rome, that bold bragging
beggar, being thus cast out, laud be it to God and our
Prince, his staff would I wish to be cast out with
him. Yea, I would wish himself to have it in his
own hand, for many poor men are daily beaten with
it, and I myself have been beaten with it ; for, as I
understand, men of worship appointed thereunto of
late have preached in their sermons, have beaten me
with the staff of the beggar, and that even for saying
that the sacrifice of the mass doth not take nor put
away sin. But I put it to your judgment to judge
what would they [say] if they durst, to our Sovereign
Lord the King, considering that he indeed doth alter
their fond foundations and put them to other use,
considering the error therein. That the Bishop of
Rome hath the conditions of an angry beggar we may
prove it thus. The angry beggar threateneth, curseth
and fighteth. The Bishop of Rome threateneth first
with interdiction all such as will not obey his froward
will. Second, he curseth with excommunication all
such as aid or counsel those which regard not his

interdiction, as the chronicles of England and of other countries maketh mention. Thirdly, he fighteth by setting princes together by the ears against him which (*i.e.* the one who) regardeth not his interdiction and great curse, promising great indulgence for they (*sic*) defending of Holy Church."

All this would have been fully approved of in previous years, ever since the breach with Rome, but indulgence in such invectives was not politic now. The real offence, however, was in what followed :—

"Then turned he to the text again, desiring all men to pray to the Good Shepherd, and according to the custom prayed. The prayers done, he stood up and said these words :—' Worshipful audience, I came not hither to recant, nor God willing, I will not recant. Yet notwithstanding, divers and many have sent letters abroad informing their friends that I should recant, to the great slander of God's word, and of me, being a poor preacher of the same admitted within this realm of England. But as for me I care not ; but yet would I wish them that they would send half so many letters informing their friends that I have not recanted. Well, God forgive them ! And yet, will they nill they, I will pray for them, will them good, and wish them good,' etc. And then he showed them that in a sermon made at the Mercers' Chapel on Passion Sunday, upon the ninth chapter to the Hebrews, he declared with the text that Christ our High Shepherd, entering into the Holy Place, once for all, not with strange blood but with his own precious blood, hath found plentiful and eternal redemption. Upon the which occasion, said he, I said, and say again, that the Bishop of Rome hath wrongly applied the Sacrifice of the Mass, making it a satisfaction for sins of the quick and dead, as he hath done the blood of martyrs oftentimes. And then he showed that to call it a sacrifice he would not stick, for a sacrifice it is of thanksgiving to our only Shepherd

He refuses to recant ;

for his once offered offering, which hath made a full satisfaction of all the sins of them which believe and cleave to him by faith. Yea, it is *Eucharistia*, which is to say *sacrificium laudis*. Yea, and it is to us a commemoration of Christ's death and Passion, according to his own words, *Hoc facite in meam commemorationem, etc.*" [1]

The Council examined Crome " upon his rashness and indirect proceedings." [2] In vain did he lay his hand upon his breast and protest that he sincerely thought that he had done everything required of him. Coxe particularly related not only the substance of the discourse but the manner in which it was delivered, accusing Crome personally of having deluded him, for he had done his best to intercede with the King in his favour. Crome was also reminded how he had been warned by Dean Haynes of Exeter to beware of yielding to the " fantasies " of his brethren in London, and particularly not to use such an expression as " that he came not to recant." [3]

The Council went back to his sermon on Palm Sunday, about which they set him to answer interrogatories in a chamber by himself. They also got from him the names of a number of persons who were friendly to him ; but what to do with them was evidently a matter for serious consideration, for some of them were by no means insignificant. [4] " Forasmuch as upon Crome's answers," they wrote next day to Mr. Secretary Petre, " we see plainly that sundry persons, of divers qualities, have otherwise used them-

---

[1] Harleian MS. 425 f. 65. The document is headed (in a different hand from the text): " Certain notes of a sermon made at Paul's Cross by Dr. Crome on Sunday the 9th day of May in the year of the reign of King Henry VIII. the xxxiii." This would be the year 1541, and it is noticed in that year accordingly in *L. P.*, XVI. 814. But the 9th May was a Monday, not a Sunday, in 1541, and it is clear the year of the reign should have been " xxxviii.," not " xxxiii."

[2] Dasent, i. 414.

[3] Cp. State Papers, i. 843 ; and *Grey Friars' Chronicle*, 51.

[4] Those implicated are said to have been " as well of the Court as of the city."—Wriothesley's *Chronicle*, i. 167.

selves with the said Mr. Crome than in our opinion is Who had encouraged him?
tolerable ; we be more desirous to know the King's
Majesty's pleasure how we shall use the calling and
ordering of them, as a matter wherein we would be
loth to offend in doing too much or too little, but as
may be agreeable with the King's Majesty's pleasure ;
whereof we require you we may by you be advertised
as soon as ye can, with sending again also the depositions and examinations, which we now send unto
you." [1]

From his answer, it appeared among others that
he had been " comforted "—that is, encouraged—by
one Lascelles, whom they had already in examination,
because he had " boasted abroad that he was desirous
to be called to the Council, and he would answer to
the prick." Next day, the 11th May, a physician
named Dr. Hewick (or Huick) [2] was brought before
them, who was on bad terms with his wife, and an
information was received from Tenterden about " a
marvellous, abominable and seditious sermon " made
there on Wednesday after Easter ; on which they sent
at once to apprehend the preacher. [3]

On the 13th they wrote again to Mr. Secretary
Petre :—

This day we look for Latimer, the vicar of St. Bride's, and
some others of those that have specially comforted Crome in
his folly.

Crome, sithens the last depositions sent to his Majesty
hath confessed that Huick, upon the sight of the articles
which he should have set forth at Paul's Cross, showed himself to mislike the same, and thought they could not be
maintained with good conscience, and that he doubted not,
therefore, but the said Crome could declare them honestly ;
by the which, and such other things as Crome hath confessed, it appeareth that he and some of those folks that he

[1] State Papers, i. 843, 844 ; Dasent's *Acts of Privy Council*, i. 414.
[2] Not Robert Huick, Principal of St. Alban's Hall, Oxford, as biographers
have supposed. From his signature (Dasent's *Acts of Privy Council*, i. 433)
his Christian name was " William." [3] State Papers, i. 844.

named in his depositions, be as much to be blamed, or more, than himself.[1]

Together with this letter the Council forwarded to Petre "a lewd bill" sent them by the Lord Mayor, which had been set up on a church door in London, against one of those who had deposed against Crome. They had also received, both from the Lord Mayor and from the Chief Baron of the Exchequer, "other lewd books and writings, with knowledge of some other light persons which meddle further in these matters than their capacities be able to comprehend."[2]

The Council at this time was sitting habitually at Greenwich, while the King was at Westminster. Mr. Secretary Petre at Westminster wrote to them the same day, conveying the King's thanks for their proceedings about Crome, whom they still kept in custody, and whom he desired them to press still further by the following message :—

> The King's Majesty, considering that Crome, in this his last submission, affirmeth again the former articles, willeth that your lordships shall cause one book to be made of the articles sent hither now by my lord of Worcester, and of those which were last agreed upon to be set forth by him; and the same being joined together, his Majesty would have him put his hand to the same, to be sent to his Highness.[3]

Latimer examined. That same 13th May the Council had before them for examination good, honest Hugh Latimer, who had been living in obscurity during all the seven years since he gave up his bishopric in 1539. During the first twelvemonth he had been committed to the custody of Bishop Sampson, and when released he had been ordered to remove from London, and to forbear from preaching and from visiting either of the universities or his own old diocese of Worcester.[4] No doubt he obeyed, but where he had spent his time since then we do not know. Perhaps the order had

---

[1] State Papers, i. 846.   [2] Ib.   [3] Ib., p. 847.
[4] Original Letters (Parker Soc.), p. 215.

been afterwards relaxed in his case as in Crome's; for he was now accused of having "devised and counselled with Crome touching his last sermon, wherein he satisfied not his promise to the King's Majesty." This seems to imply that Latimer was now resident in or near London, and the fact that Crome had taken counsel with him was all the more natural because Crome's argument against purgatory from the abolition of the chantries, was one that Latimer himself had used to the King on the suppression of the smaller monasteries.[1] In reply to the Council he now said that he had indeed been often in Crome's company since he was in Lord Chancellor Wriothesley's custody, "and that he had said somewhat touching his recanting or not recanting; couching his words so " — this was the Privy Council's report next day—" as he neither confessed the matter, nor yet uttered his mind so cleanly, but somewhat stack and appeared by the way. Whereupon we ministered an oath unto him, and delivered him certain interrogatories to answer, appointing him a place for the quiet doing of the same." But after answering two or three of these, he sent to them to say that he could proceed no further till he had leave to speak with them again. As the Council were busy with the examination of Hewick and Lascelles, of Dr. John Taylor (or Cardmaker), vicar of St. Bride's, and of a Scottish friar, they deputed Bishop Tunstall and Sir John Gage, Controller of the Household, to confer with him; but he insisted that he must address himself to the whole Council, and they put aside other matters to hear him. We may continue in the words of their report :—

At his coming he told us he was light to swear to answer the interrogatories before he had considered them, and that

---

[1] "The founding of monasteries argueth Purgatory to be. So the putting of them down argueth it not to be."—Latimer's *Remains*, p. 249 (Parker Society).

charity would that some man should have put him in remembrance of it. He told us it was dangerous to answer to such interrogatories, for that he might by that mean be brought into danger; noting the proceeding therein to be more extreme than should be ministered unto him if he lived under the Turk as he liveth under the King's Majesty; for that he said it was sore to answer for another man's fact, and besides, he said he doubted whether it were his Highness's pleasure that he should be thus called and examined; desiring therefore to speak with his Majesty himself before he made further answer; for he was once, he said, deceived that way when he left his bishopric, being borne in hand (*i.e.* persuaded) by the lord Cromwell that it was his Majesty's pleasure he should resign it, which his Majesty after denied, and pitied his condition. And finally he said, he thought there were some that had procured this against him for malice.

He mentioned specially Gardiner, the Bishop of Winchester, whose ill-will to him he inferred partly from some words they had in the King's presence at Westminster, and partly from what Gardiner had once written to Cromwell against the very arrogant sermon that he had preached to Convocation in 1536. Gardiner replied that he did him much wrong, showing that he had always "loved, favoured, and done for his person," and that he had no cause to complain of the fact that he was not satisfied with his doctrine. Latimer could say nothing in reply, and had to go on answering his interrogatories.[1]

The same day Dr. Hewick and his wife both appeared before the Council, and the grounds of their differences were examined; which we may pass over. They found that the wife had been unjustly accused, although shameful artifices had been used to entice her to misconduct.[2]

Some others examined also.

They next examined Lascelles, the vicar of St. Bride's, and the Scot. Lascelles, like Latimer, wished not to commit himself. He would not make answer about his conference with Crome so far as it touched

---

[1] State Papers, i. 848-9.   [2] *Ib.*, 850; Dasent, i. 417.

matter of Scripture, unless he had the King's express commandment and protection, giving as his reason that it was neither wisdom nor equity that he should kill himself. "Thus," wrote the Council, "you see his Highness must pardon before he know if Mr. Lascelles may have his will. The vicar of St. Bride's showeth himself to be of the same sort, but yet not so bold as the rest. And as to the Scot, he is more meet for Dunbar than for London ; for neither hath he any manner of wit or learning meet for a preacher, but is a very ignorant (*sic*), and hath framed his sayings after his audience, as, to be rid, he will say now what you will bid him."[1]

Next day, the 15th, a yeoman of the chamber was despatched to summon Dr. Shaxton (the late Bishop of Salisbury, who resigned his bishopric at the same time as Latimer) and one William Morres to answer about "these matters of Crome." On the 16th, orders were sent for three out of five persons, convicted under the Act of the Six Articles, to be executed at Colchester and two other places in Essex. On the 17th, Dr. Hewick and some other persons were committed to the Tower for having dissuaded Crome from fulfilling his promise "in the declaration of the articles." The priest of Tenterden, who had now been brought up, was committed to Newgate, and Crome's servant was sent to prison for giving evasive answers. The examination of the Tenterden priest, however, only began next day, when he was again committed for further examination about his assertion "that in the hallowing of holy bread and holy water there was heresy."[2]

On the 23rd one Powley, who had been with Dr. Crome just before his sermon, and had been ordered not to depart from London without licence, was discharged by the Council "upon submission and a good lesson," as his master, the Earl of Arundel, wished

[1] State Papers, i. 850.   [2] Dasent, i. 417-21.

to send him into Sussex on business. On the 24th two yeomen of the chamber were sent to apprehend Sir Robert Wisdom, the priest of whom we heard not long ago,[1] and to summon "one Kyme and his wife" (of whom we have heard also) to appear before the Council within ten days after receipt of the message.[2] Wisdom, as we have seen, was Dr. Crome's curate, and Kyme was the husband of Anne Askew.

So here was another unhappy couple whose differences were to be examined by the Council, and both appeared before them on the 19th June, as shown by the Privy Council record. In the interval the Council had been less occupied with cases of heresy; they had released Dr. Hewick on bail on the 29th May, and also one Robert Crome —a near relation, doubtless, of the preacher—on the 1st June.[3] But Anne Askew's case required special attention. She and Kyme being both before the Council she was asked why she would not acknowledge him as her husband, and said my Lord Chancellor knew her mind on that matter. They told her it was the King's pleasure that she should explain it to them; but she declined, saying, however, that if the King were willing to give her a hearing she would explain it to him. They said it was not meet that the King should be troubled about her, and she replied that Solomon, the wisest of kings, had deigned to hear two poor women. Kyme, on this, was allowed to return to the country till he should be again sent for; and a conversation followed between Anne and the Council, "wherein," as they placed on record, "she showed herself to be of a naughty opinion." So, judging her to be quite unreasonable, they sent her to Newgate, "to remain there to answer to the law." They also sent thither one White, "who attempted to make an erroneous book," and who, when they argued with him, "showed

Anne Askew before the Council.

[1] See pp. 379, 380.   [2] Dasent, 423-4.   [3] *Ib.*, i. 433, 440.

himself of a wrong opinion concerning the Blessed Sacrament." [1]

Anne Askew's own account of her examination by the Council is a pretty full one. It was printed by Bale next year—at Marburg, the edition is dated. But probably the date is fictitious, and the examination itself, as there published, was declared by Bishop Gardiner to be "utterly misreported." [2] We have, however, unfortunately, no other report to go by, and must give a brief account of it as it stands in Bale's publication. After refusing to answer about "Master Kyme," as she called him, she was asked by the Lord Chancellor what she thought about the Sacrament. She replied : "I believe that so oft as I, in a Christian congregation, do receive the bread in remembrance of Christ's death, and with thanksgiving, according to His holy institution, I receive therewith the fruits also of His most glorious Passion." Bishop Gardiner desired her to make a direct answer, and she said, "I will not sing a new song of the Lord in a strange land." The Bishop replied that she spoke parables, and she told him it was best for him; "for if I show the open truth," she said, "ye will not accept it." This was scarcely a modest answer to a bishop; but Gardiner knew the ways of the new school, and said that she was a parrot. She replied that she was ready to suffer all things at his hands, not only rebukes, but all that might follow, and that gladly. She then received "divers rebukes" from the Council, but was always ready with an answer and carried on the debate with them for about five hours ; after which the clerk of the Council took her to my lady Garnish.[3] It would thus seem that the Council's

Her own account of her examination.

[1] Dasent, i. 462. White's Christian name was Nicholas, according to Wriothesley (*Chron.* i. 167); but according to the *Grey Friars' Chronicle* (p. 51), he was Christopher White of the Inner Temple.
[2] Foxe, vi. 31.
[3] *Ib.*, v. 544. Although this account of her examination, written by herself, was published by Bale (interlarded with comments) in 1548, it is more convenient to refer to it in Foxe.

order to send her to Newgate was not acted on that very day.

She was, indeed, brought before them again on the day following (though no sitting of the 20th is recorded in the Acts of the Council), and asked again what she said about the Sacrament. She replied that she had said already all she could say. After a while they bade her stand aside. Then, on consulting together, they deputed Lord Lisle (Dudley, who became Duke of Northumberland in the following reign), the Earl of Essex (William Parr, the Queen's brother), and Bishop Gardiner to go and speak to her ; and they all urged her strongly to "confess the Sacrament to be flesh, blood, and bone." She told Lord Parr and Lord Lisle "that it was a great shame for them to counsel contrary to their knowledge." She evidently considered that they believed no more than she did. Bishop Gardiner tried another way with her, and said he wished to speak with her familiarly. "So did Judas," she replied, "when he unfriendly betrayed Christ." The Bishop, taking no notice of the affront, desired to speak with her alone. But this she refused, and when he asked why, she answered, "that in the mouth of two or three witnesses every matter should stand, after Christ's and Paul's doctrine." [1]

The Lord Chancellor, who seems to have come in and joined the conference, again began to examine her about the Sacrament, and she asked him in return, "how long he would halt on both sides?" He inquired where she found that, and she told him, in the Scripture. The Lord Chancellor took his departure. Gardiner then very seriously warned her that she was in danger of the stake. "I answered," she writes, "that I had searched all the Scriptures, yet could I never find that either Christ or His apostles put any creature to death. 'Well, well,' said I, 'God will laugh your threatenings to scorn.'" She was then

[1] Foxe, v. 544.

told to stand aside. Then two notable divines, Dr. Cox and Dr. Robinson, came to her, but their exhortations were equally ineffectual. They had drawn up "a bill of the Sacrament," but she would not sign it. On Sunday, which must have been the 20th, she was very ill, expecting to die, and desired to speak with Latimer; but, of course, this was not allowed, as Latimer himself was under a cloud. And it was that same day, when she was in great pain, that she was sent to Newgate.[1]

All well-meant efforts had failed to shake her constancy. Friends might have hoped otherwise; for the days had long gone by when abjuration could not save the victim of the Six Articles; and the Act, as we have seen, had few terrors now, even for those who despised the doctrine that it was meant to protect. But it was no longer a time when the King could allow it to become completely a dead letter, and that the King himself felt some anxiety about this case there is good reason to believe. The Council had left her "to answer to the law," and her case was now to come on. She was arraigned at the Guildhall[2] along with Shaxton, the late Bishop of Salisbury, the Mr. White above referred to, and John Hadlam of Essex, tailor, for maintaining heretical views on the Sacrament; and as they all confessed their heresies, no jury was required to convict them. So the awful sentence was pronounced by the "quest." She wrote a con-

She and others are sentenced at the Guildhall.

[1] Foxe, *u.s.* 544-5.
[2] The date given in Wriothesley's *Chronicle* is the 18th June; but this is impossible as she was only before the Council on the 19th, and Hadlam was only examined by them on the 22nd and 23rd, and committed to Newgate on the latter day. Wriothesley's *Chronicle*, moreover, mentions the trial at the Guildhall, which he dates the 18th, *after* Dr. Crome's recantation sermon at Paul's Cross, which he dates the 27th. The 18th, however, is certainly an error for the 28th, as will be seen by a contemporary letter printed by Ellis (*Original Letters*, 2nd series, ii. 172-8), dated London, 2nd July 1546, which first speaks of Dr. Crome's recantation sermon as delivered "on Sunday last" (*i.e.* the 27th June), and then of the trial of Shaxton, Anne Askew, and the others "on Monday following." See Appendix to this Chapter.

fession of her faith in Newgate before her condemnation; and after it she wrote a more brief one, which she enclosed in a letter to the Lord Chancellor, desiring him to submit it to the King. In the former she expressly declares the bread to be only a sign; in the latter she declares that she shall die innocent, for she abhorred all heresies. "And as concerning the Supper of the Lord," she adds, "I believe so much as Christ hath said therein, which He confirmed with His most blessed blood. I believe also so much as He willed me to follow and believe, and so much as the Catholic Church of Him doth teach; for I will not forsake the commandment of His holy lips."[1]

The prospect of a fiery death was bad enough, but worse trials awaited her. Shaxton and White, who were condemned along with her, were induced next day "by the good exhortation and doctrine of the bishops of London and Worcester" (Bonner and Heath) "and divers other doctors" to renounce their heresy and agree to the established view of the Sacrament. There seems no doubt, moreover, that their conversion was sincere; at least, Shaxton, we know, remained steadfast from this time to the end of his life in the hitherto received doctrine of the Church, and it is not unreasonable to suppose that both were convinced by men of superior learning. Great efforts were also made to persuade Anne, which are recorded by herself as follows. "On Tuesday," she says (this must be the 29th June, the day after her sentence) :—

On Tuesday I was sent from Newgate to the Sign of the Crown, where Master Rich[2] and the Bishop of London with all their power and flattering words went about to persuade

---

[1] Foxe, *u.s.* 545-6.
[2] Sir Richard Rich, Chancellor of the Augmentations, once Solicitor-General, whom Sir Thomas More accused to his face of perjury. See Vol. i. pp. 493-4.

me from God; but I did not esteem their glosing pretences. Then came there to me Nicholas Shaxton and counselled me to recant as he had done. I said to him that it had been good for him never to have been born; with many other like words. Then Master Rich sent me to the Tower, where I remained till three o'clock.[1]

It may throw some light on what follows if we here take account of traditions recorded about sixty years after Anne Askew's death. On the authority of her own nephew we learn that great search had been made for her before she was brought before the Council; and this seems to be borne out by the fact that by that time nearly four weeks had elapsed since a message had been sent out, requiring her appearance there within ten days after its receipt. So, no doubt, she concealed herself for some time. Moreover, we are told by her nephew that her discovery was effected by a letter of her own being intercepted.[2] Then another authority, the Jesuit Parsons, writing a few years before her nephew, says that the King was informed " that contrary to her oaths and protestations she did in secret seek to corrupt divers people, but especially women, with whom she had conversed; and that she had found means to enter with the principal of the land, namely with Queen Katharine Parr herself, and with his nieces, the daughters of the Duke of Suffolk, and others."[3] It would thus appear that she had been sending furtive epistles from her hiding-place into the Court itself, where she had some reason to believe that her scriptural teaching would not be altogether discouraged, at least by the Queen. This was truly alarming at a time when orthodoxy was of so much political importance! Now let us resume Anne's own narrative where we left off:—

---

[1] Foxe, *u.s.* 547.
[2] *A Historie contayning the warres*, etc., by Edward Ascu (1607), p. 308.
[3] *A Treatise of Three Conversions of England*, ii. 493.

She will not implicate any other persons.

Then came Master Rich and one of the Council,[1] charging me upon my obedience to show unto them if I knew any man or woman of my sect. My answer was that I knew none. Then they asked me of my lady of Suffolk, my lady of Sussex, my lady of Hertford, my lady Denny, and my lady Fitzwilliam. To whom I answered, if I should pronounce anything against them, that I were not able to prove it. Then said they unto me, that the King was informed that I could name if I would, a great number of my sect. I answered that the King was as well deceived in that behalf as dissembled with in other matters.

The reader will not require much information about the ladies mentioned in this extract; but he may, perhaps, desire to be told about the first, "my lady of Suffolk," that she was the widow of Henry VIII.'s favourite, Charles Brandon, Duke of Suffolk. She was the daughter and heiress of the last Lord Willoughby of Eresby—a lively and quick-witted lady enough, to judge by her letters. To continue :—

Then commanded they me to show how I was maintained in the Counter, and who willed me to stick to my opinion. I said that there was no creature that therein did strengthen me ; and as for the help that I had in the Counter, it was by means of my maid. For as she went abroad in the streets she made moan to the prentices, and they, by her, did send me money ; but who they were I never knew.

Then they said that there were divers gentlewomen that gave me money ; but I knew not their names. Then they said that there were divers ladies that had sent me money. I answered that there was a man in a blue coat who delivered me ten shillings, and said that my lady of Hertford sent it me ; and another in a violet coat gave me eight shillings, and said my lady Denny sent it me. Whether it were true or no I cannot tell, for I am not sure who sent it me, but as the maid did say. Then they said, there were of the Council that did maintain me ; and I said no.

And now comes the most dreadful part of the story :—

---

[1] A marginal note in some early editions of Foxe (though not in the first edition of 1563) says that "this councillor was Sir John Baker."

Then they did put me on the rack because I confessed no She is
ladies or gentlewomen to be of my opinion, and thereon they racked.
kept me a long time; and because I lay still and did not cry,
my lord Chancellor and Master Rich took pains to rack me
with their own hands, till I was nigh dead.

Then the lieutenant caused me to be loosed from the rack.
Incontinently I swooned, and then they recovered me again.
After that I sat two long hours reasoning with my lord
Chancellor upon the bare floor; where he, with many
flattering words, persuaded me to leave my opinion. But my
Lord God (I thank his everlasting goodness) gave me grace
to persevere, and will do, I hope, to the very end.

Then was I brought to a house, and laid in a bed, with as
weary and painful bones as ever had patient Job; I thank
my God therefor. Then my lord Chancellor sent me word,
if I would leave my opinion, I should want nothing; if I
would not, I should forthwith to Newgate, and so be burned.
I sent him again word that I would rather die than break my
faith.[1]

I cannot suppose that Lord Chancellor Wriothesley,
or even such a degraded creature as Sir Richard Rich,
loved the barbarous work to which they were committed. This, indeed, is what Foxe wishes us to
believe, but we may well expect him to make the
worst of it. The rack was never used, except by
high authority, to extract information, and in this
case it was applied to a poor woman already condemned to death. The Lieutenant of the Tower,
Sir Anthony Knyvet, in the first instance ordered
its application, and evidently with some degree of
mildness, so that she did not cry out. But no information was extracted, and the Lord Chancellor
and Rich, "throwing off their gowns"—a detail
supplied by Foxe,—administered the torture themselves. They first asked, however, if she were with
child, hoping, no doubt, to have some pretext for
not executing their full commission. "Ye shall not
need to spare for that," she said, "but do your wills
upon me." So the brutal work was done, and the

---

[1] Foxe, v. 547.

Chancellor and Rich took their way to Court. But the Lieutenant, meanwhile, taking boat, had arrived there before them, and getting access to the King, related what had occurred, asking pardon because he had declined to use severity himself without his express commands. On this, we are informed, the King "seemed not very well to like of their so extreme handling of the woman, and also granted the lieutenant his pardon." [1] We are not told that the King was really indignant at his officials having exceeded their instructions.

At last, on the 16th July, the tragedy was completed. Anne Askew was burned in Smithfield; and along with her suffered John Lascelles, a priest named Helmsley,[2] who had been an Observant friar of Richmond, and John Hadlam, the tailor of Colchester. The spectacle was witnessed by a crowd of people, in the midst of which a circular area was kept clear by barriers. Within this the victims were bound, each to a stake, a store of faggots was kept to feed the fire, and a pulpit was erected, as usual on such occasions, for a preacher. The sermon was delivered by Shaxton, the late bishop, who, with two other persons, was pardoned after sentence for the same offence for which the victims suffered. Above the crowd, on a raised scaffolding in front of St. Bartholomew's Hospital, were the Lord Chancellor, the Duke of Norfolk, and most of the Lords of the Council, with the Lord Mayor, aldermen, and sheriffs.[3]

The King, as Parsons understood the matter, had

She is burned, with others.

---

[1] Foxe, v. 547-8.

[2] "John Hemley," according to Wriothesley; but the *Grey Friars' Chronicle* gives the surname as "Hemmysley," the Christian name being apparently illegible in the MS. Hall, on the other hand, calls him Nicholas Otterden; and Foxe, Nicholas Belenian. Perhaps his Christian name is wrongly given by Wriothesley, though he gives it twice as John; but more probably he was one of those heretics who changed their names, both Christian and surnames, when they found it advisable, to avoid being tracked.

[3] Wriothesley's *Chronicle*, i. 169, 170; *Grey Friars' Chronicle*, p. 51. There is a woodcut of the scene in the old editions of Foxe.

authorised the racking of Anne Askew, to ascertain how far the ladies in the Court, including the Queen herself, had countenanced heretical utterances ; and it was at this time that Katharine Parr for a moment stood in real danger.   The story is given with some detail by Foxe, and I will endeavour to condense it here as much as possible from what Foxe himself says, for he is the only authority through whom it has reached us, and, notwithstanding his bias (for which it is not difficult to make allowance), no doubt it is true at least in substance.   Of course in Foxe's estimation Gardiner, the one strong adherent of old principles, was at the bottom of this, as of all other mischief.

Katharine Parr had conversed pretty freely with others for some time on matters of religion, and the King, since his return from Boulogne in 1544, had been well aware that she " was very much given to the reading and study of Holy Scriptures."   Daily in Lent for the space of an hour one of her chaplains had " made some collation " to her and her ladies, often discoursing on " such abuses as in the Church then were rife."   The King himself " at first and for a great time " seemed to like this very well, and at length she ventured to urge him to a more perfect reformation of abuses and superstitions.   But the enemies of " the Gospel " conspired against her, especially Gardiner and Lord Chancellor Wriothesley ; and as the King, now getting near his end, was fretful, and disliked being contradicted in argument, an opportunity at length arose.   Chafing under physical suffering, one day, as she spoke about religion, he suddenly broke off and changed the conversation.   At the end of their interview he bade her farewell " with gentle words and loving countenance." But after she had left he broke out in the presence of the Bishop of Winchester, who had heard their conversation : " A good hearing it is when women become such clerks, and a thing much to my comfort

Queen Katharine Parr in danger.

to come in mine old days to be taught by my wife!"
Needless to say, the Bishop was ready enough to blow
the coals. He "seemed to mislike that the Queen
should so much forget herself" as to argue with His
Majesty, whom he extolled to his face "for his rare
virtues, and especially for his learned judgment in
matters of religion," beyond that even of professed
doctors, till his discourse at length turned on the
danger of a prince suffering "such insolent words at
his subjects' hands." He even went on to insinuate
that the Queen's views tended to the destruction of
government, leading to a belief in the community of
goods; and though he durst not speak his knowledge
without assurance of the King's protection, yet he and
other faithful councillors could within short time
"disclose such treasons, cloaked with this cloak of
heresy, that his Majesty should easily perceive how
perilous a matter it is to cherish a serpent within his
own bosom."

These audacious insinuations had their effect upon
the King, who, "to see belike what they would do,"
authorised Gardiner and his friends to consult together
and draw up articles against the Queen, assuring them
that he would not spare her if they had any "colour
of law" to countenance their charges. But first of all
they proposed to accuse, under the Act of the Six
Her ladies. Articles, some of the ladies who were intimate with
her, especially her sister Lady Herbert, afterwards
Countess of Pembroke, the Lady Lane, her cousin,
and the Lady Tyrwit, who, like Lady Lane, was of
her privy chamber. When these ladies were apprehended their coffers were to be searched (the usual
process after important arrests), when it was expected
something would be found in their papers which
would implicate the Queen herself, and justify her
being arrested and conveyed to the Tower by night.
This plan, it seems, had the King's own approval,
"who (belike to prove the bishop's malice how far it

would presume) like a wise politic prince, was contented dissemblingly to give his consent and to allow of every circumstance."

We really must pause after quoting words like these to admire—not merely the social morality of Henry VIII. in countenancing a plot against his own wife (for of Henry VIII., of course, we can credit anything), but the commendation that the plan receives from an earnest votary of the new religion in the sixteenth century. The King, it is true, was acting a double part. He dissembled, in Foxe's opinion, when he gave his consent to a secret investigation of his wife's conduct in religious matters ; he dissembled, and was not indignant, when he was told that she might turn out to be a serpent in his bosom. But such dissembling only showed him to be " a wise and politic prince." Whoever else is to be blamed, you will never find a true gospeller like Foxe expressing any kind of reprobation of Henry VIII.'s moral conduct. He may at the utmost deplore that the King was misled by evil counsel to persecute good men. That a despot who had no superior on earth to control him should dissemble and cabal against his own wife, listening to secret accusations which he might at once have repressed and punished if they were unjust — this was only high and princely policy. But that a bishop of the old school should seek every occasion, under a most oppressive tyranny, to maintain, as far as possible, old principles of religion as he understood them, against high and low alike, was to Foxe unpardonable malice and wickedness. It is well to bear this in mind when we read Foxe's moral estimates of men. Whether they be men of his own school, or those of an opposite school, his expressed opinion of them is never to be trusted.

I quote again ; for though I condense as much as possible, an exact statement of facts is important :—

The King at that time lay at Whitehall, and used very seldom, being not well at ease, to stir out of his chamber or privy gallery; and few of his Council, but by special commandment, resorted unto him,—those only except who, by reason of this practice, used oftener than ordinary to repair unto him. This purpose so finely was handled that it grew now within few days of the time appointed for the execution of the matter, and the poor Queen neither knew nor suspected anything at all, and therefore used, after her accustomed manner, when she came to visit the King, still to deal with him touching religion as before she did.

The King allowed her to go on, "not out of any evil mind or misliking (ye must conceive) to have her speedy despatch, but rather, closely dissembling with them, to try out the uttermost of Winchester's fetches." As the critical time drew near, "it chanced" (a very curious accident, surely, in such a deep dissembler) :—

that the King, of himself, upon a certain night after her being with him, and her leave taken of him, in misliking her religion, brake the whole practice unto one of his physicians, either Dr. Wendy or else Owen, but rather Wendy, as is supposed; pretending unto him as though he intended not any longer to be troubled with such a doctress as she was; and also declaring what trouble was in working against her by certain of her enemies; but yet charging him withal, upon peril of his life, not to utter it to any creature living; and thereupon declared unto him the parties above named, with all circumstances, and when and what the final resolution of the matter should be.

Unknown to the Queen things advanced so far that articles were not only drawn against her, but were actually signed by the King's own hand — although this, too, was done "dissemblingly, you must understand." But the document, having been dropped by one of the councillors, was picked up by "some godly person," who took it at once to the Queen. Naturally, the poor lady was terrified and in a great agony of apprehension, "bewailing and taking

on in such sort as was lamentable to see, as certain of
her ladies and gentlemen, being yet alive, who were
then present about her, can testify." By these words
Foxe gives such assurance of the truth of this incident that we cannot doubt the fact. We may,
indeed, doubt whether the King really dissembled, as
Foxe intimates, in putting his hand to the bill, or
whether, during the whole business, it was with
Gardiner or with his wife that he dissembled chiefly.
But dissemble he certainly did in a manner singularly
heartless. Hearing, however, that alarm had made
her seriously ill, he sent his physicians to her, and
Wendy, who knew well enough what was the matter,
was able to give her some comfort to quiet her apprehensions; advising her, however, to show herself very
submissive and conform herself to the King's mind.
On this advice she acted, and, telling her ladies to put
away all their contraband heretical books, she sought
the King's chamber.

She found him in converse with certain gentlemen of the Chamber, but he at once broke off
his talk with them to salute her, and began speaking with her about religion, propounding certain
doubts on which he wished to know her opinion.
Her reply is given as a set speech in which she *How she*
expressed herself at some length, wondering how a *softened*
King of such great gifts should ask counsel of woman's *the King.*
inferior nature; and when the King said she had
become a great doctor, better fitted to teach him than
to be taught by him, she answered that that was not
her feeling; for though she had made bold, with his
leave, to maintain some opinions to him, it was only
to minister talk, partly hoping that it might soothe
his pain, and partly that it might elicit some learned
discourse from him by which she might profit.

"And is it even so, sweetheart?" said the King;
"and tended your arguments to no worse end? Then
perfect friends we are now again as ever at any time

heretofore." He embraced and kissed her, and said her words were more welcome than a present of a hundred thousand pounds.

Next day, in the afternoon, he and the Queen being in the garden with the above three ladies, the Lord Chancellor made his appearance with forty of the guard at his heels, intending to apprehend both her and the ladies instead of taking the ladies first, according to the original plan. The King, however, called the Chancellor aside, and some subdued conversation took place, the Chancellor being upon his knees. What was said the Queen and ladies could not hear, except that the King replied to him with the words, " Knave! Beast! Fool!" and bade him depart out of the presence. This gave the Queen occasion, after he was gone, to express a hope that she might intercede for the Lord Chancellor, who seemed to be in her husband's displeasure ; and the King answered, " Ah, poor soul! thou little knowest how evil he hath deserved this grace at thy hands."[1]

It is a strange story altogether, and Foxe himself, gathering it up from hearsay, seems not to have known how to make it into a harmonious whole. He is inconsistent in his theory of the King's dissimulation, at one time suggesting that he never really intended the Queen's arrest, but ultimately that he quite laid aside his purpose. Strange as it is, however, we cannot say that what is known of Henry VIII.'s personal history makes it at all inconceivable,[2] and we

---

[1] The whole of the above will be found in Foxe (v. 553-61, in Townsend's edition) under the heading, " The Story of Queen Katharine Parr."

[2] As early as February this year the Imperial ambassador wrote that there were rumours in London of a new Queen, though he could not find out why. Some thought that Katharine would be divorced for her sterility ; others said there would be no change while the war lasted. The Duchess of Suffolk was talked about (she would scarcely have been less Protestant than Katharine). But the King showed no change of his demeanour towards his existing Queen, though she was annoyed, even then, at the reports about her (*Spanish Calendar*, viii. p. 318). Reports were current also in the beginning of April as to some impending change " with regard to the feminine sex " (*Ib.*, p. 373).

have seen already that Foxe vouches for its truth by the evidence of witnesses living when he wrote. Moreover, Parsons, the Jesuit, in his comments on Foxe, accepts it all as true, except that he maintains the Queen was saved, not by her submission and renewed favour in the King's eyes, but by the King's mortal illness and death; for the date, as he infers from Foxe, was the very last year of the King's reign.[1] Here, however, I think Parsons is mistaken, and Foxe is right, for the King lived some months longer, and during that interval we find rather less evidence than before of the King's zeal against heresy. No doubt the tragedy at Smithfield was a very effective warning.

On the 27th June, the day before the trial of Anne Askew, Dr. Crome at last made an effective recantation in a sermon at Paul's Cross;[2] and on the 7th or 8th July proclamation was made in London, "with a trumpet and an herald at arms," of a number of English heretical books, chief of which were Tyndale's and Coverdale's translations of the New Testament, and the works of Frith, Tyndale, Wycliffe, and a number of others named, any copies of which were to be brought in by the last day of August, and delivered up to the Lord Mayor or the Bishop to be burned.[3]

---

[1] Parsons's *Three Conversions*, ii. 491-2. Foxe's dating, indeed, is very loose; for though he places the story after the martyrdom of Anne Askew and her fellow-sufferers, and of one Rogers, who suffered "about the same time" in Smithfield, he begins it with the words, "*About* the time above noted, which was *about* the year after the King returned from Boulogne." Now, Henry VIII. both went to and returned from Boulogne in 1544, and the year after would be 1545. Still, he has a preliminary remark that "after these stormy stories [of Anne Askew, etc.], the course and order, as well of the time as the matter," required him to speak of the Katharine Parr incident, which in that case must belong to the year 1546.

[2] "And the 27th day of June, which was the Sunday after Corpus Christi day, he was commanded to preach at Paul's Cross again, and there recanted and denied his words." (*Grey Friars' Chronicle*, p. 51.)

[3] Wriothesley's *Chronicle*, i. 168-9; Foxe, v. 565. The date of the proclamation is 7th July in the former authority, in the latter the 8th. The list of prohibited books given after it in Foxe (pp. 566-8) seems not to be of Henry VIII.'s time, as Foxe at first supposed, but of Mary's, and that, no doubt, is the reason why it was suppressed by Foxe himself after his first edition, though it has been replaced in the modern edition of Townsend and Cattley.

Indeed, it seems that more victims might very well have been burned about that time besides Anne Askew and her three fellow-sufferers but for special favour; for Sir George Blagge, one of the Privy Chamber, had got himself into trouble by loose talk about the Sacrament. According to Foxe he was falsely accused on one point, when he was sent for by Lord Chancellor Wriothesley on the Sunday before Anne suffered; then next day he was carried to Newgate, and thence to Guildhall, where he was condemned the same day, and was to have been burned on the Wednesday following. This would have been apparently two days before Anne's execution, which took place on a Friday. For though it would seem the words imputed to him could not be proved, he was questioned about Dr. Crome's sermon, at which he was present, and admitted that the preacher had said that the mass profited neither the quick nor the dead. What was it good for, then? "Belike," said Blagge, "for a gentleman, when he rideth a hunting, to keep his horse from stumbling." But when the news of his condemnation reached the Court,

the King being sore offended with their doings, that they would come so near him, and even into his Privy Chamber, without his knowledge, sent for Wriothesley, commanding eftsoons to draw out his pardon himself, and so he was set at liberty; who coming to the King's presence, "Ah, my pig!" saith the King to him (for so he was wont to call him). "Yea," said he, "if your Majesty had not been better to me than your bishops were, your pig had been roasted ere this time."

But events also, perhaps, contributed to mitigate the King's zeal for orthodoxy. The Council of Trent had no terrors for him if it did not create a powerful combination abroad, or if Scotland, aided by France, were not likely to invade the northern counties, and publish at last the papal bull of excommunication issued so many years before. His armies had given

Scotland some very severe lessons; but now a still more effective blow had been struck to secure him from molestation in that quarter. A plot had been long on foot with his connivance for the assassination of Cardinal Beton, and it took effect this year on the 29th May. Then France, worn out with the long struggle, made a peace with England, which was proclaimed in London on Whitsunday, 13th June. In August the French Admiral d'Annebaut came over to ratify it, and was received with the greatest possible distinction. Henry was no longer in so great fear of what the Pope might do to him. He was rather considering how to turn the situation still further to his advantage, and get Francis to take part with him against the Pope, so as to put an end to the Council. For this—indeed, a good deal more than this—is distinctly indicated in a conversation which took place between Archbishop Cranmer and his registrar, Ralph Morice, in the following reign; and the record of what was said is altogether so remarkable that we had better read the very words :—

"I am sure you were at Hampton Court," quoth the Archbishop, " when the French King's ambassador was entertained there at those solemn banqueting houses, not long before the King's death; namely,[1] when after the banquet was done the first night, the King was leaning upon the ambassador and upon me : if I should tell what communication between the King's Highness and the said ambassador was had, concerning the establishing of sincere religion then, a man would hardly have believed it; nor had I myself thought the King's Highness had been so forward in those matters as then appeared. I may tell you, it passed the pulling down of roods and suppressing the ringing of bells. I take it that few in England would have believed that the King's Majesty and the French King had been at this point, not only, within half a year after, to have changed the mass in both the realms into a communion (as we now use it) but also utterly to have extirped and banished the Bishop of

An international proposal.

---

[1] "Namely," *i.e.* especially.

Rome and his usurped power out of both their realms and dominions. Yea, they were so thoroughly and firmly resolved in that behalf that they meant also to exhort the Emperor to do the like in Flanders and other his countries and seigniories, or else they would break off from him. And herein the King's Highness willed me," quoth the Archbishop, " to pen a form thereof to be sent to the French King to consider of. But the deep and most secret providence of Almighty God, owing to this realm a sharp scourge for our iniquities, prevented for a time this their most godly device and intent, by taking to his mercy both these princes."

Is it no part of history to take note of the daydreams of princes? When schemes are seriously talked about they may be very far indeed from realisation, and after ages may think them utterly incredible, they are so unlike reality. They were mere visions at the time, and even to the diplomatists themselves their realisation may have been very doubtful. Months and years rolled on, and they were lost in the darkness of oblivion. But nothing brings the past before us more truly than the picture of what might have been, or even of what able men might have conceived possible. The Papacy was not so feeble a thing, even in the days of Napoleon Bonaparte, as it was in the first half of the sixteenth century—so feeble, that is to say, in the eyes of this world's rulers. Henry did not despise it more than Francis I. or than Charles V. himself. What thought the Emperor of the Papacy during the sack of Rome? What thought Francis, the ally of the Turk? The Pope was a convenient figurehead, perhaps; but England had shown that she could do without him, Germany had almost done without him also, and Francis, too, might have been induced to think about having a national religion in France, free from papal interference. There was life enough, at least, in the suggestions to weaken a little the respect for what was going on at Trent.

But no doubt it was true that Henry VIII. was nearing his end, and Francis I. soon followed him.

Henry died on the 28th January 1547, five months after the French admiral's visit to England; and the story of those five months is of political rather than religious interest.

APPENDIX TO CHAPTER III

The following contemporary letter, which is referred to in a footnote at p. 449, is of very special interest in connection with some of the events related in the last few pages, and the reader will undoubtedly be glad to learn what was said at the time by an outside observer.

Otwell Johnson, a Merchant of London, to his Brother, John Johnson, of the Staple at Calais (then living at Glapthorne, Northants).

[From Ellis's *Original Letters*, Second Series, ii. 172-8.]

At LONDON, *the 2nd in July* 1546.

[The first part of the letter relates to domestic and business matters. Then a rumour is reported that the Emperor is going to raise men, "and that his quarrel against the Germans was not for any cause of religion, but for their certain disobedience against him in things that concern the Empire. Most men else think otherwise; but *vous connoissez l'homme.*"]

Our news here of Dr. Crome's canting, recanting, decanting, or rather double canting, be these :—That on Sunday last,[1] before my lord Chancellor, the Duke of Norfolk, my lord Great Master, Mr. Riche, Mr. Chancellor of the Tenths, with the Suthwells, Pope, and other nobles and knights, and on the other side the Bishops of London and Worcester, all principal doctors and deans, besides gay grey amices[2] and a rabble of other marked people, the reverend father just named openly declared his true meaning and right understanding (as he said, and according to his conscience) of the six or seven articles you heard of, as he should have done upon the second Sunday after Easter,[3] but that he was letted from his said true intent by the persuasions of certain perverse minded persons and by the sight of lewd and ungodly books and writings ; for the which he was very sorry and desired the audience to beware of such books, for under the fair appearance of them was hidden a dangerous

---

[1] 27th June.   [2] Furred tippets worn by the clergy.   [3] 9th May.

accombrance of Christian consciences, and so exhorted all men to embrace auncientnes of Catholic doctrine, and forsake new fanggelnes.

On Monday following [1] quondam Bishop Saxon, Mrs. Askewe, Christopher White, one of Mrs. Fayre's sons, and a tailor that come from Colchester or thereabout, were arraigned at the Guildhall and received their judgment of my lord Chancellor and the Council to be burned, and so were committed to Newgate again. But since that time the aforesaid Saxon and White have renounced their opinions, and the talk goeth that they shall chance to escape the fire for this viage; but the gentlewoman and the other man remain in steadfast mind; and yet she hath been racked since her condemnation (as men say), which is a strange thing in my understanding. The Lord be merciful to us all!

---

[1] 28th June.

CHAPTER IV

RESULTS UNDER HENRY VIII.

WHAT, then, was the main thing done as regards religion under Henry VIII. ? Scarcely any one has seriously denied that he was a tyrant, and it is a popular impression that he forced religion into a new mould,—some consider that he actually changed it. That he did force it into new conditions seems to me undeniable ; but if he made any essential change we shall be driven to consider whether the new religion was not actually a departure from old revealed truth, or at least from a divinely ordained authority. In answer to this suggestion, there is one consideration, at least, on which we may safely rest. It is not in the power of tyranny to deflect the rays of divine truth ; and no community or nation that had really parted company with vital Christianity could hope to maintain its place in a progressive civilisation. True enough, there are always doubters, and many positive unbelievers. There were such in the sixteenth century, and there are many now. The world at all times seems too much for the Church, and when secular interests and secular thoughts become too powerful for conventional restraints, it is amazing how little regard is paid to old guarantees for the maintenance of a pure national faith, and the sacredness of nationality itself as a thing ordained of God.

But in such revolutions a rough justice may still be found. Hypocrisy is to some extent unveiled, and the unreality of much affected reverence is laid aside. Abuses, too, are corrected by a severe scourge; but essential truth remains. Religion may pass under new conditions: a yoke which seems quite insufferable may be laid upon it in one age; but the ultimate result must be that men know better than before for what they ought to live, or be prepared to suffer. Divisions, too, may result, which ought certainly to be deplored among Christians; but these will be mitigated if not effaced by examining the essentials of religion, not merely by the light of the individual reason, but by thoughtful contemplation of the whole history of the Church of Christ.

Tyranny cannot crush the truth;

Things which abide in religion must have truth in them. Heresies fluctuate and change their character. The heretical thinker may, indeed, have his own message to the world, and the Church itself must take in whatever neglected truth he is endeavouring to enforce; after which his mission is over. But the fabric of sound dogma cannot be overthrown or mutilated. What has really been ascertained must remain for ever. There may be a danger, indeed, in forcing dogmas which are over-subtle on general acceptance; for even truths, when forced, are in danger of becoming untruths to the vulgar, just because they cannot be truly apprehended. And above all things it is desirable that what truths a man once receives, even in his childhood, shall dwell in his heart through life, and bear fruit in his general conduct. If he is troubled about his faith, let him consider what things have been generally agreed on by Christians of all ages, and be assured that they were not agreed on without inquiry. The things which abide in religion must be true.

but new conditions must be studied.

Yet we are not absolved from the contemplation of new conditions which have been imposed upon religious life in different eras, and of our inheritance in those conditions. The Reformation may be the

fruit of tyranny at a time when able state-craft had
made England a positive despotism ; but it does not
follow that good has not come of evil ; for here, too,
we must consider the things that abide.   The overthrow of papal jurisdiction was effected by the
principle of Royal Supremacy over the Church ; and
Royal Supremacy, though brutally enforced by Henry
VIII., was nevertheless a true principle and remains
with us still.   It has other enemies besides the
votaries of Rome ; but all their enmity is in vain.
The principle of an Established Church, however at
variance with theories which pious minds are too easily
led to entertain, is one which, when once laid down,
can never be set aside.   What we call in these days
Disestablishment is really Establishment over again.
The only example we have of it shows this clearly.
For the Church of Ireland is now a State Church even
more than it was before 1869.   It is a Church established by Royal Charter under an Act of Parliament ;
and it was established by a very strong exercise of
Royal Supremacy.   Just as the Church of England
came to be " established " in the political sense, under
Henry VIII., by successive steps—first by subjecting
the clergy to an extortionate fine, then driving them
to complete submission and compelling all men to
abjure the Pope,—even so the Irish Church was
disestablished, or re-established, first by a sweeping
confiscation, and secondly by inducing the clergy and
laity, as the only means of recovering part of their
lost property, to elect a body of trustees and accept
a Royal Charter.   It may be that the nineteenth
century process was milder than the sixteenth century process.   Certainly it was so, especially as
regards individuals.   But as regards the Church,
Disestablishment, like Establishment, consisted
simply in coercion.   The political principle of
Establishment cannot possibly be annulled, and if
we are to have a practical religion, and not a mere

chaos of sectarian philosophies, we must face the fact plainly.

Permanent principles of the Constitution.

Of course it is not my object here to discuss things done in our own days. But a principle that cannot be annulled is surely deserving of study. Time and experience have a wonderful influence on the life of nations, changing despotic power into popular government while the ruling principle behind both is absolutely the same. To this day the King is the centre of the Constitution, and all things pass through him. His face is on the coinage; his writ opens Parliament or dissolves it; the nation's acts are his acts, and no interference with individual liberty is justifiable except by summons, arrest, or *subpoena* in his name. It is true this does not mean personal action on his part, but action through a number of functionaries who derive their authority from him. And in matters of State it is still the same. The King cannot act without advisers, nor can he now (the suggestion, indeed, is monstrous) use advisers and instruments, as Henry VIII. did, merely to be flung to the wolves when they could no longer serve his purpose. But still our constitutional principle is the same—that the King can do no wrong, though his ministers may deserve censure. And ministers now, when dismissed, fall very softly, giving place to others who for the time are more in the nation's confidence.

"The King can do no wrong." The words sound paradoxical and untrue, just like the statement that the Pope is infallible. But no Roman Catholic thinks the Pope personally infallible; and the King, like the Pope, is not a mere living person, but an institution as well. His will has to be construed according to the Constitution; and the Constitution holds that he can do no wrong, simply because there is no higher power on earth to correct him. Here at once we come to the great difference between the mediæval and the modern world. Before the days of Henry

Essence of the change under Henry VIII.

VIII. no one doubted that kings could do very much wrong, and that there was a power to correct kings who did wrong.   Henry II. and King John felt that power and were obliged to bow to it.   Henry VIII. himself, as we have seen, was not altogether confident that he too might not have to submit in the end.   But he succeeded—partly by his own astuteness, partly through the jealousies of secular princes abroad—in avoiding or warding off every danger ; and from his day there has been no spiritual rule in England, from a foreign centre, capable of controlling the action of the sovereign.   How great a result this is, and how beneficial on the whole, we in the twentieth century have great difficulty in fully comprehending.

Before the Reformation a priest was esteemed by the devout more highly than a king.   He had really higher functions.   To dispense the sacraments—especially to give the Body of Christ to His followers—was a more awful privilege than any with which royalty was invested.   And this was not a mere matter of sentiment to each individual Christian, but the Church itself, as a spiritual community, could enforce high truths, or what were so regarded, by an organisation entirely independent of the laws of the land.   The laws of the land, indeed, respected the laws of the Church as those of a superior Power ; and any lowering of the prerogatives of the Church was considered profanity.   True enough it is that there were conflicts at times between the two jurisdictions, but the superiority of the jurisdiction of the Church was never questioned in theory.   These conflicts were at times matters for adjustment, or attempted adjustment, as in the famous Constitutions of Clarendon, which Becket so strongly withstood.   But adjustments could only be made with the consent of the bishops, who in matters which concerned their duty to the Church were not the King's subjects but the Pope's ;   and so arrangements were finally made in many matters between the Sovereign and the Pope.

Then as secular powers, towards the close of the Middle Ages, grew continually stronger, they were commonly treated with no small deference by the Holy Father at Rome, and were nowise tempted to defy a spiritual authority with which they could always make very good terms for the effective government of their own kingdoms. Moreover, secular princes could use the sword against their enemies, and the gibbet against disloyal subjects, while the Church had no coercive power except that of excommunication. So the Church had no positive control over a prince whose deeds were not bad enough to merit such a penalty. He might even overrule the Church's supposed rights in some things, and must be allowed to have his own way, unless the Holy See were prepared to use the strongest spiritual weapons against him.

How much latitude, then, could the Pope allow to princes in violating the prescriptive rights and ignoring the authority of the Holy See? Practically a great deal was allowed; for princes might be at war with the Pope himself without being declared enemies of the Papacy as a principle. They might be excommunicated, too, but the sentence was always liable to revision. Popes themselves, moreover, were temporal princes, and even Popes might be wrong in their worldly policy. An adjustment was sure to come some day between secular and spiritual authority. The one unprecedented feature in the case of Henry VIII. was that, when he saw no other way to vindicate his own self-will, he threw off papal authority altogether, and not only did so himself as sovereign but caused all his subjects likewise to repudiate it; which in fact they almost all of them did, taking an oath to him as Supreme Head of the Church of England, however some might mumble between their teeth " as

far as the law of Christ permits." That such a qualification was largely made in the hearts and minds of his
oppressed and discontented subjects there is no reason
whatever to doubt. But what else could they do?
A whole nation could not allow itself to be butchered
piecemeal as traitors till other nations, laying aside
their jealousies, could agree on a crusade against that
Turk in the West, who was really far more cruel to
the Saints of God than the Turk who overran Hungary.
Machiavellism had paralysed all political action for
good; and as regards the duty of the individual subject, did not religion itself admit that he was bound
to his prince? Men settled down into silent acqui-
escence with a new spiritual authority, half believing,
at first, that it could not, in the nature of things,
last long. But time brought no relief to those who
still adhered to the old ideal; and subjects threw
the responsibility of the change upon their sovereign.
Even Irish chieftains—universally, so far as we can Even Irish
tell—each severally renounced the Pope, and gave chieftains
in his submission to Henry VIII. after he had assumed the Pope.
the title of " King of Ireland." [1]

It was, indeed, one of the most singular proofs of
the success of Henry's policy that towards the end of
the reign, after laying aside that inferior title, " Lord
of Ireland "—which only pointed to the fact that
dominion over the island was a papal gift inherited
from Henry II.—and calling himself King of that
country, he succeeded, to all appearance, in bringing
it into more complete subjection than at any time
before. All that he required to secure himself against
the world and against Rome, was to bring Scotland
into a like obedience; which he attempted, as is well
known, by a cruel war waged to enforce a matrimonial
project for the union of the northern and southern
kingdoms. That object he could not attain; and

[1] See *Calendar of the Carew MSS.*, vol. i., Nos. 159, 160, 163, 164, 165,
167, 171, 172, 173, 184.

yet his success in warding off interference from Scotland, first by playing off Scottish factions against each other, secondly by ruthless invasions, and thirdly by procuring the murder of Cardinal Beton, just as England was about to make peace with France, and thereby deprive Scotland of aid from her old ally, was surely very remarkable. In matters of high policy moral scruples never stood in his way; and his political insight was clearer than that of any other contemporary sovereign.

As in his foreign, so too was it in his domestic policy, particularly in Church matters. From the day that he took that bold and unprecedented step, which he put off as long as possible after threatening to take it for years—repudiating papal jurisdiction and making himself Supreme Head of the Church in his own kingdom,— he was well aware that it must be enforced by the most cruel laws wrung from a really reluctant Parliament, composed, as even that Parliament was, of his own creatures. By these laws, and by the atrocious cruelty with which they were executed, the spirit of the nation was completely tamed. But amid the sad spectacle of national oppression we may still note the fact that the tyrant invariably sought plausible arguments to justify his procedure, giving his subjects, if possible, no ground for rebellion, and foreign princes no ground for interference. Of such pretexts, both his timorous subjects and foreign princes who were not at war with him were only too willing to avail themselves; and the fact that he was himself an adept in technical theology and a subtle casuist, gave all the greater weight to his authority. Who could dispute matters with a king who had a reason for everything he did, and could confound any ordinary objector by his logic no less than by his laws? Nay, some of his own ablest bishops, like Gardiner and Tunstall, withstood him in argument now and then

Henry used plausible arguments in defence of his tyranny.

just as far as they dared, and then tendered a wise submission.[1]

He had taken the Pope's place and become the Supreme Spiritual Ruler of his own realm. The claim was admitted because it could not be withstood. He had acted with great solemnity as Supreme Judge in a case of heresy, and had sentenced a poor man to the flames, as no King of England had done before. But for the most part he acted as Spiritual Ruler behind a screen ; Cranmer, or Cromwell, or the bishops, were to bear all the responsibility. The

---

[1] Tunstall had a controversy with the King on the subject of Royal Supremacy which has not been noticed hitherto by Church historians, owing to the blunders of editors and the misdating of documents ; so I take this opportunity of putting the facts in a true light. In 1531, when the See of York was vacant, Tunstall naturally presided in the York Convocation, where there was only one bishop besides himself, the Bishop of Carlisle. The Southern Convocation had already passed the article with the qualified recognition of the King as " Supreme Head " of the Church, and the Northern assembly was expected to do the like. But even with this qualification Tunstall protested against the title—indeed the qualification itself, he pointed out, might be taken for an admission that by the law of Christ the King was Supreme Head of the Church in spiritual things as well as earthly. This protest is not dated in the register of Convocation from which it was printed by Wilkins ; but it was notified to the King by a letter dated 6th May 1531, which Henry answered at great length in another letter, first printed in the collection called *Cabala* in 1663. The editor of the *Cabala* most unfortunately places at the head of this letter (p. 244) the title "King Henry the Eighth to the Clergy of the Province of York, *Anno* 1533," though the very first words of the letter show that it is addressed to a single bishop only, and internal evidence proves the year to have been 1531. The false heading, nevertheless, is repeated by Wilkins (vol. iii. p. 762), and has misled everybody.

This reply to Tunstall's objections is a good specimen of Henry VIII.'s *finesse* as a theological controversialist. So also is another letter that he wrote to Tunstall (*L. P.*, v. 820) in answer to another protest by him. Tunstall had felt it necessary to remonstrate on the subject of a publication issued by the authority of the King and Council against the pre-eminence of the Pope and the Church of Rome, which would be construed as showing an intention on the King's part to separate the Church of England from the Church of Rome. Henry says in reply that he is supported by virtuous and learned men in the opinion that it is no schism to separate from the Church of Rome ; that the supremacy of the Pope is usurped ; that to follow the Pope is to forsake Christ ; and that no Christian princes will abandon him on that account.

As to Gardiner, his own words in writing to the Protector Somerset about his relations with Henry VIII. are remarkably significant. *See* Foxe, vi. 36. But while he probably used greater freedom in remonstrance with the King than any other bishop, his independence must have sadly given way when he wrote not only his able defence of Royal Supremacy (*de Verâ Obedientiâ*), but also, dreadful to say, a justification of the death of Fisher. Under Mary, he bitterly repented his past subservience.

Ten Articles were superseded by the *Institution*, and the *Institution* by the *Necessary Doctrine*, and Cromwell's Injunctions came before and after the *Institution*; so that if there were any disputes men might blame Cromwell, the bishops, or Cranmer, just as they thought fit, for no one, of course, would dare to blame the King. And the authorities, in fact, did not agree with each other, nor did Cranmer himself agree with any one of them; for, as we have seen, he pursued a policy of his own not sanctioned by either books or injunctions, forcing his own clergy in some things, especially his prebendaries at Canterbury, to obey his orders simply as Metropolitan.

Strange to say, there was not a written order or proclamation, whether of Cromwell, the bishops, or the King himself in matters of religion—for that which was called "the King's Book" in contradistinction to "the Bishops' Book" expressed far too high sacramental doctrine even for Cranmer at the time it was issued—by which the Primate of all England felt himself bound. Not only did he go in advance of existing rules and formularies, as when he declared that all images were idols, showing clearly that he would like to have them all removed one day in spite of an express sanction of their use in every one of the three authorised formularies,—not only did he countenance positions which he said he could defend before an indifferent judge, provided that judge were obtained from Germany,—but he had even once gone himself in the teeth of the Six Articles in a lecture on the Sacrament of the Altar, declaring that it was only a similitude.[1]

Cranmer a spiritual despot. Cranmer, in short, was a spiritual despot, supported by the despotism of the King. The terrors of the Act of the Six Articles were no terrors to him; and his clergy stood in awe of him. The Court was above the law, and the Primate, as a most important member

[1] See p. 374 *ante*.

of the Court, was above the law too. He did not indulge, of course, in the open profanity of the men of Windsor or of Sir George Blagge, but his sacramental views, we may well suspect, never were so high as those required by that statute which his master took so remarkable a part in persuading the House of Lords to enact, even in the face of opposition from the Anne Boleyn bishops. And though he was obliged to take a painful part in the prosecution of the unhappy Nicholson, refuting the heretic's arguments—with what casuistry or mental reservations we cannot tell,—it may be that the very fact that he had done so created secret remorse in his own mind, as the martyrdom of Stephen did in that of St. Paul. It was melancholy, indeed, that the Church of England—or, at least, a considerable part of it—should be under the control of such a Primate; for what can be worse than that authority should contradict authority? But still we must not do Cranmer, the man, injustice. We cannot vindicate his career; but we may, at least, admit its difficulties. It was not by his own will that he was set in a position where he must either domineer or be lost. The one original weakness on his part was recommending himself to Court favour by the suggestion of an appeal to the universities. Henry at once saw the value of that advice, and of the man who could give it. On the first opportunity he made Cranmer Archbishop, to do him further service; and Cranmer, not without a strong presentiment of the things that would be imposed upon him, delayed coming home from the Continent as long as he reasonably could. At last, when seated on the Archiepiscopal throne, and familiar with the conditions under which it seemed to him Religion must live in his day, he framed for himself a religion of Royal Supremacy—an ideal of Christianity subject to earthly power, which was his guiding principle even to the very end.

But it is not in the power of one man, or even of three or four men, placed in high positions, of themselves to bring on a religious revolution. The elements of the great change which was now gathering strength had been in the Church, as we have seen, long before Henry's Act of Supremacy. They were in their own nature elements of lawlessness; but, favoured by the power of the Sovereign, they could no longer be treated as lawless. The reader has seen what Lollardy was long before the Reforma-

Principles of Lollardy unchanged in Henry VIII.'s day.

tion. He has seen also what it was in Sir Thomas More's day; and I need but refer to the analysis of More's *Dialogue* which will be found at the end of the first volume of this work,[1] to show that its principles remained precisely what they had been. It was only that the printing press, the circulation of Tyndale's Testaments, a touch of Lutheranism at the universities, and, most of all, the encouragement given to heresy by the King himself as soon as he saw that he could not obtain his divorce by the authority of the Church, had combined to favour Lollardy in a way that had not been seen before. The stock complaints against the old Religion were precisely the same as they had been. Images were idols, pilgrimages and prayers to Saints were gross abuses. Scripture was the one rule of faith, and the burning of Tyndale's Testaments showed that the Church authorities hated the diffusion of pure Christian truth. The so-called heretics claimed to be the true Church of Christ, though their methods of advancing truth were not plain-spoken and aboveboard.

Henry made use of them for his own purposes.

Now Henry VIII.'s reformation of the Church, it will be seen, was precisely on Lollard lines. Lollardy did not suggest Royal Supremacy, but Royal Supremacy, when the King had made up his mind to it, suggested his seeking the support of Lollardy. Not that this was a consistent but a variable policy; for

---

[1] Appendix to Chapter V. of Book II.

he could disown Lollard support whenever convenient,
and there were times when it was desirable to do so.
But those who favoured Lollardy could never afford
to disown him; because it was only by the fact that
papal authority was excluded from the realm, and
even episcopal authority liable to be overruled, that
heretics could expect to have their own way in anything. So, after the Supremacy had been vindicated
by cruel butcheries, and the monasteries, which depended more on Rome than the clergy at large did,
had been overthrown, Royal power began to act more
openly upon Lollard principles, setting itself against
images and pilgrimages and things that savoured of
superstition in a way to which men had not been
accustomed. It was not a question with the King
or Cromwell, or even with Cranmer, how much good
there might still be in old institutions like the
monasteries whose best days of usefulness were
past, nor what might still be pleaded for other old
observances. It was enough that there were some
abuses and some symptoms of decay. The spirit of
destruction was let loose, to prevent a return to
Rome.

The wonderful thing is really, not how much was
destroyed but how much was preserved—a fact which
is all the more striking as the destructive policy long
survived Henry VIII., and was even carried further.
But conservative principles still maintained themselves in the Church, and preserved the Church itself.
Bishops were absolutely necessary to the policy, alike
of Henry VIII. and his successors, though abbots
and priors were not; and the old bishops, though
sadly at a disadvantage with such a king, still made
their influence felt in many things. We have seen
already how stoutly they fought the battle in Convocation against those very influences which the
King was doing his best to foster, how they brought
back the authorised teaching of the Church from the

But con-
servative
principles
fought
hard.

vagueness of the Ten Articles to a more and more
clear enunciation of old principles ; and though they
were thwarted by double-dealing in high quarters,
they still preserved both King and realm to some
extent from the reproach of apostasy and the hostility
of other nations.

The story of Lollardy and the Reformation does not
end with Henry VIII. ; it had in truth made but a
beginning when he died.   Lollardy, by itself, was a far
older thing ; but Lollardy as a driving power, though
it was no longer called Lollardy, had entered on a new
career entirely.   The King, invested with a spiritual
authority hitherto quite unknown, had made large
use of it for his own ends ; but for his own interests,
likewise, he had to keep it under some control.   And
this he could do effectually, first, because he was
wise and politic, and secondly, because religious innovators had no other refuge and were bound to support
the new spiritual jurisdiction that he asserted.   After
he was gone the flood-gates were not so easily closed,
and Henry was regretted by conservative souls as a
strong and able sovereign who at least knew how to
maintain order.

As for the Reformation, it must not be identified
merely with Henry's repudiation of the Pope and
assertion of Royal Supremacy.   That, indeed, was
the one great fact which has dominated the history
of men and nations ever since.   A new era had
begun, and no spiritual power on earth was able to
bring back the past.   Truth must grow and flourish
henceforth, if it were to grow and flourish at all,
under the protection of Royal Supremacy.   It was
no longer to be scientifically defined and authoritatively imposed on men by General Councils.   It
must have scope to move and work ; it must be
discussed among common men, even though the
arguments might lead to blows and civil war before
they found a settlement.   Lollardy certainly had

A freer
atmosphere
under
Royal
Supremacy.

broken into the Church, unrecognised but powerful; and it could not be met and eliminated in the old fashion when once it had secured its footing there. The unhappy attempt to burn it out in the Marian reaction was a failure.   Royal Supremacy again asserted itself under Elizabeth with a tyranny almost as cruel as before.   But Lollardy, in the forms of Calvinism and Puritanism, reasserted itself likewise, and almost vied with Romanism at times in disrespect for that Royal Supremacy by which the bondage of Rome had really been thrown off.   The poor Romanists could be fined and persecuted; but it was Puritanism that would not be controlled, and the bishops were no longer the sort of men to control it. Bishops themselves took up positions that might well have been called Lollard, though the word had gone out of use.   Opposite schools of thought were developed within the National Church.   Yet truly Catholic principles were never lost sight of.   The desire was to include, not to exclude, all thinkers of whatever tendency; and it is remarkable what a broad basis was laid down, even in Elizabeth's day, for the reformed religion which we still profess.   It does not seem possible, indeed, that we can make it broader now.

INDEX TO VOLS. I. AND II.

Candish, Mr., i. 349, 350
Canon law, revision of the, ii. 412
Cannonis, Master, ii. 64
Canterbury, heretic at, reclaimed by Henry VII., i. 273-4
Cathedral of Christchurch, ii. 212, 365
preachers in, i. 315
prebendaries of, complain of Cranmer, ii. 394
refoundation of, ii. 359
All Hallows Church, ii. 385
St. Alphege's Church, ii. 368
St. Alphege's Church, parson of (H. Chirden), ii. 370
St. Augustine's monastery, ii. 156
St. George's, parson of (John Tofer), ii. 360
St. Sepulchre's, i. 453
Canterbury, Archbishops of. See Sudbury, Simon (1375-81); Courtenay, William (1381-96); Arundel, Thomas (1396-1413); Stafford, John (1443-52); Bourchier, Thos. (1454-86); Warham, William (1503-32); Cranmer, Thomas (1533-56)
Archbishop invested with new powers, i. 475
Canterbury, Convocation of, i. 299, 300, 388, 403, 445-7, 462; ii. 90, 91, 260, 265-6, 295, 350, 412
Canterbury, St. Thomas of. See Becket
pilgrimages to, ii. 172. See also Becket
Canyng, Thomas, Mayor of London (1456), i. 231
Capon, John, abbot and bishop. See Salcot
Cardine. See Cawarden
Cardmaker (or Taylor), Dr. John, ii. 443-5
Carlisle, Bishops of. See Lumley, M. (1430-50); Aldridge, Robert (1537-56)
Carlisle Cathedral Monastery to be a college, ii. 212
Carlstadt (Carlostadius), the German theologian, i. 578
Carne, Sir Edward, ambassador, i. 330-1; ii. 187, 217
Carthusians. See Charter House
Castillon, French Ambassador, ii. 184, 189-91
Castilten, W., Abbot of Wymondham, ii. 98
Castleacre Priory, a cell of Lewes, ii. 110-11

Catton, Robert, Prior of Norwich, ii. 103
Caultam, a place of pilgrimage, ii. 172
Cawarden (Cardine), Sir Thomas, ii. 401-3, 406, 407
his wife Elizabeth, ii. 404, 407
Caxton, W., the printer, i. 265-6
Celibacy of the clergy, ii. 179
Cephas, error about the name, i. 62, 225
Ceremonies, ii. 337
Cesarini, legate, i. 163, 164
Chaloner, Sir Thomas, ii. 350 n.
Chamber, Geoff., Receiver-General of Augmentations, ii. 123
Chamberlen, Thomas, Abbot of Wymondham, ii. 97
Channel Islands, spiritual jurisdiction in, i. 306
Chantries, Act for dissolution of, ii. 435-6
Chantry priests, ii. 82, 83
Chapel (or Holbeche), Robert, chaplain of Oldcastle, i. 125
Chapuys, Eustace, Imperial Ambassador, i. 444, 450; ii. 5, 51, 71, 81, 188, 190, 276, 347, 349
Charles IV., Emperor and King of Bohemia, i. 120
Charles V., Emperor, i. 291, 292, 304, 324; ii. 181-7, 189, 191, 193, 204, 217, 346-8, 413, 431-2, 434, 464
Charterhouse monks, martyrs, i. 304, 311, 477-8, 483, 486, 488, 503; ii. 4, 136-7, 147
Charterhouse, London, i. 421-9; ii. 9, 26, 29, 36-43, 49, 55
suggested orders for, ii. 14, 16
order for, ii. 16
Chartreuse, the Grande, ii. 20, 22
Chatrys, William. See Sawtré
Chaucer, the poet, i. 5, 37, 251
Chauncy, Maurice, Carthusian, and his writings, i. 423-4, 426; ii. 10, 16, 28, 30, 36, 40, 42
Chelsea, More's house at, i. 503
Cherdian. See Chirden
Chertsey, abbey, ii. 74, 108, 113
Abbot of, i. 146. See Cordrey, John
Chester, St. Werburgh's Abbey, ii. 115
to be a college, ii. 212
rood of, ii. 172
Chichele, Henry, Archbishop of Canterbury (1414-43), i. 89, 93, 124, 126-8, 133-4, 144, 151, 156, 162
censured by Pope Martin V., i. 135-9, 262
his appeals, i. 140-4

Holbein, the painter, ii. 223
Hollins, Margaret, nun of Blackborough, ii. 99
Holm Cultram, Cumberland, relic at, ii. 115
surrender of monastery, *ib.*
Holme, Richard, friar, i. 173
Holt, John, Titular Bishop of Lydda, Abbot of Wymondham, ii. 98
Holt, William, i. 415
Hooper, John, Bishop of Gloucester (1550-3), and of Worcester (1552-3), i. 320-1
Hoper, ——, a servant of Oldcastle, i. 151
Horde, Dr., Prior of Hinton, Somerset (Carthusian), ii. 13, 20
Horn, William (Carthusian), ii. 38
Horsey, Dr., Chancellor to the Bishop of London, i. 279
Horwod, John, monk of Winchcombe, called *Placet* or *Placidus*, ii. 64-6, 68 *n.*
Houghton, John, Prior of the London Charterhouse, martyr, i. 421-9, 435-7 ; ii. 5, 7, 8, 10, 17-19, 21, 22, 33
Hounden (or Hunden), Richard, burnt, i. 159, 161
Howard, Queen Katharine, ii. 290, 350
Huchyn. *See* Tyndale, W.
Huick. *See* Hewick
Huiskin (Hausschein). *See* Œcolampadius
Hull Charterhouse, ii. 30-34
Hulme, St. Benet's, abbey, ii. 104
Humerston, Justice of the Peace, i. 351
Hungary, i. 256-7
Hungerford, Walter, Lord, Lord Treasurer, i. 134
Hunne, Richard, i. 111-13, 278, 282, 309, 310, 512, 574 ; ii. 227
Hunniades, John, Governor of Hungary, i. 256
Huntington (John), a priest, ii. 428
Hus, John, the Bohemian martyr, i. 88, 102, 111, 118, 120-3, 337, 574
his followers in Bohemia, i. 143, 161-3 (*see* Bohemia)
Husee, John, correspondent of Lord Lisle, i. 465 *n.* ; ii. 111, 124, 127, 167, 194-5, 320 *n.*
Hussey, Archbishop Cranmer's registrar, ii. 394-6
Hussey, Lord, ii. 15
Hwyskyn (Hausschein). *See* Œcolampadius

Hyde, near Winchester, Abbot of. *See* Salcot, John

Idols and images, ii. 371
Images, i. 317; ii. 334, 360-4, 370. *See* Idols
Incent, John, Dr., Dean of St. Paul's (1540), ii. 382 *n.*
Indulgences, i. 256, 289
Ingeam, Vincent, of Sandwich, ii. 392
Ingworth, Richard, Suffragan Bishop of Dover, ii. 160-2
Innocent III., Pope, i. 53
Innocent VIII., Pope, i. 269, 273, 279, 280
Inolde (or Enold), Curate of Rye, ii. 332-3
"Institution of a Christian Man," the (called "The Bishops' Book"), ii. 108, 279, 305, 323, 328-32, 337, 345, 352, 355-6, 359, 370, 372, 375, 475
Ipswich, Our Lady of, i. 555, 561 ; ii. 149, 150, 172
Grey Friars of, ii. 160
Ireland, John, of Eltham, ii. 411, 412
Ireland, Church of, ii. 469
chieftains of, renounce the Pope, ii. 473

Jacopo, a nuncio, i. 148
James IV. of Scotland, his widow Margaret, i. 381
James V. of Scotland, ii. 151
James, William, Lollard, abjures, i. 126
Jaye. *See* Joye
Jerome of Prague, i. 118, 120, 122, 123
Jerome, William, burnt in Smithfield, ii. 289, 381
Jervaux, monastery of, i. 247
Jessopp, Dr., his *Visitations of the Diocese of Norwich*, ii. 106
Jewel, Bishop, i. 363
Joan of Navarre, Queen of Henry IV., i. 558
John of Gaunt, Duke of Lancaster, i. 13, 21, 22, 31, 32, 34 *n.*, 36, 40, 63
John III. of Portugal, i. 294
Johnson, John, merchant, ii. 465
Johnson, Otwell, letter of, ii. 465
Johnson, Thomas (Carthusian), ii, 38, 39
John XXII., Pope, i. 9, 13, 33 *n.*, 257, 260
John XXIII., Pope, i. 66, 103, 119
John Palæologus II., Emperor, i. 167
Jonas, Justus, the German Reformer, ii. 316
Jourdelay, John, heretic, i. 145

CORRECTION

I AM sorry to find that in Vol. II. p. 308 I have made a misstatement about the Convocation which met at St. Paul's on the 9th June 1536. I have said that it was a special Convocation, in which the clergy of the Northern Province sat along with those of the Southern. This, on further consideration, I believe not to have been the case, though the Archbishop of York and the Bishop of Durham signed the Ten Articles elaborated in that assembly. Wake, in his *State of the Church*, p. 491, finds no evidence in the registers that the Convocation of York was summoned at this time, although he believes that the bishops of that province, and possibly some select persons of their clergy, assisted at the framing of the Articles.